WILDLIFE TOXICOLOGY

Courtesy Michigan Department of Natural Resources (Bob Harrington photo).

WILDLIFE TOXICOLOGY

Tony J. Peterle

Professor Emeritus
Department of Zoology, The Ohio State University
Columbus, Ohio

VAN NOSTRAND REINHOLD
New York

Copyright © 1991 by Van Nostrand Reinhold

Library of Congress Catalog Card Number 90-22781
ISBN 0-442-00462-1

Printed in the United States of America.

Van Nostrand Reinhold
115 Fifth Avenue
New York, New York 10003

Chapman and Hall
2-6 Boundary Row
London, SE1 8HN, England

Thomas Nelson Australia
102 Dodds Street
South Melbourne 3205
Victoria, Australia

Nelson Canada
1120 Birchmount Road
Scarborough, Ontario MIK 5G4, Canada

16   15   14   13   12   11   10   9   8   7   6   5   4   3   2   1

Library of Congress Cataloging-in-Publication Data

Peterle, Tony J.
    Wildlife toxicology / Tony J. Peterle.
        p.   cm.
    Includes bibliographical references and index.
    ISBN 0-442-00462-1
    1. Pesticides and wildlife.   2. Pesticides—Toxicology.
    3. Pollution—Environmental aspects.   I. Title.
QH545.P4P497   1991
591.2'4—dc20   90-22781
                                                                                          CIP

To my former students, who through their enthusiasm, questions, and responses kept me learning throughout my academic career.

Contents

Foreword

Wildlife toxicology, keyed to awareness of environmental problems, began its development as a science in response to the need to know the effects of DDT. Birds died after DDT applications, and scientists and the public protested—but a causative effect was denied or its magnitude minimized by DDT advocates. A lack of controlled experiments was cited as evidence sufficient for dismissal of the problem. Soon, controlled laboratory studies confirmed the field effects, but skepticism continued.

Environmental problems increased, from songbird mortality to contamination of food-chain organisms, to egg-shell thinning and impaired reproduction of birds of prey. Biologists and chemists pooled their skills and knowledge to develop new methods and proceeded step-by-step in laborious experimentation, guided by and integrated with intensive ecological study. Results were confirmed and accepted. That was the beginning. Soon there were new chemicals and new problems, but these were considered more solvable as scientific knowledge developed and grew. These were worldwide problems and many countries were involved—scientists in Great Britain, Sweden, and the Netherlands made major innovative contributions.

This book provides a clear picture of today's knowledge of environmental pollution as it affects wildlife. An understanding of principles is developed through examples, which examine key chemicals and their environmental actions. It both enlightens and informs, and will be appreciated by both laypersons and students.

The author is particularly able to provide this knowledge and perspective. He was there as a research investigator in the 1960s and has continued in active participation as scientist and research director. He has addressed environmental problems as consultant and member of many national and international groups. He has been Chairman of the Zoology Department at The Ohio State University, and a member of the faculty since 1959. His many graduate students include more than a dozen who have received doctorates in the field of Wildlife Toxicology.

Awareness of environmental problems and concern for pollution effects is widespread today. This book will sharpen this awareness with knowledge and vision.

Lucille F. Stickel
Former Director
Patuxent Wildlife
Research Center
USFWS, USDI

Preface

It is a bit presumptuous to assume that any author or group of authors could present as broad a topic as wildlife toxicology in one or even several volumes. We have brought to this manuscript a bit of our understanding of the subject matter, together with some of the literature. Collectively, we have been involved in studying the effects of toxic substances on wildlife for nearly a century. The book is meant to provide some background information on toxic substance effects for wildlife biologists, ecologists, and students. It is meant primarily for those who have not been directly involved in wildlife toxicology, although we hope those who are involved in this area might also find something of interest as we view the subject matter from our own perspective.

Acknowledgments: Chapter 1, by J. O. Keith, is an important contribution to the historical perspective of wildlife toxicology and I am grateful to him for this effort. My academic colleagues, J. Bart, T. A. Bookhout, and J. D. Harder, sometimes lectured on these topics in my absence. They greatly assisted me in clarifying my thoughts and presentations. My time spent on various committees of the USEPA Science Advisory Board, The National Academy of Sciences, and reviews done for various agencies and universities exposed me to a variety of technical problems, learned people, and information. I am grateful for these experiences; they helped to improve this manuscript. I wish to express my gratitude to my wife, Thelma, who supported me throughout my professional career with her good cheer and encouragement.

Introduction

Modern study of wildlife toxicology began shortly after the turn of the century when there was some concern about wildlife mortality related to the use of arsenicals, and mixtures of copper and lead to control pests. The greatest impetus for research came after World War II when the widespread introduction of synthetic organic chemicals such as the chlorinated hydrocarbons and later the organophosphates and pyrethroids began to affect wildlife. Later, research was extended to heavy metals and other industrial contaminants such as PCB and dioxins when they were also observed to have an impact on wildlife. Overall, the record of effects of toxic substances on wildlife is quite good and the research done by both private and public agencies has been exemplary. Despite all our knowledge concerning direct and indirect effects of a great variety of toxins on wildlife, we are still not capable of fully predicting the impacts on some species, populations, and ecosystems.

Although the effects of plant and animal toxins are important to many wildlife species, we deal mainly with the xenobiotics, those compounds introduced into the ecosystem by humans either as inadvertent pollutants in the industrial process or as a result of direct use or application for plant or animal pest control. Pesticides have been of greatest interest because of their widespread use, transport, and distribution in the global ecosystem. For many species of wildlife, we do not know the lethal or chronic effects of many of these compounds. Because most wildlife species are exposed to several contaminants simultaneously, prediction of cause-and-effect relationships is even more difficult. As the sophistication in the detection of lower and lower residues became available, the results of contaminant surveys and monitoring could be interpreted only to the extent that they could be corroborated by laboratory research. Early research dealt mainly with the determination of lethal effects, but progressed in later years to the study of behavioral, reproductive, and physiological effects of low chronic doses under controlled conditions. Use of several common wildlife species for laboratory studies (bobwhite, pheasant, mallard, blackbirds; all scientific names are provided in the Appendix) provided some insight into potential effects at the population level. We know that extrapolation of toxic substance data among species is not reliable, so for many species of wildlife we do not know how to evaluate either lethal or chronic effects of many of the thousands of chemicals now in production. Organic chemists continue to synthesize new and more effective toxins in order to control plant and animal pests. Testing protocols established by law under TSCA and FIFRA (see Acronyms) provide some basic information on laboratory and some wild species. It is up to the biologists who study wildlife toxicology to determine whether new compounds will present undue hazards to the great diversity of wildlife species. Surveys and monitoring programs can also be effective in calling attention to serious wildlife hazards. Direct lethal effects are sometimes obvious following release of a toxin, but they might also be slow and difficult to observe if the physiological functions or reproductive success of a species are affected by low-level exposure of a persistent toxic compound in the environment. Because of non-point sources of input into natural systems and long-distance transport, the sources of toxic substances cannot be identified and reduction of exposure might be impossible. We know this to be true for migratory species that obtain body burdens in different locations during their migrations.

The identification of toxic effects on wildlife is difficult, not only at the individual organism levels because of multiple exposures, but at the level of the population and ecosystem. We hope this book will help wildlife biologists become more aware of possible effects of toxic substances on species of concern and on the welfare of the ecosystems in which they are found. Ultimately, toxic substance effects on wildlife can become important to human welfare and survival. Perhaps the information available here will make us more aware of the potential affects of toxins, help us to call attention to such effects, and possibly alleviate or reduce the potential impact on wildlife species that are important to our own future welfare and survival.

Acronyms

AA	Assistant Administrator, EPA
AChE	Acetylcholinesterase
ACP	Alternative Chemicals Program, EPA
AH	Adminstrative hearings, EPA
APHIS	Animal Plant Health Inspection Service
ATSAC	Administrators Toxic Substance Advisory Committee, EPA
AQCR	Air Quality Control Regions
AWQS	Ambient water quality standards
BPCTCA (BPT)	Best practical control technology currently available
BAT	Best available technology
BCF	Bioconcentration factors
BCT	Best control tecnology
BLM	Bureau of Land Management
CAA	Clean Air Act
C&ED	Criteria and Evaluation Division, EPA
CAG	Cancer Assessment (Advisory) Group, EPA
CAS	Chemical Abstract Service
CASAC	Clean Air Science Advisory Committee, EPA
CBI	Confidential Business Information
CBIB	Chemical and Biological Investigation Branch, EPA
CDC	Centers for Disease Control
CEQ	Council on Environmental Quality
CERCLA	Comprehensive Environmental Response, Compensation and Liability Act (Superfund)
ChE	Cholinesterase
CIS	Chemical Information System
CNS	Central Nervous System
CSIN	Chemical Substances Information Network
CWA	Clean Water Act

DMR	Discharge monitoring reports
DOE	Department of Energy
EA	Economic Analysis Branch, EPA
EAI	Effective Avoidance Index
EEC	European Economic Community
EIS	Environmental Impact Statements
EMB	Ecological Monitoring Branch, EPA
EMS	Enforcement management system, EPA
EXAMS	Exposure analysis modeling systems
FDA	Food and Drug Administration
FARM	Field agricultural runoff monitoring
FCPC	Federal Committee on Pest Control
FEPCA	Federal Environmental Pesticide Control Act
FFDCA	Federal Food, Drug, and Cosmetics Act
FIFRA	Federal Insecticide, Fungicide,and Rodenticide Act
FIFRA/SAP	FIFRA Science Advisory Panel
FPCRB	Federal Pest Control Review Board
FWGPM	Federal Working Group on Pest Management
GLP	Good laboratory practices
HEMB	Human Effects Monitoring Branch, EPA
HES	Hazard Evaluation System, EPA
HHS	Health and Human Services
IB	Information Branch, EPA
ICPC	Interdepartmental Committee on Pest Control, EPA
I/M	Inspection and maintenance
IPM	Integrated pest management
IRLG	Interagency Regulatory Liaison Group
ITC	Interagency Testing Committee, EPA
IUA	Integrated Use Analysis, EPA
KDR	Knock-down resistance
LH	Luteinizing hormone
MAG	Management Advisory Group to Municipal Construction Division, EPA
MSSS	Mass spectral search system (CIS)
MCL	Maximum contaminant levels
MFO	Mixed function oxidase
MSHA	Mine Safety and Health Administration
NAAQS	National Ambient Air Quality Standards
NAMS	National Air Monitoring Stations
NAS	National Academy of Sciences
NCI	National Cancer Institute
NEPA	National Environmental Policy Act

NEPMN	National Envronmental Pesticide Monitoring Network
NESHAPS	National emission standards for hazardous air pollutants
NIEHS	National Institute of Environmental Health Science
NIH	National Institutes of Health
NIOSH	National Institute of Occupational Safety and Health
NIPDWR	National Interim Primary Drinking Water Regulations
NMFS	National Marine Fisheries Services
NOAA	National Oceanic and Atmospheric Administration
NPDES	National Pollution Discharge Elimination System
NPMP	National Pesticides Monitoring Program
NSF	National Science Foundation
NSPS	New source performance standards
NTIS	National Technical Information System
OA	Office of Administration, EPA
OAQPS	Office of Air Quality Planning and Standards, EPA
OD	Operations Division, EPA
ODW	Office of Drinking Water, EPA
OE	Office of Enforcement, EPA
OECD	Organization for Economic Cooperation and Development
OER	Office of Exploratory Research, EPA
OGC	Office of General Counsel, EPA
OHM	Oil and Hazardous Materials (CIS)
OIG	Office of Inspector General
OMB	Office of Management and Budget
OPM	Office of Planning and Management, EPA
OPP	Office of Pesticides Programs, EPA
OPRM	Office of Policy and Resource Management, EPA
OPTS	Office of Pesticides and Toxic Substances, EPA
ORD	Office of Research and Development, EPA
OSHA	Occupational Safety and Health Administration
OSPR	Office of Special Pesticide Review, EPA
OSW	Office of Solid Waste, EPA
OSWER	Office of Solid Waste and Emergency Response, EPA
OTI	Office of Toxics Integration, EPA
OTS	Office of Toxic Substances, EPA
OWHM	Office of Water and Hazardous Materials, EPA
OWPS	Office of Water Planning and Standards, EPA

PAH	Polycyclic aromatic hydrocarbons
PBBs	Polybrominated biphenyls
PCBs	Polychlorinated biphenyls
PCDDs	Polychlorinated dibenzo-para-dioxin (Dioxin)
PCRC	Pesticide Chemical Review Committee, EPA
PERS	Pesticide Episode Reporting System, EPA
PM	Project Manager, EPA
POTW	Publicly owned treatment works
PPAC	Pesticide Policy Advisory Committee, EPA
PPQP	Plant Protection and Quarantine Program
PRRPB	Pesticide Research Review and Priority Board, EPA
PSAC	President's Science Advisory Committee
PSD	Prevention of significant deterioration
PSI	Pollutant Standard Index
PWS	Public Water Systems
RCRA	Resources Conservation and Recovery Act
RET	Reviewability Evaluation Team, Registration Division, EPA
RMAC	Regional Management Analytic Centers, EPA
RPAR	Rebuttable presumption against registration
RPDWR	Revision primary drinking water regulations
RTECS	Registry of toxic effects of chemical substances (CIS)
SAB	Science Advisory Board, 80 members, 5 committees, EPA
SANSS	Structure and nomenclature search system (CIS)
SAP	Science Advisory Panel—7 members, recc. by NIH, NSF
SCP	Substitute Chemical Program, EPA
SCR	Suspect Chemical Review, EPA
SDWA	Safe Drinking Water Act
SEA	State/EPA Agreements
SIPS	State Implementation Plans, EPA (air quality)
SLAMS	State/Local Air Monitoring Systems
SNARLs	Suggested no adverse response levels
PRZM	Pesticide root zone model
QSAR	Quantitative structure—activity relationships
SLSA	Simplified lake and stream analysis
SSB	System Support Branch, EPA
TCE	Trichloroethylene
TSCA	Toxic Substances Control Act PL 94-469
TSD	Technical Services Divsion, EPA

TSP	Total suspended particulates
TSPC	Toxic Substances Priority(ies) Committee, EPA
UIC	Underground injection control
USAID	Unites States Aid for Independent Development
USDA	U.S. Department of Agriculture
USEPA	U.S. Environmental Protection Agency
USHHS	Health and Human Services Department (former HEW)
USFS	U.S. Forest Service
USFWS	U.S. Fish and Wildlife Service
WARF	Wisconsin Alumni Research Foundation
WDROP	Water distribution register of organic pollutants (CIS)
WHO	World Health Organization
WQM	Water quality management
WQS	Water quality standards

1

Historical Perspectives

James O. Keith

All organisms are greatly influenced by alterations in their environments. Change threatens some species, while survival of others is enhanced. In pursuing their own interests, humans have considerably altered the earth's environment and have decreased the probability of survival for many other species. There is a question whether humans as environmental manipulators have increased or decreased their own chance of survival. It might prove to be that humans would have persisted longer as a species if, as all other organisms on earth, they had pursued the course of adaptation rather than manipulation.

As agriculturalists, humans changed the physiognomy of continents, especially in the Northern Hemisphere. Centuries of intensive land use and habitat alteration certainly have had a greater influence on other organisms than anything else humans have done. This process of change continues today at an accelerating rate, particularly in the developing countries of the Southern Hemisphere. The Industrial Revolution ultimately led to a different kind of influence on the earth's environment. During only the last 40 years, increasing technological pollution has seriously degraded the quality of natural environments. Entire continents have been affected, and pollutants now contaminate the oceans, the atmosphere, and thus the entire biosphere.

The development and intensive use of synthetic chemicals, heavy metals, oil, and petrochemical products are responsible for today's most serious pollution problems. These activities also created most of the increased wealth in the world today. Therefore, current practices will con-

This chapter was contributed by James O. Keith, Denver Wildlife Research Center, U. S. Department of Agriculture. An earlier version of this manuscript appeared as part of Czechoslovak–American Symposium on Toxic Effects of Environmental Contaminants upon Production and Reproduction Ability in Free-living Animals, edited by P. Kacmar and J. Legath, University of Veterinary Medicine, Kosice, Czechoslovakia, 1983.

tinue and pollution problems will intensify. Regulatory and technological controls offer the best hopes for limiting the impact of pollution on the environment.

Broad concern about the environmental effects of pollution began only recently. In the United States, it came with the realization that chemicals used to control rodents and predators on western rangelands could also poison other animals (Pierce and Clegg 1915, Lindsdale 1931, Ward 1931). With the increased use of inorganic and botanical pesticides, studies were begun to determine mortality of wildlife in treated areas. Evaluations were made of the use of arsenicals for control of grasshoppers (Pollack 1929, Whitehead 1934), gypsy moths (Frost 1938), and aquatic weeds (Surber and Meehean 1931). Similar studies were made of pyrethrums (Leonard 1942), mercury, cryolite, ryania, and copper sulfate (Rudd and Genelly 1956) used in agriculture. Concern for wildlife increased with the development of methods for the aerial application of pesticides to agricultural lands and forests (Tragardh 1935). Until 1945, rodenticides and arsenicals were the principal pesticides used in the United States. Conflicts between pest control and wildlife were identified and discussed (Strong 1938, Zimmerman 1938). Few intensive studies were conducted, but wildlife mortality was documented (Rudd and Genelly 1956). The abundance of some species decreased after pesticide treatments, and indirect effects through reduction in food supplies were suspected. However, considering what was to come, these programs did not cause many serious problems.

World War II brought on intensive research into the use of chemicals for both positive and negative purposes. The insecticidal properties of DDT were discovered, and during and after the war, DDT was used to control disease vectors threatening military personnel and civilian populations. Research on DDT also identified the potential insecticidal and herbicidal properties of other related chlorinated hydrocarbons. Military research on nerve gases during the war led to the development of the organophosphates for insect control. Similarly, research on rodent control to protect troops and cities from disease produced the new rodenticide, Compound 1080 (Aceto Chemical Co., Flushing, NY), which later was adapted for use in controlling predators.

At the end of World War II, a variety of new, synthetic chemicals was available for control of pests that had plagued humans since crops were first planted. In 1945, private firms in the industrialized countries began to manufacture and market these new chemicals. Agricultural acreage had greatly increased in the United States during the war; and elsewhere in the world, normal agricultural production had to be quickly reestablished. This coincidence of need and availability of pesticides created a large and instand demand for products and an explosive increase in their use throughout the world. Basic toxicity and efficacy data were rapidly developed, but widespread use was begun without knowledge of the ultimate fate and effects of the chemicals in the environment.

THE EARLY YEARS

Fortunately, biologists were alert to the potential hazards of the new synthetic pesticides. In 1946, the U. S. Fish and Wildlife Service conducted field studies on pesticides in seven states and ran numerous laboratory trials (Nelson and Surber 1947). Most research was on DDT because more of it was being used than all of the other insecticides combined. Many publications appeared in 1946, including those on the effects of DDT for control of mosquitoes (Couch 1946) and gypsy moths (Hotchkiss and Pough 1946), DDT effects on birds (Kozlik 1946; Stewart, Cope, Robbins, et al. 1946) and nestlings (Mitchell 1946), DDT effects on mammals (McDermid 1946, Stickel 1946), and general discussions of the biological effects of DDT (Coburn and Treichler 1946, Cottam and Higgins 1946, Storer 1946).

Some interesting characteristics of DDT were discovered during initial studies. The accumulation of DDT in adipose tissue of animals was demonstrated (Woodard, Ofner, and Montgomery 1945; Kunze, Nelson, Fitzhugh, et al. 1949). Milk from mammals exposed to DDT was found to contain residues (Woodard, Ofner, and Montgomery 1945), and chickens fed DDT were shown to lay contaminated eggs (Rubin, Bird, Green, et al. 1947). Jones (1952) defined the stability of DDT; Finnegan, Haag, and Larson (1949) described the distribution and elimination of residues from animal tissues, and the estrogenic activity of DDT was discovered by Fisher, Keasling, and Schueler (1952).

By 1950, 15 insecticides and fungicides were in common use (Bunyan and Stanley 1983). As applications of other chlorinated hydrocarbon insecticides increased, wildlife studies were broadened to give them scrutiny along with DDT (Baumgartner 1948, Post 1949, Barnett 1950). DDT, aldrin, dieldrin, chlordane, and toxaphene sometimes caused wildlife mortality when used in grasshopper programs (Harris 1951, Eng 1952), in orchards (Odum and Norris 1949, Kelsall 1950), in cotton (Young, Hulsey, and Moe 1952; Eyer, Faulkner, and McCarty 1953), and in rice (Rudd and Genelly 1955). The acute toxicity and gross effects of these chemicals on reproduction were assessed in laboratory studies (Dahlen and Haugen 1954, DeWitt 1955, Genelly and Rudd 1956).

The first widespread use of organophosphate insecticides began in the 1950s. Field applications were evaluated (Barnett 1950; Mohr, Telford, Peterson, et al. 1951), and the first of many poisonings of geese with organophosphates was reported (Livingston 1952). Organophosphate persistence was evaluated (Fahey, Hamilton, and Rings 1952), and the technique of chloinesterase measurement was used to monitor exposure (Stearns, Griffiths, Bradley, et al. 1951). Organophosphates, in general, were more toxic than the chlorinated hydrocarbon insecticides, and concern over human hazard restricted their acceptance. Their use increased with knowledge of how to monitor human exposure and how to safely apply the chemicals by air. In these early programs, the higher toxicity of the organophosphates did not result in more frequent wildlife deaths, as some had feared.

By 1955, several hundred papers had been published on the effects of pesticides on wildlife. Acute toxicity data existed for many chemicals against laboratory animals, fishes, and a few species of wild birds. In general, birds and fishes appeared more susceptible to pesticide poisoning than mammals, reptiles, and amphibians (see discussion by Walker 1983). Insecticides were shown to be more toxic to wildlife than other pesticides, although the toxicity of insecticides differed considerably among compounds and wildlife species. Field experience showed that the acute toxicity of pesticides did not necessarily depict their hazards to wildlife when used in the field. Some highly toxic pesticides did not persist long enough to be hazardous, while less toxic materials persisted and had serious sublethal effects. Field studies had identified the insecticides and rates of applications that were most hazardous to wild animals, and the potential for reproductive effects was documented in both field and laboratory investigations.

Robert L. Rudd and Richard E. Genelly of the University of California compiled the available knowledge on pesticides in their encyclopedic reference book, *Pesticides: Their Use and Toxicity in Relation to Wildlife* (Rudd and Genelly 1956). This book was the first classic publication in the wildlife pesticide field, and it continues to be a valuable reference today.

MAJOR PROGRAMS

From the beginning, biologists were especially concerned about pesticide programs that each year treated extensive areas of important wildlife habitat. Improved techniques for aerial application of pesticides enabled treatment of thousands of hectares of forests and rangelands. Equally disturbing was the widespread use of toxic seed dressings and the multiple treatments (up to 20) being applied each year to some wetlands for mosquito control.

Insect Control in Forests

High rates of DDT (2–7 kg/ha) were applied to forests for control of spruce budworm (Hope 1949, Cope and Springer 1958), Dutch elm disease (Benton 1951), and Japanese beetles (Fleming and Hawley 1950). These programs caused bird mortality, reduced populations, and sometimes affected reproduction (Adams, Hanavan, Hosley, et al. 1949; Langford 1949). Use of DDT in control of Dutch elm disease consistently caused high mortality of birds (especially robins), and some populations were severely decimated in local areas (Hickey and Hunt 1960; Wallace, Etter, and Osborne 1964; Wurster, Wurster, and Strickland 1965).

During the 1950s, concern over the mortality of fishes and forest wildlife resulted in a reduction in application rates of DDT. Satisfactory insect control was achieved with much less DDT, and the incidence of bird and fish mortality decreased (Hoffman, Janson, and Hartkorn 1958). Continued use of DDT in forests undoubtedly contributed to global contamination with DDT residues, but that problem had not yet been identified in the 1950s.

Biologists in the United States (Pillmore and Finley 1963) and Canada (Fowle 1966, Pearce 1971) worked with forest entomologists (Benedict and Baker 1963) for over two decades to make forest applications safer for wildlife. Gradually, the less toxic chemicals malathion, carbaryl, and the synthetic pyrethrins replaced DDT in many programs, but use of some organophosphates such as phosphamidon still caused bird mortality (Finley 1965, Fowle 1972). Thorough evaluation of the most recent, and one hopes the last, use of DDT in forests again clearly illustrated its lethal and sublethal effects on wildlife (Herman and Bulger 1979; Henny, Maser, Whitaker, Jr., et al. 1982).

Fire Ant Eradication

A program to eradicate the imported fire ant in the southeastern United States was begun in the 1950s and is still underway. Applications of insecticides in baits were made to extensive areas of woodlands, pastures, and farms during most years. Heptachlor and dieldrin were used during the first decade of this program, and biologists documented high bird mortality and population decreases after treatments (Clawson and Baker 1959, Rosene 1965). Residues of heptachlor epoxide were found in many species of birds (Stickel, Hayne, and Stickel 1965), including woodcock, whose eggs on Canadian breeding grounds also contained residues (Wright 1965).

Mirex (Allied Chemical Corp., Hopewell, VA) was later substituted in the fire ant program, but it also was highly persistent, accumulated in wildlife (Oberheu 1972), and was toxic to terrestrial and aquatic life (Galbreath 1965, Baker 1967). Kepone (Allied Chemical Corp., Hopewell, VA) bait has since been used, and new, less hazardous materials are currently being tested for this program.

The history of the program to eradicate the fire ant illustrates the hazards to animals of large-scale, blanket treatments of farmlands, woodlots, and wild areas that in the aggregate constitute important habitats for wildlife. Many species are exposed, and this increases the probability that some will be vulnerable to either mortality or sublethal effects. Using bait formulations is especially hazardous, as they are often highly palatable to birds that feed on the ground.

Seed Dressings

In the large programs involving the use of insecticides as seed dressings, mortality was the primary effect on wildlife. During the 1950s and early 1960s, seeds were commonly treated with aldrin, dieldrin, heptachlor, and mercurial fungicides in the United States and western Europe. Extensive areas were planted with treated seeds. The seeds of many agricultural crops were treated as were most seeds planted in forests and rangelands. Such practices caused extensive primary and secondary poisoning of birds, the evidence of which was annually compiled and published in the United Kingdom (Bunyan and Stanley 1983, Walker 1983).

The hazard of seed dressings is rather straightforward. Poisons are put on seeds; wild animals that eat the seeds are poisoned and they die. Scavengers that feed on the dead animals can also be killed. Still, it took 25 years to ban most hazardous seed dressings, and that experience is indicative of the resistance that was usually encountered in changing use practices once they became established. Aldrin-treated rice seeds were still killing birds in Texas in the early 1970s (Flickinger and King 1972) and heptachlor on seeds killed geese in Oregon in the late 1970s (Blus, Henny, Lenhart, et al. 1979).

Mosquito Control

Mosquitoes are a nuisance to humans, and adults and larvae are controlled over large areas of the United States. Wetlands are commonly treated, which subjects a variety of wildlife species to exposure. Heavy applications of DDT were made to marshlands and estuaries for many years, and wildlife effects were commonly documented (Tarzwell 1947, Knedel 1951, Springer and Webster 1951, Hanson 1952). As multiple treatments often were made each year, this use of DDT greatly contributed to the contamination of aquatic food chains that would later be identified. Within a decade, such intensive use of DDT resulted in the development of resistant mosquito populations. Other chlorinated hydrocarbons were effective for only short periods before resistance developed. Organophosphate insecticides then became the only effective means of controlling mosquitoes. Tests with wildlife (Keith and Mulla 1966, Hill 1971) indicated the hazards of organophosphate insecticides like fenthion, but the low toxicity of fenthion to mammals made it safer for humans to use than other insecticides such as parathion. Fenthion came into wide use and repeatedly has caused bird losses throughout the United States (Seabloom, Pearson, Oring, et al. 1973; DeWeese, McEwen, Settimi, et al. 1983).

In California, mosquito populations ultimately developed a resistance to all insecticides. This set off a rapid search for alternate means of mosquito control. As has happened whenever use of chemicals was restricted, entomologists quickly found promising alternatives. Synthetic juvenile hormones that interrupt larval development are now on the market. Also BTI (*Bacillus thruingiensis var. Israelensis*) and certain chemical amines were found effective in controlling mosquitoes and are being developed for widescale use.

Grasshopper Control

Grasshoppers have been controlled on western rangelands in the United States nearly every year since 1934; areas treated annually have averaged about 800,000 ha (McEwen 1982). Many chlorinated hydrocarbon insecticides are effective against grasshoppers, and most have been applied to control grasshoppers and other rangeland insect pests. Such uses consistently killed birds, and sometimes mammals, fishes, reptiles, and amphibians. Applications of chlorinated hydrocarbons were discontinued after 1965 in the major control programs, but their use has continued in some states. Wildlife hazards and relationships were thoroughly documented, and wildlife ecologists worked with entomologists to demonstrate the greater safety of malathion and carbaryl to wildlife (McEwen 1982).

The newest approach for grasshopper control is most encouraging because of its safety to wildlife. Combinations of carbaryl bait and a bait containing spores of protozoans are aerially applied. The instant action of the insecticide coupled with the residual effect of the parasite give good grasshopper control without poisoning wildlife.

The reduction of grasshoppers itself adversely affects wildlife, as grasshoppers are a principal food of rangeland birds, especially during the birds' breeding season. Control of grasshoppers essentially diverts energy produced on rangelands from food chains of small insectivores into the food chains of herbivores, especially livestock. Such indirect effects of grasshopper control may have greater influences on wildlife populations than the mortality caused by insecticide use.

Herbicide Programs

More herbicides have consistently been used each year than any other type of pesticide. Herbicides account for two-thirds of the pesticides used in the United States (Maddy 1983). Most of this use is to control weeds in crops, but considerable amounts are applied to forests, rangelands, and other important wildlife habitats. Laboratory trials have shown that most herbicides are not highly toxic to birds and mammals, and field investigations have seldom shown lethal effects (Rudd and Genelly 1956).

The greatest concern about the use of herbicides has been their possible indirect effects through altering habitats. Indeed, herbicides are widely used by wildlife biologists to manage vegetation for the benefits of wildlife. Still, herbicides applied to eliminate brush (Goodrum and Reid 1956), to maintain right-of-ways (Bramble and Byrns 1958), and to control marsh vegetation (Hanson 1952) have adversely influenced wildlife populations.

Indirect effects of herbicides on wildlife are difficult to assess. Usually, treated habitats already have been disturbed and the availability of food and other life requirements of animals are seldom clearly understood either before or after herbicide treatments. In one study where food supplies, food habits, and population changes could be measured, the herbicide 2,4-D reduced food abundance, which in turn altered food habits and severely reduced numbers of pocket gophers (Keith, Hansen, and Ward 1959).

The influence on wildlife of dioxins, the highly toxic contaminants in certain herbicides, was never thoroughly evaluated. They had great potential to adversely influence animals, but working with dioxins was extremely hazardous. Now herbicides containing dioxins have been banned.

Evaluations of the major programs concentrated on abundant species that occurred in treated areas. Biologists reasoned that if pesticides caused mortality or reproductive problems, those effects should be most obvious in animals directly exposed to applications. Studies often documented the death of wildlife and enabled modification of programs so as to reduce or prevent further mortalities. Important effects on reproduction were seldom observed. This work accomplished a lot, but biologists were slowly learning that serious problems had developed elsewhere.

RESIDUE CONTAMINATION AND BIOACCUMULATION

In the late 1950s, biologists investigated a mortality in western grebes at Clear Lake, California. Birds contained high levels of DDD in their adipose tissue and apparently had died from DDD poisoning. DDD had been applied to the lake to control midge larvae as the adult midges were a nuisance to humans that resided on the lake shore. But how had the birds been exposed? The ensuing research documented for the first time the phenomenon of bioaccumulation of insecticide residues in animal food chains. This pioneer work by Hunt and Bischoff (1960) initiated a line of research that ultimately led to the banning of most chlorinated hydrocarbon insecticides and thereby to saving a number of species endangered by those chemicals.

Subsequently, investigations of fish-eating bird mortality in marshlands in England (Prestt 1966) and the United States (J. O. Keith 1966) showed that birds had accumulated sufficient chlorinated hydrocarbon residues to kill them. These studies documented that insecticides used in agriculture were being transported in waste irrigation water into untreated natural habitats, where they accumulated in aquatic food chains and ultimately poisoned predaceous species.

Dispersal of Residues

Hooper and Hester (1955) measured pollution of streams by runoff water from agricultural fields, but consideration was given only to the immediate lethal effects on aquatic organisms. In the United States, nationwide surveys were conducted to determine the levels of pesticide contamination in streams receiving waste agricultural water. Results consistently showed only trace amounts of residues at most sampling stations. However, these findings were largely erroneous. Sampling was done with carbon filters that were easily clogged with detritus and sediments. Sand prefilters were used to divert material that was suspended in water. Measurements, therefore, were of pesticides in water solution; chlorinated hydrocarbons are relatively insoluble in water.

Later work showed that most pesticides transported in water are adhered to suspended organic debris (J. O. Keith 1966). Organic matter in water is fed upon by small invertebrates, and this initiates the contamination of aquatic food chains. This organic debris often contains higher residues (20–80 ppm) than those found in invertebrates, fishes, and the fat of birds; but it is present in only very small amounts. Bioaccumulation, therefore, must be viewed in terms of the quantity of pesticide accumulated as well as the proportional amount in parts per million. In the final analysis, it is the number of molecules or weight of poison that becomes important.

Soil is the matrix that remains to become contaminated from repeated treatments of crops with pesticides. Residue levels in soil and their persistence after treatments were measured in many studies, such as one by Chisholm and Koblitsky (1959). Most studies implied that loss of contamination over time illustrated the rate of pesticide degradation in soil. That suggestion was often incorrect. Residues usually disappeared from soil by moving into the atmosphere and by being carried off in irrigation water.

Measurements of aerial applications consistently have shown that deposits on treated areas seldom exceed 50 percent, and often are as low as 10 percent, of the amount applied. Herbicides applied to rice fields in California were finally identified as the cause of death to fruit trees in orchards 30 km downwind. Probably the most spectacular finding was that residues of pesticides used in Africa were being transported on dust particles across the Atlantic Ocean to the Western Hemisphere in the southeasterly tradewinds (Risebrough, Huggett, Griffin, et al. 1968). Airborne fallout on Iceland also contained DDT and PCB residues (Bengtson and Sodergren 1974).

Residue Surveys

Evidence was gradually accumulated that residues of chlorinated hydrocarbons were dispersing widely and often persisting much longer than expected. Interestingly, this information primarily came from wildlife biologists and not from agricultural scientists. Surveys of residues in birds, mammals, fishes, reptiles, and amphibians were conducted throughout the United States and in more than 30 other countries. Results provided convincing evidence that insecticides in air and water were contaminating untreated wildlife habitats. The homerange of many species containing residues simply did not include areas where direct applications had been made. It was evident that not all animals received equal exposure. As a group, birds carried greater amounts of residues than mammals. Flesh-eating birds had higher levels than herbivores. Residues of DDT and its metabolites were consistently found in more samples and at higher levels than any other chlorinated hydrocarbons (Keith and Gruchy 1972). Residue levels of the more toxic compounds (e.g., endrin, dieldrin) were lower than those of slightly less toxic ones (e.g., chlordane, heptachlor). Apparently, the more toxic ones killed before high levels could be accumulated, whereas the less toxic ones accumulated and later sometimes caused mortality when animals were stressed (Keith 1968). Mortality was the only real effect noted in most species during these early surveys, but levels in living birds were often high enough to cause concern about sublethal effects.

Migratory birds were thought to be exposed on wintering grounds and subjected to the hazards of accumulated residues while breeding after migration. This potential existed for snow geese (Flickinger 1979), white-faced ibis (Capen 1977), white pelicans (J. O. Keith 1966, Knopf and Street 1974), peregrine falcons (Cade, White, and Haugh 1968), woodcock (Wright 1965), and many other species. Measurement of exposure during migration proved difficult, but winter exposure in species showing breeding debility was finally shown for brown pelicans (Anderson, Jehl, Risebrough, et al. 1975) and peregrine falcons (Henny, Prescott, Riddle, et al. 1982). Risebrough, Menzel, Martin, Jr., et al. (1967) reported some of the first residues from marine fishes. Their findings that fishes in the oceans were being exposed to insecticides stimulated a number of additional surveys. Results showed that even fishes in the middle of oceans carried insecticide residues (Risebrough 1969). Subsequently, contaminations were found in marine mammals in Sweden (Jensen, Johnels, Olsson, et al. 1969), in Arctic ringed seals (Addison and Smith 1974), in British grey seals (Heppleston 1973), and in many other sea mammals. DDT and DDE were found in Antarctic mammals and birds (Tatton and Ruzicka 1967, Brewerton 1969), in birds of Greenland (Braestrup, Clausen, and Berg 1974), animals in Iceland (Bengtson and Sodergren 1974), and in eggs of green sea turtles from Ascension Island (Thompson, Rankin, and Johnston 1974).

Chlorinated hydrocarbons were being used throughout the world, but only a small proportion of each continent had received treatments. Even in California, which accounts for 10 percent of the world's annual pesticide use (Maddy 1983), only an average of 15 percent of the land is treated each year. The United Kingdom is an example of the exceptions: 85 percent of the land is in agriculture, and most is treated with pesticides. Dispersal of these persistent chemicals from areas of use had created a global contamination, the total effects of which were not yet clearly understood.

Residues in Ecosystems

Several ingenious studies helped to describe the fate and involvement of insecticides in ecosystems. Radioactive-labeled DDT was applied to a marsh, and levels in different substrates were analyzed over time (Meeks 1968). Hickey, Keith and Coon (1966) and J. A. Keith (1966) successfully documented the source and food chain contamination of DDT that influenced herring gulls in Lake Michigan. The fate of malathion in a forest was studied with labeled insecticide (Giles 1970). Korschgen (1970) followed aldrin from the soil of treated fields into wildlife food chains, and Wood-well, Wurster, and Isaacson (1967) documented biological concentration of DDT in an estuarine environment.

Most studies of insecticide dynamics dealt with relationships within treated areas, and attention was primarily given to agricultural basins and other areas of intense and annual pesticide use. Animals were continuously exposed to residues, but it was seldom clear whether that exposure came primarily from current applications or from those made in the past. Where single applications were made to study areas, chemicals sometimes persisted and contaminated food chains for many years (Herman, Garrett, and Rudd 1969; Dimond, Belyea, Kadunce, et al. 1970; Forsyth, Peterle, and Bandy 1983), whereas in other instances residues appeared to quickly degrade and only briefly contaminate food chains (Keith 1968, Meeks 1968). This contrast was most evident in a study of two lakes treated with toxaphene to control undesirable fishes (Terriere, Kiigemagi, Gerlach, et al. 1966). Trout were successfully stocked in one lake within months following treatment, but in the other lake toxaphene killed introduced trout each year for 8 years. The process and rate of toxaphene degradation differed considerably between the two lakes.

Woodwell, Wurster, and Isaacson (1967) used the concept of half-life to describe the persistence of DDT, and others have continued to use this term. The concept is misleading and should not be applied to pesticides. Pesticides, unlike radioactive materials, do not have a predictable half-life. Pesticide degradation rates are governed by the kinds and intensity of factors that metabolize pesticides in the environments where residues occur. For instance, Brown and Brown (1970) convincingly showed that DDT persistence is exceptionally lengthened in the subarctic compared with its persistence in more temperate climates. It is known that the persistence and involvement of a pesticide can vary among environments, but not enough is known to enable a prediction of its fate and influence at a particular site. It becomes difficult, therefore, to generalize the rate of residue degradation, which is the basis for a half-life value.

A rather unusual method was used by biologists in an attempt to evaluate the cumulative effects of environmental contamination on bird populations. Life tables were developed for periods before and after the advent of modern pesticides. Comparisons were then made of the dynamics of populations with and without the influence of pesticides. Population problems were indicated in some species that had been shown in other studies to receive high exposure (Henny 1972, Franks 1973).

Residue Effects in Animals

Laboratory scientists became involved in diverse kinds of studies to evaluate the hazards of DDT and other persistent chemicals. Considerable effort was made to document the lethal toxicity of pesticides to wild animals. Handbooks were published of acute toxicity to fishes and invertebrates (Johnson and Finley 1980) and to birds and mammals (Tucker and Crabtree 1970; Hudson, Tucker, and Haegele 1984). Lethal levels of pesticides in the diet of birds were reported (Heath, Spann, Hill, et al. 1972; Hill, Heath, Spann, et al. 1975). Lethal toxicity data indicated the physiological susceptibility of animals to different poisons. Such information provided a valuable perspective on the potential for lethal effects on animals. Once pesticides are applied, however, this potential is modified by the ecological vulnerability of species to exposure. Species killed may not be the most susceptible ones on treated areas. Animals whose foods are contaminated become vulnerable and are most likely to be poisoned. Mortality reduces the abundance of animals; but it was ultimately found that chronic effects, which decrease survival and reproductive success, had a greater impact on populations than acute mortality.

Rates of uptake and loss of pesticides received considerable study in poultry (see review by Stickel 1973). Residues in poultry were a serious problem, as contaminated birds and eggs could not be marketed. Some of these studies misled biologists, as domestic hens often proved to be less susceptible than wild birds to the effects of pesticides.

Studies defined the residue levels in tissues that were indicative of pesticide poisoning. Brain residues best correlated with mortality (Bernard 1963; Stickel, Stickel, and Christensen 1966; Stickel and Stickel 1969). Residues in adipose tissue of birds were shown to be mobilized with fats during stress (Sodergren and Ulfstrand 1972), and this often caused mortality (Van Velzen, Stiles, and Stickel 1972). The various types of stress found to cause death in contaminated birds included starvation and weight loss (Bernard 1963), molting (Stickel, Stickel, and Spann 1969; Stickel and Rhodes 1970), and disturbance of captive birds (Stickel 1965).

The effects of many pesticides on reproductive success in penned birds were evaluated (Dahlen and Haugen 1954; DeWitt 1955; Genelly and Rudd 1956; Azevedo, Hunt, and Woods 1965; Jefferies 1967; Neill, Muller, and Schutze 1971; Haegele and Hudson 1973). These studies often showed that pesticide exposure resulted in decreased egg production and reduced hatchability. Other studies suggested that chlorinated hydrocarbons delayed ovulation (Jefferies 1967), increased estradiol metabolism (Peakall 1970b), stimulated production of liver microsomal enzymes that led to hydroxylation of steroids (Gillett, Chan, and Terriere 1966; Peakall 1967), and altered thyroid secretion (Jeffries and French 1972) and adrenal structure (Lehman, Peterle, and Mills 1974). Wurster (1969), Stickel (1973), and Risebrough (1986) reviewed the relationships between pesticides and avian reproduction.

Wild animals contaminated with chlorinated hydrocarbon residues must often be faced with the additional stresses of disease and food shortage. In such situations, the combined effects could be additive and create a severe challenge to animals. Studies evaluating pesticide–disease interactions were made by Friend and Trainer (1974a and b) and Thompson and Emerman (1974). Keith (1978) tested the combined effects of DDE and food restriction on reproductive success. These studies showed that pesticides can seriously aggravate the debilities caused by natural limiting factors.

Concern among biologists was heightened by these accounts of environmental contamination and wildlife effects from pesticides. They reasoned that if pesticides killed some animals, then certainly survivors containing high residue levels could be subject to sublethal effects on reproduction and survival. All of these fears, backed by the evidence that caused this concern, were convincingly presented by Rachel Carson (1962) in her book, *Silent Spring*. This book successfully informed the public of the hazards of pesticides to wildlife and is now regarded as giving rise to the environmental movement that has become so dominant in decision-making processes today.

POPULATION STUDIES

Ultimately, it was the study of declining avian populations that provided definition of the specific debilities caused by exposure to chlorinated hydrocarbon insecticides. Biologists in several countries were investigating populations of birds that had slowly declined to critical levels. The species all carried residues of DDT, its metabolites, other chlorinated hydrocarbon insecticides, polychlorinated biphenyls, and other chemicals. Nesting success was lower than normal in all affected species, but the exact nature of the debility affecting birds was not clear (see discussion in Cade, White, and Haugh 1968). Species of concern included osprey (Ames 1966), bald eagles (Stickel, Chura, Stewart, et al. 1966), Bermuda petrels (Wurster and Wingate 1968), herring gulls (J. A. Keith 1966), and brown pelicans (Schreiber and DeLong 1969).

A British biologist, Derek Ratcliffe, had tenaciously struggled for 10 years to understand the relationships involved in the decline of sparrow hawks and peregrine falcons in the United Kingdom. This inquiry finally led him to considerations of raptor eggshells; measurements proved that shells of eggs laid after World War II were lighter in weight than those of eggs laid before the war (Ratcliffe 1967). He postulated that the use of chlorinated hydrocarbon insecticides had somehow caused eggshell thinning in raptors.

Ratcliffe's ideas immediately stimulated an assessment by biologists of the incidence and cause of eggshell thinning in birds. Anderson and Hickey (1972) measured over 23,000 eggshells of 25 species. They found shell thinning in 22 of those species and illustrated that thinning was correlated with DDE residues in the eggs. Experimental work with mallards (Heath, Spann, and Kreitzer 1969) and American kestrels (Wiemeyer and Porter 1970) soon showed DDE, a metabolite of DDT, caused eggshell thinning. Since those early studies, it has become clear that DDE is the primary cause of shell thinning in many kinds of birds. Gallinaceous species were not affected. A tremendous amount of effort has gone into study of eggshell thinning, and results have been reviewed (see Cooke 1973, Stickel 1973). Eggshell thinning was definitely a major cause of low reproductive success and population decline in some species, but chlorinated hydrocarbons probably contributed to declines in other ways. Many adults of some contaminated species did not attempt to breed in some years, and desertion of eggs and nestlings was commonly observed. Preliminary studies suggested such behavior could be caused by DDT and polychlorinated biphenyls (Peakall and Peakall 1973, Haegele and Hudson 1977). Later, intensive work more fully described the aberrant behavior and reduced productivity caused by chlorinated hydrocarbons (Keith 1978) and the hormonal basis for these debilities (McArthur, Fox, Peakall, et al. 1983). Continued investigations of this nature are needed to assess the potential for other persistent chemicals to adversely affect the behavior and breeding performance of birds.

Populations of several species of wild birds were severely affected by DDE, but other chlorinated hydrocarbons contributed to the decline of some species. Exposure often was from specific, identifiable sources. Osprey populations probably were influenced by DDT used for mosquito control. Bald eagle abundance decreased over much of North America due to contamination of agricultural waters with DDE and dieldrin; DDE caused eggshell thinning, while dieldrin caused direct mortality. Regional populations of brown pelicans probably were reduced by endrin poisoning (King and Flickinger 1977) and by DDE-caused eggshell thinning (Keith, Woods, and Hunt 1970). In both instances, chemicals originated primarily from manufacturing plants. White-faced ibis apparently received (and continue to receive) greatest exposure to DDE on their wintering grounds outside of the United States. Osprey, bald eagles, and pelicans eat fishes, whereas ibis eat earthworms. Their foods were easy to identify and sample for residues. The situation with peregrine falcons was more complex.

Dieldrin mortality reduced populations in the United Kingdom, but after dieldrin use was curtailed, DDE effects prevented population recovery (Bunyan and Stanley 1983). Peregrines feed on a variety of prey species, and the specific sources of contaminations in their prey have seldom been determined, either in Europe or the United States.

Field investigation of problems in avian populations will continue to offer one means of monitoring effects of chemical contaminations in the environment. It is not the best way, as problems often must be serious before they can be recognized. It is hoped that better predictive models can be perfected in the future to help identify problems before they become detrimental to wildlife populations.

AFTER THE BANS

Restrictions on the use of DDT and other organochlorine insecticides in the United States that were begun in the early 1970s resulted in a decreased exposure of some birds to DDE (Johnston 1974), to endrin (Blus, Henny, and Grove 1989), and to other harmful residues. Population productivity improved immediately in brown pelicans (Anderson, Jehl, Risebrough, et al. 1975). Wiemeyer, Bunck, and Krynitsky (1988) found residues in osprey eggs had declined by 1979 in New Jersey. Bald eagle reproductive success in the Chesapeake Bay area was improved by 1986 as DDE residues declined (Ohlendorf and Fleming 1988). Anderson and Gress (1983) followed the recovery of brown pelicans in California between 1970 and 1980. Dramatic increases in the annual number of breeding adults (750 to 2,244), the number of young fledged (1 to 1,515), and in productivity (0.002 to 0.68 young per nest) were documented.

However, peregrine falcons continued to accumulate pesticides in Latin America (Henny, Prescott, Riddle, et al. 1982), and their prey in the western United States were still contaminated in 1980 (DeWeese, McEwen, Hensler, et al. 1986). Five addled peregrine eggs collected in Arizona between 1978 and 1982 contained residues of 15 chlorinated hydrocarbons, and highest residues continued to be those of DDE (Ellis, DeWeese, Grubb, et al. 1989).

Eggshells of osprey in the Chesapeake Bay area remained 10 to 24 percent thinner than normal in 1977 and 1978 (Ohlendorf and Fleming 1988); however, organochlorine residues in eggs were lower than in earlier surveys. Between 1978 and 1980, single eggs collected from 220 nests of black-crowned night herons all contained DDE (Henny, Blus, Krynitsky, et al. 1984). As DDE residues increased in eggs (4 to 25 ppm), shell thinning increased (3 to 17 percent) and fledgling success in the 220 nests decreased (79 to 22 percent). In isolated Mississippi wetlands, even waterbirds resident in the United States had accumulations of DDE in eggs and showed eggshell thinning in 1984 and 1985 (White, Fleming, and Ensor 1988). High DDE residues also persisted in wildlife from New Mexico and Texas (White and Krynitsky 1986). White-faced ibis in Nevada were gravely influenced by DDE in 1985 and 1986 (Henny and Herron 1989). Forty percent of the nesting population was sufficiently contaminated to reduce breeding productivity by 20 percent.

These studies showed the continued presence of DDE and other insecticide residues in the United States long after use restrictions were imposed. Some contaminations probably are due to prolonged persistence of residues, others to illegal use of the insecticides. Residues in migratory birds could represent exposure in other countries of both predaceous and prey species. The use of chlorinated hydrocarbon insecticides has not been restricted in many countries, and residues will continue to create problems for local birds and also for migratory birds that visit those countries.

Documentation of chlorinated hydrocarbon effects on wildlife populations led to bans on some insecticides and to greater restrictions on use of others in the United States. This, in turn, prompted rapid development of the organophosphates, carbamates, synthetic pyrethroids, bacterials, synthetic juvenile hormones, and other types of insecticides to replace the banned materials.

Although registrations were canceled and use restrictions were imposed on the "dirty dozen" in the United States, considerable use of chlorinated hydrocarbons continued in other parts of the world during the 1980s. Information compiled by Hirano (1989) gives a good indication of world trends. Sales of chlorinated hydrocarbon insecticides decreased by 20 percent ($500 to $400 million) between 1983 and 1986, while organophosphate sales ($1,600 to $1,900 million) and carbamate sales ($1,000 to $1,100 million) increased 18 and 10 percent, respectively. Sales of the synthetic pyrethroids more than doubled ($600 to $1,300 million), while sales of other insecticides increased 38 percent ($400 to $550 million).

Many predicted that if chlorinated hydrocarbon insecticides were banned, greater wildlife mortality due to insecticides would occur. That is exactly what happened—with greater use of organophosphate and carbamate insecticides, reports of wildlife mortality increased (Seabloom, Pearson, Oring, et al. 1973; Zinkl, Rathert, and Hudson 1978; Stone 1979; Flickinger, Mitchell, White, et al. 1986; Hill and Fleming 1982; White, Mitchell, Kolbe, et al. 1982; White, Mitchell, Wynn, et al. 1982). Of the six organophosphate insecticides that made up 50 percent of total use between 1978 and 1981, five are highly toxic to wildlife. Carbofuran, the carbamate insecticide that received greatest use, also is extremely toxic to birds and mammals (Smith 1987).

Grue, Fleming, Busby, et al. (1983) found over 400 reports of wildlife mortality due to organophosphate poisoning. Of the unintentional poisoning in North America, 74 percent involved either diazinon, fenthion, parathion, or phosphamidon, while seed treatments with carbophenothion and chlorfenvinphos caused most losses elsewhere. Wildlife numbers involved in each incident ranged from a few individuals to estimates of 2.9 million.

The mechanisms of insecticide exposure that cause wildlife mortality have been clearly identified. Exposure can be dermal (Pope and Ward 1972; Guzman and Guardia 1978; Bruggers, Jaeger, Keith, et al. 1989) or through inhalation (Weeks, Lawson, Angerhofer, et al. 1977; Berteau and Chiles 1978), but most often it is caused by ingesting contaminated food. Birds often die after consuming contaminated vegetation (Stevenson 1972; Nettles 1976; Stone 1979; White, Mitchell, Kolbe, et al. 1982; White, Mitchell, Wynn, et al. 1982), contaminated insects (Mills 1973; Stehn, Stone, and Richmond 1976; DeWeese, Henny, Floyd, et al. 1979; White, King, Mitchell, et al. 1979; Bruggers, Jaeger, Keith, et al. 1989), or contaminated vertebrates (Mills 1973; Mendelssohn and Paz 1977; Hall and Kolbe 1980; Balcomb 1983; Bruggers, Jaeger, Keith, et al. 1989). Seed treatments pose hazards to granivores (Hamilton and Stanley 1975, Stromborg 1977, Stanley and Bunyan 1979, Smith 1987).

Wildlife mortality due to chlorinated hydrocarbon insecticides was reduced in the 1950s because research proved that pests could be controlled with considerably lower rates of applications than those first used. In the 1980s, documented evidence of mortalities shows that application rates now recommended for many of the more toxic organophosphate and carbamate insecticides are sufficient to kill wildlife (Smith 1987). It seldom will be possible to reduce rates at which these current insecticides are being applied without limiting efficacy.

In the United States and elsewhere, wildlife mortality has not often been a sufficient reason to restrict use or to cancel registration of a pesticide. Usually, a real threat to populations of rare or endangered species must be shown. This was the case recently in the United Kingdom. Use of carbophenothion as a seed treatment caused unexpected mortalities in geese wintering in Scotland. As a large proportion of the world's population of these geese were killed, carbophenothion use as a seed dressing in Scotland was banned (Hart 1990).

There is no evidence that mortalities due to organophosphate and carbamate insecticides are causing population declines in any wildlife species in the United States. The subject has not received adequate study, as most current research has been conducted under laboratory and pen conditions. However, these controlled studies of chronic and sublethal effects have provided adequate reason for concern about the threat of organophosphates and carbamates to wild populations of birds and mammals.

Grue, Fleming, Busby, et al. (1983) and Smith (1987) reviewed the sublethal effects of organophosphates and carbamates on wildlife. An abundance of laboratory and controlled studies have shown effects in birds ranging from reduced food consumption (Herbert, Peterle, and Grubb 1989) and general fitness of animals (McEwen and Brown 1966) to reduced reproductive performance and poor reproductive success (Grue, Fleming, Busby, et al. 1983; Peakall and Bart 1983).

Field studies of mammals have documented reduced productivity of adults and lower survival of young in areas treated with organophosphates (Giles 1970, Buckner and McLeod 1975). Dosing of wild nestling starlings with dicrotophos reduced cholinesterase levels and caused mortality, but there were no lasting effects on survivors (Stromborg, Grue, Nichols, et al. 1988). Other field studies have documented exposure of birds (minor reduction in cholinesterase levels) to organophosphates and carbamates in agricultural areas without mortality or other adverse effects (White and Seginak 1990; White, Seginak, and Simpson 1990). In contrast, a similar study clearly indicated severe exposure and considerable mortality in sage grouse exposed to agricultural sprays (Blus, Staley, Henny, et al. 1989). These inconsistencies appeared related to the relative toxicity of the insecticides and the susceptibility of the birds studied.

Laboratory studies have documented a unique effect of organophosphates on birds that would be very difficult to either recognize or evaluate in the field. Exposure of chickens has caused a delayed neurotoxicity characterized by axonal degeneration and demyelination of nerve bundles that produce symptoms of ataxia and paralysis (Davies and Richardson 1980). Recent studies have shown that the commonly used insecticides fenthion and fenitrothion are capable of causing these delayed, long-term effects (Farage-Elawar and Francis 1987, 1988).

Another class of insecticides in which there has been much interest are those that inhibit the synthesis of chitin in insects and thereby cause mortality (Marx 1977). Diflubenzuron has received most attention and study. It has a low toxicity to wildlife (Wilcox and Coffey 1978), and field studies suggest it can be safely used in wildlife habitats without adverse effects on birds and mammals (Bart 1975; Bruckner, McLeod, and Lidstone 1975; Richmond, Henny, Floyd, et al. 1979).

By 1986, pyrethroid insecticides were in use worldwide, and 25 percent of the insecticides used to protect crops were these relatively new, photostable, synthetic materials (Hirano 1989). Four are registered for use in the United States: permethrin, cypermethrin, deltamethrin, and fenvalerate (Day 1989). The pyrethroids are generally about 100 times more toxic to insects than the other classes of insecticides (Elliott 1989) and are used for household, public health, and veterinary purposes as well as in the protection of cotton and other agricultural crops (Haya 1989).

The pyrethroids are lipophilic, are rapidly adsorbed onto materials in water, and readily contaminate aquatic organisms (Demoute 1989). They are extremely toxic to fishes (Elliott 1989, Haya 1989) and aquatic invertebrates (Coats, Symonik, Bradbury, et al. 1989), especially crustacea (Day 1989).

In contrast, the pyrethroids are quickly metabolized and have a low toxicity to birds and mammals (Elliott 1989). They are more rapidly excreted (within a few days) from birds and mammals than from insects and fishes (Demoute 1989). They do not persist or accumulate in the environment. With low vapor pressures, they are not readily carried in air currents and have not been found to be subject to aqueous leaching (Demoute 1989, Elliott 1989).

The severe toxicity of the pyrethroids to fishes and aquatic arthropods raises a question about their use in aquatic ecosystems. Fish mortality following pyrethroid applications has not been common, suggesting that adsorption to other materials in natural waters may protect fishes (Demoute 1989). Their effects on nontarget organisms have been reviewed (Mulla, Majori, and Arata 1979; Hill 1985; Natl. Res. Counc. Canada (NRCC) 1986; Smith and Stratton 1986).

SOME FINAL THOUGHTS

The indirect effects of pesticides on habitat quality have the potential to seriously influence wildlife populations, and more attention should be given to such possibilities (Bunyan and Stanley 1983). Many human activities contribute simultaneously to habitat changes, and it is difficult to isolate alterations due to pesticides and to identify their particular influence on animal populations. Little is known of the life requirements of most species, so these evaluations will demand additional ecological and life history information. Pesticide studies have been exciting because they often required the gathering of such data. Research on pesticides has contributed much new knowledge about the habits, behavior, reproduction, foods, and population dynamics of species.

Pesticide mortality has created a genetic resistance in a few vertebrate populations to some insecticides. This has occurred in frogs (Boyd, Vinson, and Ferguson 1963), pine mice (Webber, Hartgrove, Randolph, et al. 1973), and mosquitofish (Ferguson 1963). Resistant frogs and mosquitofish accumulate much higher residues when exposed to chemicals and pose a greater hazard to their predators (Rosato and Ferguson 1968). The frightening potential of this process has not been thoroughly assessed, and further work is needed.

Wildlife mortality from the more toxic carbamate and organophosphate insecticides remains a problem. Use of these insecticides must be restricted, and additional data are needed to fully illustrate their hazards. It is generally accepted that carbamate and organophosphate insecticides neither persist in the environment nor accumulate in food chains. This assumption is sometimes false. Residues of organophosphates can persist for long periods in certain environmental substrates. As with chlorinated hydrocarbons, this occurs in situations where residues are isolated from factors that metabolize them. These relationships are poorly understood, as they have not been studied. Techniques are available to investigate the environmental fate of organophosphates, and such information should be generated.

Organophosphates can persist, and they also can accumulate in food chains. Concentrations have been measured in fishes (Mulla, Keith, and Gunther 1966), tadpoles (Hall and Kolbe 1980), and frogs (Fleming, de Chacin, Patee, et al. 1982). Some predators fed contaminated tadpoles and frogs in these studies died from organophosphate poisoning. Apparently, fishes and amphibians do not produce the enzymes that rapidly degrade organophosphates. Birds and mammals have such enzymes, and residues have not been found to accumulate in their bodies. Field and laboratory investigations of food chain accumulations of organophosphates and their hazards to birds and mammals are needed.

In the past, much effort was given to evaluating effects of polychlorinated biphenyls and mercury on wildlife. These chemicals were widely distributed in the environment and accumulated in animals. Mortality and other sublethal effects were documented (Bailey and Bunyan 1972; Heath, Spann, Hill, et al. 1972), and toxicity and sublethal exposure were evaluated in the laboratory (Dahlgren and Linder 1971, Heinz 1974). Seed dressing with mercury has been discontinued, and other uses of mercury and the uses of polychlorinated biphenyls are increasingly being regulated to prevent contamination of the environment and wildlife.

The problems created by heavy metals, oil pollution, and acid rain are subjects that deserve attention along with the remaining questions about pesticides. Although a number of biologists are working on toxic substances in the environment, new problems seem to arise before the older ones are completely solved. Still, it is evident that sufficient progress in identifying problems has been made to enable regulation of chemicals that pose the most serious threats to wildlife. Adequate regulations must be promulgated and vigorously enforced to ensure protection of the environment and wildlife resources from toxic substances.

2

Laws, Regulations, and Agencies Dealing with Toxic Substances in the Environment

The myriad laws, acts, regulations, ordinances, and agencies that deal with toxic substances have an impact on wildlife and the environment at the global, international, national, state, and local levels. Regulations promulgated by such agencies as the World Health Organization (WHO) or USAID might have a direct effect on wildlife populations where pest control chemicals are used throughout the world in both developed and lesser developed countries. For example, residue tolerances set by various countries that import commodities can alter application of pesticides in nations that export to those countries.

Within the United States, some states may set more rigid guidelines for the production, transport, and sales of toxic substances than the federal government. Counties, townships, and cities also establish regulations on transport, sale, use, and disposal of toxic substances that influence, directly or indirectly, wildlife species, populations, and their habitats.

This chapter cannot review all of these important regulatory statutes, but serves to introduce the important federal laws that regulate the production, testing, registration, and use of toxic substances in the United States. Also included are brief accounts of some federal agencies responsible for research and regulatory actions related to toxic chemicals, and a few notes on other countries for comparative purposes.

The registration, licensing, and labeling of toxic chemicals, including pesticides, has greatly improved the potential for screening and prevention of risk to humans and the environment. A brief acquaintance with these laws and processes is important to understanding the development, production, distribution, use, and potential environmental impacts of the thousands of chemicals in use in our highly developed economic system.

TSCA

History

The Toxic Substances Control Act became Public Law #94-469 in 1976. The primary purpose of the law was to prevent any unreasonable chemical risk to man or the environment.

TSCA was initiated by a 1975 National Academy of Sciences (NAS) study sponsored by EPA through its Environmental Studies Board. The NAS Committee formed to conduct this study was entitled "Decision-making for Regulating Chemicals in the Environment." The following major conclusions by the committee were important to the formulation of TSCA.

1. Burden of proof that society will benefit from a new chemical or a new use of an old chemical rests with those proposing the use.
2. Once government makes a reasonable case challenging an existing use as a possible excessive hazard to human health or to the environment, the burden of producing evidence shifts to those proponents of continued use to show it is desirable.
3. Statutory provisions should not preclude use of information in the decision-making process. All information must be available.
4. Congress should provide statutory guidance on the relative importance of human health, environmental, and economic factors in the regulation of chemicals.
    (Altogether there were 33 recommendations from the committee. Numbers 5–32 are deleted from this list.)
33. A generic approach to the regulation of chemicals should be adopted.

As a result of the committee report, TSCA was drafted and passed by Congress in 1976 as Public Law #94-469. The Environmental Protection Agency (EPA) is responsible for actions under this law, but the Office of Management and Budget (OMB) may negate any agency order.

A low in EPA activity and morale that greatly affected implementation of TSCA occurred when a former EPA administrator accepted and suggested reductions in personnel and budgets. Reductions for 1983/84 were estimated up to 60 percent. Subsequent changes in administrative leadership have greatly improved the agency. Recent discussions have involved the passage of enabling legislation to make EPA a cabinet agency. This should further improve both budgeting and personnel actions concerning TSCA.

TSCA Activities

EPA administration of TSCA includes the following four major activities:

1. Gather information on chemicals.
2. Require testing of chemicals identified as possible risks.
3. Screen new chemicals proven to present risks.
4. Control chemicals proven to present risks.

The goal is to prevent unreasonable chemical risks. EPA deals with about 44,000 chemicals under TSCA with the addition of several hundred new chemicals each year. Currently about 65,000 chemicals are in use by industry in both public and private sectors.

Eight product categories are exempt from TSCA. These are: tobacco, nuclear materials, firearms, ammunition, pesticides, food and food additives, drugs, and cosmetics. These products are regulated under different laws administered by EPA, the Food and Drug Administration (FDA), and the Alcohol Tax Bureau.

Gather Information

This first major TSCA activity includes the inventory of what, where, and how much of the chemical is manufactured, the existing stores of chemicals, and the production of new chemicals. Much of this information was not available before TSCA; it was considered proprietary information (CBI, or confidential business information) by the manufacturers, who felt the release of this information was a possible infringement related to patents and trade secrets. Manufacturers are permitted to make confidentiality claims to their chemicals, and then only the generic names are listed by EPA in the chemical summaries.

Require Testing

Potentially hazardous compounds and chemicals require added testing. Industry must report, upon request by EPA, information on persistence, environmental fate, ecological effects, health effects, carcinogenicity, mutagenicity, teratogenicity, and behavioral effects of chemicals they manufacture. Recommendations for testing and reporting to EPA under TSCA have been described in the *Federal Register* of 9 May 1979. Further Proposed Health Effects Test Standards for TSCA Test Rules were published in the *Federal Register,* 26 July 1979.

There is a legal basis for rules and the reports should be available in the public record. The Natural Resources Defense Fund has forced EPA to make more of the industry reports available to the public, but some test results are still considered CBI. Some components of the required testing include Chronic tests, in which two laboratory species, one non-rodent, (usually rats and dogs) are used. These animals are tested from birth to weaning; for dogs this is up to 24 to 30 months total if oncogenic effects tests are required. The manufacturer must submit a study plan to EPA at least 90 days before the tests are initiated and qualified personnel must be available and in some instances they must be licensed (pathologists). There must be a complete chemical description of the compound being tested. Diets of the test animals must be carefully monitored and must include the prescribed levels of minerals, protein, and so on. Reporting requirements are clearly defined. Suggestions are provided concerning the selection of test animals; age of the animals at the start of the exposure; housing and care of the control groups; route of exposure; and numbers of animals at each dose level. Usually there is a high dose level (HDL) which should be slightly toxic; there should be a maximum tolerated dose (MTD) as well as a low dose (LD). The low dose is usually about 1/100 of the HDL. Clinical procedures must be defined as well as the pathological examinations, which include about 40,000 tissue sections per chemical tested. These examinations of tissues must be reported according to the Systematized Nomenclature of Pathology (SNOP), created by The College of American Pathologists.

All data sets must be made available to EPA and there are requirements for record keeping and calibration of instruments. Any effects on personnel during the testing must reported. EPA has agreed to make testing for TSCA as consistent as possible within the law with the Federal Insecticide, Fungicide and Rodenticide Act (FIFRA). There are rules related to confidentiality, public participation, economic analyses, a requirement for quality assurance, and statements on the legal bases for the testing and how they become matters of public record. Toxicity tests under both TSCA and FIFRA include: acute oral; acute dermal; acute inhalation; primary eye irritation; primary dermal irritation; dermal sensitization; subchronic oral; subchronic 90-day dermal; and subchronic inhalation. They generally require mutagenic tests, and test standards have been proposed for heritable chromosomal mutations, the effects on DNA repair, or recombination as an indicator of genetic damage may also be tested.

Procedures for necropsy and sectioning are spelled out. The animals should be autopsied no longer than 16 hours after death; a qualified pathologist must be on-site, methods for preservation, fixation, and slide preparation are described; tissue sections are usually 3 to 6 microns but must not be more than 10 microns thick. Methods for statistical treatment of the data are described; the company must provide means, standard errors, and standard deviations for all data sets.

An example of a testing procedure under TSCA could be an acute oral toxicity study. The study design would be described as follows: species—lab rat—young—both male and female; dose—one above, another below the estimated LD-50; five animals per sex; dose up to 5 mg/kg; no animals died, no further testing required.

If testing produced mortality of 10–90 percent the LD-50 must be calculated for both males and females together with the 95% confidence level. The LD-50 must be obtained from at least three dose levels; size of groups in each dose may vary, but there must be equal males and females in each. The control group must be of sufficient size to statistically determine any effect of the carrier. Dosing is by gavage; no more than 4 or 5 ml per animal, with the same volume for all dose levels. Duration of the test is 14 days. Animals are fasted 1 day before administration of the test doses. Animals must be observed frequently, but no less than every 12 hours. All test animals must be sacrificed and necropsied. The data set from this testing must include dose response by sex, time of death, LD-50 for each sex, 95 percent confidence interval on LD-50, dose response curve and slope, and methods for calculation of dose response curve.

Screen Chemicals

EPA appointed the Interagency Testing Committee (ITC) to recommend chemicals that might be posing a potential risk for priority testing under TSCA. Members of the ITC included EPA, the Occupational Safety and Health Administration (OSHA), Council on Environmental Quality (CEQ), National Institute of Occupational Safety and Health (NIOSH), National Science Foundation (NSF), National Cancer Institute (NCI), and the Communicable Disease Centers (CDC).

The ITC originally listed 33 chemicals ranging from acetonitrile to xylene and suggested that these be tested first. Since that time they have added 16 more chemicals and decided to list new chemicals under seven categories.

According to TSCA, any individual can notify EPA that a chemical has a substantial risk, but sufficient information must be included to substantiate the statement. EPA must then review the chemical and decide if testing by the producer is necessary. The agency can obtain any privately done health and safety studies if they need them to make decisions on a new or old chemical. EPA requires that industry keep health and safety records for all personnel for up to 30 years and for any consumer or environmental effects for 5 years.

Premanufacture Notice   Under TSCA, all chemical manufacturers must submit a premanufacture notice to EPA before processing or using a substance. Any compound or chemical not listed in the 1980 revised inventory of chemicals must go through the premanufacture notice procedure. Items that must be provided by the manufacturer include trade or common name, chemical identity and molecular structure, production amounts, use categories, disposal methods, work-place exposure, by-products, impurities, related products, any and all test data available.

EPA publishes all premanufacture notices in the *Federal Register*. The usual 90-day review by EPA can be extended to 180 days to provide EPA with added time for review and decision. EPA can approve the manufacture and use of the chemical, or it may issue and order to regulate its use because of lack of data. If regulated, the manufacturer can go to court and obtain an injunction for continued use on a limited scale until the data on risk assessment is available.

Control Chemicals

Finally, EPA is authorized to control any chemical found to pose an unreasonable risk to human health or to the environment. They may prohibit production, processing, distribution, use of, or disposal of the chemical. This may vary from a complete ban to simply labeling for specific uses or limits. EPA must publish the basis for the decision on any chemical in the *Federal Register,* where they also must list possible substitutes available as well as any possible economic consequences.

An example of such action was the ban of PCB. As a result of TSCA, EPA published a final rule in the *Federal Register* on May 31, 1979, which banned all use of PCBs in other than a totally enclosed manner (TVs, air conditioners, microwaves, capacitors). Chloroflurocarbon use limitation is also being considered as it relates to possible effects on ultraviolet radiation and possible weather or human effects.

CERCLA

The Comprehensive Environmental Response, Compensation, and Liability Act (CERCLA) of 1980 establishes the so-called "SuperFund" to be used to clean up dump sites that present hazards to humans and the environment. SuperFund monies are obtained by a tax on chemical production. SuperFund extension came up for discussion and voting in 1986. The House recommended extension of the authority by $10 billion, the Senate by $7 billion, and the administration by $3 billion. Besides deciding on the amount of funding, discussions also centered on additions to cleanup of below-ground storage tanks included by the House and the various methods for raising the monies to be appropriated. The Senate preferred to tax the final manufactured products; the House recommended collection of some funds from the petroleum industry as well. Finally, in October 1986, President Reagan signed the 5-year extension of the Super-Fund Bill (PL 99-499) providing $9 billion for further cleanup of toxic waste sites. As part of the bill, $500 million was provided to assess and clean up underground storage tanks found to be leaking. Deadlines were established for the cleanup of sites, the standards for cleanup were set, and right-to-know provisions were included to allow communities to gain information on the contents and hazards associated with local dump sites. Monies to support the fund are to be obtained from petroleum, general corporate taxes, general revenues, interest on the fund, and monies recovered from companies associated with the dump sites. Both the House and Senate passed the bill with overwhelming majorities.

FIFRA

History

The original 1947 Federal Insecticide, Fungicide, and Rodenticide Act was administered by the U.S. Department of Agriculture (USDA) and dealt mainly with registration, efficacy, and recommended uses of pesticides. The act simply assured users that the materials contained in a product were as described and would be useful in killing whatever species was indicated in the instructions. The original act was amended twice: first as the Federal Environmental Pesticide Control Act (FEPCA), passed as Public Law #92-516 in October 1972, and again amended as Public Law #94-140 in November 1975. The main intention of these revisions in the original FIFRA was to change a largely registration-oriented statute to one that was regulatory. The law also changed the administration of the law from the USDA to EPA.

The amended law governs manufacture, labeling, transport, use, purity, and effectiveness of insecticides, fungicides, and rodenticides. Under the law, EPA has broad authority, not only to register and re-register but to regulate use. Other pesticide authority is under the Federal Food, Drug, and Cosmetic Act (FFDCA), which is administered by FDA and controls residues in food and cosmetics.

According to law, EPA must determine whether a pesticide is efficacious for control of the target organisms or species and that it will not result in unreasonable adverse effects on human beings or the environment. An efficacious pesticide is defined simply as one that kills the pest species. However, deciding what might be considered as an "unreasonable" adverse effect on human health or the environment is much more complicated. Defining "unreasonable" is a basic problem in the administration of the law. By law, EPA must balance benefits and risks in their decision-making.

The revision of FIFRA has been delayed for years in debates among the various power groups such as the National Agricultural Chemicals Manufacturing Association, EPA, members of Congress, and a coalition of conservation organizations such as the Sierra Club, Natural Resources Defense Council, National Audubon Society, and others. Early in 1986 these groups met in a series of meetings and drafted new pesticide laws that have been introduced into Congress. The central theme for the settlement was related to an extension of the patent rights time period requested by industry and a reduction in the time allowed for re-registration of about 600 pesticides by the conservation organizations. A $150,000 re-registration fee was also written into the law to provide funds to EPA for the re-registration process. Under this settlement, EPA will also be able to regulate inert ingredients and the public will have the right to review registration data before action is taken by EPA. The time period for registration or cancellation has also been reduced from a possible 7 years with all the appeals to only 1 year. Some questions remain unresolved, such as the desire by EPA to eliminate reviews of compounds that have low use and/or exposure, liability suits for users against producers if problems result from proper use, and some regulations on contamination of ground water. Nevertheless, the coalition and discussion has produced the best legislation that has been introduced concerning the revision of FIFRA.

Patent extensions have not been supported by all. Some congressmen, such as Ohio's Howard Metzenbaum, are against the proposal because it will lead to a greater monopoly by a few major chemical companies that already have a major share of the market. Patent life on some popular herbicides has been extended to 26 years. Some companies have been issued second patents because of changes in composition or methods of production. Some claim that as a result of patent protection, prices for some high-use pesticides and herbicides remain too high and the farmer/consumer must pay the costs.

EPA Involvement under FIFRA

Under FIFRA, EPA is involved at several levels in the pesticide industry:

1. Manufacturing Use Product—this is the initial chemical that is sold to formulators to be mixed and labeled and sold for many uses. (Most effort is at this level.)
2. Formulated Product—bagged, or in a container with label containing directions and restrictions for use.
3. Technical Grade Product—technical grade of the actual pesticide that has a stated level of purity, used most frequently for toxicity testing and analytical work.

In most cases for registration and re-registration EPA will use a single "standard" for each pesticidally active ingredient. Usually formulated, end use products are not tested, except for efficacy as indicated on the label.

Under FIFRA each manufacturer must provide EPA with data in the following categories:

1. *Product identity:* disclosure of ingredients, name, trade name, company code number, technical grade name used in formulated products, statement of formula identifying each substance included, inert ingredients, reaction products, degradation products, molecular weight, structural formula for all organics.
2. *Description of manufacturing process:* composition of materials for start of production—intermediate products, basic process of manufacturing, flow sheet, chemical reactions, purification, materials to package, formation of unintentional ingredients, inert or active, reactions either during manufacture or in storage.
3. *Declaration and certification of ingredients:* quantities, limits, product life, and expiration dates.
4. *Analytical methods:* how to measure ingredients or impurities, step-by-step detailed descriptions for the manufactured use product and the formulated product; other ingredients or impurities; data sets on five samples; data from spectral analyses, NMR, infrared, mass spectrometer or UV, or ECGC (electron capture gas chromatography).
5. *Physical and chemical properties:* color, odor, melting point, solubility, stability, octanol/water partition coefficient, physical state, density, specific gravity, boiling point, vapor pressure, ph, storage stability, flammability, oxidizing or reducing action, explosiveness,

miscibility, viscosity, corrosive characteristics, dielectric breakdown voltage. The manufacturer must also submit a sample to EPA
upon request.

6. *Environmental chemistry:* physico-chemical degradation—metabolism, mobility, field dissipation, accumulation in living plants or
animals, direct consequences to humans (user–field exposure to
workers and applicators), indirect consequences related to possible
loss of land-use, water, or wildlife; potential environmental exposure, possible food-chain accumulation, material balance, and a
quantitative accountability. Reports are required to indicate possible
use patterns such as terrestrial, aquatic, crops, greenhouse, fruit and
nut trees, vegetable crops, aquatic crops, non-row crops, indirect
discharge, direct discharge, as well as possible disposal in sewerage
at the time of manufacture.

Physico-chemical degradation, both hydrolysis and photodegradation data are required.

• Metabolism: aerobic soil metabolism, anerobic soil, anerobic
aquatic, aerobic aquatic, microbial metabolism, effects of microbes
on the pesticidal qualities, effects of pesticide on the microbes,
activated sludge metabolism.
• Mobility: volatility, adsorption/desorption, leaching, water dispersal.
• Field dissipation: dissipation and mobility under field use, the data
should be collected until 90 percent has dissipated or until pattern
of decline is established by sampling through time. Some specific
requirements may be requested depending on site of use or application areas; some long-term data may be required, up to 3
years.
• Accumulation: rotational crops, irrigated crops, fish accumulation
determined by flow-through or static tank tests usually using two
species such as bluegill sunfish and channel catfish.

Under the Resource Conservation Recovery Act of 1976 (Public Law
#94-580) the manufacturer must provide EPA with information on stor-
age, possible disposal methods, transport restrictions, and potential addition to hazardous wastes. For some compounds, special chemistry requirements are requested: Tolerance clearance must be obtained if there
are any anticipated residues on foods and feedstuffs. Tolerance levels
must be approved by FDA and EPA and listed on the label. Pesticides in or
on tobacco are also regulated and residues must be determined not only for
the tobacco but for the smoke as well.

Hazard Evaluation for Wildlife and Aquatic Organisms

EPA requires tests for pesticide effects on wildlife and aquatic organisms. Usually the manufacturing use product is tested, but technical grade material or even pure or active-only material may be required in the testing program. If there is any indication of environmental problems with the formulated product, tests may be required on inert ingredients, any contaminants or impurities, any known metabolites, formulations, or synergists. Decisions are based on a tiered testing program (Figs. 2.1–2.3).

Wildlife Testing Programs   EPA makes recommendations concerning the care and selection of organisms and requires that the manufacturer describe the rationale for the selection of the species to be tested. This must be related to the use characteristics of the compound, where it moves in the environment, and ultimately what organisms it is likely to affect. Recording sex, age, and dosing methods as well as weights of the test animals is required. Methods of observation; housing conditions including light, temperature, humidity, type of floors, cages and animals per cage or tank; water sources; dilutions used; determination of any LD-50 or LC-50 levels; calculations performed; and references used must be reported.

In avian testing, mallard ducks and bobwhites are usually recommended, but pheasants may also be used in some tests although they are resistant to some pesticides, especially as related to DDT and eggshell thinning. Avian tests are done with birds aged 16 weeks old or older. Data must be supplied on diets, fasting, food preparation, and mortality.

Reproduction tests may be done on any species, but frequently the mallard is used. Yearlings are fed the chemical for 10 weeks prior to breeding. Eggs are collected, stored for specified periods, and incubated. Viable embryos are determined, and any change in eggshell thickness or cracking, numbers of total eggs laid, number set for incubation, number hatched, and the number of 14-day survivors must be reported. Any abnormal development of embryos or ducklings must also be noted.

For mammalian testing, EPA simply suggests that any wild mammal may be used in testing, more expressly those species that are expected to be exposed to a given pesticide. In most instances these are microtines.

Additional Legislation, Regulations, and Programs under FIFRA

The Federal Food, Drug and Cosmetic Act (FDCA), passed in 1938, has had many amendments. This act regulates pesticides and other toxic substances in foodstuffs and cosmetics. The Miller Pesticide Amendment of 1954 and the subsequent Delaney Clause of 1958 further regulated pesti-

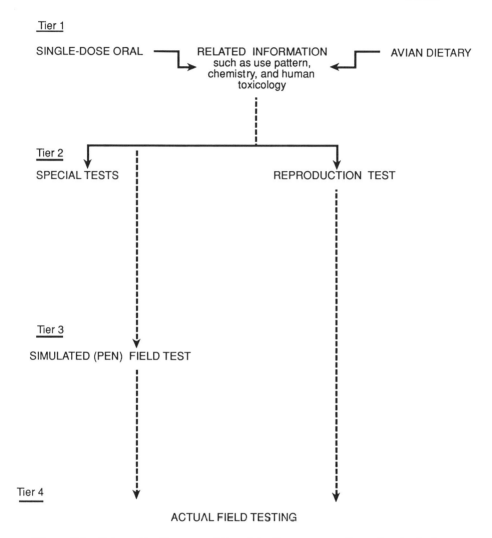

Figure 2.1 Schematic diagram of tiered testing program for avian toxicology. USEPA.

cide residues in foods. The Delaney Clause requires that no (zero toler-ance) oncogenic pesticide residues appear in processed food. This is not true of raw foodstuffs and residues are permitted if benefits outweigh the risks. This is determined by USEPA. Many products registered before 1978 have not been appropriately tested for carcinogenic properties nor

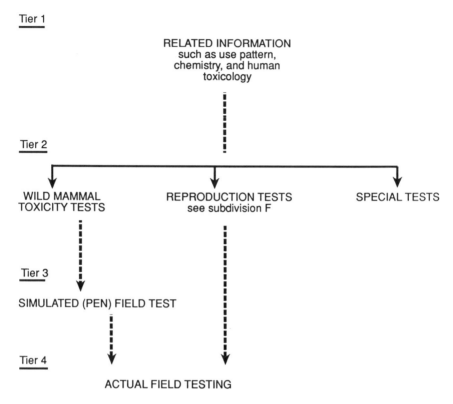

Figure 2.2   Schematic diagram of tiered testing program for mammalian toxicology. USEPA.

have accumulation and residue patterns been determined. Many of these products must be re-registered, but the process has been very slow and USEPA has not met several deadlines established by Congress. A new revision of FIFRA, currently in Congressional discussion, requires additional data and sets new time limits on re-registration. Residues of pesticides that increase cancer risk are now being permitted on raw foodstuffs. In terms of risk estimates, tomatoes are the most hazardous and grapes the least hazardous: 8.75 cancer risks for every 10,000 people who eat tomatoes throughout their lifetime to 1.9 cancer risks for grapes. Beef and potatoes are second and third on the list. EPA could regulate residues of these compounds under current law if they determine the risk is unacceptable.

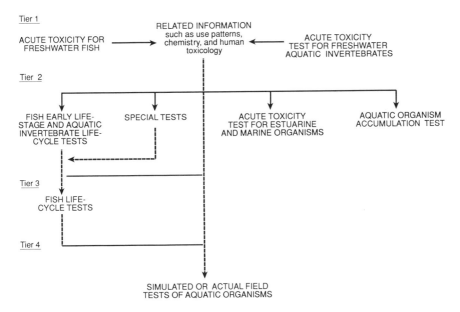

Figure 2.3   Schematic diagram for tiered testing program for aquatic toxicology. USEPA.

Risk Assessment

Uncertainty is inherent in risk assessment. Any reduction in potential adverse effects, as a result of a wide diversity of risks, has a certain probability of happening and as a result of effort, usually the expenditure of funds, the risks may be reduced. Some authors (Wilson and Crouch 1987) compare a wide variety of risks in discussing toxic substance effects. Whether this is reasonable or not is a matter of judgment. Home accident risks are about one-half those possible related to motor vehicles, but how this might be related to exposure to a carcinogen that may accumulate over a lifetime is uncertain. In terms of carcinogenicity, the HERP (human exposure/rodent potency index) values of normal tap water, for example, are 0.001 percent; those for well water in contaminated areas of Silicon Valley, California, quadruple to 0.004 percent. PCBs in normal dietary intake per day are 0.0002 percent, while beer is 2.8, wine 4.7, and vocational exposure to EDB (ethylene dibromide) is rated at 140 percent. Equating risks does not seem to be very satisfying to the general public because of basic differences associated with the source of the risk. The fact that living near a nuclear power plant, in terms of health risk, is the same as driving an extra 3 miles per day is somehow not very satisfying. Long-term risk/benefit assessments of environmental contaminants are some of the most difficult to make. Decisions concerning residues of many common toxic substances have been very contentious and time-consuming.

Congress, OMB, and EPA are all involved in debating the promulgation of risk reduction for carcinogens. Congress has even reduced a portion of the OMB budget to indicate their displeasure with the delay in approval of recommended EPA regulations (Marshall 1986b). Most recent discussions (1990) relate to the removal of differences in allowable residues in raw and processed food under a single negligible risk standard of one-in-a-million cancer cases over a lifetime. The determination of such a single risk standard must also consider benefits. Recent statements by scientists in the USSR (Yablokov 1990) suggested there is no lower limit to pesticide effects and even low dosages can produce substantial negative effects on human health.

NEPA

The National Environmental Policy Act (42 USC 9341, Public Law #94-53, Public Law #94-83 1975) was established to encourage harmony between humans and their environment and to prevent damage to the environment and biosphere. The law also was initiated to enrich understanding of ecological systems. The act established the Council on Environmental Quality (CEQ) and required that environmental impact statements (EIS) be prepared by responsible officials in any development utilizing federal funds. CEQ is the coordinating agency for all EIS work required by the federal agencies. Private industry must also prepare EIS statements if there are possibilities of any adverse effects on the environment as a result of construction or chemical use. CEQ initially requires an environmental assessment statement (EAS), which is reviewed by any interested federal agency to determine whether or not an EIS is required. This is done by "scoping," "piggy-backing," and pre-planning so that one EIS can satisfy all of the federal agencies. The EIS must consider productivity, long-term effects, alternatives, short-term effects, or any irreversible or irretrievable effect on the environment.

Some of these EIS have been required for the use of pesticides. The U. S. Forest Service had to prepare an EIS to use aerial sprays for tussock moth control as well as for the use of herbicides. The U. S. Department of Health has to prepare an EIS if they request emergency use of an insecticide to control an insect vector related to human health or disease transmission.

Endangered Species Preservation Act

The Endangered Species Preservation Act of 1966 and its subsequent revisions requires that the federal agencies must protect wildlife species threatened with extinction. As a result, this act, and subsequent revisions, the latest in 1988, has a direct bearing on the use and distribution of toxic chemicals in the environment identified as critical to the maintenance of such species. This might involve reviews of the use of chemicals for disease vector control by public health agencies, pesticide use to stop the spread of or eliminate exotic agricultural pest insects, or the use of herbicides by such agencies as the Forest Service. In many cases EIS are prepared and if there is any potential that such activities might affect an endangered species, alternatives must be found and use of the chemicals may be stopped. Such actions may be taken whether the endangered species is being affected directly by a chemical, or as a result of alteration or loss of habitat for the species. As more and more species of plants, invertebrates, and vertebrates are added to the list of threatened or endangered species, more and more land and water areas of the nation are required to be protected from toxic substances as a result of the Endangered Species Act. This further enhances the protection of all forms of wildlife from potential toxic substances.

FEDERAL AGENCIES

Regulation and control of toxic substances is a very complex and convoluted system. Among the federal agencies that have an influence or some regulatory power over toxic substance use are: USEPA, HUD, DOT, Army Corps of Engineers, DOD, FDA, USDA, CDC, NIH, NIEHS, OSHA, USDI, NCI, HHS, and CEQ.

In addition to these federal agencies, all 50 states have similar organizations to control toxic substances and in addition to these there are about 3,000 counties, 18,500 municipalities, and 17,000 townships. These agencies relate to control of toxic wastes such as in sewage treatment plants and solid waste dump sites.

USEPA

The USEPA was organized by a law passed by Congress on December 2, 1970. Congress requested EPA to do an unreasonable task in an unreasonable time with limited resources of budget and personnel. Since the organization of EPA, the time period to re-register all pesticides has been extended several times and the deadline has not been met 20 years after the agency was organized. There are many conflicts to be resolved that include economic, social, aesthetic, and political considerations. In addition, human health matters are involved together with environmental degradation. Congress is now tampering with EPA and with the laws by considering individual items related to toxic substances control as separate acts. This further complicates the activities of EPA and their function. Special interest groups with political power manage to influence a sufficient number of Congressmen to introduce specific bills dealing with pesticides or toxic substances. EPA has further been hampered by actions of OMB (Office of Management and Budget) and the political influences of some administrations.

Figure 2.4 shows an organizational chart breaking the EPA down into offices and regions of jurisdiction. I will go into a little more detail on some of these offices in the following paragraphs.

Office of Pesticide Programs

The Office of Pesticide Programs (OPP) is a major division related to pesticides, regulation, tolerance, registration, monitoring, efficacy, hazards, evaluation, incidents, research impact statements, and training. The various sections of OPP include:

1. *Program Development and Evaluation and Administration:* in-house reorganization and review, supervision.
2. *Policy and Regulatory Affairs:* plans and coordinates.
3. *Operations Division:* enhances government effectiveness, program policy, recommends legislation, training, state model legislation, coordination with other federal agencies, investigates incidents and accidents.
4. *Registration Division:* reviews all pesticide labels, up to 25,000 per year for all formulated/use products. Sets tolerances in cooperation with FDA, tolerance levels are not absolute, there are in-house EPA agreements on what is "an actionable" level. Reviews wording on labels, efficacy as indicated, methods for analysis, ecological effects, establish product manager teams within EPA.
5. *Technical Services:* monitors and analyzes physical and biological samples from the environment, develops assay techniques and bioassay methods, information and support to other divisions, library reference services, provides analytical reference standards to qualified investigators (these are high purity, small quantities from Research Triangle Park, a catalog is available, and there is no charge for small quantities of pesticides).

6. *Criteria and Evaluation (C&E):* comes up with chemical methodology, methods for testing effects and efficacy, standards for residues and tolerances, safety analysis, risk/benefit analyses, establishes guidelines for monitoring needs.

Office of Special Pesticide Review (OSPR)

This section is organized into four branches with four branch chiefs and 20 program managers. They review any pesticide for which there is an RPAR (rebuttal presumption against registration). RPAR may lead to suspension or cancellation of the designated uses of a pesticide, and arises if the pesticide (ingredient, metabolite, or degradation product) exceeds certain criteria for risk. The risk is estimated based on a review of the published literature on the pesticides and all testing data available, and is also related to a review of data on acute toxicity hazard to humans, domestic livestock, or wildlife (chronic effects are also considered). All information is weighed by teams established by the program managers and if there is sufficient evidence, a "trigger" is indicated and a full investigation to prepare a decision paper for the EPA administrator is undertaken. The 20 program managers chair working groups made up of representatives from the Assistant Administration for Pesticides, Office of General Counsel, Office of Planning and Management, Office of Enforcement, and Water and Hazardous Materials. If the compound is a suspected carcinogen, a member of the Cancer Advisory Group is included in the working group.

Procedure for Review   Manufacturers are notified of the investigation and intent to cancel or withdraw registration or specific uses of their pesticide. They have 45 days to respond; this may be extended to 60 days upon request.

The EPA then announces the manufacturer's response. If there is a rebuttal, use continues. If the manufacturer does not respond with a rebuttal, OSPR reviews risk/benefits (R/B) analysis for up to another 180 days. Dependent on results of R/B analyses, use of the pesticide is continued or the OSPR confers with USDA concerning alternatives, economic effects, and special uses.

Sixty days are allowed for additional hearings. EPA then issues a statement on continued normal use, restricted use, or cancellation. Hearings may last 1 year or more.

If the working group under the program manager has sufficient information, the Administrator of EPA may declare a substance an "imminent hazard" and cancel all uses with a suspension of the registration until more study or information results in a final cancellation. DDT was cancelled in

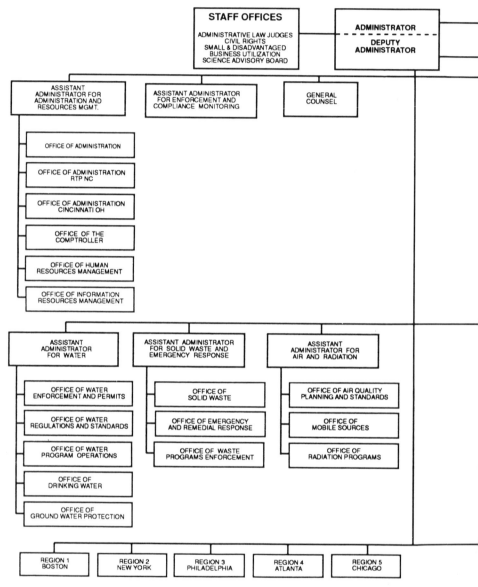

Figure 2.4 Organizational plan for the United States Environmental Protection Agency. USEPA.

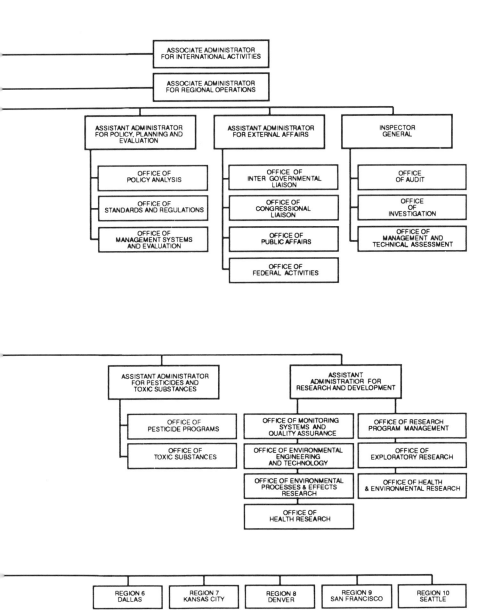

ASSOCIATE ADMINISTRATOR
FOR INTERNATIONAL ACTIVITIES

ASSOCIATE ADMINISTRATOR
FOR REGIONAL OPERATIONS

ASSISTANT ADMINISTRATOR
FOR POLICY, PLANNING AND
EVALUATION

OFFICE OF
POLICY ANALYSIS

OFFICE OF
STANDARDS AND REGULATIONS

OFFICE OF
MANAGEMENT SYSTEMS
AND EVALUATION

ASSISTANT ADMINISTRATOR
FOR EXTERNAL AFFAIRS

OFFICE OF
INTER GOVERNMENTAL
LIAISON

OFFICE OF
CONGRESSIONAL
LIAISON

OFFICE OF
PUBLIC AFFAIRS

OFFICE OF
FEDERAL ACTIVITIES

INSPECTOR
GENERAL

OFFICE
OF AUDIT

OFFICE
OF
INVESTIGATION

OFFICE OF
MANAGEMENT AND
TECHNICAL ASSESSMENT

ASSISTANT ADMINISTRATOR
FOR PESTICIDES AND
TOXIC SUBSTANCES

OFFICE OF
PESTICIDE PROGRAMS

OFFICE OF
TOXIC SUBSTANCES

ASSISTANT
ADMINISTRATIOR FOR
RESEARCH AND DEVELOPMENT

OFFICE OF MONITORING
SYSTEMS AND
QUALITY ASSURANCE

OFFICE OF ENVIRONMENTAL
ENGINEERING
AND TECHNOLOGY

OFFICE OF ENVIRONMENTAL
PROCESSES & EFFECTS
RESEARCH

OFFICE OF
HEALTH RESEARCH

OFFICE OF RESEARCH
PROGRAM MANAGEMENT

OFFICE OF
EXPLORATORY RESEARCH

OFFICE OF HEALTH
& ENVIRONMENTAL RESEARCH

REGION 6
DALLAS

REGION 7
KANSAS CITY

REGION 8
DENVER

REGION 9
SAN FRANCISCO

REGION 10
SEATTLE

41

1972—others were aldrin, dieldrin, and Hg pesticides; the predator control poison 1080 and others have been suspended, such as chlordane and heptachlor (Table 2.1).

Risk/Benefit Analyses

EPA must consider group risk, in terms of the total human population exposed, as well as individual risk from continued use of a pesticide. These two evaluations are not easily compromised and EPA must also evaluate the competency and value of the risk assessment itself. The national policy on risk/benefit analyses is political, not scientific. There is always the potential for judicial review of any EPA decisions, either by industry or by health, conservation, or resource agencies.

EPA Research in Wildlife Toxicology

Much of the wildlife toxicology research done by EPA is conducted by the Wildlife Toxicology Research Team at the Corvallis Environmental Research Laboratory in Corvallis, Oregon. Although EPA is largely a regulatory agency, there are basic needs for information to better test and regulate toxic substances as they impact wildlife. The team was organized

Table 2-1 Regulatory Status of Some Organochlorine Compounds Used in the United States During the Past Three Decades

Chemical	Regulatory status[a]
Aldrin	Canceled except for limited use, 1974
Chlordane	Cancelled except for limited use, 1980
DDT	Cancelled except for limited use related to human health, 1972
Dieldrin	Cancelled except for limited use, 1974
Endrin	Uses restricted, 1979—environmental applications not uncommon
Heptachlor	Uses restricted; total phase-out for most uses, 1983
Kepone	Cancelled, 1978
Mirex	Cancelled, 1977
PCBs	Manufacturing, processing, and distribution prohibited, 1979
Toxaphene	Cancelled, 1982—use of existing stocks permitted

[a] The regulatory status presented here is an oversimplification of use regulations, but summarizes restrictions of major environmental importance. See EPA's Suspended and Cancelled Pesticides (1979) for additional details. Adapted from Fleming, Clark and Henry 1983, 187. Trans. N. A. Wildl. Nat. Resour. Conf. Wildlife Management Institute, Washington, D.C. Permission granted.

in 1983 with minimal staffing and visiting scientists and since has been expanded to include a team leader and several full-time scientists. The program responds to six major areas: evaluation of current toxic substance testing guidelines, field validation of hazard assessment techniques, interspecies comparative toxicology, development of sublethal tests of toxicity, development of a wildlife toxicology database, and technical assistance to the various offices and divisions of EPA. The program has been enhanced by the construction of a modern animal holding facility and some research is being contracted to university scientists. Species being used in field and laboratory tests include bobwhite quail, mallards, valley quail, various species of blackbirds, and some native small mammals. Techniques and standards for blood and brain cholinesterase analysis have been developed. Behavioral, reproductive, physiological, and field testing programs are being conducted to assist administrators in the regulatory process.

EPA Advisory Committees

EPA has established many permanent and temporary advisory boards and committees to review policy and in some cases specific decisions or changes in administrative decisions. Some of these include: Administrators Toxic Substances Advisory Committee (ATSAC); Clean Air Science Advisory Committee (CASAC); FIFRA Science Advisory Panel (FIFRA/SAP); Management Advisory Group to Municipal Construction Division (MAG); National Air Pollution Control Techniques Advisory Committee (NAPCTAC); National Drinking Water Advisory Council (NDWAC); and the Science Advisory Board (SAB). The SAB can appoint subcommittees for specific topics, for example, the Transport, Fate, and Effects Committee that reviewed site-specific water quality standards, policies, and methods.

Other Federal Agencies Involved with Toxic Substance Control

Numerous pesticide coordinating bodies have been developed among the federal agencies that have a legal interest in regulation. These date back to 1940 when the Interdepartmental Committee on Pest Control (ICPC) was formed. This included the USDA, USDI, Army, Navy, and the USPHS and it met three times each year. In 1961, the Federal Pest Control Review Board (FPCRB) replaced the earlier organization and included the same agencies. In 1963, the Federal Committee on Pest Control (FCPC) was organized and established subcommittees on research, public information, monitoring, program review, and safety. By 1969 this had evolved to a

Cabinet Committee on the environment which had a subcommittee and working group on pesticides. Besides the other agencies, the new group included representatives from the Department of State and the Department of Transport. In 1970 this was dissolved as a cabinet committee and was made responsible to CEQ. The Federal Working Group in Pest Management (FWGPM) included the already named agencies plus the newly organized EPA, Department of Commerce, and the Department of Labor. These agencies were responsible for the publication of the *Pesticides Monitoring Journal* that has been published ever since.

USDA

The U. S. Department of Agriculture is responsible for user recommendations, extension activities, the Agricultural Experimental Station research on crop/livestock uses; users' instruction and classwork for state licensing, and public contacts. The Denver Research Center of APHIS deals mainly with testing vertebrate animal control chemicals and techniques. The center, formerly a part of the U. S. Fish and Wildlife Service, has a long history of toxicity testing on a great number and variety of wildlife species. Many compounds, numbered DRC-XXXX have been tested in the laboratory for both lethal and chronic effects, but also in the field for use as possible animal control chemicals. DRC-714 is a rodenticide called "Gophicide" used to control gophers. DRC-1339 is an avicide and repellent called "Starlicide" used to control various species of blackbirds. In addition to laboratory testing, the Denver Research Center also does field testing of vertebrate control chemicals and provides technical assistance to such agencies as WHO and USAID in countries abroad.

USFS

The Forest Service mainly uses pesticides for insect and vegetation control and obtains special permits and licensing for forest pest control and applications to National Forest lands.

Department of Commerce

This agency is involved with registration and technical input to the trade laws, and the Federal Trade Commission regulates monopolies, and trade regulation in pesticide marketing.

FDA

The source of human foods related to the Federal Food Drug and Cosmetic Act is the responsibility of the FDA.

HEW or HHS (Human Health Services)

The Centers for Disease Control in Atlanta is the lead group related to the use of pesticides in human health and disease control, i.e., rabies, insect vectors, and rodent control.

USDI

The Fish and Wildlife Service mainly does surveys and research on effects of pollutants on wildlife. These are conducted at national laboratories at Patuxent, Maryland, and Jamestown, North Dakota, and the Wildlife Health Laboratory at Madison, Wisconsin. No single agency or laboratory has had as great an impact on wildlife toxicology research than the Patuxent Wildlife Research Center. Initial studies of toxicity and chronic effects began in the 1950s and have continued to date. The field and laboratory studies done by Patuxent personnel have formed a broad basis for subsequent wildlife toxicology research throughout the United States as well as in other countries. Major findings by Patuxent personnel were crucial to the development of the federal DDT hearings by USEPA and the ultimate decision by the administrator to ban DDT in 1972. Studies by Patuxent have not only dealt with many important pesticides and their effects on species and ecosystems, but also with other chemicals such as PCBs and many important heavy metal contaminants such as lead, mercury, zinc, and cadmium. Toxicological research done at Patuxent for nearly 40 years serves as a landmark accomplishment for responsible efforts by a federal agency to provide a research base to enhance and protect our wildlife and their environments.

STATE AND LOCAL AGENCIES

State Agencies

Many states have organizations and functions that parallel those of the federal government. The state EPA handles all EIS for a particular state. They coordinate with federal EPA on all toxic substance laws; and air, water, and solid waste disposal. They handle enforcement duty, National Pollution Discharge Elimination System (NPDES) permits, and prepare water and air quality plans for approval by USEPA. TSCA pre-empted the states' rights in the area of toxic substances, but EPA has now relegated some enforcement duties to state EPA. States deal with licensing of pesticide applicators, and recommendations on use of pesticides through state Extension Services.

State Departments of Agriculture recommend uses; operate animal health laboratories for animal disease and poisoning; monitor pesticide levels in water, animals, and foods; establish training programs for licensed users of pesticides for both general or restricted uses (these courses must be approved by USEPA). State Departments of Agriculture maintain animal health and food inspector systems, and operate agricultural experiment stations for testing new pesticides. State Agriculture Departments may permit unregistered use of a pesticide in certain circumstances. For specific uses, states may also obtain experimental permits to test new compounds for pest control.

State Departments of Natural Resources (DNR) are responsible for enforcement of some dumping laws; they investigate fish kills, pesticide use on public lands, regulation of use of wild animals related to possible toxic substance exposure in human foods; investigate spills and accidents that result in fish or wildlife kills; and can take industry to court and assess damages and fines.

Local Agencies

City-County-Mosquito Abatement Districts (MAD) are organized by law and can assess taxes for control of nuisance or disease-vector mosquitos. Cities are also involved with toxic substances when they pass health laws; take insect control measures; require food inspections; create laws on sale, use, and transport of toxic substances; mandate vector control; or implement control programs affecting rats, dogs, cats, wild animals, and birds. Some counties have rigid zoning and planning commissions that make decisions governing regulation of agricultural, lands, solid waste dumps, and other areas where toxic substances may be involved.

MONITORING PROGRAMS

Toxic substance monitoring was a piecemeal sampling program by many agencies up to 1964, performed mostly by the Fish and Wildlife Service at Patuxent Wildlife Research Center. Samples of waterfowl wings were sent to the center by hunters for sex and age studies, and samples of grackles and starlings were collected by shooting. Regular aquatic sampling stations were operated by the Columbia Fish Pesticide Laboratory.

In 1964, the President's Science Advisory Committee (PSAC) recommended a network of monitoring stations for air, water, wildlife, fish food, estuaries, animal feeds, and agricultural crops.

The National Pesticides Monitoring Program (NPMP) was established but never very effective because its operation was split among many federal agencies with split budgets and responsibilities. In 1972, EPA was designated as the lead agency for monitoring but never was given proper budget/personnel authority to carry out their mandate. The 1972 EPA Act requires the administration to develop a National Pesticide Monitoring Plan. One was reviewed and critiqued by Battelle Laboratories but nothing ever came of it; there was never a firm central authority established and no appropriate funding of any one agency.

Problems involved the coordination of various department personnel; financing; and the fact that there was no control of accountability. Publication and analyses lagged 3 or 4 years behind sample taking; and there were also problems with inter-laboratory quality control in analyses.

What is being monitored and what should be monitored? Samples include meat, poultry, and eagles, so there is difficulty in coordinating what chemical is used to what is sampled and what to look for in samples. There are critical short-term versus long-term problems relating to species, sample sizes, costs of collection and analyses, timeliness of data, publication of results that lag behind, and analytical procedures that are difficult to coordinate between laboratories. EPA should take the lead by law, but they lack budgeted funds, direction, personnel, and management authority over non-EPA personnel.

There is high use and release of pesticides: 45,000 products were registered in 1980; 2.5 billion pounds (active ingredients) of pesticides were used in 1980 (Maddy 1983). In 1986, an estimated 661 million pounds of pesticide were used (Gianessi 1986). How and where to monitor is a real problem, not only nationally, but globally.

One of the best examples of monitoring that has been conducted over a long time span has been the waterfowl wing analyses done by the Patuxent Wildlife Research Center, USFWS. The report of the analyses for 1979–80 (Cain 1981) showed that DDE was found in all mallard and black ducks analyzed. Residues had declined since 1976, but significantly so only in the Pacific Flyway. All DDT metabolites except DDE declined. PCB levels were also reduced, but the number of positive samples had increased. Alabama and New Mexico samples were highest. More recent monitoring in Arizona and New Mexico of waterfowl and other species of wildlife has shown the potential for more recent contamination by DDT. In New Mexico, data for bats, starlings, songbirds, and waterfowl showed higher residues of DDE. In Arizona, fish, starlings, and waterfowl wings were also high in DDE. DDT may be illegally used; or the contamination might be coming from dump sites, or as a manufacturer's contaminant in 10 or 12 pesticides currently being used, especially dicofol, which may contain 6 percent DDT and 9 percent DDE (Clark and Krynitsky 1983b).

The Commission of the European Communities, the Federal Environmental Agency of West Germany, and the USEPA sponsored an international workshop on monitoring environmental materials and specimen banking in 1978. Some of their important recommendations (adapted from Luepke 1979) are as follows:

1. Establish system to monitor environmental exposure for substances that have or may have adverse effects.
2. Establish specimen banks.
3. Pilot specimen banks.
4. Maintain quality control of banks and analyses.
5. Establish living tissue specimen banks—adaptation processes to toxic substances.
6. Coordinate internationally.
7. Legal and ethical considerations by countries.
8. Collection areas should allow for extrapolation.
9. Samples should reflect terrestrial, aquatic, and urbanic systems.
10. Species selected for monitoring and those in specimen banks should have some relationship.
11. Plant species recommended.
12. Monitor invertebrates—honey bees, carabid beetles, earthworms.
13. Monitor birds/mammals—availability—ducks mallard/starling; specimen banks should include gonads, thyroid, kidney, adrenals, bone, adipose tissue, blood, liver, lung, skeletal muscle, spleen, feathers, hair, thymus, bursa, teeth, eye lens, brain.
14. Aero-plankton collection and banking and analyses are important.
15. Analytical quality control is important.
16. Pollutants to be monitored relate to exposure, size of population at risk, severity of effects.
17. High priority pollutants include those that show accumulation, persistence, and chronic/acute ratios that are low.
18. Determine environmental exposure/concentration in indicator species; investigate normal concentrations and those related to effects.
19. Utilize pre-screening data on new chemicals in the design of monitoring programs.

INTERNATIONAL POLICIES

Toxic substances residues are controlled worldwide largely by tolerance limits on residues on imported foodstuffs. Europe was first to lower the tolerance on DDT residues in meat/fat, so the United States had to lower tolerances in order to ship meats and poultry to Europe. West Germany lowered the arsenic tolerance on apples to zero, so the French had to reduce tolerances as well in order to sell French apples in Germany. Most developing countries have no tolerance levels because foodstuffs are imported, not exported.

The European Economic Community (EEC) has a Codex Committee on pesticide residues within the EEC. The Organization for Economic Cooperation and Development (OECD) also has cooperative committees on monitoring and residues. Most countries do not have laws on export products; this is regulated by the country that is importing, either related to pesticide products or residue tolerances.

Other international organizations involved with toxic substances include those under the auspices of the United Nations such as the World Health Organization (WHO). They are primarily concerned with human disease problems and utilize large quantities of pesticides to control vectors for transmissible disease such as malaria and typhus. WHO continued to use DDT in lesser developed countries long after the 1972 ban in the USA. USAID (US Aid for Independent Development) also assists lesser developed countries by controlling insect and vertebrate pests with chemicals. Field testing and evaluations of impacts on non-target species are now being conducted by USAID in some African countries prior to large-scale field applications for control. Some problems develop as a result of these international programs in that pesticides are shipped from many countries and printed instructions are not understood by local applicators. Materials are partitioned into smaller unmarked containers that sometimes results in misuse and accidental poisoning. On occasion, large quantities of controlled chemicals are shipped to locations of pest outbreaks and subsequently not used. Disposal of these stores presents a problem to the local environment, wildlife and humans as well. Initially, large international organizations such as WHO were interested only in the prevention of disease and starvation and not concerned about long-term environmental or human hazards from persistent toxic substances. Fortunately this situation is changing.

Following is a brief description of toxic substance policies in eight countries.

In Britain, there are no formal laws; companies more or less abide by gentleman's agreement to register and control residues, impose voluntary restrictions, and have committees to discuss and suggest regulations. A *Pesticides Safety Protection Scheme* is published for industrial review.

Japan requires registration, government review, and applicator guidance. There is some evidence of overuse and accidents have been reported such as Minimata disease and Ouch-Ouch disease in humans and some domestic pets.

In the Netherlands, market basket surveys for residues are done and there is government licensing and review.

Sweden has ordinances on products hazardous to health and the environment. The Swedish code of statues 1973.334 requires that the manufacturer or importer prevent ill effects. The state has surveillance authority to intervene and to regulate manufacture and safe handling. County administrations hire safety inspectors and public health committees are organized at the county level. A Products Control Board charges a fee to investigate for licensing; there are 10 members appointed from agencies, the public, and business. They handle registration, labeling, and revocation of labels.

Pesticide use in India greatly increased following World War II. A law passed in 1979 requires registration. Some human cases of poisoning have been reported. Residues of DDT in human fat for 1963–1966 was 13.7 ppm.

In 1974 Mexico used 10,423 metric tons of pesticide on cotton alone. Pesticides and fertilizers caused 12.4 percent of all human accidental deaths in 1969/71. The General Bureau of Standards handles labeling and tolerances. Other federal agencies involved with pesticides include the General Bureau of Plant Protection, Ministry of Public Health, and Department of Environmental Improvement.

France requires that agricultural chemicals be regulated through registration in order to minimize residues on human and animal feeds. There is an Investigatory Commission on the Use of Toxic Substances in Agriculture with 17 members. A Commission on Pest Control Products for Agricultural Use deals with labeling and classification of hazards, and residue limits on foods (Commission des Toxiques for Registration).

The West German Plant Protection Law of 1968 deals with registration, labeling, tolerances, testing, residue data, and monitoring. A 12-person council on environmental questions has been appointed. There is some local and state control of toxic substance use.

3

Elements, Chemicals, and Compounds found in Environmental Pollutants

What is a toxic substance?? Major components of such a definition are related to dose and time (Fig. 3.1). Both natural as well as synthetic chemicals present contaminant problems. In broad classes, these include:

1. Natural chemicals, such as those found in earth's crust, and normal dietary components; nitrites; nitrates; elements such as selenium, zinc, lead, and mercury; and trace minerals.
2. Natural fungal and plant toxins, such as aflatoxins.
3. Organic/inorganic mixtures in air, water, at occupational sites, and volatile substances.
4. Synthetic chemicals, such as agricultural chemicals, pesticides, food additives, and industrial chemicals.

Table 3.1 depicts toxic elements in the environment. Some are non-critical; others are toxic but not generally available, or insoluble; while others are highly toxic and accessible (Wood 1974).

ENVIRONMENTAL POLLUTANT CATEGORIES

Inorganics

Some important inorganics related to environmental problems are listed (Table 3.2) in the National Drinking Water Standards. Inorganic pollutants (organometallic compounds) include salts and compounds of many of the elements in Table 3.2, especially the heavy metals such as mercury, zinc, nickel, cadmium, chromium, selenium, arsenic, and copper.

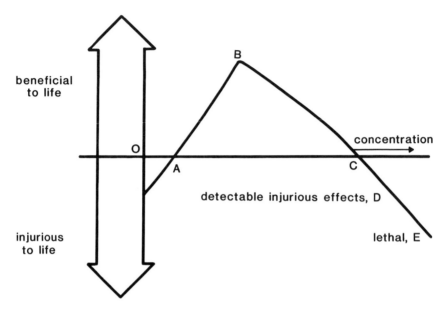

Figure 3.1 The relationship between time, dose, and effects of potential toxins. Modified from Horne, R. A. 1972. *Science* 177(4055)1152–1153. Copyright 1972 by AAAS.

Table 3-1 Toxic Elements in the Environment

Non-critical			Very Toxic, Relatively Accessible			Toxic but Very Insoluble or Very Rare		
Na	C	F	Be	As	Au	Ti	Ga	Hf
K	P	Li	Co	Se	Hg	La	Zr	Os
Mg	Fe	Rb	Ni	Te	Cu	W	Rh	Nb
Ca	S	Sr	Pd	Pb	Zn	Ir	Ta	Ru
H	Cl	Al	Ag	Sb	Sn	Re	Ba	
O	Br	Si	Cd	Bi	Pt			
N								

From Wood, J.M. Biological cycles for toxic elements in the environment, *183, pp. 1049-521, 1974. Copyright AAAS.*

Table 3-2 Toxic Elements, Sources, and National Drinking
Water Standards

Element/ Compound	Sources	National Drinking Water Standard (mg/l)
Arsenic	Runoff, mining, smelters, pesticides	0.05
Asbestos[a]	Industrial, wallboard, insulation, talc	
Barium	Clinical tests, radiation testing	1.0
Beryllium[b]	Acid mine drainage, industrial, natural	0.5 Recom. for irrigation water
Cadmium	Industry, mining, pesticides	0.01
Chromium	Industrial	0.05
Copper	Industrial	1.0
Lead	Mining, industry, autos, pesticides	0.05
Manganese	Mining	0.05
Mercury	Mining, seed dressing, natural	
Nickel	Mining, oxide powder, sulfides	
Selenium	Agricultural runoff, mining	0.01
Zinc	Industrial	5.0
Arsenicals	Lead arsenates	
Silica gels	Aerosols, dessicants	

From ReVelle and ReVelle 1974. Sourcebook on the Environment—the Scientific
Perspective. *Houghton Mifflin, Boston, pp. 62–66. Permission granted.*
[a] *Carcinogen*
[b] *lung disease*

Many inorganic compounds can accumulate in plants and result in toxic
effects to animals and humans. Asbestos has presented many problems in
industry, in academic institutions, as well as in many public buildings
where it was used for years in pipe insulation, ceiling tiles, and in many
areas where a fire-retardant material was desirable. All of these areas now
have to be sealed, or the asbestos-containing material must be removed at
high cost. There has been some federal assistance for removal of the
asbestos hazard from public buildings and schools. EPA has proposed a
ban on future asbestos production that would phase out all uses in 10
years. This would add about $1.8 billion to the cost of alternative products.
EPA considers that any exposure to asbestos is not without risk. Dinman
(1972) has suggested a threshold of activity exists at 10^4 atoms within a cell.
About 30 million tons of asbestos were used between 1900 and 1980; during
1984, 240,000 tons were used in the United States. Currently it is estimated

that between 3,000 and 12,000 cancer deaths occur each year as a result of asbestos exposure; about 65,000 people suffer from asbestosis (Sun 1986b).

The economics and risk benefit assessment for the removal of asbestos hazards from public buildings have been debated and discussed. In terms of dollar cost, the application of these large sums to other health benefit programs, seems, in some cases, more helpful. If asbestos is in place and in good condition, the hazard might be contained and best left in place rather than to risk the removal and disturbance involved. Hazards increase for workers as well as building residents when asbestos is disturbed. Removal of asbestos may cost as much as $28 to 60 million per life year saved (Dewees 1986).

As a result of the discovery of a high concentration of selenium at Kesterson Refuge in California (Zahm 1986), 23 sites in nine western states were surveyed for high concentrations. Selenium concentrations of over 600 ppb were found in seven states: Arizona, California, Montana, Nevada, New Mexico, South Dakota, and one other unnamed by the survey (Marshall 1986a). The Department of the Interior is reported to have a plan under way to deal with high selenium levels as well as other heavy metals on migratory bird refuges as a result of agricultural drainage and industrial contamination.

Many inorganic chemicals are also found in the insecticide, pesticide, fungicide, rodenticide, miticide, and herbicide categories listed in the following pages.

Organics

Organo-halogenated compounds include those containing fluorine, bromine, chlorine, iodine, and astatine. Examples include compounds such as PCB, PBB, dioxins, solvents, propellants, and some pesticides.

Although organics are found in many of the environmental pollutant categories that follow, there are several used mainly for industrial purposes that will be described in this section.

The many organic compounds produced by various water treatment practices have been of concern for a long time. Most of these are chloro- or bromophenol, acetonitrile, or aldehyde compounds. Some of them are acids. Several have been found to produce carcinomas in animals and others have resulted in teratogenic effects in rodent studies. Production, distribution, and effects of these compounds are not well understood in human drinking water or in the natural environment (Health Effects Research Laboratory 1987).

DNOC Dinex

Methyl dinitrophenol alters and uncouples phosphorylation, is a neuro-toxin, increases oxygen consumption, and is metabolized very slowly. There is an oral toxicity in bees of 18 μg; in rats, 300 μg/g; dogs, intrapa-ritoneal IP 10; and pigeons, intramuscular (IM) 5 μg/g. It is used as an insecticide and fungicide (O'Brien 1967).

Polychlorinated Biphenyls (PCBs)

In Aroclor #1016, a common PCB, the latter two digits indicate the percentage of chlorine. Many PCB compounds are made in numerous countries for a wide variety of industrial uses, including 1221, 1232, and 1254. The most common used in testing is 1254. These isomers are used in askarels (large transformers), carbonless paper, paints, the electronics industry, coolants, and for several other purposes. They are found throughout the environment. LC-50s for 1254 are bobwhite, 604 ppm; pheasants, 1091 ppm; and mallards, 2699 ppm (Heath, Spann, Hill, et al. 1972; Brown, Bedard, Brennan, et al. 1987).

Polybrominated Biphenyls

PBBs were mainly released in Michigan where they were produced as a fire retardant and accidentally mixed with animal feed and spread throughout Michigan and other nearby states. Mink are highly susceptible to PBB; reproduction and kit survival are influenced by 1 ppm in the diet. There is 90 percent mortality in adults fed 6.25 ppm (Sleight 1979).

Other closely related toxic industrial compounds are polychlorinated napthalenes and halowax (1014, 62% chlorine). Other organics that are toxic and enter natural systems from industry include benzyl chloride, methane, ether, bromochlomethane chlorophenol, tetrachlorophenol, and methyl phenol. Trichloroethylene (TCE) is a serious contaminant of un-derground water supplies including dimethyl-dintro phenols, phenyla-mines, ethanes, and ethylenes.

PCBs are reduced in toxicity by both aerobic microbial degradation and reductive dechlorination. Various decay products have been identified in sediment spill sites and the higher, more toxic PCBs seem to be reduced first. Rates are not known (Brown, Bedard, Brennan, et al. 1987).

Dioxin—PCDD (polychlorinated dibenzo-para-dioxin)

This toxic compound is found in chemicals and in industrial wastes in about 75 different isomers. These low-level contaminants concentrate in fat and are highly toxic and carcinogenic to a variety of species. Lethal, reproductive, teratogenic, mutagenic, immunotoxic, and histopathologic effects have been demonstrated. Residues of over 0.01 ppt in aquatic systems may prove harmful. Low exposures of 0.1 μg/kg in mice produced teratogenic effects in young. This low-level exposure also produced carcinomas in rats (Eisler 1986a).

Future Organic Problems

The synthetic fuel industry will create many toxic substances from coal extraction, coal shale, biomass conversion, and tar sands.

Synthetic fuels will be produced from coal because it has a high (35–65%) efficiency of conversion to fuels. Biomass conversion is 35 to 55 percent effective. For shale, 10 to 40 gallons of crude oil is produced per ton of shale processed, and the 85 percent waste is increased to 125 percent of the original volume through the process of extraction. A shale conversion plant producing 55,000 barrels of oil per day uses 30 million tons of shale per year. This annual production will result in the necessity of disposing of 500 million cubic feet of spent shale. The leachable salts include arsenic. Oil shale production is expected to produce 3 million bbls per day by the year 2000 and 8 million bbls per day by the year 2010 (Schriesheim and Kirshenbaum 1981). Drops in crude oil prices from the Middle East have delayed development temporarily, but the recent Gulf crisis has reversed the trend.

The production of synthetic fuels and the increased development of new organic chemicals in industry are the greatest potential problems. There are now about 70,000 chemicals regularly produced and used. The Chemical Abstract Service (CAS) lists about 6 million chemicals. Current regulatory mechanisms and survey/research programs are not sufficient.

An excellent source of information on chemicals is the Chemical Information System CIS, which is publically accessible by computer terminals. CIS was developed by USEPA and NIH, and currently contains the physical/chemical structure, toxicological information, and regulatory data on about 200,000 chemicals and compounds including chemicals from about 20 countries. The annual subscription fee is $300 and an hourly user fee is between $55 and $85.

Pesticides and/or Insecticides

Chlorinated Hydrocarbons

Chlorinated hydrocarbons, used in both pesticides and insecticides, include: DDT, DDE (see Fig. 3.2), DDD, TDE, aldrin, dieldrin chlordane,

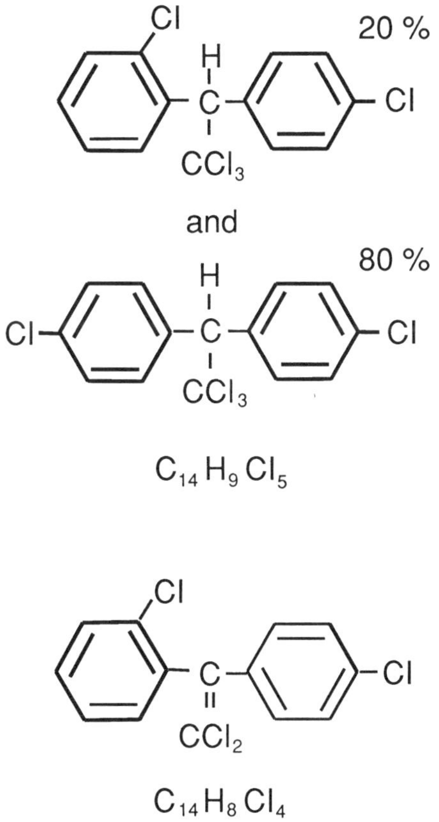

20 %

and

80 %

$C_{14}H_9Cl_5$

$C_{14}H_8Cl_4$

Figure 3.2 Chemical structure of technical DDT, mixed isomers and o, p′ DDE, a common environmental metabolite. U. S. Government Publication.

heptachlor, nemagon, DBCP, methoxychlor, BHC, lindane, endrin, toxaphene, kelthane, dicofol, prolan, bulan, dilan, isodrin, telodrin, and thiodan. These are neurotoxicants with low vapor pressures and most are highly persistent. Toxicity is highly variable between compounds; endrin, one of the most toxic, will kill some species of fish at a concentration of 0.2 ppb (USEPA 1971). These chlorinated compounds are not readily absorbed across the skin barrier, but they will pass across the gill integument easily. The most common example of this class of compounds is DDT, which has a low vapor pressure of 1.5×10^7 mm at 20°C. It is apolar and has high chemical stability, being relatively insensitive to sunlight. Water solubility is low, 0.2 to 1.2 ppb, and the oil/water partition coefficient is large; for olive oil it is 923/1 (O'Brien 1967). DDT metabolizes to

DDE, DDMU, DDMS, DDOH, and DDA. DDE is most common and this metabolite is still capable of producing toxic effects in many species; it also accumulates in organisms and systems. Many of these cyclodienes convert by epoxidation to more toxic substances and also to glucuronides. Another common example of this class of compounds is hexachlorocyclohexane: BHC, HCH, or lindane. This compound has a much higher vapor pressure and was commonly used in vaporizers for insect control. Toxicity for the rat is 125 mg/kg, for the American roach 5.0, mosquito 3.0, and rabbit 200 mg/kg (O'Brien 1967). Toxaphene has been used extensively and is very hazardous to aquatic life. Lethal exposures can be as low as 10 μg/l in freshwater organisms, with adverse effects on reproduction and physiology as low as 0.05 μg/1. It is highly persistent in water and soil, up to 9–11 years, but is readily metabolized by warm-blooded animals. At high doses, it is mutagenic and carcinogenic (Eisler and Jacknow 1985).

Organophosphates

Organophosphates (Fig. 3.3), used in pesticides and insecticides, are toxic organic compounds containing phosphorous with the general structure $(RO)_2 P(A)X$, where R = methyl or ethyl, A = sulfur or oxygen, and X = highly variable.

Other common organophosphates include parathion, malathion, diazinon, dichlorvos, guthion, ronnel, coumaphos, mevinphos, bidrin, TEPP, demeton, schradan, dimefox, chlorthion, sumithion and azodrin. The organophosphates are strong inhibitors of cholinesterase by direct or indirect

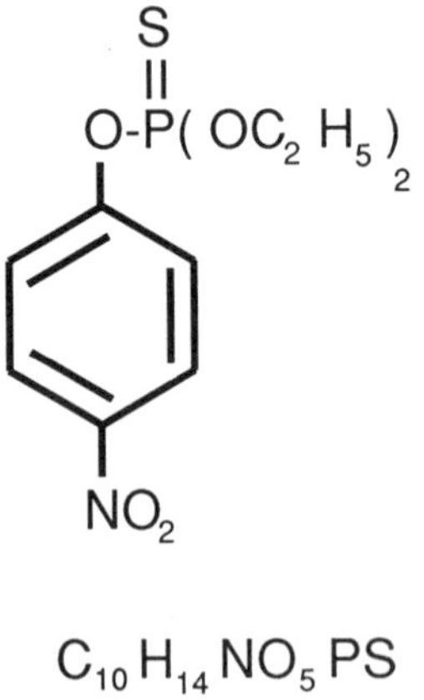

$$C_{10} H_{14} NO_5 PS$$

Figure 3.3   Chemical structure of typical organophosphate insecticide, ethyl parathion. U. S. Government Publication.

latent inhibition, which requires activation of the compounds to analogs such as malaoxon and paraoxon. Death results from CNS effects or by action in the peripheral nervous system. Demyelination of the nerve sheaths occurs. Some LD-50s for some organophosphates are sumithion (fenitrothion) for mallard 1190 mg/kg, pheasant 55.6, bobwhite 27.4, and sharp-tailed grouse 53.4. Azodrin (monocrotophos), an insecticide used commonly on cotton in California, is more toxic; LD-50s are as follows: mallard 4.76 mg/kg, bobwhite 0.9, Canada goose 1.58, and pigeon 2.83 mg/kg. Toxicities are highly variable. In the case of diazinon, the red-winged blackbird is more sensitive (2.0 mg/kg) than the pheasant (4.33), the bobwhite (10), and the European starling (110 mg/kg) (Smith 1987). This is true of many toxic substances and prevents extrapolation of toxic substance testing across species or genera.

Carbamates

These insecticides (see Fig. 3.4) are derivatives of carbamic acids, both aromatic and phenolic. The carbamates include a broad group of toxic compounds used as insecticides, fungicides, and herbicides.

Carbofuran (furadan) is a common carbamate used on a variety of crops. About 7 million pounds are used each year. Aquatic invertebrates are affected at levels as low as 200 ppb and some bird species show evidence of toxicity at 238 ppb. The LC-50 for larva of a marine crab is 2.5 ppb. For mammals, tolerance is higher, at about 2,000 to 9,000 ppb. Fish are affected at concentrations of 15 ppb maximum allowable toxicant concentra-

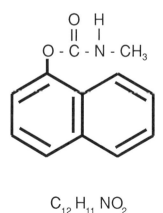

$$C_{12} H_{11} NO_2$$

Figure 3.4 Structure of a typical carbamate insecticide, carbaryl or sevin. U. S. Government Publication.

tion (MATC). Thousands of waterfowl have been killed by use and misuse of carbofuran. Half-life may be as long as 16 years in soils with low ph. At normal ph, carbofuran degrades in about 30 days. Microbes can detoxify the compound rapidly, especially under anaerobic conditions (Eisler 1985b).

Other chemicals classed as carbamates include carbaryl, zectran, isolan, carbofuran, pyrolan, matacil, baygon, chloro IPC (herbicide), diallate (herbicide), ziram and zineb, both fungicides. Carbamates are also cholinesterase inhibitors with highly varied toxicity to insects. Bees, for example, are highly sensitive to sevin, while the German cockroach is essentially immune. The LD-50 for the water flea is 1 ppm, for the American roach 500 ppm. Mammalian toxicity also varies, but generally carbamates are less toxic to mammals than are organophosphates (O'Brien 1967).

Pyrethroids

Pyrethroids (Fig. 3.5), some of the oldest organic insecticides known, were sold on a commercial basis to control insects as early as 1828. These chemicals were extracted from chrysanthemum flowers up until about 1950, when commercial synthetics were developed.

Many new and more toxic synthetic compounds have been fabricated since that time and include allethrin, barthrin, cypermethrin, deltamethrin, dimethrin, fenvalerate, permethrin, phenithrin, pyrethrins, resmethrin, and tetramethrin. No good mode of action has been described and the

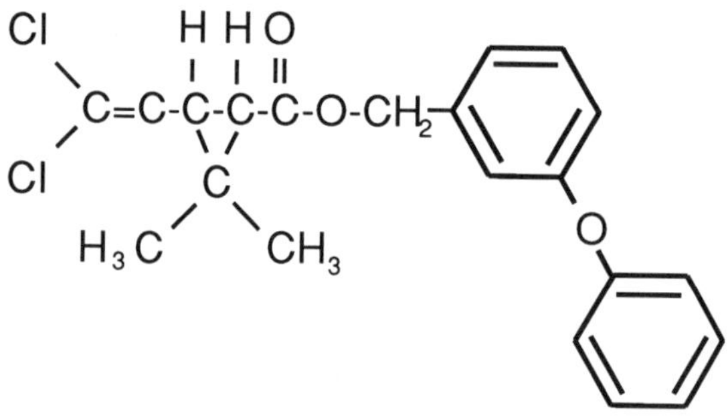

$$C_{21}H_{20}Cl_2O_3$$

Figure 3.5 Chemical structure of typical synthetic pyrethroid, mixed isomers of permethrin. U. S. Government Publication.

newer fourth or fifth generation of synthetic pyrethroids are highly toxic; some can kill aquatic invertebrates at less than 1.0 ppt. These synthetic toxins can remain in the environment as long as 400 days or more. However, mammals are relatively immune to their effects; the LD-50 is 2949 mg/kg for rats given permethrin in water (Leahey 1985).

Nicotinoids

These tobacco extracts were recommended for use as insecticides as early as 1746. They have been synthesized in the laboratory, but extracts from tobacco leaves are cheaper. Nicotinoid insecticides are alkaloid nicotine and methyl pyridine, and the sulfate form is also used. Black-leaf 40 is the best example. Nicotinoids are neurotoxins that mimic acetylcholine. Toxicities are highly variable; topical applications in the American roach produce an LD-50 of 650 mg/kg, but for the silkworm, it is only 4.0 mg/kg. Oral LD-50s for the rat are 55 mg/kg, for the mouse 24 mg/kg. Intravenous injections produce LD-50s of 0.8 mg/kg in mice, 1.0 in rats, 9.0 in rabbits, and 5.0 mg/kg in dogs. Nicotine is readily metabolized by the liver (O'Brien 1967).

Rotenoids

These are insecticides and picicides produced from extracts of the tuba root *Derris elliptica*. They were used by natives for obtaining fish and for insecticides as early as 1848. Toxicity is variable; for the bee the LD-50 is 3 mg/kg, for the American roach it is 1,000 mg/kg. Toxicity is produced in chickens at 906 mg/kg, mallards are relatively immune (LC-50 2600 ppm). The rat oral LD-50 is 132 mg/kg (O'Brien 1967; Hill, Heath, Spann, et al. 1975).

Fungicides

Some common compounds used as fungicides include captaful, captan, thiram, diphenyl mercury, zineb, and ceresan. The more important toxic effects of fungicides have been found in their mutagenicity and carcinogenicity. Toxicity for cerasan m (LC-50) is 57 ppm for bobwhite, about 50 ppm for the mallard, and 146 ppm for the pheasant (Heath, Spann, Hill, et al. 1972).

Rodenticides

These are used widely both in urban areas as well as in orchards and in grain storage areas. They include antu(napthylthiourea), diphacinone, warfarin, gophacide, 1080, and talon. Some secondary hazards to birds of prey, such as owls, have been demonstrated as a result of orchard use of some rodenticides (Hegdal and Colvin 1988, Mendenhall and Pank 1980). The LD-50 for gophacide is 24 mg/kg for mallards, 161 mg/kg for pheasants, and 2–5.0 mg/kg for golden eagles (Tucker and Crabtree 1970).

Miticides (Acaracide)

These compounds are used mostly as innoculants in soils and include dicofol or kelthane, ovex, mevinphos, phosdrin, omite, or comite, propargite. Ovex is used to control eggs and larvae of mites. It has a low mammalian toxicity (Rat LD-50 2050 mg/kg) but is persistent (Matsumura 1975). Mevinphos (phosdrin) is highly toxic to both mammals and birds. The LD-50 for the rat is 3.7 mg/kg, for the starling 3.9 mg/kg, mallard 4.6 mg/kg, and sharp-tailed grouse 0.75–1.5 mg/kg (Smith 1987).

Other highly toxic organic compounds that have been used for pest control include the fluroine-fluoro-organics, especially fluroacetate. These are activated to fluorocitric acid and used as insecticides and rodenticides; they are highly toxic to mammals. They have been generally withdrawn from use, but some consideration is being given to allow the use of 1080 in special circumstances for control of predators. The intravenous LD-50 for dogs is 0.06 mg/kg; for cats, 0.2 mg/kg; the rat intraparitoneal (IP) is 5.0 mg/kg and the oral dose LD-50 for man is 2 to 10 mg/kg. The compound fluoroacetamide has been withdrawn in Britain where it was known as Tritox (O'Brien 1967).

Herbicides

There are two broad groups of herbicides, the phenoxyacids such as 2,4-D or 2,4.5-T; and the ureas such as monuron, diuron, and fenuron. See Figure 3.6 for the chemical structure of a typical herbicide.

Other common herbicides include butoxyethanol ester, BEE; propylene, glycol, butyl ester, PGBE; isosytle ester IOE, 2,4-D, simazine, 2,4,5-T, arsenite, dalapon, dicamba, dinoseb, diquat, paraquat, and diuron. The phenoxyacids are relatively non-toxic to birds; the LC-40 for bobwhite, pheasant, mallard, and coturnix for 2,4-D is in excess of 5,000 ppm (Heath, Spann, Hill, et al. 1972). Paraquat, on the other hand is more toxic; the LC-50 for bobwhite is 981 ppm in feed. Diuron is toxic to bobwhite at LC-50 1730 ppm.

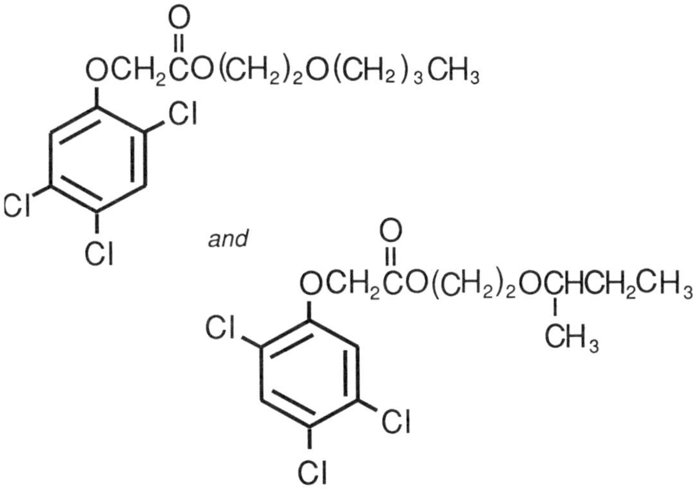

$$C_{14}H_{17}Cl_3O_4$$

Figure 3.6 Chemical structure of typical herbicide, 2,4,5-T butoxyethanol ether esters. U. S. Government Publication.

HALF LIFE AND DISAPPEARANCE RATES

The concept of physical and biological half-life, $T_{1/2}$ or $t_{1/2}$, originated from radiation studies.

The sign for physical half-life is T_p, which equals the time for disintegration of one-half the atoms of a given ratioactive substance. Half of all ^{36}Cl atoms will decay in 410,000 years. We used ^{36}Cl to label DDT in a marsh and meadow study (Meeks 1968; Forsyth, Peterle, and Bandy 1983).

T_b, the biological half-life equals the time a chemical takes to leave the body following ingestion or injection. It includes both the physical half-life as well as the excretion rate in air or in body wastes. The physical half-life of ^{32}P is 14.2 days; if injected into the body, the biological half-life is 1155 (bone) days before half of the phosphorus is excreted. Combining both the physical and biological half-life gives the effective half-life in the body of 14.1 days. How applicable is the term *half-life* to toxic substances?

There is much confusion between half-life and disappearance rates and breakdown rates. Gunther and Jeppson (1960 : 82) have defined half-life as "the time required for half of the residue to react or otherwise dissipate." In closed ecosystems, dissipation simply means the chemical has moved to another site in its original state or as a metabolite. If it retains its toxicity, the problem of effects and accumulation persists through time. For some toxic substances such as the heavy metals, $T_{1/2}$ is not useful because the metallic elements do not break down, although some of the more toxic compounds such as methyl or ethyl mercury are altered in the environment and become less biologically active. Conversion and breakdown can result in a more or less toxic substance, for example, malathion to malaoxon, which is more toxic; parathion to paraoxon, which is also more toxic; but DDT to DDE to DDMU, the latter being less toxic. $T_{1/2}$ can be measured in a variety of ways. Usually in the laboratory the substance is placed on glass plates and exposed to known light, temperature, humidity, and wind. $T_{1/2}$ is also tested by innoculation in soils, either sterile, reconstituted, and/or in-situ. Some pesticides are tested for half-life on leaf surfaces.

$T_{1/2}$ is related to a great variety of both physical and biological effects in addition to the initial type, structure, and application methods or release situation (air, water, sewerage, solid waste, etc.). These factors include temperature (cold generally inhibits dissipation and breakdown—DDT lasts longer on-site in the Arctic, Brown and Brown 1970); ph; light, including ultraviolet spectral qualities; presence of organisms and what kind and how many; oxygen; animal digestive tracts (rumen organisms); substrate; soil type (mainly organic matter and water holding capacity); solubility; volatility; vapor pressure; method of application in spray, granule, surface or sub-surface; carriers used; emulsifiers; presence of other chemicals in the system; wind; humidity; rainfall; days of sunshine; snow cover; and the chemical characteristics of the substance (for example, does it break down to substances that are physically/chemically altered in terms of how they interface with the physical and biological environment?).

Persistence vs. Disappearance

In relation to many pesticides, the term *persistent* is frequently used; DDT is a persistent chlorinated hydrocarbon. There are few studies done that actually measure persistence and differentiate between actual breakdown versus disappearance from the site. Persistence refers to both and infers the compound or element is present or its metabolites are still present and toxic properties are still present. In the case of heavy metals, all of them would be persistent, but some metabolites may not be biologically available and could be considered non-toxic. Some inorganics are very stable and long-lasting. The organics are usually less stable, but there are excep-

tions such as PBB, PCB, and DDT. The half-life of DDT has been estimated as 10 to 20 years (USEPA 1975). It may be longer if DDE is
considered as a toxic metabolite. Generally, the organophosphates are less
persistent and the organochlorines are more persistent.

Examples

DDT has low solubility in water; in one experiment, 3.0 ppb was altered to
not detectable (ND) in 1 month (Meeks 1968). DDT was banned in Arizona
in 1969, but although milk and crop residues declined, soil levels remained
constant for 4 years (Ware, Esteson, and Cahill 1974). In a treated old-field
ecosystem, soil residues declined by 45 percent over a 5-year period
(Forsyth, Peterle, and Bandy 1983). Ten pounds per acre of DDT was
applied to a Miami silt loam with 3.8 percent organic matter; 22 percent
was recovered from the soil after 42 months. In a muck soil with 40 percent
organic matter, 33 percent was recovered in 42 months (Lichtenstein and
Schulz 1959). In aerobic soil DDT is metabolized to DDD in 166 days; in
anaerobic soil DDT is altered to DDD in 46 days (Burge 1971). Several
chlorinated hydrocarbons were degraded by actinomycetes at the rate of
25 percent in 6 days, but 8 different fungal species had no effect on
metabolite production (Chacko, Lockwood, and Zabik 1966). Radiation
does break down DDT. 160 K rads of gamma radiation with the presence of
oxygen will break down 85 to 90 percent of DDT (Kanitz, Costello, and
Orlando 1971).

Disappearance

Many physical factors influence disappearance rates: leaching; solubility;
volatilization; vapor pressure; absorption and desorption rates; bioaccumulation; and rates of transport in water, wind, in organisms. Decomposition, structure, and metabolism in organisms are also related to the
kinds of organisms and their physiological systems.

Conversion of DDT to DDE is pH-dependent. Higher pH increases the
rate as well as the presence of MgO (Nash, Harris, and Lewis 1973). In a
forest soil, DDT was applied at the rate of 4 pounds per acre for 6 years,
and the $T_{1/2}$ was estimated at 10 years (Woodwell 1961). There was an
increase in soil DDT after the cessation of application as a result of
"rain-out" from the foliage (Woodwell and Martin 1964). Aldrin applied
to a muck soil at 21 g per acre for 4 years resulted in 0.07 ppm aldrin and
0.21 ppm dieldrin. In our research experience, we applied 1 pound of DDT
per acre in a granular form from the air; very little DDT moved in surface
or subsurface water, routes of accumulation varied by species even between two species of shrews, and accumulation in the some of the biota

increased for 6 to 7 years (Forsyth, Peterle, and Bandy (1983). Residue content in some species, such as earthworms, declined, while others such as plants and *Microtus* increased in residue content. (We will discuss more of these results in the chapters on transport and accumulation.) For many toxic substances, including pesticides, the decrease at the site of application or release is not a matter of simple reaction kinetics, but usually some form of logarithmic rate and for some the decrease is bi-phasic. Experimental plots were treated once with 9 kg/ha of DDT, then dieldrin or heptachlor and residues in earthworms were assayed over a 20-year period. "Half-times," defined as the time necessary for half the body burden in earthworms to disappear, were for DDE, 5.7 years; for dieldrin, 5.4 years; and for heptachlor epoxide, the half-time was 4.3 years (Beyer and Krynitsky 1989).

DDT on crops decreases rather rapidly, in a matter of days. $T_{1/2}$ for DDT on alfalfa is 5 to 7 days, citrus 38 to 50 days, clover 10 to 14 days, lettuce 2 to 3 days, peaches 8 to 11 days, and peach leaves 14 to 18 days (Gunther and Jeppson 1960:82).

Persistence is sometimes defined as time in residence at site of treatment or release. All of the varied physical and biological considerations must be applied in any discussion of persistence, disappearance, and $T_{1/2}$. In areas treated with DDT for 10 or more years: an orchard still retained 40 percent of the total DDT applied (USEPA 1975); a vineyard still had 22 percent of the total DDT after 24 years of treatment (Kuhr, Davis, and Taschenberg 1972). Arizona banned the use of DDT on alfalfa as a result of residues in commercial milk sales; 4 years after the ban there was no observable drop in DDT soil levels (Ware, Esteson, and Cahill 1974). Soil residues in sprayed forest areas equal 0.213 g/m^2 and in unsprayed forests the soils contained 0.004 g/m^2 (Woodwell, Craig, and Johnson 1971). An orchard area contained 6.0 to 11.4 g/m^2 DDT. Crops grown on DDT-contaminated soil reduce soil levels to about 0.1 to 2.62 g/m^2. DDT is found in air (Bidleman and Olney 1974, Lloyd-Jones 1971), co-distills with water, and in sprayed areas rain has been assayed at up to 190 ppt pp'DDT (Tarrant and Tatton 1968). In one of our studies, we detected 40 ppt of DDT in Antarctic snow from Polar Station (Peterle 1969). The average concentration of DDT in rain has been measured at 60 ppt. Residence time of DDT in air has been estimated at 3.3 years (Woodwell, Craig, and Johnson 1971). Point sources can be important to wildlife contamination; at Wheeler Refuge in Georgia, 10 years after production ceased a mallard had maximum residues of 6900 ppm (lipid wt. basis) in muscle, a crow 1470 ppm, and a cottontail rabbit 79 ppm of DDTR (O'Shea, Fleming, and Cromartie 1980). In our DDT study site, about 3 percent of the DDT ultimately ended up in the above-ground biota (Grau and Peterle 1979).

BREAKDOWN AND METABOLISM

Breakdown

The breakdown of compounds is defined as physical or chemical alteration of these compounds to form daughter products. Toxicity may increase, decrease, or be reduced to nil as a result of these changes in chemical structure. Many effects relate to breakdown; several have already been discussed in the sections on $T_{1/2}$, persistence, and disappearance rates.

Photodegradation is an important factor in the breakdown of many compounds. Both quantity and quality of light affect this process; the photolytic rate is also related to the chemical being broken down and its surface environment. Photodegradation may be continuous, periodic, or dynamic. The rate is also affected by water, surface, temperature, atmosphere, and organic films. In addition, there are some pH-regulated photodegradation rates.

Metabolism

Metabolism results in detoxification or activation of the chemicals being metabolized. There are four major types of metabolism: oxidation, reduction, hydrolysis, and synthesis. The oxidation of aromatic rings, oxidation of side chains to form alcohols and to ketones, sulfoxide formation, and N-oxide formation are the major oxidation reactions. This occurs mainly by means of the mixed function oxidase (MFO) system in the liver and cytochrome P-450.

Reduction includes dehydrogenation as well as dehydrohalogenation as with DDT to DDD, DDMU, DDNU, DDOH, and DDA. Reduction also occurs as a result of dehalogenation to aldehydes and alcohols, such as DDT to TDE.

Hydrolysis usually takes place in the form of hydrolytic reactions with water that lead to cleavage of esters and amides to yield alcohols, esters, and acids. This occurs mainly with the organophosphates and carbamates.

Synthesis includes exchange reactions such as 0 for S in parathion.

A secondary metabolic process includes conjugation by adding OH. This alters substances into water-soluble compounds, including amides, metal complexes, sulfates, glucosides, and glucuronic acid (Matsumura 1975).

Radioisotopes such as ^{32}P, ^{35}S, and ^{14}C have been used extensively to study the metabolic pathways in organisms and in systems. Most of the effort has been with animals, both invertebrate and vertebrate. In any study of metabolism in organisms, there is a problem with changes through post-mortem time. While some compounds continue to metabolize in dead organisms, others do not. There has been some limited work with metabolism in plants, especially cultivated crops.

Plants

Pesticides can be metabolized by plants, and different parts of plants can metabolize compounds at different rates and through different routes. Carrots and peanuts, for example, can convert aldrin to dieldrin. Breakdown rate is very species-specific. Sweet corn, for example, will rapidly metabolize the herbicide simazine, but field corn will not (Menzi 1966). Marine algae can metabolize DDT (Rice and Sikka 1973).

Microorganisms

Microorganisms form one of the most important groups of animals that break down and metabolize all sorts of toxic substances, including organochlorines, phosphates, carbamates, and the heavy metal compounds. They convert synthetic organics to inorganics and may detoxify or create new toxic substances—these are via co-metabolism, dehalogenation, deamination, decarboxylation, methyl oxidation, hydroxylation, nitrogen oxidation, nitro-metabolism, hydration, oxime metabolism, and nitrile/amide metabolism (Alexander 1981).

Fungi mycelium was treated with DDT at 1 ppm for 8 days with a total recovery of the application of 42 percent; of the total, 47.5 percent was found in the aqueous phase. Presence of other chemicals may inhibit or enhance metabolic rates (Anderson, Lichtenstein, and Wittingham 1970).

Proteus vulgaris alters DDT to DDD and then to DDE, which does not further metabolize. *Escherichia coli* changes DDT to DDD; yeast converts DDT to DDD; and many forms of bacteria convert DDT to DDD. DDD (rothane) is still considered toxic.

Invertebrates

A large number of insect species have developed specific enzyme systems to metabolize toxic compounds. Many convert aldrin to dieldrin and then to hydrophilic compounds. Insects are capable of metabolizing DDT to seven or more other compounds.

Vertebrates

Rates of metabolism and conversion are highly varied and depend on the compound, the kinds of animals, sex, age, reproductive state, time of year, food habits, dose, concentration, and time. Many toxic substances, including some pesticides, are capable of inducing liver enzyme activity in a variety of vertebrates. Therefore, metabolism in many vertebrates is studied in vitro through the use of liver homogenates. We have done this with bobwhite quail to show that birds treated with DDT more readily metabolize hormones such as progesterone and testosterone (Lustick, Voss, and Peterle 1973). In marine species, DDT is converted to DDE—in the bluegill, 50 percent of the DDT taken in is excreted in 32 days (Gakstatter and Weiss 1967). Conversion and excretion are related to whether the route of intake is across the integument or in food (Jarvinen, Hoffman, and Thorslund 1976).

Aldrin fed to rats at 4.3 μg/g/day leads to enhancement of microsomal oxidation by liver enzymes whether it is injected or taken orally. The rate of excretion and intake are balanced at about 8 weeks. There are varied ratios of excretion in the feces and urine (Menzie 1966).

The composition of an organism's intestinal flora may dictate the pathway of metabolism for DDT. Pesticides are excreted in the bile to the intestinal tract, some is resorbed, some excreted; the more hydrophilic compounds are excreted in urine. In some cases, such as with BHC, the metabolized compound as well as some undecomposed compound is excreted in urine through the kidneys. The rabbit produces six metabolites of dieldrin. Rats, dogs, and cows metabolize heptachlor to hepachlor epoxide. Ratios of different compounds being excreted in the kidneys in urine versus that in the feces varies and is not predictable. Rates of excretion are highly variable between species, sex, and age classes. Hyroxylation of biphynel and chlorbiphynel compounds is highly variable. The rate of breakdown in cats, brown trout, adult rabbits, rats, guinea pigs, hens, and fox is very low. Metabolic rate or breakdown in mice, coypus, hamsters, common frogs, and young rabbits and rats is very high (Creaven, Parke, and Williams 1965).

Compounds are highly variable in rates of metabolism and excretion; some are excreted unchanged, some are metabolized to compounds that are highly soluble and non-toxic; still others are metabolized to more toxic substances. The herbicide 2,4-5-D is excreted in sheep and cows unchanged, about 96 percent is excreted within 72 hours in the urine, about 1.4 percent in the feces (Menzie 1966). Rats excrete parathion via the kidney, *not* in the bile.

Organochlorines

These are reduced by dehalogenation, for example, DDT to DDE; specific enzyme systems are enhanced in insects especially to rapidly break down some insecticides and this is related to both oral and dermal resistance.

Some organochlorine doses can be readily reduced and excreted. Insects produce as many as seven metabolites of DDT, most to the hydroxy analog DDE (Menzie 1966). Among mammals, DDT is also degraded to DDE and in some instances to DDA and is found in both bile and feces. Some organochemists feel that DDD is a necessary intermediate step. There are many species differences; rhesus monkeys and hamsters, for example, will produce DDA as an excretory product but no DDE, the usual metabolite of DDT (Menzie 1966). Isomerization of DDT also occurs in some mammals. Rats will alter o,p DDT to p,p DDT. Organochlorine breakdown in fish is not very rapid. In one study only about 10 percent of the injected DDT was metabolized and excreted in brook trout over a 5-week period (Menzie 1966). The rate of metabolism and excretion in fish is related to the route of intake. Substances taken orally in foodstuffs will follow a more rapid breakdown than those taken in across the gill membranes and integument (Jarvinen, Hoffman, and Thorslund 1976). Birds convert DDT to DDE.

Organophosphates

In most cases, there is a reduction of the nitro groups to hydroxylamines-parathion to aminoparathion. The MFO system is very important to the breakdown of phosphates and is related to the P–O cleavage. Ultraviolet light can be important to the oxidation of S-ethyl and S-phenyl moities in substances such as parathion. There is isomerization of some organophosphates at high temperatures (Matsumura 1975). Methyl parathion on cotton leaves is altered to parathion and paraoxon within 24 hours. Other plant work shows some breakdown to phosphoric acids. Insects reduce parathion to the more toxic paraoxon-dealkylation to thiophosphates. In mammals, the liver enzyme systems readily convert parathion to aminoparathion; this is also true for fish and birds. This conversion is usually by reduction to paraoxon and then to aminoparathion. In humans who have ingested parathion, the metabolite nitrophenol shows up in the urine. In rats, parathion follows a similar pathway and residues are found in salivary glands, cervical fat, liver, and kidney. Excretion is from the kidneys, not the bile. In fish, liver homogenates have also been shown to degrade parathion; the bullhead is three times better than the sculpin at breakdown (Hitchcock and Murphy 1967).

Carbamates

The MFO system is also important to the degradation of carbamates by hydroxylation. In the case of carbaryl, metabolism is to 1-napthol, sulfates, and glucuronic acids. Sevin or carbaryl can be reduced by ultraviolet light. In the cockroach, absorption is low and excretion is very rapid leading to some resistance. The house fly produces three metabolites of sevin, mainly by hydrolysis. Among mammals, cows will metabolize sevin to napthol and it is excreted in the urine only. In rats and guinea pigs, 85 percent of the sevin can be recovered in the urine within 24 hours; 1-napthol is the most common metabolite. Napthol labeled with ^{14}C in rats showed no labeled material in CO_2, but in methyl and carbonyl labeled with ^{14}C, about 11 percent and 32 percent were found respectively in the CO_2. In rats, about 88 to 99 percent is excreted; very little remains as residue in tissues. About 10 metabolites are found in rat urine. The metabolite 1-napthol is the most common and is found in about 15 different species. Dogs excrete about 35 percent in feces and 40 percent in urine. In cows, the metabolites appear in milk (Matsumura 1975, Menzie 1966).

Plant Products

Nicotine is reduced by methylation and excreted in the urine of humans; in dogs as isomethonium. Nicotine can also be metabolized by soil organisms and is altered by insects and plants to cotinine. There may be as many as four metabolites in insects and these vary with the species. In humans and dogs, the common metabolite is cotinine (both desmeythyl and hydroxy cotinine), and it is excreted in the urine; about 95 percent in 36 hours in dogs (Menzie 1966). The hamster is about six times more efficient in metabolizing nicotine to cotinine than the rat (Matsumura 1975).

Heavy Metals/Hg

There is a close relationship between levels that are inhaled with levels in both blood and urine in humans. At levels below 50 $\mu g/m^3$ of air, there do not seem to be any adverse effects on humans. Occupational exposure is usually to organo-mercurials, which vary greatly in their toxicity. Breakdown is by the cleavage of the C–Hg bond, then to the inorganic form. Inorganic Hg usually accumulates in the kidneys, in rats about 29 percent is in the kidneys in four hours post-injection (Clarkson 1969). Ethyl mercury is more slowly metabolized, but still more rapidly than methyl. In some species there does not seem to be a dose-related build-up in the brain through time-post injection. Organo and other mercury compounds used as diuretics are rapidly excreted. Mercuric salts are more slowly distributed in the body through time and somewhat equally distributed in various tissues. Up to 80 percent of mercury excretion usually occurs through the bile.

ENVIRONMENTAL PARTITIONING

Partition Coefficients

The concept of partition coefficients is very important in relation to both liposolubility and toxicity, *but not directly and not always*. Coefficients are usually given as oil/water and equal to P. They are sometimes given as octanol/water as well. For example: PC + a constant; P = partition coefficient, C = concentration (external) necessary to produce an effect such as LD_{50} or LC_{50}, for example barbital for tadpoles. P oil/water = 1.38; C = 0.03 (M); PC = 0.041. For barbital, the molecular weight is 184.19, dissolved into 1 liter of water at 1,000 g; there is a concentration of 0.184 ppt, therefore 184 ppm × 0.03 equals 5.52 ppm to produce some effect (O'Brien 1967). Some partition coefficients (PC) are given for olive oil/water for some substances, for example, dimethoate, 0.34; paraoxon 4.06; dieldrin, 64.40; and DDT, 316.0 (Matsumura 1975). Partition coefficient is also related to CF, or concentration factor. Kosian, Lemke, Studders, et al. (1981) found the ASTM method for measuring BCF over 28-day tests proved to be satisfactory with the BCF for hexachlorobenzone (HCB) at 35,000 ($\pm 3,300$) and for DDE it was 50,000 ($\pm 4,800$). Besides the ASTM method, they calculated the BCF using both BIOFAC and CANDLES programs and found higher values of 52,000 and 48,000 for HCB and 180,000 and 110,000 for DDE. The CF is time-dependent, and species- as well as temperature-related. After over 242 days in a quarry with water containing about 1 ppt DDE, trout showed a DDE level of 171.9 ppb, for a CF of 1.81×10^5. For bluegills in a similar situation, the CF after 81 days was 1.08×10^5 (Hamelink and Waybrant 1973). We will discuss partition coefficients because many environmental compartments and factors are related to these changes.

Factors Important to Environmental Partitioning

Several factors are most important to environmental partitioning. These include hydrophilic characteristics, biological availability, and affinity. Three major pathways related to environmental partitioning include:

1. Physical transport—simple spatial change and distribution.

2. Interfacial processes: (a) no change in the compound and these include absorption, adsorption, chelation, ionic interactions, volatilization, dissolution; (b) all chemical structure; oxidation/reduction, photolysis, ionic reactions and radical reactions. These factors can be integrated with affinity, transformation and degradation estimates with fugacity equations to predict concentrations throughout the ecosystem (Mackay and Paterson 1981).
3. Non-interfacial transformations—abiotic, chemical, photodecomposition (National Academy of Sciences 1981).

Main Compartments of Transfer

Air/Water

Some factors related to transfer between these compartments are temperature, pH, whether in salts or other compounds, surface oils, suspended particulates, physical disturbance of surface, spray, wind, waves, rapids, waterfalls, rate of wind, moisture in wind, type of compound related to vapor pressure, solubility, rates of adsorption and desorption, water evaporation rates, and humidity.

Sediment : Soil/Water

Soils and sediments are important sinks. Some factors related to sorption and release include temperature, pH, organic content of soil, particle size, water flow rates, turnover, mixing, compound, vapor pressure, solubility, how applied, carrier, granule, ultra low volume (ULV) spray, solubilizer mixed in, interstitial water in soil, water-holding capacity, and the adsorption/desorption characteristics of the compound.

Air/Soil

Few actual field measurements are available to show air/soil movement, but some related factors include temperature, pH, salts, velocity of air, soil surface texture, shape, particle size, organic matter, moisture, plants on surface, field capacity of soil, and slope.

Biota/Water

Transport across various integuments is important to bioconcentration and subsequent effects. Some contributing forces include temperature, pH, water chemistry, sediment load, surface area characteristics of particles, characteristics of the compound, solubility, species involved, sex and age, season of the year, fat levels in the organism, breeding condition, and characteristics of the organism such as mode of feeding, movement, and microhabitat (sediment vs. fast water, slow water, etc.).

Biota/Sediment-Soil

Soil organisms are important to detoxification as well as being initial food sources for bioaccumulation. Some relationships include temperature, pH, moisture, soil capacity, type of species, integument of species, sex, age, compound, solubility, surface area of soil organism, fat levels, excretion rates, mortality, "rain out" from above the surface, plant leaves, burrowing habits of soil organism, and depth of penetration into soil.

Biota/Biota

Many biological factors such as learning and behavior as well as physical factors influence biota transfer. Some of these include temperature, species, sex, age, food habits, type of digestive system, phenology, metabolic rate (shrew vs. reptile), rate of food intake, excretion rate, storage, fats, reproduction, and mobility of predator versus prey.

Examples of Environmental Partitioning

Marine phytoplankton at maximum growth rates will partition DDT 1.2 to 2.9×10^5 times from water (Cox 1970). The vapor pressure of DDT is 1.5×10^7 mm Hg at 20°C. Air contains about 10 to 20 ppb DDT. The water solubility of DDT is 1.2 ppb, so it partitions from water to air.

If water contains 100 ppb DDT, it will drop about 52 percent in DDT content over a 24-hour period at 25°C (Acree, Beroza and Bowman, 1963). The DDT concentration and temperature influence the rate of co-distillation from water to air. Lower concentrations and higher temperatures show a higher percentage of loss to air. DDT total (p,p'; o,p'; and DDE) is found in air associated with particulate matter. Levels as high as 150 ppb have been measured (Risebrough, Huggett, Griffin, et al. 1968).

DDT is also found in rain samples; levels in rain sampled near London have ranged from 35 to 120 ppt (p,p' DDT) with an average of 61 ppt (Tarrant and Tatton 1968).

Snow in Hawaii has been found to contain 15 ppt (Bevenue, Ogata, and Hylin 1972). We measured DDT in Antarctic snow at Polar Station and found 0.04 ppb (Peterle 1969). If we assume equal distribution of this level in Antarctic snow, there could be 2.4×10^6 kg of DDT in Antarctica. Little is known about the transfer of DDT from snow to air.

DDT will move from soil to air. Treated sites have been known to lose 5 kg of DDT/ha/year, or about 2 to 2.2 percent per day (Farmer, Igue, Spencer, et al. 1972). In laboratory studies with soil, p,p' DDT hydrolyzes to DDE, which is more readily volatilized. Vapor density of DDE increased from 0 to 1.4 ng/l in 65 days post treatment with 100 μg/g of DDT in Gila silt loam (Cliath and Spencer 1972). DDE was intensively studied in a stone quarry and after 3 months, 85 percent of DDE introduced into the water appeared in the sediment; DDE was concentrated in the invertebrates. Of the lindane introduced, 72 percent was still in the water after 3 months (Hamelink and Waybrant 1973). Some of our own work has shown that little DDE is lost in surface runoff. After DDT treatment, we found none in water run-off after the first 20 days. DDT did not move below 25 cm in the soil and only about 3 percent was concentrated in the above-ground biota following application. Levels in plants increased over time. Residues in two species of shrew differed, and body burdens in *Microtus* increased over a 4-year period (Forsyth, Peterle, and Bandy 1983).

Fugacity

These are criterion for equilibrium of a chemical between phases or units of pressure (Pa) which relate to the "escaping tendency" the substance exerts from a given phase or compartment to another (see Fig. 3.7). At low concentrations, fugacity is linearly related to concentration:

$$C = fz \text{ where } \begin{aligned} C &= \text{concentration in mol/m}^3 \\ \text{Pa} &= \text{atmospheric pressure} \\ f &= \text{fugacity} \\ z &= \text{fugacity capacity} \end{aligned}$$

Fugacity for atmosphere is more or less equal to partial pressure.

$$\begin{aligned} \text{Water} - f &= X \gamma P^S \\ X &= \text{mol. fraction} \\ P^S &= \text{vapor pressure of pure liquid solute at system} \\ & \quad \text{temperature} \\ \gamma &= \text{liquid phase activity coefficient on a Raoult's law} \\ & \quad \text{convention when } X \text{ is unity and gamma is unity.} \end{aligned}$$

Raoult's Law states that molar weights when dissolved in a given solvent lower the freezing point and raise the boiling point, reducing vapor pressure equally for all such solutes.

Fugacity for water is only true if the solute is in a *truly* dissolved form. Use of partial pressures must be obtained from either solid or liquid forms of the solute, *not both*.

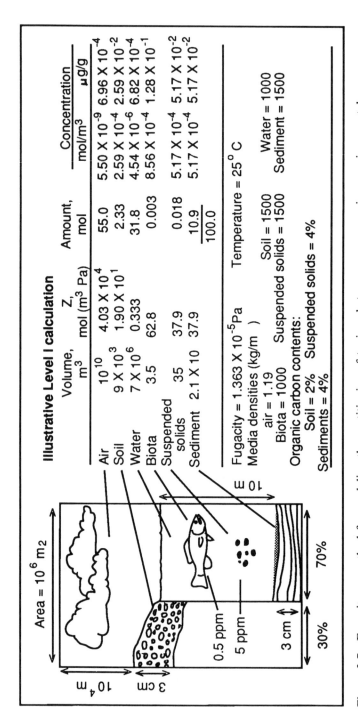

Illustrative Level I calculation

	Volume, m^3	Z, mol (m^3 Pa)	Amount, mol	Concentration mol/m^3	Concentration $\mu g/g$
Air	10^{10}	4.03×10^4	55.0	5.50×10^{-9}	6.96×10^{-4}
Soil	9×10^3	1.90×10^1	2.33	2.59×10^{-4}	2.59×10^{-2}
Water	7×10^6	0.333	31.8	4.54×10^{-6}	6.82×10^{-4}
Biota	3.5	62.8	0.003	8.56×10^{-4}	1.28×10^{-1}
Suspended solids	35	37.9	0.018	5.17×10^{-4}	5.17×10^{-2}
Sediment	2.1×10	37.9	10.9	5.17×10^{-4}	5.17×10^{-2}
			100.0		

Fugacity = 1.363×10^{-5} Pa   Temperature = 25° C

Media densities (kg/m)
  air = 1.19   Soil = 1500   Water = 1000
  Biota = 1000   Suspended solids = 1500   Sediment = 1500

Organic carbon contents:
  Soil = 2%   Suspended solids = 4%
Sediments = 4%

Area = 10^6 m₂

10^4 m   3 cm

0.5 ppm

5 ppm

30%   70%

3 cm

10 m

Figure 3.7 Fugacity, a method for modeling the partitioning of toxic substances among various environmental compartments. Modified from Mackay, D., and S. Paterson. 1981. Reprinted with permission from *Environ. Sci. Technol.* 15(9): 1006–1014. Copyright 1981, American Chemical Society.

Sorbed phase is defined as sediment or suspended: at equilibrium fuga-
cities sorbed and dissolved are equal:

$$F = HC = C_S/Z_S$$
$$Z_S = C_S/HC$$
$$H = \text{Henry's Law Pa} \cdot \text{m}^3/\text{mol}$$
$$P_a = \text{partial pressure of atmosphere}$$
$$C = \text{concentration in water mol/m}^3$$
$$K_P = \text{coefficient water/suspended solids or sediments}$$
$$K_{OW} = \text{octanol/water partition coefficient}$$
$$P_S V_S = \text{solubility}$$
$$P_S/V_S/RT = \text{vapor pressure}$$

In measuring the biotic phase, K_b = biotic concentration factor is used
rather than partition coefficient in biota on wet weight basis; when refer-
ring to the octanol phase, Z_O = fungacity capacity for octanol. Octanol/
water partitioning is an indicator of hydrophobicity for hydrophobic organic compounds; γ_O is fairly constant in the range of 1 to 10. In the pure
solid/liquid phases, fungacity = vapor pressure. Concentration rates are
Z ratios (Mackay and Patterson 1981).

SAMPLING METHODS

Study Types

Four major types of studies used in sampling environmental pollutants are
survey, monitoring, incident sampling, and research.

Surveys ascertain what toxic substances occur in an array of living and
non-living materials at a given time and place. The purpose is to determine
exposure/distribution, hazard, and possible cause-and-effect relationships. Some examples include radiation fallout surveys and surveys of
pesticides in human tissue/milk, and market basket surveys.

Monitoring implies consistent sampling of specific materials/species
through time on a regular basis—usually at given locations. The purpose is
to determine trends in accumulation and distribution, predict possible
future hazards, and decide upon the need for a more intensive survey or
added research.

Incident sampling involves studying a specific point source, spill, application, or accident. The purpose is to determine the immediate hazard, the
distribution, and disappearance of the chemical; and prevention of mortality and additional damage or injury.

When using the *research* method, usually a given toxic substance, sometimes isotope-labeled, is released into open or closed systems for a specific purpose to determine a specified result. These studies are carefully controlled and intensively sampled.

A common adage to remember when designing a sampling scheme is the world out there is all "skewed" up. Equal distribution is rare, so scientists must be concerned about numbers of samples taken, volume, storage space and conditions, analyses time and cost, and also about urban area effects. In the case of vertebrate sampling, public relations may also become a problem.

Sources Sampled

Air

When sampling air the following variables must be taken into account: filters, desorption rates, flow rate, volume, levels of substances expected, weather patterns, prevailing winds, time since last rain or last precipitation, elevation, location, quantity of particulate matter, pre-filter, temperature, volatility of materials expected, impinger trains, and the types of solvents used.

Water

Water sampling requires working with the following concerns: grab samples, physical location, near shore, edge of river flow, should sediment be included, particulate matter filters, water chemistry, preservation, degradation following collection, pumps, flow rates, adsorption/desorption rates, carbon filters and soxhlet extraction, where to sample soil/water interface, concern about flow rates in rivers, and time since last high water.

Soils

Soil sampling involves knowledge of soil types, aerobic or anerobic, microorganisms included or not, organic matter content, particulate size, efficiency of extractions, moisture content, water table, water flow, flushing rate, runoff, depth, Berleze funnel use to extract macroorganisms, grinding of samples, efficiency of soxhlet extraction, and the solvents used for extraction.

Vegetation

There is not much interest in sampling vegetation. Only low up-take of most pesticides occurs in plants. Some root crops do concentrate insecticides. When studying vegetation, one must keep in mind that plant parts sampled will be different. Some plants act as collectors, and those with heavily dissected leaves seem to collect more air pollutants. Waxes on leaves hold organic pollutants. Some plant species are now being used to monitor movement of PCBs from dump sites. Concentration of lead and selenium in plants may produce subsequent toxic effects. When sampling vegetation, researchers must keep in mind the fact that light may break down chemical pollutants. The height of the vegetation must be taken into account, as must method of contamination, and whether or not animal matter may be present on leaf surfaces.

Organisms

The concept of total stress on organisms is important: this includes all physical and biological factors, including toxic substances. The difficulty is in how to select individuals or populations for sampling, genetic selection for resistance, choosing a reference species, determining prior history of exposure, influence of uptake on current body burdens and vice versa, clumped distribution of organisms, sample sizes, body parts, sample volume, species identification, post mortem metabolism, methods of extraction, storage, and analytical costs.

Invertebrates When sampling in invertebrates, one must be familiar with distribution, species, collection and extraction, numbers, sample volumes, life stages, turnover time; the fact that there may not be exposure to toxic substances in some life stages, those that feed as adults and those that do not, total life span, trophic level of species, the fact that aquatic or terrestrial systems differ greatly, and use of sessile species such as oysters and clams as monitors.

Vertebrates Vertebrate sampling takes into account distribution, mobility, integration of exposures through space and time, numbers, subsamples of body parts, how many and what, sex, age, time of reproduction, migration, emigration, public relations problems, availability at time of collection, handling time for large species, collection method biases, trophic level characteristics and preferred foods, and use of domestic animals/pets and/or human tissues.

Problems with vertebrate collection also include sampling, storage, shipment, analyses, containers, freezing versus freeze drying, reference samples, specimen banks, use of zoo animals, all analytical problems including verification, and inter- and intra-laboratory quality control.

Point vs. Non-point Sampling Problems

Point

These studies usually involve a known substance or compound from a spill, pipe, stack, mine, or other use. A concentration gradient is to be expected from the source or release site. Transport is determined and predicted from known characteristics of the substance, including toxic effects. Specific species are sampled, and distribution through time is predicted, the hazard estimated, and reduction and clean-up methods for environment are suggested.

Non-point

The major problem is to identify major elements, compounds, and metabolites in the system. A survey of presence must be made, and the extent of distribution must be determined, along with major pathways of distribution and uptake, and levels of accumulation in selected species or compartments. Potential effects must be estimated and sensitive species determined. Data must be obtained on production and use. Time sequence sampling must be performed to estimate whether levels are increasing or decreasing, and evaluation of potential human effects related to carcinogenic, mutagenic, and teratogenic effects must be carried out.

MONITORING TOXIC TRACE ELEMENTS

Fourteen elements are usually of concern because of their toxicity and availability. These include **antimony,** arsenic, **beryllium,** boron, **cadmium,** chromium, cobalt, copper, **lead, mercury,** nickel, **selenium,** tin, and vanadium. Those of highest toxicity appear in boldface and are of greatest concern. Those found in highest amounts in the earth's crust in descending order include V, Cr, Ni, Cu, Co, and B. Those found in largest concentrations in the ocean include B, and Ni; and As, Cu, and Sn, which are found in nearly equal amounts. In fresh water, Cd, Se, B, Ni, and Cu, in descending order, are the toxic elements that appear most frequently. Those in highest commercial production for industrial uses are Cu, Pb, Cr, B, and Ni.

These toxic trace elements often transfer to plants and animals. To determine the extent of transfer and discover which elements are present in plants, vegetation is sampled for air pollutants, fallout, sewage, biocides, and industrial wastes. Animals, including humans and their food, air, and skin, are sampled in both aquatic and terrestrial systems. Biological monitoring of trace elements is done to determine gradients of concentrations in local, regional, or national areas. Some monitoring is also done on a global basis through cooperative programs (NATO, OECD). Sampling is based on toxicity; levels of manufacture, use, and distribution; and hazard to humans and domestic livestock. Global priorities have include the monitoring of As, Cd, and Pb.

Monitoring for trace toxic elements provides valuable information in the following areas: First of all, early warning of toxic effects can be given. Areas of impact and sites of concentration become apparent, and possible pathways to humans, an illustrated. A baseline over geographic areas is established. Trends over time can be seen. Data gathered in monitoring provides a means to integrate exposure and body burdens with environment, and to relate a particular toxic substance to possible other environmental problems. Finally, monitoring information may signal a need to evaluate possible control measures if a hazard is developing.

Sometimes *accumulators* or *concentrators* (species) are used as samples to determine concentrations and to measure impacts or effects. An accumulator takes in and stores toxins; the intake is greater than excretion. A bioconcentrator selectively takes up and sequesters toxins in body parts such as hair, feathers, and organs. Some elements found in high concentrations in mammals and fish include Cd, Cu, Pb, and Hg; in mollusks–crustacea: As, Cd, Cr, Cu, Pb, Hg, and V; in plants: As, B, Cd, Cr, Co, Cu, Pb, Ni, Se, and Sn; in mosses and lichens: Cd, Cr, Cu, Pb, and Ni. Herbivores magnify (concentrate) the following trace elements: Sb, As, Cd, Cr, Cu, Pb, Hg, and Se. Carnivores concentrate Hg and Cd. Aquatic herbivores form high concentrations of Sb, As, Cd, and Hg; aquatic predators: Cd and Hg.

There may also be biominification of elements, defined as a reduction in body burden based on intake levels, or a high rate of excretion/metabolism. For some elements, there may be no change in body burdens related to intake.

The selection of which species to sample for toxic trace elements is based on rate of toxin accumulation; availability; geographical distribution, ease of capture; size (adequate to sample specific tissues); occurrence in impact areas and in unpolluted areas; correlation to environmental levels of substance; availability of background data on the species; and availability of specimen bank samples. Specific organs or systems are sampled for some elements: public relations problems must also be considered.

For example, human hair has been sampled for Sb, As, Cd, Cr, Pb, and Hg; mammal organ sampling includes liver, Hg; kidney for As, Se; spleen for Cr; bone for Pb; bird feathers for Pb and Hg; and fish for Hg. The National Environmental Pesticide Monitoring Network (NEPMN) included studies on human hair, Norway rats, cows, pigs, sheep, pigeons, starlings, eagles, poultry, many human food plants, mosses, lichens, fish, marine and freshwater species, mussels, oysters, crabs, and lobsters. Some monitoring examples appear in the following section.

Examples

DDT

DDT was most widely monitored in a great variety of habitats globally. Studies were conducted on changes in use, distribution, measures of volatility from different substrates, various metabolites, food chain accumulation, bioaccumulation in long-lived species, whole body checks, and specific organ assays (blood, brain, fat, muscle). Much sequential sampling as well as incident sampling has been done. Most monitoring research has been on the chlorinated hydrocarbons.

PCBs

PCBs were introduced by Monsanto in 1929; they had widespread use and long half-life. (More details on PCB effects and uses will appear later in this book.) Much environmental contamination occurs as a result of improper use, improper disposal, and illegal dumping of PCBs. Manufacture and use of PCB has been banned, but much remains in the environment. Some species have hundreds of parts per million in whole-body samples, particularly species associated with aquatic systems near point sources of PCB, such as the Hudson River. Contamination of foodstuffs, feed, and milk has been documented. There have been correlations between high PCB levels and disease, but not cause-and-effect demonstration. Table 3.3 shows the results of a general survey of vegetation in areas of West Germany.

PBB

PBB is a hexabromobyphenyl known as "Firemaster," a fire retardant that was made by Michigan Chemical Co. Dow Chemical also produced a FR-250 octabromobiphenyl, but chose not to manufacture it because of stability and possible environmental problems. After an error in bagging caused PBB to be used as a feed additive, which contaminated livestock and humans in Michigan, about 88 percent of people in Michigan now have residues of PBB. The initial problem in this incident was defining the contaminant. It was finally found about 6 months after the initial problem

Table 3-3 A Survey of PCB Levels in
West German Vegetation

Species	Autobahn Site Near Industry (ppm Dry Weight)	Sites in Alps (ppm Dry Weight)
Mosses	0.13	0.06
Heather	0.28	0.08
Rasberry leaves	0.15–0.27	0.11
Rushes	0.12	0.07
Fir	0.31	0.09–0.10[a]
Oak	0.50	NS[b]
Larch	0.95	NS

From Klein, W. Organohalogenated compounds in plants. In Monitoring
environmental materials and specimen banking, ed. N-P. Leupke, pp.
354–358. Reprinted by permission of Kluwer Academic
[a] Dwarf fir;
[b] None sampled.

was reported. Studies sampled foods, feeds, humans, wildlife, and there
was trouble with tolerance limits, politics, and court suits (Chen 1979,
Halbert and Halbert 1978). More on PBB can be found in chapter 8 on
Classic Examples.

Mercury

Mercury has been widely monitored as an element; and in organic salts,
inorganic salts, and alkyl mercury compounds. Biomethylation is an important process by which microorganisms convert mercury to methyl
mercury, which is biologically active. Contamination may result from
runoff from natural levels in surface or distributed surfaces for roads and
mine sites; in soil; in water as a natural contaminant; and leaching from
cinnebar mines.

Industrial uses of mercury include fur processing, coal, electrical, dental, paper, plating, paints, fossil fuels, seed dressing, and cement manufacture. Mercury in systems is a result of both point and non-point sources.
Lakes Ontario and Erie are contaminated from point sources, for example,
paper mills. Japan's Minimata disease was traced to Minimata Bay, a
manufacturing location that led to subsequent seafood contamination;
there were some human deaths and injuries (Hammond 1971). Sweden has
Hg problems stemming from the paper industry and seed dressing, and
fallout from industrial Europe. Sweden has done much fish and human

sampling and surveys of biological availability of Hg. They estimate that a daily intake of fish containing 0.3 mg of Hg will cause human effects (Hammond 1971). There are also examples of high natural mercury levels. Kuskokwim River in Alaska releases about 18,000 kg of Hg per year from some old cinnebar mine sites, as well as natural soil contamination; any disturbance of surface soils will increase run-off. Mercury has been analyzed from the Greenland Ice Sheet. Ice samples pooled from 800 BC to 1946 contained an average of 60 ppb; ice samples pooled from 1956 to 1965 contained an average of 125 ppb mercury (Weiss, Koide, and Goldberg 1971).

Lead

There are many lead sources; most important is aerial distribution from automative exhaust. Lead also comes from industry, paints, natural lead in plants from soil uptake, industrial contamination, lead in pottery, lead from plumbing, and from illegal whiskey production. There is some suggestion that people were poisoned in early Roman times by lead cooking vessels (Berry, Osgood, and St. John 1974).

4

Transport and Distribution in Natural Systems

At least four major factors must be taken into account when trying to understand the transport and distribution of toxic substances in the environment. These are:

1. *Characteristics of the pollutant*—solubility, vapor pressure, breakdown and metabolism rates, partitioning, and persistence.
2. *Total production and use*—initial quantity and distribution in economic systems, nationally and globally; possible industrial point-source pollution prior to release; following non-point distribution.
3. *Formulation*—types of uses: used only in manufacturing-stability or containment until final disposition in landfills or through incineration or chemical destruction; how applied: to surfaces, below ground, as spray, carrier, emulsion, ULV sprays, granules, oil, water carrier, paints, below ground use only.
4. *Rates and types of applications*—granular, oil, water, spray, droplet size, aerial, ground, leaf surfaces, dormant season, types of ground cover, manipulation of soil surfaces, time to first precipitation, total rainfall, temperature, pH, etc.

AIR

The 1970 Clean Air Act (42 USC 7409) is up for review and renewal. Five basic "criteria" pollutants listed in the Clean Air Act are ozone (O_3), nitrogen dioxide (NO_2), carbon monoxide (CO), sulfur dioxide (SO_2), and total suspended particulates (TSP). The act required the standardization of monitoring efforts and a uniform air quality index or Pollutant Standard Index (PSI) based on the National Ambient Air Quality Standards (NAAQS). A PSI of greater than 100 is considered unhealthful, greater than 200

85

is very unhealthful, and greater than 300 is considered hazardous. Cities with PSIs higher than 100 over 30 percent of the time include Chicago, Denver, Los Angeles, New York, Ontario, Riverside, and San Bernardino. These problems are related to sulfur oxides (SO), oxidants, and TSP. Grand Rapids, Michigan, and Buffalo, New York, have high TSP; some of their problems result from local industries such as smelters and power plants. Total suspended particulates are also related to vehicle traffic levels and dust storms. The current NAAQS are given in Table 4.1. State Implementation Plans (SIPs), are being required of all states indicating how they will meet the NAAQS. Some states have been prompt with SIPs, whereas others have delayed for years.

Transport in Air

Global air circulation patterns are important in terms of transport between continents and to ocean surfaces.

The quantity and quality of solar irradiance and ultraviolet light are difficult to measure, but they are crucial to chemical breakdown in air and

Table 4-1 Current National Ambient Air Quality Standards

Pollutant	NAAQS Value	Additional Information
TSP	$75 \ \mu g/m^3$	Annual geometric mean.
O_3	0.08 ppm averaged over 1 hour	There are adverse human effects at 0.15 to 0.25 ppm; discussion that standard may be altered upward to 0.10 or even 0.12 ppm, or $235 \ \mu g/m^3$/hr. (ReVelle and ReVelle 1974).
CO	9 ppm over 8 hours as a mean, maximum of 25 to 35 ppm recommended for 1 hour	Much of this is from auto emissions; the current emission standard is 68 grams/mile and this will be reduced to 15 g/mile as a result of New American Quality Act.
NO_2	$100 \ \mu g/m^3$	Annual arithmetic mean.
SO_2	$80 \ \mu g/m^3$	Annual mean.
	$365 \ \mu g/m^3$	24-hour period maximum.
Pb	$1.5 \ \mu g/m^3$	Mean monthly level.

thus influence toxic effects from fallout. Photochemical breakdown includes oxidation, reduction, photonucleophillic displacement or elimination, and isomerization. Many of these photochemical reactions take place during aerial transport. Transport is usually higher in winter than summer (Weibel, Weidner, Cohen, et al. 1966).

Characteristics of the chemical being transported are equally important, not only the volatility and vapor pressure, but the solubility as well because many compounds co-distill with water into air.

For example, in PCBs, the vapor pressure decreases with increasing numbers of chlorine atoms. We measured DDT in Antarctic snow at 0.04 ppb (Peterle 1969). Some metabolites and isomers are more volatile than others, o,p DDT is more volatile than pp'DDT—at 30°C the atmosphere would contain 62 percent op'DDT, 16 percent op'DDE, 14 percent pp'DDE, and 8 percent pp'DDT (Spencer and Cliath 1972). Over agricultural areas, DDT has been assayed at 5 to 23 ng/1,000 mm^3 (Tabor 1966).

Particulate matter in the air is another major factor; many organics are associated with particulates (dust-pesticides, associated with dust) in air. Cities with high TSP also have high chemical air pollution (Abbot, Harrison, Tatton, et al. 1966; Antommaria, Corn, and DeMaio 1965; Emanuel, Olson, and Killugh 1980).

In agricultural areas, concentrations of up to 22 ppb of DDT have been measured in air (Tabor 1966). DDT does move from soil to air and this has been estimated at up to 2 lb per acre in summer and 0.3 lb per acre in winter (Lloyd-Jones 1971). Organic pollutants were reported in air and rain samples at Enewetak Atoll in the North Pacific. Levels of DDT, dieldrin, chlordane, and PCBs were detected (Atlas and Giam 1981).

Contaminants in air are scrubbed out by rain, snow, or they simply settle out if they are heavy enough. As they settle out, they become part of the hydrogeologic cycle.

Volatilization—Water to Air

An equation for rates of transfer from water to air may be given as:

Mass Flux = Mass Transfer Coefficient × Concentration (driving force)
$$N(mol/m/s) = K(m/s) \times delta \ C(mol/m^3)$$

Fick's Law and the Whitman two-film theory and Henry's Law constant apply. Some water-soluble pollutants are gas-film controlled, such as SO_2. Some less soluble pollutants are water-film controlled, such as chlorinated hydrocarbons. Mass flux rates between water and air can be calculated within about 5× magnitude orders (Mackay and Cohen 1976). Transfer to air is greatly influenced by temperature. For example, the loss rate of PCBs to air can be increased by 40× by doubling the temperature. Surface configurations are also important. The lower PCB 1224 as opposed to 1254 has a greater loss to air at the same temperature.

Examples

- In May–July 1980, four sites were sampled intensively 24 hours a day, 7 days a week. These were at Houston, St. Louis, Denver, and Riverside; 44 organic chemicals were found, including chloroalkenes, 89 μg/day; haloethanes and halopropanes, 140 μg/day; and halomethanes at 197 gμ/day. St. Louis had the cleanest air. For these cities, the total aromatic hydrocarbon exposure for an average human male of 70 kg breathing 23 m^3 was 1394 μg/day (Singh, Salas, Smith, et al. 1981).
- Air over Pittsburgh was sampled and contained 1.36 μg/1,000 mm^3 of pp′DDT in particulate matter (Antommaria, Corn, and DeMaio 1965). Evaporation of DDT at 20°C = 3 × 10^{-3} μg/cm^2/hour. It is estimated that about half the DDT applied was lost to air. Air was sampled in the Barbados in 1968 and presumably represented air moving west across the mid-Atlantic from Africa and Europe; 1 to 164 ppb chlorinated hydrocarbons was found, about 41 ppb by weight in dust. It was estimated that aerial input to the oceans was equal to input from all of the major river systems, and that this fallout is higher in winter months (Risebrough, Huggett, Griffin, et al. 1968). When air and dust was sampled at LaJolla, California, on an oceanside pier to sample the landward airflow from the open Pacific, a mean level of chlorinated pesticides of 7.0 × 10^{11}g/m^3 of air was found (Risebrough, Huggett, Griffin, et al. 1968). In 1965, air over some agricultural areas was sampled and at Lake Apooka, Florida. The highest DDT level in one 4-hour sample was 8500 ng/m^3. This was similar to an urban area with a mosquito control program where 8000 ng/m^3 was found during application of DDT (Tabor 1966).
- In the Randers/Meadows global model for DDT, the authors suggest that the airborne fraction of DDT and metabolites is 0.4. In 1970 about 150,000 metric tonnes of DDT was used/year and an additional 35,000 metric tonnes/year was used for mosquito-malaria control. Randers and Meadows estimated the half-life in the atmosphere from a few days to 1 month. They said about 30 percent is deposited on land and 70 percent in the oceans, the ratio of land to ocean (Randers and Meadows 1971).
- Volatilization of DDT from soil to air is temperature controlled. At 30°C the vapor pressure of DDE is 109 ng/l and for DDT, 13.6 ng/l (Cliath and Spencer 1972). There are differences in geographic areas related to use

and distribution. In 1964, both agricultural and urban areas were sampled for total DDT $\mu g/24$ hours. In Georgia agricultural areas it was 0.3 to 9.9 ng/m^3 (Tabor 1966). Some have estimated that the total air mass could contain up to 40 percent of the total annual production of DDT (Randers and Meadows 1971).

- Equilibrium of DDT in air is about 3×10^{-6}g/m^3 or about 2.0 ppb. If, at this equilibrium rate, the entire atmosphere was saturated up to the troposphere, the air would contain about 10^{12} grams of DDT. The mean residence time in the atmosphere is estimated at about 3.3 to 4 years (Woodwell, Craig, and Johnson 1971). There is some suggestion that the maximum levels of DDT occurred in the atmosphere in 1966 (Woodwell, Craig and Johnson 1971). The rates of decay of many organics in the atmosphere are unknown. Rates of decay depend on whether the compound is in actual vapor or whether it is sorbed to particulate matter, what kind of particulate, sunlight, ultraviolet light, temperature, and so on. Vapor transported PCBs are differentially accumulated by plant species. Studying relationships between atmospheric and foliar concentrations may be an economical way for monitoring levels of PCBs in transport (Buckley 1982). Goldenrod had higher PCB levels than either staghorn sumac or trembling aspen foliage. Levels around landfills were found to be higher.

Acid Rain

Much has been written and studied on the subject of acid rain, but political and economic considerations have sometimes influenced biological interpretation. Usually rain below a pH of 5.6 to 5.7 is considered acid rain. Acid is formed from sulphates and nitrates inserted into the atmosphere by humans and by natural events such as volcanoes. In the eastern United States it is now common to have rain with a pH as low as 4.5 or even down to 4.0. On some occasions pH measurements in individual rain storms have been as low as 2.0. (USEPA 1980: 204). In the past 25 years there has been a 50-fold increase in acid rain events. Problems are primarily aquatic, although leaching of trace metals (Al is important as well as Cd), pesticides, and other organics as a result of acid rain are a problem. Some vegetative effects have been suspected, mainly spruce tree die-offs in NE USA and Canada. There is also direct effect on man-made objects and on the biota. Spring run-off periods may be critical to fish or reptile reproduction (USEPA 1980).

The United States now has at least 429 exhaust stacks over 200 feet tall that have been built since 1970, about 283 of them by electric power plants. These exhaust stacks insert sulfur and nitrous oxides higher in the atmosphere to travel longer distances before they precipitate. Currently there are 27,000 major sources of air pollutants; that is, sources with over 100 tons/year emissions. Standards are now applied by EPA to Air Quality Control Regions (AWCR), which permits averaging of pollutants over broader areas. The law does state that exhaust levels that produce acid rain elsewhere may not exceed regional air quality standards. The Clean Air Act allows EPA to disapprove SIPs if the air quality in another region may be reduced. Proof of origin of acid rain is being questioned by some, primarily as it relates to cost of cleanup.

In Norway, under the auspices of Organization of Economic Cooperation and Development (OECD), 11 European countries have contributed $2 million per year to study the acid rain problem in northern Europe. They have found that contaminants move from 1 to 2 kilometers above ground. In one 8-day period, 4000 tons of sulphate and sulfuric acid aerosols were deposited over a 20,000 km^2 area in southern Norway. In these areas, there is a lowered buffering capacity because of the amount of bedrock present. A high flush of acid in the spring snow melt coincides with the spawning season for several fishes; the autumn rains coincide with the movement of newly hatched fry. Some lakes in southern Norway now have a pH of 3.5 to 4.0. Another problem is leaching of aluminum from soil, which causes toxic problems as well. Aluminum and lowered pH reduce cellular breakdown and nutrient cycling. Salmon (Atlantic) and sea (brown) trout do not reproduce below a pH of 4.5 to 5.0. Researchers have also found reduced plant growth by leaching of minerals as a result of acid rain (O'Sullivan 1976).

In areas of high population concentration, automotive exhausts and the industrial contaminant hydroxymethanesulfonate has been found attached to fog droplets. Concentrations near Bakersfield, California, were as high as 300 micromoles per liter. These concentrations can play an important role in the formation of acidity and result in transformation of SO_2 and long-distance aerial transport (Munger, Tiller, and Hoffmann 1986). Near Los Angeles, fog has been measured with a pH of 2, the most acidic precipitation ever measured in the world (Roberts 1982).

It was found that tree canopies intercept large volumes of airborne particulates and for some elements, the needs for growth are satisfied by uptake from air. Hardwood canopies retained 50 to 70 percent of the free acidity and nitrogen intercepted but released calcium and potassium. Atmospheric deposition supplied 40 percent of the nitrogen requirements for growth and 100 percent of the sulfur requirements (Lindberg, Lovett, Richter, et al. 1986).

Several environmental organizations and states have sued EPA to restrict the sulphate emissions from midwestern industries. Lawsuits over the tall stacks that emit sulfur from power production have also been initiated. EPA has not taken the lead in resolving the acid rain problem. A joint report issued by the United States and Canada requested that $5 billion be set aside to develop and demonstrate low-cost technologies to reduce emissions (Sun 1986a). Few are satisfied with the report. Some dissatisfaction is because of the cost involved; others feel it does not require a major reduction in emissions, and ultimately the cost of applying the new technologies would be too great in order to affect a major improvement in air quality.

The sea-air partitioning of mercury may be particularly important in areas such as the equatorial Pacific Ocean where cold, nutrient rich, biologically productive waters reach the surface. The surface waters are saturated with respect to elemental Hg and this may result in a global transfer of Hg to the atmosphere equal to all anthropogenic emissions (Kim and Fitzgerald 1986) (Fig. 4.1).

Atmospheric dispersal of DDT is still high in offshore areas where DDT is still being used in some quantities. Concentrations in air over the Arabian Sea and Indian Ocean are 25 to 40 times higher than in the North Atlantic, where DDT has been banned since 1972. Pesticides move as a result of droplets from spray applications (about 3 percent) and as a result

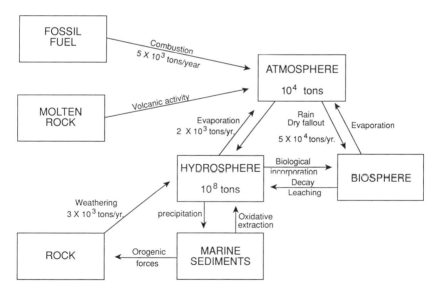

Figure 4.1 Exchange and balance of mercury in the global environment. Modified from Peakall, D. B., and R. J. Lovett. 1972. *BioSci.* 22(1):20–25. Copyright 1972 by the American Institute of Biological Sciences.

of volatilization (about 35 percent). In one Austrian study, 75 percent of the damage caused by herbicide sprays was a result of vapor transport (Pimental and Levitan 1986).

WATER

Surface Water Pollution

Polluted surface waters receive much attention because they can be seen and smelled. For example, a great deal of attention was devoted to the Cuyahoga River at Cleveland several years ago when the river caught fire. It was a national news item: a river so polluted it burns. As a result of public awareness of water pollution problems on a national basis, there has been some improvement in surface water quality over the past few years. EPA is now initiating a program to permit a change in the National Water Quality Standards for site-specific locations. States will be able to petition EPA to request alteration in national water standards for specific substances based either on chemical changes connected to specific local water characteristics, or changes in biological information related to species. For example, if the National Water Quality Standard was based on laboratory exposures with rainbow trout and no trout ever have or ever will exist at a specific site, within a certain state, that state would then be responsible for gathering the data sets necessary for EPA to adjust the standard accordingly; if they have limited workers and funds, industry may contribute. These are preliminary discussions and are not yet implemented.

Examples

Surface water problems usually relate to heavy metals (Pb, Hg, Cd) and in some areas to pesticides (Lower Mississippi, California, East Coast, Florida). These contaminants come from both point and non-point sources. The James River kepone incident was related to an industrial manufacturing site on the river and illegal dumping; the PCB problem in the Great Lakes is both point, from industrial effluent; and non-point, from sources such as aerial fallout. The most serious PCB problem in the Hudson River is related to an industrial source. In some of the Great Lakes, fish and shellfish have been declared as unfit for human consumption because of PCB contamination.

Reduction of lead levels in air as a result of reduced emissions from lead-free gasoline have been questioned. One positive result has been observed in that lead being transported by the Mississippi River has decreased by 40 percent over the past 10 years. This was demonstrated by both water samples and lead levels in sediments. Because about 90 percent of the lead is associated with suspended sediments, most of it is a result of runoff from urban areas and from industrial sites. Most of the lead is deposited within 3 km of the mouth of the Mississippi and is not readily leached to lower soil horizons (Trefry, Metz, Trocine, et al. 1985).

Petroleum pollutants transported on the oceans' surfaces are difficult to sample. Boersma (1986) has suggested that seabirds (*Procellariiformes*) be used to sample ocean surface contaminants. The birds readily regurgitate when captured, so the sampling methods do not require death of the bird. The storm-petrel species (fork-tailed, Leach's, sooty) are widely distributed over all the oceans, they feed on the surface, oil from the food accumulates and is digested slowly, and they feed over wide areas. Food samples from captured birds seemed to show some relationship to the availability of low level contamination in their feeding areas.

Other surface water problems relate to phenols, and cyanides from industrial areas. There is an agreement between Canada and the United States concerning pollutants in the Great Lakes. This agreement covers phosphorus loading, which is still too high, and a suggested level of PCB in fish of 0.1 $\mu g/g$ (many predator fish in the Great Lakes exceed this level). DDT is declining in the Great Lakes biota. Dieldrin is still found at low levels; mirex has been found in Lake Ontario and in some Great Lakes fishes Hg levels are still in excess of recommended tolerance limits of 0.2 $\mu g/g$.

National Pollution Discharge Elimination System (NPDES) permits are being used to reduce the discharge of toxic wastes into surface waters. Both state and federal EPA must approve of the permit system; this has been completed in at least 33 states and up to 1980 about 60,000 permits had been issued. In February 1980, 63 percent of the permits issued to municipal treatment facilities were not in compliance and EPA had issued fines totaling $7.5 million from 52 cases, mostly non-municipal, non-public sources. In terms of non-point source pollution, erosion is a most serious problem; currently it is estimated at 4.8 billion tons per year in the United States. This comes from agricultural lands in addition to construction, silviculture, urban runoff, mining, and livestock operations.

Ground-Water Pollution

Serious problems occur with ground-water supplies, where the flow is five times that of surface waters. Half the people in the United States use springs or wells for water. Here, the pollutant problems are often hidden from sight and smell. Because of a current over-use or mining of ground water in some areas, water tables are dropping. There is also good evidence of contamination of ground water by organic chemicals, and some ground-water supplies for drinking have been declared unfit for human consumption. Concentrations of synthetic organics in ground water may be orders of magnitude higher than in surface waters or drinking water originating from rivers or reservoirs. Many organics are odorless and tasteless, yet they may present hazards as carcinogens or mutagens at levels as low as 10 ppb. There is very little protection by federal law for subsurface waters.

Examples

In Massachusetts, the water supplies from underground wells for 22 towns were analysed. Of those surveyed, one-third were declared unfit for use, and some had up to 900 ppb TCE. TCE is trihloroethylene, a toxic organic that has been used for numerous purposes, including cleaning out septic tanks (Tangley 1984). The EPA action level for TCE is 10 ppb. In California, 37 public wells have been closed as a result of TCE contamination of up to 600 ppb. These wells served 400,000 people; they had to find alternative supplies of potable water. EPA has begun a ground-water contamination survey, but with budget cuts and reduction in force it is a long way from completion. Underground water contamination is a serious problem because breakdown and metabolic rates of toxic substances are very slow in the underground environment; it is dark, cold and in many cases abiotic and anaerobic. Some underground water pools have a long turnover time and slow recharge. Under the Safe Drinking Water Act of 1974, EPA does have a set of maximum contaminant levels (MCLs) if water is used for household purposes. Levels have been set for toxaphene, methoxychlor, endrin, lindane, 2,4-D, 2,4,5-T, and for some of the trihalomethanes. The Federal Water Pollution Control Act of 1971 and 1977 charges EPA with a huge and unwieldy task: to "Restore and maintain the chemical, physical and biological integrity of the nation's waters."

Another problem with ground water has been the insecticide Temik (aldicarb). This is a relatively soluble compound that is leached through porous soils with low organic content. It is a systemic used for control of potato beetles and nematodes in potatoes. Because potatoes are frequently grown in sandy soils, the transport of the chemical to ground water is enhanced. There have been contamination problems on Long Island. Aside from the problem on Long Island, about 100 private wells sampled across the nation have been found to be contaminated with residues of aldicarb. There are some estimates that it might take 100 years for aldicarb residues to be flushed from some Long Island ground water sources if no degradation occurs (Back 1985, Marshall 1985b).

Transport of toxic substances from agricultural drain waters is becoming an increasing problem in many states. If, as predicted, irrigation increases, the problem will become more widespread. In the San Joaquin Valley of California, the Bureau of Land Management (BLM) is subsidizing the availability of water to cotton growers that are being subsidized to produce a surplus crop and the resultant waste water is creating an environmental hazard. Study plans proposed by BLM have been inadequate (Marshall 1985a).

Movement of Toxicants in Water

Toxicants move in water as a solution by runoff and percolation to ground water, and secondly by adsorption on particulate matter through erosion. See Figure 4.2 for a simple model of water transport. Varying solubilities are important: for DDT, solubility is about 1.2 ppb; for PCBs (Aroclor 1254), it is about 56 ppb (Haque, Schmedding, and Freed 1974). The characteristics of the receiving water are also very important; sodium carbonate will remove 75 to 99 percent of DDT from water. Other factors related to water transport include amount of precipitation, adsorption, pH, suspended sediments, the structure of the chemical and its physical properties, whether the water is aerobic or anaerobic, presence of organisms in the water (micro, macro, and vertebrates), temperature, oxidation and hydroxylation, photochemistry, partition coefficients for the compound (octanol/water, oil/water), flow rates, types of aeration, water depth, particulate matter, type of sediment/water interface, and rates of surface to ground water transport.

The importance of particulate matter was illustrated when rainwater samples taken in England showed higher mean organochlorine levels in areas with dirty air such as London. Residues in rain vary throughout the

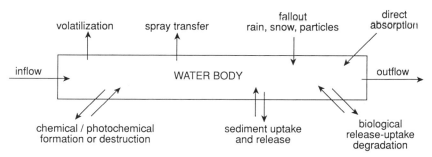

Figure 4.2 Simple schematic model for exchange of toxic substances in aquatic systems.

year. They are not directly related to agricultural areas or time of treatment. Fallout from rain is a global, worldwide distribution and independent of total rainfall. Residues in rainwater from England were BHC 5 to 230 ppt, dieldrin 1 to 40 ppt, and DDT 6 to 190 ppt (Tarrant and Tatton 1968). Rainwater in Hawaii to $\overline{X}$ = 4.0 ppt organochlorines mean = 4 ppt (Bevenue, Ogata and Hylin 1972).

pH is another important controlling factor in water transport. For example, the half-life of chloroform in water at 25°C at pH 4 is 32,000 years; at pH 7, it is 3500 years; and at pH 10, it is 10.5 yrs.

Ocean Pollution

In oceans, the thin oily film on the surfaces of most waters forms as a result of organisms or human-made pollutants and is important to the distribution of pollutants in the water column. The highest pollutant levels are on the surface; they are not uniformly mixed (Seba and Corcoran 1969). As a result of this, oily film on the surfaces of oceans contains the highest levels of residues, and most are moved back to air as a result of surface turbulence. Rainout of pollutants to abyssal depths is usually in dead organisms. Once these pollutants are in the depths of the oceans, breakdown is very slow because of the cold temperatures, darkness, and lack of organisms. Residues of organochlorines have been found in abyssal organisms. DDT and lindane were applied to an oligotrophic quarry; there was a concentration of about 200 ppt in the epilimnion and 50 ppt in the entire quarry. DDT and then DDE as a result of metabolism were rapidly sorbed onto particulate matter and DDE disappeared 15 times faster than the lindane. After 3 months, 85 percent of the DDE was in the sediment, 72 percent of the lindane was still in the water (Hamelink and Waybrant 1973).

DDT and PCBs were studied in the Atlantic Ocean 66°N 35°S—*all* organisms analysed had higher PCB than DDT levels. These concentrations did not appear to have come from food-chain accumulation in gilled organisms; mixed plankton had 200 μg/kg of PCB residues, and mesopelagic organisms had levels about 10 times lower. No horizontal concentration gradients were found. The PCB/DDT ratio was about 30 for surface organisms and a ratio of 3 in higher predators and midwater organisms. This shows the distribution of the organochlorines varies with depth (Harvey, Miklas, Bowen, et al. 1974). Based on a series of samples taken between 26°N and 63°N in the North Atlantic, the average PCB concentration in water was 20 ppt. The upper 200 m of seawater in the North Atlantic could contain 2×10^4 metric tons of PCBs (Harvey, Steinhauer, and Teal 1973). Based on these and other estimates, the environmental half-life of PCBs seems much longer than DDT. Based on surveys of hydrocarbons in ocean waters, Brown and Huffman (1976) suggested that hydrocarbons in ocean waters may be removed by absorption on particulate matter and subsequent settling in the abyssal depths. Deposition in the deep ocean may also result from zooplankton fecal pellets (Elder and Fowler 1977).

ORGANISMS

Two important factors influencing how organisms transport toxic substances in the environment are that (a) the organismal compartment size, in terms of total biomass, is small; and (b) the concentration of toxic substances can be very high, but the total quantity of toxins residing in the organismal compartment at any one time is small. Our studies of ^{36}Cl DDT in a meadow (Forsyth, Peterle, and Bandy 1983) showed that about 3 percent of the DDT applied was contained in the above-ground biota, including all plants and animals. Partitioning and concentration in organisms is related to the characteristics of the chemical itself; and the type of organism, its state of health, reproductive stage, and the microhabitat it occupies.

Another important organismal transport consideration is whether the organisms are terrestrial or aquatic. Uptake in terrestrial systems is generally slower and occurs mostly by ingestion, while in aquatic systems uptake is usually very rapid and takes place through the gills or integument. The organism itself in relation to surface body size ratios can alter the uptake of a toxic substance, particularly in aquatic systems or in soil.

Whether the animal is active or passive in its life processes can also alter the potential for accumulation of toxic substances. Animals that are active can move to or from sites of contamination. This is especially important in marine systems, where the ultimate deposition of toxic substances is related to death and rainout to the abyssal depths and sinks. Animals can obtain residues from point or non-point sources and integrate local or regional differences in toxic substances deposition and concentrations. The organism has the ability to metabolize the compound to more or less toxic substances; it may sequester the substance and in animals that become resistant, higher doses can be passed on to predators or scavengers in the food chain. Predators might continue to feed on preferred prey or prey might become more vulnerable because of chronic exposure to a toxin. Buffer species may become more important and could be contaminated at higher or lower body burdens and thus alter the potential exposure to the predator. Seasonal differences may be important as they relate to migration, hibernation, aestivation, and reproduction. For lipposoluble substances, the relative fatness and body condition of the prey could alter body burdens and the potential transport in the food chain and to other areas. Rates of uptake in accumulators or bioconcentrators (some animals may also be considered biominificators) varies greatly depending on the species and its location in the food chain and in the environment. There may be vertical changes in freshwater, terrestrial, and marine systems and animals that occupy different levels in the environment will be exposed at different rates. Rainout from upper foliage may be important to the availability of a compound to soil macro- and microorganisms. This group of fauna then may act as a route of transfer to ground-dwelling insects, shrews, moles, and mice. Organisms are also important to concentration of toxics in aquatic systems, where they may partition a compound from the water and concentrate it thousands of times in a few hours or days. In the marine system, the neuston, or surface layer traps organic compounds and initiates the concentration in the food chain because microorganisms and small invertebrates feed in the surface film and become available to higher organisms including marine fish, birds, and mammals. A sampling transect from Grennock Station off the coast of Scotland to India Station, 400 miles to the west, showed mean concentrations of dieldrin, DDT, and PCB in plankton to be 0.040 ppm wet weight, 0.046 ppm and 0.34 ppm at Grennock (Sta. 1); at India Station (Sta. 7), the mean levels in plankton were about 0.002 ppm for dieldrin, 0.008 ppm for DDT, and 0.03 ppm for PCB (Williams and Holden 1973). These plankton residues are then available for uptake by higher order organisms in the food chain. In invertebrates, the partitioning of toxins from water into the organisms is very rapid and very high. A variety of organisms were exposed to 1 to 16 ppb of PCB in water for 4 to 21 days and the following concentration factors (CF) were recorded: daphnia, 47,000; midge 25,000; scud 27,000; mosquito larvae 18,000; and glass shrimp 17,000. In 21 days, crayfish concentrated the PCB 5,100 times (Eisler 1986b).

Rates of uptake and accumulation in vertebrates is highly variable and not only depends on the compound and its distribution and the species, but the season, sex, age, and reproductive and nutritional states of the individual animal. Toxins may be sequestered, stored in fat, and mobilized at different times. Rates of excretion vary with diet and reproductive condition. Vertebrates are more mobile and capable of transporting toxic substances long distances from contaminated agricultural and industrial areas to relatively pristine environments where toxic substances are not directly applied or released. Perhaps the best examples are the birds of prey that migrate from the high Arctic to Central and South America, where they obtain toxic residues and transport them to their breeding grounds. Ocean fishes and mammals also travel long distances and could transport toxic substances from high concentration outfalls along industrialized coasts to Arctic or Antarctic oceans. Concentration in ocean fishes ranges from 10 to more than 100 times the residues found in the marine plankton (Harvey, Miklas, Bowen, et al. 1974). Some concentrations of PCBs in Great Lakes fishes have been reported as follows (all in mg/kg): Lake Superior—lake trout 1.79, walleye 3.6, whitefish 3.6, lake trout 47.4; Lake Huron—perch 3.9, brown trout 1.9, lake trout 5.7; Lake Erie—perch 1.34, catfish 3.85 to 5.65; Lake Ontario—lake trout 18.3, brown trout 15.1, catfish 12.4, smallmouth bass 16.17 (Swain 1980).

This shows both geographical as well as species differences in uptake and potential transport in the system, to other organisms and to humans.

Organisms may be used to determine minimal contamination levels in remote areas where direct application does not occur. In Antarctica, species such as krill, marine fish, skua, Adelie penguins, and crabeater seals have been found to be contaminated with DDT and DDE (George and Frear 1966; Sladen, Menzie, and Reichel 1966; Tatton and Ruzicka 1967). In remote areas, ratios of body burdens of the various contaminants such as DDT/PCB or DDT/DDE can be used to suggest origins of the body burdens and movements of the organisms following initial contamination. Widely distributed species, such as the marine fish, the grey mullet, found on most coasts of the world can be used to determine uptake, accumulation, and transport of toxic substances from coastal outfalls (Luepke 1979). In terrestrial systems, blood samples from peregrines show they accumulate toxic substances on their wintering grounds in Central and South America. DDE measured in blood samples in spring migrants showed that about 10 percent of the population had residues high enough to potentially influence reproduction. Residues declined from 1979–80, suggesting a decrease in contamination (Henny, Prescott, Riddle, et al. 1982). Biomagnification in organisms in oxbow lakes in Louisiana was evident for 13 different compounds in 15 different species. DDT-R = DDT plus known metabolites and PCB were most frequently found. Tertiary consumers had the highest residues (largemouth bass, water and cottonmouth snakes, green-backed herons, spotted gar). Primary consumers had low residues (crayfish, threadfin shad). In most of the lakes surveyed, the spotted gar had the highest residues, about 28 ppm DDE and 19 ppm PCB. Among the avian species sampled, the greenbacked heron usually had the highest residues (Niethammer, White, Baskett, et al. 1984).

Transport by organisms in any system is closely tied to the compartmentalization of the compound within the system and consequently its availability to resident and migratory species. In our studies of isotope-labeled DDT in a meadow system, we found the following changes in compartmentalization and uptake by the various components of the ecosystem over a 6-year period (see Table 4.2).

Total quantities of DDT-R residues in soil and biotic compartments of

Table 4-2 Total Quantities of DDTR Residues in a
10-acre Old-field Ecosystem Treated with ^{36}Cl DDT

	Total DDTR (grams)		
Compartment	1969	1972	1974
Soil	2692	2144	1779
Roots	18	18	18
Grasses (*Poa* sp.)	16	205	352
Forbs (*Daucus, Achillea*)	46	65	130
Earthworms	131	14	8
Grasshoppers	0.002	0.02	0.05
Microtus pennsylvanicus	0.0	0.02	0.01
Blarina brevicauda	0.22	0.02	0.03
Sorex cinereus	0.001	0.002	0.001
Total in system	2905	2447	2289
Total in biota	213	303	510
% in biota	7	12	22
% volatilized	37	4	5

*Adapted from Forsyth, Peterle, and Bandy 1983. Persistence
and transfer of 36 ClDDT in the soil and biota.* Ecology 64(6)
1620–1636. Permission by Ecological Society of America.

the study area were estimated by combining residue data and peak biomass, at the Urbana, Ohio, 10-acre study site (Forsyth, Peterle, and Bandy
1983).

SINKS AND RECIRCULATION

Many toxic substances are long-lived, persist in the environment, and
ultimately end up in sinks. Little is known about rates of deposition,
metabolism or breakdown in situ, uptake by organisms, or recirculation.
Sediments in fresh and marine systems can act as sinks. Sediments analyzed in the Santa Barbara Basin showed deposition of PCBs beginning in
1945 and DDE in 1952, with a peak in deposition in 1967. Quantities
of DDE in the sediment in 1967 were deposited at the rate of 1.9×10^{-4} g/m^3/year and PCBs were being deposited at the rate of 1.2×10^{-4}g/m^3/year (Hom, Risebrough, Scintar, et al. 1974).

Deposition in marine sediments in offshore areas influenced by industrial contamination can be high, but rainout in the open ocean to the
abyssal depths can also result in accumulation. Ninety percent of the total

hydrosphere is beyond the 200 m isobath and the temperature of most waters at these depths is about 4°C; they are essentially sterile, with a low concentration of suspended matter and sparse stocks of organisms. Xenobiotics may be deposited in these areas from continental currents or runoff, or from open oceanic areas from floating matter and turbidity. Livers of demersal fish off Cape Hatteras, North Carolina, have been found to contain 5.4 ppm of DDE. These abyssal sediments may be the ultimate repository of the halogenated hydrocarbons, but we know that the accumulation of carbon in these systems is very slow and we do not know much about potential for recirculation into the upper water column and back into organisms. We know that livers from deep sea fish collected at 3200 m do show induced cytochrome P-450 induction by xenobiotics, demonstrating they are exposed to organics (Stegeman, Kloepper-Sams, and Farrington 1986).

Chlorofluromethanes have been found in the depths of the Greenland and Norwegian Seas. Their distribution is similar to isotopes from bomb fallout. Models developed suggest a mixing time of about 40 years and lateral mixing between the basins of about 20 to 30 years (Bullister and Weiss 1983).

The Amoco Cadiz tanker catastrophe was the most intensely studied oil spill in history and resulted in the deposition of 223,000 metric tons of oil in the ocean. Of the total oil lost, 13.5 percent became directly dissolved in the water, 8 percent was deposited in sub-tidal sediments, 28 percent washed into intertidal zones, and 30 percent evaporated. At sea, about 10,000 tons were degraded microbiologically. After 3 years, hydrocarbon concentrations were still high in affected estuaries (Gundlach, Bohem, Marchand, et al. 1983).

Residual time for toxic substances in sediment sinks is related to the rate of deposition in streams, lakes, or ponds. With rapid sediment build-up, compounds are quickly buried and remain in the site for long periods. Whether the sediment is aerobic or anerobic and the numbers and kinds of organisms that burrow in the sediment relate to the permanence of the sink as a repository for long-lived toxic substances. Whether light can penetrate to the sediment surface is also important.

Sediment sinks can act both as a sink and as a source of contamination if the sediment is washed out or resuspended in the water column. Dredging also promotes resuspension of the toxic substances in the water column, either directly or from leachate in dredge spoil disposal sites. PCB sediments in Lake Superior have been measured at up to 90 μg/kg. In Manistique Harbor in Lake Michigan, one site measured 17,500 μg/kg; in Lake Huron, 20 μg/kg; Lake Erie, 800 μ/g/kg; and in Lake Ontario one site was 245 μg/kg PCB in sediment (Swain 1980).

Residues are strongly influenced by industrial contamination and urban runoff. More recent contamination of fish and wildlife in the Lower Colorado River has been observed as a result of movement from sediment or illegal use of DDT. Some fish in 1978–79 were assayed at 31.5 ppm (channel catfish); DDE and DDE in birds was measured at up to 81 ppm DDE wet weight in a laughing gull (White and Krynitsky 1986). Some of these levels were considered high enough to have physiological effects (White and Krynitsky 1986). A former industrial site at Mission, Texas, may have been the source of the contamination. Aerial transport and subsequent deposition in sediment is an important route of contamination. The sediment in Siskowit Lake on Isle Royale in Lake Superior was examined and 560 ppt of octachlorodioxin was found in surface sediment. Air sampled in urban areas has been shown to contain OCDD; in Washington, DC, up to 200 ppb OCDD was found; and in St. Louis, 170 ppb of octachlorodibenzo-p-dioxin (OCDD) (Czuczwa, McVeety, and Hites 1984).

Aerial transport of precursors of acid rain cause leaching of heavy metals to sediments and suspension in the water column. Aluminum is readily mobilized and is hazardous to fish at levels of 100 ppb. Avian eggshell thickness is also influenced by dietary Al. Calcium and Al are biologically interactive, thus Al might compete for Ca binding sites; it is also neurotoxic. Other metals mobilized in soil and sediment as a result of acid deposition are cadmium, zinc, arsenic, and selenium (Maugh 1984).

Ice and permanent snow fields could also act as sinks for toxic substances. Rates of deposition or sublimation back to air from snow and ice surfaces are not known. Toxic substances have been measured in glaciers, in snow and ice from polar areas, and in organisms from the Arctic and Antarctic. Global circulation patterns promote the deposition of particulate matter at the poles where downdrafts are common. Some toxins move to the sea with ice, some are re-volatilized back to the air, and some are buried for long periods.

Other sinks include burial waste dumps and the disposal of liquid wastes in deep wells. Whether these sites act as permanent sinks is not known, but some contamination of ground water has been detected and some toxic wastes have posed human health problems when they leach to the surface.

The entire area of the dynamic nature of sinks, rates of deposition, and recirculation is relatively unknown in terms of impact on the environment and on wildlife populations. Monitoring programs do show, on occasion, increases in body burdens for unknown reasons. Sometimes these have been associated with water systems and one potential source could be the circulation of toxic substances from sinks. This has been observed from river sediments and there is some suggestion that even the sediments of the abyssal depths of the oceans are not permanent sinks, that they too are subject to recirculation. The manufacture, use, and distribution of long-lived toxic substances and their final disposal will continue to present problems related to wildlife toxicology far into the future.

5

Accumulation in Organisms

Accumulation of toxic substances within an organism is a very complex process related to both physical and biological laws. Partitioning of the compound in the environment, called fugacity (Mackay and Paterson 1981) determines the availability of the toxic substance to the habitat or microenvironment occupied by the organism. Perhaps a better understanding of accumulation and partitioning has become available for aquatic systems largely because of the potential for study and containment.

Bioconcentration factors (BCF) for fish for organic chemicals have been modeled and predicted based on the log P (N-octanol/water). Veith, DeFoe, and Bergstedt (1979) and Veith, Macek, Petrocelli, et al. (1980) have described this relationship (see Figure 5.1).

This first-order uptake model was developed by exposing fathead minnows to a variety of organic compounds for up to 32 days. The model is summarized by the equation

$$\log BCF = 0.85 \log P - 0.70.$$

Biological magnification of chlorinated hydrocarbons in lentic environments has been defined by Hamelink, Waybrant, and Ball (1971). This model relates the exchange between fat, blood, gills, and water in predicting the BCF for specific compounds. Some examples from Hamelink, Waybrant and Ball (1971) are shown in Table 5.1.

Although these approximations are useful for aquatic habitats and organisms, there are few useful models to predict partitioning and uptake in terrestrial organisms. In studies of DDT partitioning in a meadow ecosystem, 91.8 percent remained in the soil horizons after 1 year (Grau and Peterle 1979). Some compartments of the meadow ecosystem decreased in residues after 5 years; others increased. Plants contained more DDTR residues after 5 years as did the herbivore *Microtus* (Forsyth, Peterle, and Bandy 1983, see Figure 5.2). Residues also increased in isopods, field

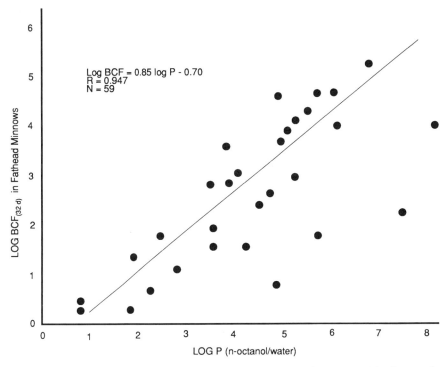

Figure 5.1   The relationship between Log p, the octanol/water partitioning coefficient and log of the bioconcentration factor (BCF) in fathead minnows. Modified from Veith, G. D., D. L. DeFoe, and B. C. Bergstedt. 1979. *J. Fish. Res. Bd. Canada*. 36(9):1040–1048.

crickets, and carabid ground beetles. Soil levels 5 years after application contained about 38 percent of the DDT applied; the total biota contained 22 percent.

Many other physical and biological factors govern the transport and accumulation of toxic substances from the point of release through the

Table 5-1 BCF Predictions for Specific Compounds

Compound	Water Solubility (ppm)	PC Water/Fat	BCF
Lindane	10	1×10^3	1×10^2
Toxaphene	3	1×10^4	1×10^4
Dieldrin	0.25	1×10^5	1×10^4
DDT	0.037	1×10^6	1×10^5

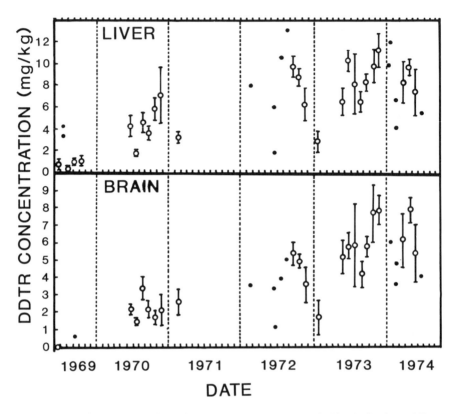

Figure 5.2 The accumulation of DDT-R over a 6-year period in the brain and liver of field voles in a meadow area treated with DDT once in 1969. Modified from "Persistence and transfer of 36 Cl-DDT in the soil and biota of an old-field ecosystem: a six year balance study" by D. J. Forsyth, T. J. Peterle, and L. W. Bandy. *Ecology* 1983. 64(6):1620–1636. Copyright © 1983 by the Ecological Society of America.

environment and into the living organisms. Sufficient knowledge is not available for most toxic substances to be able to predict the final residues and their potential chronic or lethal affects in terrestrial organisms.

ROUTES OF INTAKE

Routes of intake are directly related to storage, transport, and metabolism within the organism. As a result, the actual route of uptake of a toxic substance, as well as the form of feeding, can also be directly related to lethal or chronic effects. Woodcock given doses of an organochlorine pesticide dissolved in corn oil can withstand 3000 to 8000 mg/kg in a single oral dose. Much of the toxic substance is not absorbed in the gut and is excreted without harm, but if the woodcock is dosed with 2 to 3.0 ppm of an organochlorine over time given in contaminated earthworms, it will die (Stickel, Dodge, Sheldon, et al. 1965; Stickel, Hayne, and Stickel 1965).

The dynamics of intake, storage, and excretion of environmental pollutants was studied in herring gulls over a period of about one year. Body burdens at any given time of the year are variable, despite constant intake, as a result of changes in dietary foods and residue levels in various foods; altered physiological states of the birds; the state of sexual maturity; and the interactions between the physiological systems and various combinations of pollutants (Anderson and Hickey 1976).

In the fathead minnow, DDT intake and concentration from food sources over time might be as low as 1.2 times, but concentration from water might be 100,000 times. The DDT taken in from food had a short retention after 60 days but the DDT taken up from water was almost completely retained after 60 days (Jarvinen, Hoffman, and Thorslund 1976). Carp, taken from a marsh 1 month after treatment with 0.22 kg/ha of ^{36}CL labeled DDT had 3.76 ppm DDTR residues in ova (Peterle 1966).

The major routes of toxic substance intake are oral, dermal, and inhalation.

Oral

Trophic transfer of the compound from the environment into the organism might occur from live prey, from plant tissues, detritus, soil, or sediment. Chironomid (midge) larva might obtain the toxic substance from sediment, earthworms from soil, a caterpillar (gypsy moth) from plant leaf surfaces, a white-footed mouse from seeds or grass stems, a cotton-tailed rabbit from leaf surfaces, the bald eagle might obtain the compound by eating the rabbit, and wolves would obtain compounds from prey such as white-tailed deer or snowshoe hares. Herbivores obtain toxic substances that volatilize and adhere to leaf surfaces, those that are translocated into the plant from roots or surfaces and from seeds and fruits. Pesticides are not readily translocated into seeds; in field crops, soybeans contain about 10 percent of soil levels, corn and barley about 1.0 percent of soil levels; but a seed with higher oil content such as peanuts can concentrate soil residues of some toxic substances by 4 to 7 times (Lichtenstein 1959; Lichtenstein and Schulz 1965; Bruce, Decker, and Wilson 1966). Omnivores and detritus feeders obtain toxic substances directly as a result of application, from rainout, and from direct primary mortality of invertebrates or vertebrates in the system. Carnivores obtain toxic substances directly from prey and this could be in concentrated doses as a result of accumulation in primary consumers or in primary predators.

Pine voles from pesticide-treated orchards in New York were fed to captive American kestrels. Residues in voles included 48 ppm DDE, 1.2 ppm dieldrin, and 38 ppm lead. Kestrels accumulated only 1 ppm lead in livers, but 232 ppm DDE and 5.9 ppm dieldrin (wet weight), in carcasses after 60 days. One bird died after 31 days on the vole diet (Stendell, Beyer, and Stehn 1989).

Both primary and secondary poisoning may be important wildlife hazards for vertebrate control chemicals such as zinc phosphide, strychnine, 1080, and anticoagulants such as diphacinone and brodifacoum (Colvin, Hegdal, and Jackson 1988). Predators also might preferentially kill affected prey because of modified behavior and susceptibility to predation. Examples would be peregrines, wolves, in terms of the lichen (*Cladonia*), caribou transfer that we know occurred in the case of isotopes (cesium), and in some of our studies on a marsh treated with isotope-labeled DDT we found different uptake rates in mallards and scaup exposed to the same area for the same period of time (Dindal and Peterle 1968). This was also true for two different species of shrews on a meadow treated with labeled DDT (Forsyth, Peterle, and Bandy 1983). Six species of bats were sampled in the southwest and residues of DDT and metabolites in the herbivorous species averaged 0.51 ppm. In the insectivorous species, the combined DDT residues averaged 46 ppm, wet weight (Reidinger 1976).

In a thorough review of kinetics of pollutants in small mammals, Talmage and Walton (1991) found a relationship between contaminants in soil or food and selected target tissues. Heavy metals showed a close relationship, with the kidney as the best assay organ. Bone was best for lead and fluorine and the liver for organic contaminants. Other ways to document pollutant effects on small mammals included population dynamics, organ histology, genotoxicity, and enzyme changes. Insectivores had highest levels of contaminants, herbivores the lowest. Seventeen different organochlorines were detected in a collection of 69 small cetaceans from 10 different South Atlantic and Pacific Ocean species. DDT isomers and metabolites were most common; the highest residues were found in a coastal bottlenosed dolphin off the California coast; total DDT residues in blubber were 2695 ppm (O'Shea, Brownell, Clark, et al. 1980). Moriarty (1972) felt that rates of accumulation and excretion in the individual organism might be more important in accumulation than its position in the food chain.

Oral intake is also influenced by the initial metabolism of the compound either on plant surfaces or as it is stored in prey species. In some cases this might be a more lethal compound such as the conversion of malathion to malaoxon, or the metabolite might be less toxic and easily excreted such as DDA or DDMU.

In any discussion of oral intake, questions of avoidance by smell or taste can also be important, regurgitation or emesis might occur and the animal could leave the treated area during or directly after treatment. Bennett and Schafer (1988) found potential avoidance problems in avian LC-50 tests. While it is not direct oral intake, we should also mention transfer across the placenta in mammals and the transfer of toxic substances directly into the egg in birds. Toxic substances are also transferred in the milk of mammals and in prey brought to young of both birds and mammals.

Dermal

This may include transfer across the surfaces of both plants and animals and is related to the type of chemical involved, the carrier, chemical structure, molecular configuration and ionic charge, and the surface coating on the plant and animal tissue exposed. There seems to be little effect of dermal intake in terrestrial systems except for the invertebrates directly involved and the soil-dwelling organisms such as earthworms.

Dermal uptake is more important in aquatic systems where there is very rapid equilibration between the organism and the toxic substance if it is water soluble. Uptake is related to the type of organism, the total body surface, ventilation rate of structures such as gills and siphons, and the body water turnover time of the organism itself. Relatively large molecules such as insulin can be moved directly across the gill membrane of fish and increased ventilation rate is sometimes a result of toxic substance exposure.

Skin and eye tests are usually done for registration and as a general rule, organophosphates are more readily transferred across the skin than are organochlorines. Skin and eye tests with vertebrates are being reduced or eliminated in preference for invertebrate tests.

Inhalation

Little is known about the uptake of toxic substances by wildlife as a result of inhalation. Most of the research has been done with laboratory species such as mice, rats, and dogs. For some toxic substances such as asbestos, some forms of radiation (plutonium), and some carbon compounds that might be carcinogenic, inhalation can be considered important. The use of red deer antlers for retrospective analyses of heavy metals has been demonstrated (Samiullah and Jones 1990). Lead in antlers of red deer from the Island of Rhum has decreased from 2.9 ng/g in 1960–61 to 1.8 μg/g in 1977–85.

Newman (1979) summarized reports of effects of air pollution on birds and mammals for the United States and Europe. In one early incident in Germany in 1936, 60 to 70 percent of the red deer, roe deer, and European rabbits died in a forest area as a result of arsenic emissions. In recent times, fluorides have been important in roe deer dental anomalies (Kierdorf and Kierdorf 1990). Urban English sparrows (polluted inland air) have been found to have more macrophages in their lungs than rural (coastal clean air) sparrows (McArn, Boardman, Munn, et al. 1974). We know that NO_x can have serious effects on human and laboratory animal lung function and there is no reason to believe that wild animals exposed would not also be affected in a similar manner. We also know that exposure to NO_x can influence the organism's response to other disease organisms such as pneumonia. Studies of human volunteers show that 81 to 87 percent of the exposure of NO_2 at levels of 0.5 to 5.0 ppm in air is absorbed by the lungs at normal respiration rates; at maximal respiration rate this is increased to over 90 percent. Mortality of laboratory species (rats, mice, guinea pigs, rabbits, dogs) occurs after 1 hour of exposure at concentrations of 75 to 95 mg/m^3 or 40 to 50 ppm. Rabbits and dogs are least susceptible; monkeys are more susceptible. Pathology of the lungs occurs after 24 hours of exposure at levels of 13.16 mg/m^3 or 7.0 ppm. Human mortality occurs at sudden high exposures of 150 ppm with death in 3 to 5 weeks (National Academy of Sciences 1977). Short-term exposure to humans increases the risk of bacterial pneumonia. This has been documented in many instances of high level pollution both in the United States and abroad. We don't know whether or not there are highly susceptible wildlife species that might be affected by air pollutants.

Prior Exposure

For most of the wildlife species, exposure to multiple sources and kinds of contaminants is the rule rather than the exception. Prior exposure to one compound does alter the subsequent storage, metabolism, and excretion of a second compound.

In experimental work with dogs treated with DDT at 12 mg/kg and/or aldrin at 0.3 mg/kg the resultant body burdens were quite different. In male dogs being fed only DDT, body burdens in fat were 204 to 210 ppm (total DDT); males fed both DDT and aldrin had 288 to 1019 ppm. In females fed only DDT, fat residues were 260 to 277 ppm and those being fed both pesticides had fat residues of 247 to 642 ppm (Deichmann, MacDonald, and Cubit 1971). Pregnancy or lactation would have altered the values for females to be even greater than those for males.

In laboratory rats being treated with 10 ppm of dieldrin and either 0.0,

5.0, or 50.0 ppm of DDT, dieldrin residues were highest in those being fed dieldrin along with DDT (67.5 ppm), less in those treated with 5.0 ppm DDT (43.9 ppm), and least in those treated with 50.0 ppm DDT (11.2 ppm in fat) (Street and Blau 1966).

Some toxic substances have been used to control vertebrates by dermal transfer such as an endrin compound used to control birds as a result of transfer through the feet. In other cases stickers and wetting agents are sometimes used to enhance dermal pesticide transfer to increase mortality.

STORAGE SITES AND ORGANS

Storage and transport within the organism is influenced most by the characteristics of the compound, primarily whether it is lipo- or hydrophyllic. The rate and route of intake are also important; for instance, there are major differences in transport and storage between dermal and oral intake. Storage and transport within wildlife species is highly variable. Body condition in terms of the proportion of lipid to whole body weight is important to the retention and transport of lipophyllic substances such as organochlorines. The organism's condition related to food stress, reproductive status, migration, and the status of available fat pools (kidney, subcutaneous, brain) and sometimes special fat pools such as brown fat in bats, all can influence the storage and transport of the toxic substance within the animal. The organism's metabolic rate and added stress can mobilize stored compounds and produce lethal effects such as was demonstrated in cowbirds and grackles at Patuxent (Stickel, Gaylen, Dyrland, et al. 1973). Cage stress during capture some weeks after treatment resulted in lethal effects (Stickel 1965).

Other more subtle factors might influence uptake and storage of toxic substances. Dominant bluegills held in tanks with subdominants stored less of the 32 ng/l of zinc to which they were exposed and survived longer. When the tanks were provided with shelters for subdominant fish, the differences in residues of body burdens in zinc were reduced. The mechanism of how dominance plays a role in uptake of toxic substances is unknown, but perhaps in the case of the bluegills the ventillation rate changed with dominance and aggression (Sparks, Waller, and Cairns Jr. 1972).

Uptake of lead has been studied in depth as a result of lead poisoning in waterfowl. In one study, lead versus a combination lead/iron shot were fed to mallard ducks, a single pellet deposited in the proventriculus. Lead levels in blood, kidney, and liver in ducks fed lead shot as opposed to those fed a combination of lead and iron were about twice as high. Residues in kidneys and livers reflected the different lead doses of 100 and 200 mg. Residues in kidneys and livers of females were higher, and in wing bones, lead residues in females were 10 times those of males. In females the number of eggs laid was correlated with the residues in the wing bone. The higher the residue, the greater the number of eggs produced. Wing-bone residues in females given all-lead shot ranged from 2.3 to 270 ppm. During active bone metabolism in laying females, apparently lead competes with calcium for deposition (Finley, Dieter, and Locke 1976). Residues of lead in livers of tits taken from contaminated forests in Poland had levels as high as 21.16 μg/g dry weight; those from uncontaminated forests 5.3 ug/g (Sawicka-Kapusta, Kozlowski, and Sokolowska 1986).

Hair has been used to assess lead levels in humans. Adult antique hair (1871–1923) had higher levels of lead (93.36 μg/gm dry weight) than contemporary hair (1971) that had residues of 6.55 μg/g (Weiss, Whitten, and Leddy 1972).

In the differential storage of dietary treatments, the enhancement of microsomal action in the liver is most important and will be dealt with in a later section.

In the storage of toxic substances in organisms, there are sometimes strong correlations between residues in various organs for some substances, particularly the organochlorines. In the case of DDT, there are strong correlations between such organs as the breast muscle, pancreas, gonads, brain, and adrenal gland (Dindal 1970). Others have found relationships between total body burdens and the wings; this is used especially in the Fish and Wildlife Service's monitoring program where hunters submit the wings of waterfowl for species/sex/age ratios in the kill and the wings are also used for monitoring toxic substances (Prouty and Bunck 1986).

Storage in organs of a variety of wildlife species is reflected in the list of organs recommended for sampling by the EEC and other environmental agencies (Luepke 1979). These include for birds and mammals the gonads, thyroid, adrenal, bone, adipose, kidney, liver, lung, skeletal muscle, and the spleen. Specifically for heavy metals, residues of lead are found in bone; nickel and mercury in the liver; and cadmium in the kidney and liver.

Bile and the bile duct are important to the metabolism and excretion of toxic substances and may relate to secondary resorption by the lower gut and further transport within the body. Blood is used as a tissue to reflect the current status of a toxic substance in the body and is being used more frequently in wildlife sampling programs (Henny and Meeker 1981). The brain is considered the critical tissue related to LD-50 levels. It is sampled most often in postmortem studies and residues can be directly related to lethal effects (Stickel, Stickel, and Spann 1969).

The time since exposure is most important in that residues are transported within the body, stored, metabolized, excreted, or sequestered. Cleansing agents might have been taken in or other toxic substances that compete for binding sites such as mercury and selenium or various isomers of organochlorines can alter the storage location and kinetics within the body.

Mobilization of toxic substances from stored sites during times of stress such as food deprivation, moult, or migration in birds and during reproduction can result in mortality if residues reach sufficient levels in critical tissues such as brain and other nervous tissues (Van Velzen, Stiles, and Stickel 1972). A merlin found dead during autumn migration contained brain residues of 1800 ppm (lipid weight) DDE, 4.4 ppm dieldrin, and 96 ppm heptachlor epoxide (Henny, Bean, and Fyfe 1976).

Bats during the critical spring period of food stress and birds during migration have been known to die of toxic substance exposure following mobilization from stored sites. Brain levels of DDE in cowbirds dying 9 or 40 days after exposure and up to 4 months after exposure had ceased had similar residues of DDE in the brain (Stickel, Stickel, and Coon 1970).

Storage of toxic compounds within the body may be a protective measure and an avoidance of direct toxic effects. *Coturnix* treated with dieldrin can survive brain residues of 1.1 to 3.0 μg and body burdens of 860 μg to 2100 μg. Liver residues (lipid weight) reached 491 ppm in live birds and 1301 ppm in dead cowbirds. Dose/time variables alter the time to reach LD-50 levels in brain tissue. Grackles fed mirex at 250 ppm died at about 38 days with residues of 225 to 458 ppm in the brain. At 2250 ppm in the diet, birds died at 5 days with about the same residue levels in the brain. Approximately 177 ppm in the brain was considered lethal. Brain residues do not decrease in an even expotential manner because brain fat levels are related to total fat in the body (Fig. 5.3). Following cessation of treatment with oral doses of mirex, grackles were sampled at 0, 1, 4, 8, 12, 20, and 28 weeks. Brain residues decreased from 130 ppm at the termination of feeding to 15.4 ppm at 12 weeks, but residues increased to 37 ppm for weeks 20 and 28. Brain lipids remain more or less constant and residues of lipophyllic compounds such as DDE in the brain are inversely related to percentage of body lipids (Stickel and Stickel 1969; Stickel, Stickel, and Coon 1970; Stickel, Stickel, Dyrland, et al. 1984a,b; Stickel, Gaylen, Dyrland, et al. 1973).

In crayfish (Red and White River), water soluble fractions of crude oil were concentrated in the cehpalothorax and in the hepatopancreas (Tarshis 1981). Fuel oil residues were rapidly lost when the crayfish were placed in clean water. Earthworms can concentrate heavy metals from soils many times the soil levels. Earthworms found in soils with 2.0 ppm

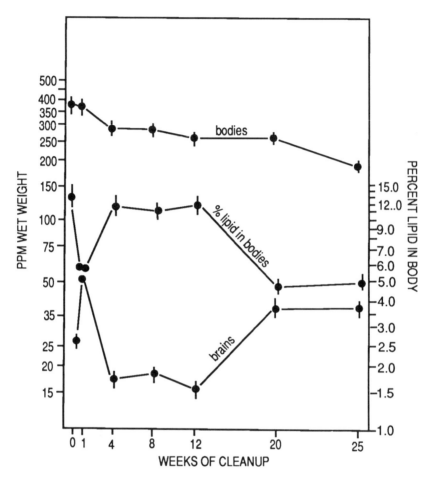

Figure 5.3 The compartmentalization of body residues of mirex in birds related to the level of fat in brain and body. These relationships are inverse, as body fat declines, residues in brain fat increase. These relationships are important to potential mortality as a result of loss of body weight/fat and accumulation of sufficient toxins in the brain to kill the organism. Modified from ''Toxicity and persistence of mirex in birds.'' W. H. Stickel, J. A. Gaylen, R. A. Dyrland, et al. 1973. In *Pesticides and the environment: a continuing controversy*, pp. 437–467. Symposia Specialists, North Miami, FL.

cadmium contained 100.0 ppm of the heavy metal (Beyer, Chaney, and Mulhern 1982).

In aquatic systems the water quality can alter uptake rates of most toxic substances. Soft waters form complexes with heavy metals and the actual availability of the species of heavy metal at the site is important to uptake in fish and other aquatic organisms. Storage sites in Lake Michigan coho salmon varied in DDT-R residues. Whole salmon steaks contained 14.9 ppm. Abdominal adipose fat had the highest residue of 66.0 to 92.33 ppm, belly fat 69.66 ppm, dorsal median fat 61.1 to 62.82 ppm, and lateral line fat 34.31 to 41.1 ppm (Reinert 1970; Reinert, Stewart, and Seagran 1972).

In a marine fish, the spot, exposure to 1.0 ppb of PCB water for 58 days resulted in a plateau at 14 to 28 days. Accumulation of 3.7×10^4 the levels in the water in the whole body was stored in descending order of importance in the liver, gills, whole fish, heart, brain, and least in muscle. Whole body residues had decreased about 73 percent after 84 days on clean food (Hansen, Parrish, Lowe, et al. 1971).

In birds, there are good correlations among various tissues in terms of DDT-R residues. Dindal and Peterle (1968) reported on residues from mallard and scaup ducks exposed to a marsh treated with radio-labeled DDT. Because waterfowl wings are used in the national monitoring surveys, correlations were compared among residues found in the wing and other body tissues (see Table 5.2).

Table 5-2 Correlations among Wing and Various Tissues of Mallard and Scaup Ducks Exposed to a DDT-Treated Marsh

Tissue Type	Mallard (r)	Scaup (r)
Wing	1.0	1.0
Breast skin	0.73	0.82
Kidney	0.61	0.76
Breast muscle	0.68	0.78
Uropygial	0.55	0.69
Adrenal	0.63	0.82
Pancreas	0.48	0.69
Brain	0.66	0.66
Gonads	0.27	0.62
Liver	0.18	0.50
Thyroid	0.32	0.37
Breast feather	0.31	0.12

r = *correlation with wing residues.*
From Dindal and Peterle 1968. Wing and body tissue relationships and metabolic residues in mallard and lesser scaup ducks. Bull. Environ. Contam. Toxicol. *3(1):37–48. Permission by Springer-Verlag, Heidelberg.*

The r values were significant at $P < 0.01$ for mallard at $r = 0.32$ and for a scaup $r = 0.37$. In some later studies of body burden correlations in black ducks, heptachlor and Aroclor 1254 residues were correlated among tissues, but endrin was not. R^2 values for endrin residues between carcass and wing fat were 67 to 73 percent; for heptachlor and Aroclor, they were 90 to 97 percent. Permissible residues in wildlife related to human food and potential population effects on species may be monitored by measuring residues in wing samples on a lipid-weight basis (Hall, Haseltine, and Geissler 1989). The mallard wing monitoring program has exposed high residues from certain areas of industrial contamination, such as Wheeler Refuge in Alabama. Mallard wings from the local area contained mean residues of DDE of 4.40 ppm; the statewide means of DDE for Alabama were 0.69 ppm in 1976 (Fleming and O'Shea 1980). Maximum body burdens of 480 ppm (DDTR) have been reported in mallards from Wheeler Refuge (O'Shea, Fleming, and Cromartie 1980).

High residues of total DDT and PCBs were reported in peregrines from southwestern North America (California and Texas coasts). Total DDT in a migrant bird equaled 5,000 ppm lipid weight, and 1,420 ppm PCBs. In an adult from California, total DDT was 2,600 ppm and PCBs 1,980 ppm lipid weight (Risebrough, Rieche, and Peakall 1968). Nutrition stress in DDE-treated cockrels resulted in brain residues of 63 to 219 ppm; birds fed full levels of food had residues of 29 to 64 ppm in the brain. Residues of about 35 ppm were considered lethal (Ecobichon and Saschenbrecker 1968).

Brown and white fat in bats contained varying levels of DDE residues. Even though brown fat contained lower lipid levels than white fat, there was 28 percent more DDE in brown fat samples from big and little brown bats and in the eastern pipistrelle. Because brown fat is important at the time of arousal from hibernation, lethal levels could be mobilized from brown fat reserves (Clark and Krynitsky 1983a).

EXCRETION AND METABOLISM

The rates of toxic chemical excretion and metabolism are dependent on several important factors including the type of chemical involved, whether it is water or liposoluble, the route of intake, and the prior exposure history of the organism.

Water soluble chemicals are excreted very rapidly related to the total body water pool and the rates of turnover of the body water pool. Lipophyllic compounds are stored in fat in different parts of the body at different rates and the compounds are metabolized and excreted or mobilized to other storage sites related to the condition of the animal, its sex, and reproductive state.

The rate and route of intake ultimately determine the plateau levels reached within the organism and whether chronic or lethal effects become evident during exposure and excretion. In aquatic systems, uptake from the water occurs at a much higher rate than concentration from food sources and excretion is slower from compounds taken in across the integument (Jarvinen, Hoffman, and Thorslund 1976). Intake from food results in higher residues in eggs and young. The rate of intake is important in terms of toxic effects, storage without toxic effect, rates of metabolism, and ultimate resistance to the chemical's toxicity. Low rates of intake over long periods of time may build immunity in the organism and permit higher concentrations to accumulate within the body without toxic effects (Hill, Spann, and Williams 1977). Plateau levels are related to the species, rate of intake, the sex, age and reproductive status, the nutritional state of the animal, and prior exposure to compounds that could potentially enhance metabolic rates, and enzyme breakdown in the liver.

Excretion of the chemical, either as the original parent compound or as a metabolite, is through the urine, feces, skin, hair, feathers, the reproductive process, or through exhalation. Rates of excretion or half-time, $T_{1/2}$, are quite variable. In mallard drakes, for example, the uptake of mercury was rapid, as was loss. The $T_{1/2}$ was 84 days, but there was no loss between days 7 and 56 (Stickel, Stickel, McLane, et al. 1977). The half-time of mercury for humans is 76 days, but for some species of fish it is much longer. In contaminated waters of Finland, pike weighing 4 kg with mercury residues of 2.2 ppm lost residues at the rate of 0.13 ppm per year (Nuroteva, Lodenius, and Nuroteva 1979). Uptake of mercury in perch in Wisconsin seepage lakes is controlled by pH, alkalinity, and sediment concentration (Cope, Wiener, and Rada 1990).

The liver and kidney are major organs for excretion and metabolism and excretion curves are frequently biphasic; there is a rapid loss for the first few days, then a plateau and a more gradual loss thereafter. Excretion rates in feces and urine are usually equal, but not in all instances. The bile is an important route of excretion into the intestine and intake of fats can influence the breakdown and excretion rates and possible resorption of lipophyllic compounds from the lower intestine following excretion in bile.

The oil gland in birds is also an important route of excretion of lipophyllic compounds and distribution on the feathers and possible re-ingestion may occur. After about one month of dietary intake, residues in the oil gland are about equal to that found in the diet of mallards (Nauman 1969; Peterle, Lustick, Nauman, et al. 1974).

We know very little about excretion by exhalation in wildlife; it is obviously related to the type of compound and the organism involved.

The reproductive process is an important route of excretion for females. In the wild, females fequently have lower total body burdens as a result of excretion in eggs, placenta, in fetuses, and in milk. Mallard hens fed 40 ppm DDE for 96 days were subsequently allowed to lay eggs. In the first reproductive period, body burdens ranged from 311 to 362 ppm in lipid and the eggs averaged 714 ppm DDE. Approximately 11 months later, without further exposure, body burdens were about 79 ppm and egg lipids contained 107 ppm (Haegele and Hudson 1974). Common tern populations declined in the Great Lakes during the 1970s, but residues of PCB and DDE in eggs measured in 1981 showed an 80 to 90 percent decline from 1969 through 1973. Residues of organochlorines in tern eggs were lower than those in caspian terns or herring gulls (Weseloh, Custer, and Braune 1989). In big and little brown bats, the chlorinated hydrocarbons are transmitted across the placenta and in the milk. PCB is transmitted across the placenta in bats at a 2 or 3 times higher rate than is DDE. Most of the DDE found in young bats is transmitted in the milk from the mother (Clark and Lamont 1976a, b).

Excretion in feathers and hair have been measured and samples of human hair have been used for forensic purposes to determine exposure to toxic substances. After 56 days of expsure on a DDT-treated marsh, feathers from mallards and scaup contained up to 17.5 ppm DDT-R, some of which might have been adsorbed to the surface in oil or particulate matter (Dindal and Peterle 1968). Mercury was found in great blue heron feathers at levels of 2.7 to 12.5 ppm at a Lake Erie rookery (Hoffman and Curnow 1973). Berg, Johnels, Sjostrand, et al. (1966) used feathers to study mercury levels in Swedish birds over a 100-year period. Levels increased from about 2 to 29 mg/g. Rates of excretion by the various routes are highly variable. Bald eagles fed DDT excreted the parent compound or metabolites at about 0.4 to 0.8 percent per day. The rates may be calculated by: $\log_e$ (content at time 2/content at time 1)/ days (Stickel, Chura, Stewart, et al. 1966). Rates of excretion are not constant but relate to the remaining residues in the organism and the rate of intake. DDE residues in grackles were lost at a rate of 0.30 percent per day after being treated with 1500 ppm in the diet for 7 days. The half-time was estimated to be 229 days, with residues being lost from the brain tissue most rapidly. Brain residues were in proportion to total body fat after 25 days (Stickel, Stickel, Dyrland, et al. 1984b).

Half-time of a toxic substance in an organism is related to age because in the case of young mammals, the bile duct does not become functional for some time following birth and exposure to toxic substances can produce a higher rate of mortality because of the individual's inability to excrete toxics, such as mercury (Ballatori and Clarkson 1982).

SPECIES, SEX, AND AGE

Species Differences

Species responses to accumulation of toxic substances are highly variable. Metabolic rates, as related to existence as a poikilotherm or homeotherm, directly influence the rates of uptake and excretion. The organism's body size related to total body surface determines the extent of intake across the integument, as does the organism's habitat: terrestrial or aquatic, or whether it lives above or below ground. The organism's place in the food chain can influence rates of intake; that is, whether the animal is an omnivore, detritivore, carnivore, or herbivore influences where and how it might be exposed to a toxic substance. The total life span, time to sexual maturity, and frequency of reproductive cycles can also affect the uptake and excretion of toxic substances.

The mobility, home range, migration, and sequence of movements and behavior patterns can serve to integrate point and non-point sources of pollution to which the animal might be exposed. We know that in some migratory birds, exposure to toxic substances during their winter migration may influence their reproductive success on the breeding grounds. This has been demonstrated for black-crowned night herons migrating to the southwestern United States or to Mexico (Henny and Blus 1986). Some species have highly sensitive senses of taste and/or smell and may be able to avoid contaminated food or habitats. The relationship of the population or individual to sources of contamination such as agricultural areas, industrial, or dump sites could influence exposure and accumulation. Whether or not the organism may aestivate or hibernate and the time and length of various life stages could influence intake of toxics. The rate of population turnover influences selection for resistance, rates of metabolism, and removal of the toxic substance from the environment.

Pintails in California showed low (below 1.0 ppm) residues of pesticides, but levels increased during the wintering period. Residues in diving ducks (canvasbacks, lesser scaup) were slightly higher, but rarely over 1.0 ppm. Organochlorine residues were not sufficiently high to result in effects on the waterfowl sampled (Ohledndorf and Miller 1984).

The total stress concept is probably related to toxic substance kinetics and effects. Organisms living under highly stressful conditions, physical, social, or nutritional, would react differently to toxic substance exposure than one existing under optimum conditions. Toxins could impinge on many points in the neuro-endocrine system (Fig. 5.4).

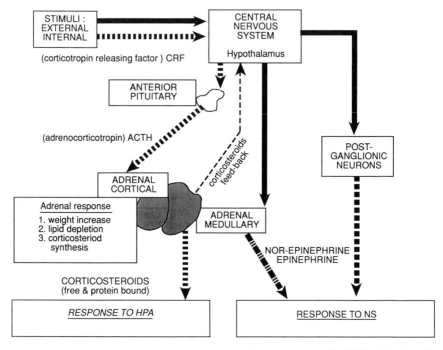

Figure 5.4   General diagram of the neuro-endocrine system in birds. Toxic substances may interact at many points of the system by mimicking hormones, in addition to the reduction of hormone levels by MFO induction in the liver. Modified from Siegel, H. S. 1980. "Physiological stress in birds." *Biosci.* 30(8):529–534. Copyright 1980 by the American Institute of Biological Sciences.

Sensitivity to toxics is highly variable among species and for this reason, the prediction of toxic substance effects on species and ecosystems is extremely difficult. Some species are highly susceptible to low-level exposure. Catfish exposed to 0.5 ppb of endrin in the water will die in 2 hours. The 96-hour LC-50 for channel catfish is 0.32 ppb (Johnson and Finley 1980). Tolerance level median (TL_m) values for 96-hour exposures to several compounds were provided by Henderson, Pickering, and Tarzwell (1959). These are shown in Table 5.3.

In a survey of a variety of species found in the vicinity of a smelter in Pennsylvania, residues of lead were highest in earthworms, 310 ppm. Litter contained 500 ppm, upper soils 150 ppm, and lower soils 17 ppm. Other species found contaminated were slugs (53 ppm), millipedes (27 ppm), toads (13 ppm), short-tailed shrews (109 ppm), white-footed mice (17 ppm) and wood thrushes (49 ppm) (Beyer 1983; Beyer, Pattee, Sileo, et al. 1985).

Table 5-3 96-Hour TL_m in Minnows, Bluegill, and Goldfish

	Species		
Compound	Fathead Minnow (ppb)	Bluegill (ppb)	Goldfish (ppb)
Aldrin	33	13	28
Dieldrin	16	7.9	37
Endrin	1.0	0.6	1.9
Chlordane	32	22	82
Heptachlor	94	19	230
Toxaphene	7.5	3.5	5.6
DDT	32	16	27
Methoxychlor	64	52	56
Lindane	62	77	152
BHC	2300	790	2300

From Henderson, Pickering, and Tarzwell 1959. Relative toxicity of ten chlorinated hydrocarbons. Trans. Amer. Fish Soc. 88(1):23–32.

Long-lived species do accumulate high levels of toxic substance residues. In a sample of California condor leg muscle tissue, the dry weight residue of DDE was 200 ppm. Other residues included dieldrin (0.87 ppm), toxaphene (0.27 ppm), DDMU (11.0 ppm), and 5.3 ppm of PCB (Wiemeyer, Krynitsky, and Wilbur 1983).

Over a period from 1978 to 1981, 293 bald eagles were necropsied and DDE was found in all carcasses. Several other organochlorines were found in addition to PCB and lead. Seventeen samples had dieldrin residues of over 10.0 ppm (Reichel, Schmeling, Cromartie, et al. 1984).

Avian species do vary in the rate of transport of xenobiotics across the wall of the gut. Bobwhites, screech owls, and kestrels absorbed toxics across the gut at a higher rate than black-crowned night-herons or mallard ducks. Kestrels absorbed eight times more mercury than did mallards and two times more than screech owls. Mallards absorbed less dieldrin and mercury than did herons (Serafin 1984).

Because of the high variation in uptake among wildlife species, as well as individual variation, predictions of chronic or lethal effects from laboratory exposure of a limited number of species is not reliable. Keith (1969) sampled western grebes from Tule Lake Refuge and found DDT residues ranged from 0.07 to 995 ppm in fat in one group of 10 birds and 58 to 1282 ppm in another group of 10 birds.

Highly variable rates of uptake and accumulation of organochlorines are evident related to species as well as geographic location. Gilbertson and

Reynolds (1974) have provided the results of a broad survey of avian species in Canada for organochlorine residues in brain tissue and in eggs (Table 5.4).

Sample sizes in the above survey varied from 1 to 14 for brain residues and 1 to 55 for egg residues. Accumulation rates for other species can be much higher or lower. In snapping turtles in the Hudson River, maximum residues in fat were 7,990 ppm for PCB and 26.5 ppm for dieldrin and 57.5 ppm for DDE (Stone, Kiviat, and Butkas 1980). In contrast, toxic substance residues found in snow geese from Baffin Island were very low: eggs less than 0.049 DDT-R; and 0.13 ppm PCB and liver residues were 0.015 ppm DDT-R and 0.029 ppm PCB. These were wet weight determinations. Livers also contained some mercury and BHC (Longcore, Heyland, Reed, et al. 1983).

Because of their widespread distribution and varied food habits, Alaska sea birds, while showing evidence of a variety of environmental contaminants in their eggs, had residue levels of usually less than 1.0 ppm. PCB residues were highest (3.55 ppm) in eggs of glaucous-winged gulls from the Aleutians and DDE was highest in the same species and location (5.16 ppm wet weight). The horned puffin had low residues of 0.009 ppm DDE and 0.034 ppm of PCBs (Ohlendorf, Bartonek, Divoky, et al. 1982).

Variations of residues of chlorinated hydrocarbons in eggs among various species of birds along the California coast showed that Caspian terns had the highest levels of both DDE and PCB, 8.67 ppm wet weight for DDE and 5.67 ppm for PCBs (Ohlendorf, Custer, Lowe, et al. 1988). Forster's terns had DDE egg residues of 1.92 ppm and PCBs were 5.65 ppm. Black-crowned night herons had lower residues of 2.92 ppm for DDE and 4.84 ppm for PCBs. DDE was considered the most hazardous environmental contaminant because residues in 10 percent of the eggs were above those known to cause reproductive effects.

Sex

Sex of the organism is related to uptake as influenced by body size and composition, reproductive activities, and activities related to dominance, territorialism, fighting, differential migration, food-intake rates, and nutrition. Total stress on individuals such as might occur during incubation, rearing of young, and moulting influences the rates of intake, excretion, and effects of toxic substances. Female waterfowl for example, increase their intake of animal foods prior to egg-laying and could potentially also increase their uptake of toxic substances that might subsequently be excreted in the egg and influence reproductive success. Female *Coturnix*

Table 5-4 Residues of DDE and PCB in Brain and Egg Tissue of Avian Species in Canada (ppm dry matter, geometric mean)

Species	DDT Brain	DDT Egg	PCB Brain	PCB Egg	Location
Common loon	1.54	7.53	1.38	5.43	Alberta
Arctic loon	1.99	4.8	1.44	6.49	Northwest Territories
Red-throated loon	2.95	2.76	4.16	3.14	Northwest Territories
Eared grebe	3.96	8.58	0.54	2.92	Alberta
Western grebe	4.11		6.45		British Columbia
White pelican	21.2		11.2		Manitoba
Double-crested cormorant	22.2	86.0	63.9	140	Lake Huron
Red-tailed hawk	0.61	29.0	0.20	2.29	British Columbia
Bald eagle	5.32	164.0	1.82	140	Saskatchewan
Osprey	0.87	22.0	2.40	19.4	Ontario
Peregrine	5.42	22.0	1.96	36.1	Northwest Territories
	16.7	84.8	3.82	25.6	British Columbia
	0.84		0.63		New Brunswick
Merlin	45.5	42.1	0.003	8.64	British Columbia
Herring gull	22.8	131.0	91	565	L. Ontario
California gull	4.76	20.5	0.74	1.65	L. Ontario
Ringbilled gull	206.0	60.5	1055	379	L. Ontario
Caspian tern	29.2	57.9	43.8	174	L. Ontario
Great horned owl	0.285	23.8	0.09	3.08	Saskatchewan

Values are ppm dry matter, geometric mean.
Adapted from M. Gilbertson and L. Reynolds 1974. A summary of DDE and PCB determinations in Canadian birds, 1962–1972. Occasional Paper No. 19. Canadian Wildlife Service, Environment Canada. Reproduced with permission of the Minister of Supply and Services Canada.

held in the laboratory were less susceptible to DDT poisoning if they were in active egg-laying for the first 10 days (Gish and Chura 1970).

Age

Age influences uptake rates beginning either in the egg or during gestation in mammals. Toxic substances are deposited in eggs and some are transmitted across the placenta; individuals are then born or hatched with body burdens of some compounds. This is further influenced by intake from milk or in foods brought to the nest. Young of many species have different rates of growth, time to sexual maturity, and times of migration or emigration. Fat/body weight ratios also vary in young and adult. As a general observation, the young of most species are more susceptible to toxic substances than are adults. Young bats, for example, are about 1.5 times more sensitive to DDT than are adults, probably because of fat/body weight ratios (Clark 1981a, b).

In a meadow ecosystem treated with ^{36}Cl labeled DDT, pathways of accumulation were studied for 6 years. Among the several species of rodents exposed, the breeding adults of *Microtus, Blarina,* and *Sorex* contained whole-body residues similar to that of embryos. Residues peaked in newborns at 5 to 6 days of age, then declined as they were weaned (Forsyth and Peterle 1973).

SYNERGISM AND ANTAGONISM

Most wildlife species in natural systems are exposed to more than one toxic substance at any given time, so moderators of toxicity (both synergists and antagonists) are important. Aside from a few laboratory studies where multiple exposures have been tested, we know very little of how moderators influence the responses of wildlife to toxic substances.

Cotoxicity coefficients and synergistic ratios have been used to define multiple effects of toxic substances given simultaneously or sequentially to animals in laboratory studies. A cotoxicity coefficient is equal to the ratio of the LC-50 of the toxic substance alone to the LC-50 of the toxicant plus 1 percent synergist.

The cotoxicity coefficient for house flies, for example, when 1 percent sesamex is used as the synergist is 3.8 for endrin, 1.4 for lindane, and 29 for amiton (O'Brien 1967). The coefficient represents increased mortality. In rats and mice, exposure to paired insecticides might be synergistic in the case of malathion and trichlorfon, it may be antagonistic in paired treatments of parathion and malathion, or it might simply be additive when treated with parathion and demeton (O'Brien 1967). *Coturnix* and pheasant chicks were tested with 18 different pesticides, 13 of them in paired LC-50 tests. Some pairs of organophosphates were moderately synergistic, and others were additive. Mammals and insects seem more responsive to the effects of synergism in paired tests than do birds (Kreitzer and Spann 1973).

Many compounds, including the organochlorines, enhance microsomal action in the liver and can alter the susceptibility of an organism to subsequent intake of a toxic substance. Responses are not general, but specific to the compounds involved. Prior treatment of *Coturnix* with 5 and

50 ppm DDE in the diet enhanced their susceptibility to parathion toxicity. Exposure to chlordane was antagonistic to the toxic effects of parathion (Ludke 1977). Prior exposure of *Coturnix* to mercury enhanced their response to subsequent treatment with parathion and carbofuran (Dieter and Ludke 1975, 1978).

Combinations of heavy metals are found to be associated in both uptake and retention and in toxicity. In mussels, saturation of binding sites with zinc will permit rapid excretion or binding of cadmium and thereby reduce cadmium toxicity. Some organochlorines might cause zinc deficiency and result in higher cadmium toxicity. Simultaneous or sequential exposure to other combinations of heavy metals such as cadmium and calcium, and selenium and mercury can alter storage and toxicity (National Academy of Sciences 1980).

Single and combined treatments of mallard hens with South Louisana crude oil and DDE resulted in different effects. Oil was fed at 0.5 percent of the diet either alone or in combination with 5.0 ppm DDE. DDE was also fed as the single contaminant. There was no effect of any of the combinations on onset of laying, egg production, egg fertility, or egg size. Oil decreased hatchability, DDE had no effect, and when fed in combination there was no effect. Oil alone increased the proportion of shell, DDE decreased the shell thickness, and when fed jointly, the proportion of shell by weight increased. The proportion of yolk increased and the proportion of albumen decreased with oil treatment, but DDE had no effect on these measurements and when fed with oil, the effect was the same as with oil fed alone (Vangilder and Peterle 1983).

There are many more combinations of toxic substances to which wildlife species are simultaneously exposed and we know little about their potential combined effects, particularly at chronic levels as related to physiological function and reproduction.

PREDATOR/PREY TRANSFER

Much attention has been given to the biomagnification of toxic substances in food chains as a result of predator/prey transfer. Perhaps equally important might be the chronic effects of predators that make them less efficient at catching prey or effects on prey that make them more or less susceptible to predation. Because many of the toxic substances are neurotoxic, chronic exposure could alter the ability of the predator to search and seize prey. Presumably, predators must remain as efficient as possible in catching prey in order that they may devote more energy to survival and reproduction. Some predators are obligated to catch live prey, such as aerially feeding predators, while others prefer live prey.

Mortality or alteration of behavior among prey species could alter the ability of the predator to survive. Reduced populations of prey would concentrate predators in certain areas and increase the potential for competition and perhaps disease transfer. One of the important aspects of prey exposure to toxic substances is the concentration of the toxic chemical, especially among resistant populations, and the subsequent transfer to the predator. After 2 weeks of exposure to 500 ppb endrin, resistant mosquitofish accumulated 214.28 ppm endrin that would have been available to a predator (Ferguson, Ludke, and Murphy 1966).

The behavior of the prey might be altered to make them more susceptible to predators; their reproductive and migratory patterns could also be altered and influence the food base of primary predators. Common frog tadpoles that had been treated with 0.5 to 0.6 μg DDT were exposed to warty newt predation. Newts made 167 lunges at treated tadpoles and were successful 43 times. They lunged at untreated tadpoles only 38 times and were successful 5 times (Cooke 1971). In a mosquitofish–largemouth bass prey/predator system, mosquitofish exposed to 0.01, 0.05, 0.1 ppm mercury suffered higher predation rates than fish exposed to 0.005 ppm and control fish (Kania and O'Hara 1974). In a simulated marine ecosystem with pinfish and grass shrimp, exposure to low (0.13 μg/l) doses of mirex resulted in lower survival of shrimp following 3 days of exposure to pinfish. Percentage survival of shrimp after 1 to 3 days of predation in the control tanks was 44, 16, and 24 percent while in the mirex-treated tank, survival of shrimp was 23.0 percent, and 4 percent on days 1, 2, and 3 (Tagatz, Borthwick, Ivey, et al. 1976).

Predator/prey transfer might even be important in the case of organophosphate exposure. Cricket frogs treated with 10 ppm parathion produced mortality in a kestrel being fed these frogs that contained 4.6 ppm (Fleming, de Chacin, Pattee, et al. 1982). As early as 1962, high residues of heptachlor epoxide, dieldrin, and BHC were reported in the liver of a kestrel in Britain. Concentrations were 44 ppm for heptachlor, 42 ppm of dieldrin, and 28.8 ppm of BHC (Moore and Ratcliffe 1962) In 1964, avian samples from the field in Britain showed higher DDE and dieldrin residues in fish-eating birds compared to flesh-eaters. Breast muscle residues in herons were about 12 ppm and in a sparrow hawk, about 4 ppm (Moore and Walker 1964).

Organochlorines

A thorough study of the ecosystem in Lake Michigan, including Green Bay, demonstrated the potential accumulation of organochlorine residues in the food chain. Sediments taken from 10 to 30 m contained an average of

0.014 ppm of DDT, DDE, and TDE. Amphipods, taken from deeper waters, had 30 times more organochlorine residues than the sediments; they averaged 0.41 ppm. Fish concentrations were about 10 times higher than amphipods. For alewife, wet weight residues were 3.35 ppm; for chubs, 4.52 ppm; and for whitefish, about 5.6 ppm. Herring gulls contained residues 29 times that found in alewives; they averaged 98.8 ppm wet weight in breast muscle. Fat residues in gulls were much higher; total residues averaged 2441 ppm (Hickey, Keith, and Coon 1966). Stickel (1968) prepared a thorough review of organochlorines in the environment in 1968.

Samples of white pelican and grebe tissues from the Klamath Basin were analyzed for 12 organochlorine compounds. Residues decreased from 1969 to 1981 in general, but DDE and PCB residues did not change. PCB residues varied between different colonies, indicating different wintering areas or migration routes. Pelican and grebe eggs had different PCB/DDE ratios, showing different routes of uptake from the environment. There was an increase in white pelican eggshell thickness between 1969 and 1981, but the 1981 shells were still thinner than those analyzed in 1947. Endrin was the cause of some pelican mortality between 1975 and 1981, but the endrin residues may have been accumulated outside the Klamath Basin (Boellstorff, Ohlendorf, Anderson, et al. 1985).

Mallard duck wing samples taken in 1980 were analyzed and high levels of PCB and DDE were found in certain locations in Arizona and New Mexico. Residues of DDE were about 17 times higher from the Verde and Gila River drainages, about 6.0 ppm on a wet weight basis. High levels of PCB and heptachlor were found in mallard wings from the Pecos and Rio Grande River drainages. No abnormally high residues were detected in mallard wings from Arkansas and Louisiana (Fleming and Cain 1985). Mean levels of DDE in duck wings were higher than 0.5 ppm in only three states in the 1981–82 sample; in Delaware, Alabama, and Arizona (Jacknow, Ludke, and Coon 1986).

Many of the common organochlorines that resulted in widespread contamination from the 1950s through 1970s are still being found in a variety of vertebrates, but at lower levels than in previous years. The long-term sampling of waterfowl wing samples have shown decreasing levels of DDE both in quantity and in positive samples analyzed. DDE still occurs (1981–82) more frequently than PCB. PCB has also declined, but residues in black duck wings from the northeastern United States were higher than those from the southeast along the Atlantic Flyway. Residues for both DDE and PCB differed among flyways and regions (Prouty and Bunck 1986).

Populations of brown pelicans along the Texas coast declined drastically in the mid-1950s to 1970 from about 5,000 to almost none. In 1975, there were 18 pairs and in 1981 they had increased to 57 pairs. All unhatched eggs analyzed still contained DDT metabolites and about 7 percent of the egg residues were considered high enough to potentially cause reproductive failure. PCB and DDE levels did not decline between 1975 and 1981, indicating continued sources of low-level contamination. Eggshells were 4 to 14 percent thinner than normal, but were not considered a cause of reproductive failure. The population is increasing (King, Blakinship, Payne, et al. 1985).

Black skimmers along the Texas and Mexican coasts had lower residues of DDE and PCB, about 2.0 and 1.0 ppm. DDE was found in all carcasses and ranged up to 10.0 ppm (White, Mitchell, and Stafford 1985).

During the nesting seasons of 1977 to 1980 in the Rocky Mountains, tree swallows had higher residues of DDE than 49 other small passerine prey species examined. Pooled samples from Oregon and Montana had a wet weight residue of 10.6 ppm, and swallows from Colorado had 18.0 ppm. This was compared to starlings with 0.1 ppm. Swallows were considered to present a potential hazard to birds of prey. About 3 percent of the breeding females died on the nest for no apparent reason (De Weese, Cohen, and Stafford 1985).

DDE levels are still causing potential reproductive problems in Cooper's hawk eggs in some locales. There was significant eggshell thinning in an egg from Connecticut, but not in eggs from four other states (Maryland, Michigan, Wisconsin, Pennsylvania) (Pattee, Fuller, and Kaiser 1985).

DDE residues in snail kite eggs have declined from about 0.33 ppm wet weight in 1966 to about 0.03 ppm in 1974 (Sykes 1985). Low levels of DDE residues have been found in a variety of avifauna and other wildlife on Guam, but they are below any harmful levels and the continued decline of bird fauna on Guam must be for other reasons (Grue 1985).

Organophosphates

The treatment of large areas of rangelands with organophosphates for grasshopper control could result in a hazard to avian predators that feed on these insects. Following treatment with malathion and acephate, residues in dead grasshoppers of 2.8 ppm of malathion were measured 30 to 54 hours after application. No malaoxon, a toxic metabolite of malathion, was found. Acephate residues were higher, about 8 to 9 ppm 4 hours after spraying, but the toxic metabolite methamidophos was also measured at 2.6 to 4.6 ppm. These residues suggested that malathion residues were probably not a hazard, but because the toxic metabolite of acephate was found, these residues may have been hazardous to insectivorous birds

(Stromborg, McEwen, and Lamont 1984). Aerial application of parathion to a marsh and a borrow pit in California resulted in mosquitofish residues of 3.1 to 26.4 ppm whole body (Mulla, Keith, and Gunther 1966).

One of the recent and perhaps most notable instances of heavy metal accumulation has been in the California condor, an endangered species. In 1986 there were 2 birds left in the wild and about 12 or so in captivity. Now, all have been taken into captivity for propagation and several eggs have been successfully hatched. Several deaths have been attributed to ingestion of lead from carcasses of wounded deer or other game species. Turkey vultures sampled in the area inhabited by the California condor do carry high levels of DDE and in one instance endrin. Of the few California condors analyzed, pesticides have not been a problem. Turkey vulture eggs are about 16 percent thinner than normal. Ravens in the same area are apparently not accumulating heavy metals nor pesticides. One condor found dead had 79 ppm lead in the tarsus. Several have died of lead poisoning (Wiemeyer, Jurek, and Moore 1986).

Heavy metals have been shown to accumulate in a variety of wildlife species that occur in areas near industrial point-source contamination. In Missouri, in the vicinity of large piles of tailings from inactive lead mines, five species of riparian vertebrates were sampled. These included the water snake, bullfrog, muskrat, green-backed heron, and rough-winged and bank swallows. Herons, frogs, and muskrats all showed higher lead levels below the contamination site. The water snake had higher lead residues, but did not seem to accumulate cadmium. Residues in the swallows did not seem to reflect the local contamination. The best species to sample for local contamination was the bullfrog. A composite sample of five bullfrog livers from the contaminated area contained 6.3 ppm wet weight lead, 5.0 ppm cadmium, and 49.3 ppm zinc. Bullfrogs are not good indicators of organochlorine contamination (Niethammer, Atkinson, Baskett, et al. 1985).

Raccoons taken from Shiawassee National Wildlife Refuge at the confluence of three industrially contaminated rivers in Michigan were assayed for heavy metals and organochlorine compounds. Liver residues from adults contained 1.0 mg/kg wet weight cadmium, 0.23 mg/kg lead, 1.60 mg/kg mercury, 2.22 mg/kg selenium, and 44.1 mg/kg zinc (Herbert and Peterle 1990). Kidney and brain residues were generally lower except for cadmium in kidneys.

Smelter sites and an ash pond of a coal-fired power plant have been studied to determine residues of elements in wildlife. Elements in a fly ash pond did accumulate to a higher level in sediment; molybdenum increased significantly, but residues did not appear at elevated levels in waterbirds sampled (primarily coots). A variety of species of animals were collected in the vicinity of a zinc smelter in Pennsylvania; shrews had the highest lead levels (110 mg/kg), followed by songbirds (56 mg/kg), and then mice, carrion insects, moths, and fungi. Continued build-up of elements in the pond should be monitored (White, King, Mitchell, et al. 1986). Cadmium was highest in carrion insects, then fungi and shrews. Zinc and copper followed similar patterns to cadmium. Shrews had higher levels than mice (Beyer, Pattee, Sileo, et al. 1985). Deer had high concentrations of cadmium (372 ppm) and zinc (600 ppm) in renal tissue. Lead levels were lower (Sileo and Beyer 1985).

Heavy metal accumulation in soils, vegetation, and animals in roadside habitats was related to traffic volume. Shrews had higher body burdens of lead, cadmium, nickel, and zinc than herbivores such as white-footed mice (Scanlon 1979).

Florida manatees had low levels of organochlorines and some heavy metals, but residues of copper in the liver were the highest ever found in a free-ranging mammal. As a result of high herbicidal copper usage to control aquatic weeds, liver residues in manatees were as high as 1200 ppm dry weight. Levels may be sufficiently high to cause toxic effects when compared to other mammal species (O'Shea, Moore, and Kochman 1984).

RESISTANCE

There have been some discussions and suggestions that pest control practices either by convention or by law should be altered to avoid the development of continued resistance in insects. Some chemical manufacturers and applicators object to added regulation of pesticide use related to this prevention of resistance in insects.

Resistance can develop as a result of genetic selection, biochemical changes, changes in susceptibility at the contact site, or knock-down resistance (KDR) and combinations of mechanisms (Brattsten, Holyoke, Leeper, et al. 1986). Some insects, as a result of development of resistance, are able to extend their diversity of feeding on plant hosts in terms of being able to overcome the new host plant allelochemicals. This allows insects to move to new plants and present additional plant–pest problems.

Resistance first must be controlled by documenting the incidence. Some resistance can be alleviated by using mixutres of chemicals or synergists, and alteration of dose patterns, timing, and sequence of treatments to alter the pest insects' responses. Integrated pest management is also considered beneficial in terms of prevention of resistance development. Some (Dover and Croft 1986) have suggested changes in the philosophy of the regulatory agencies in terms of added direct regulation such as prescription treatments, while others (Delp 1986) have argued that the pesticide industry and users are already overregulated and they are already sensitive to the resistance problem. Because FIFRA requires a risk/benefit analysis, part of the risk considered should be the added cost and loss that results from insect resistance. In 1970 there were 313 insect species that were resistant to some chemicals in some parts of their range; by 1980 the number had grown to 829 species (Dover and Croft 1986). Clearly, some action must be taken to prevent the further rapid growth in resistance. Whether this is done by voluntary means by users and producers or by legal regulations remains to be seen.

Reistance to toxic substances, particularly pesticides, is worldwide and develops from the repeated exposure of individuals and populations to lethal and sublethal concentrations of the toxic substance. Selection might be based on sensitivity to the toxin, rates of and development of metabolism, and avoidance either through behavior or geographic modification, storage in non-target sites, and enhanced excretion.

Because of rapid population turnover times, most resistance has developed in invertebrate populations. Between 1970 and 1980 the number of resistant insect species nearly doubled from 224 to 448. Cross resistance to two or three insecticides is now more common. Among pests of cotton, 25 species are resistant in 36 countries, and mosquitoes show resistance to pesticides in 84 countries (Sun 1984). There was some resistance among invertebrates to the old lime, arsenical, and sulfur insecticides used in the early 1900s.

Resistance to DDT was reported as early as 1947 following its first widespread use in 1942. Sometimes there is cross resistance between and within classes of compounds, but not always. DDT provides cross resistance to methoxychlor, but not to lindane or dieldrin (O'Brien 1967). The organophosphates induce resistance very slowly and not to the same extent as the organochlorines. House flies may be 7 times more resistant to parathion, but as much as 3000 times resistant to DDT. Selection for resistance is apparently for a dehydrochlorinase and resistance is maintained through generations, but resistance to organophosphates is lost over time.

Resistance developed very rapidly in some pest species. In the tobacco budworm, the minimum lethal doses in mg/g in 1961 for DDT, endrin, and carbaryl was 0.13, 0.16, and 0.30 respectively; in 1965, it was 16.5, 12.94, and 54.57 (Adkisson, Niles, Walker, et al. 1982). The carrot rust fly is 5600 times resistant to aldrin (Stickel 1975).

Resistance among the vertebrates is not so evident and has developed slowly. Most examples have been aquatic species that occur in high treatment areas such as in cotton areas of the south. Resistance has been reported in mosquitofish, golden shiner, bluegill, green sunfish, and in yellow and black bullhead (Ferguson 1967). Resistant mosquitofish can withstand exposure to 1000 ppb of endrin for 3 weeks, the normal 48-hour TLM is 1.0 ppb. Cricket frogs and toads in southern cotton fields are up to 100 times resistant to DDT and to toxaphene, aldrin, and dieldrin in varying amounts (Ferguson and Gilbert 1967).

In some cities, rats have become resistant to frequent exposures to the anticoagulant warfarin. In a survey of 98 cities, 45 percent responded that 10 to 20 percent of the rat population was resistant to warfarin (Mlot 1985).

Even with highly lethal poisons such as 1080 used to control pest vertebrates in New Zealand, resistance has been reported. Normal rabbits and possums would have to find and eat 4.2 to 8.4 carrot baits treated with 1080 to produce 99 percent mortality. Individuals in resistant populations would have to consume 6.5 to 15.6 baits to produce a similar mortality (Batcheler 1982).

Resistance has been reported in a wide variety of animal species and plants such as arthropods, rodents, weeds, plant pathogens, and nematodes (Mlot 1985).

6

Lethal Effects on Organisms

GENERAL CONSIDERATIONS

The determination of lethal effects of toxins on wildlife in the laboratory has provided information on the relative toxicity of various compounds; the sensitivity of a diversity of species tested; the influence of diets and routes of administration; and the variance in response due to sex, age, and reproductive status. Because of these results, the extrapolation of laboratory toxicity tests to the field is, in most instances, uncertain and inadvisable. The discussion and publication of toxicity data are frequently presented with a variety of abbreviations related to the type of testing, species, routes of administration, and effects. Table 6.1 is presented to include a basis for further discussion of lethal effects through the utilization of appropriate abbreviations.

The LD-50 is the most common unit of toxicity data available for most species and compounds. This dose level is reached for all compounds when ACk_x = constant (Hansch and Fujita 1964, Hansch 1969). A describes the probability of the toxic substance reaching the target tissue or organ, C is the external concentration, and K_x is a rate constant that describes the affinity for the target. Lien (1985) refined these notions by defining QUSAR analysis; quantitative structure-activity relationships. Weil (1952) has provided convenient tables for LD-50 or ED-50 calculations. These factors all relate to the basic information needed to describe toxicity; the rate of application or availability, the effectiveness of reaching the target, and the reaction once the substance is taken into the organism. Tests involve acute doses of the compound given orally by gavage, ipr, ims, or ivn. Most testing with wildlife does not involve inhalation or dosing by other routes.

There are some general considerations related to laboratory testing of toxic effects that are applicable to both lethal and chronic exposures. The species to be tested is sometimes dictated by the needs of the agency,

Table 6-1 Key to Abbreviations

Route of Administration

ice—intracerebral
icv—intracervical
idr—intradermal
idu—intraduodenal
ihl—inhalation
imp—implant
ims—intramuscular
ipc—intraplacental
ipl—intrapleural
ipr—intraperitoneal
irn—intrarenal

itr—intratracheal
ivg—intravaginal
ivn—intravenous
ocu—ocular
orl—oral
par—parenteral
rec—rectal
scu—subcutaneous
skn—skin
unk—unreported

Toxic Effects

ALR—allergic effects
BCM—blood clotting mechanism effects
BLD—blood effects
BPR—blood pressure effects
CAR—carcinogenic effects
CNS—central nervous system effects
COR—corrosive effects
CUM—cumulative effects
CVS—cardiovascular effects
DDP—drug dependence effects
EYE—eye effects
GIT—gastrointestinal tract effects
GLN—glandular effects
IRR—irritant effects
MMI—mucous membrane effects

MSK—musculo-skeletal effects
MUT—mutagenic effects
NEO—neoplastic effects
PNS—peripheral nervous system effects
PUL—pulmonary system effects
RBC—red blood cell effects
SKN—skin effects
SYS—systemic effects
TER—teratogenic effects
TFX—toxic effects
TXDS—qualifying toxic dose
UNS—toxic effects unspecified in source
WBC—white blood cell effects

Animal Species

bdw—wild bird species
bird (other domestic or lab)
cat—cat
chd—child
ckn—chicken
cattle
dck—duck
dog—dog
dom—domestic (all other)
frg—frog
gpg—guinea pig more than 50% of food

hm—hamster
hmn—human
mam—mammal (species unspecified)
mky—monkey
mus—mouse
pgn—pigeon
pig—pig
qal—quail
rat—rat
rbt—rabbit
sql—squirrel
tod—toad

Table 6-1 Key to Abbreviations *(continued)*

grb—gerbil
trk—turkey

wmn—woman

Data Description

ALD—lowest published lethal concentration dose

LC-50—lethal concentration 50 percent kill

LD-50—lethal dose 50 percent kill

LC-Lo—lowest published lethal concentration in air

LDLo—lowest published lethal concentration level–dose

TCLo—lowest published toxic concentration in air

TDLo—lowest published toxic dose

FR—food reduction intake

REP—percentage refusing to eat more than 50% of food

LDFR—amount of chemical ingested during food reduction

Units of Measure

d—deci
c—centi
m—milli
u—micro prefixes for 10 to 10x
n—nano
p—pico
f—femto
a—atto
g—gram
kg—kilogram

M—cubic meter
mg—milligram
ng—nanogram
pg—picogram
ppb—parts per billion (v/v)
pph—parts per hundred (v/v) (percent)
ppm—parts per million (v/v)
ppt—parts per trillion (v/v)
μg—microgram

Units of Time

'—minute
C—continuous
D—day

W—week
I—intermittent
Y—year

Adapted from Christensen, H. E. (ed.). 1973.

Some Abbreviations Related to Toxicity Testing

LD-50—Dose to kill 50 percent of the test animals

LC-50—Concentration in food or water necessary to kill 50% test animals

LT-50—Time to kill at a specific concentration

TC-50—Threshold concentration to produce specific toxic effect in some time frame

TL_m—Tolerance level median, may be given as 96-hr, 47-hr, or 24-hr, used for temperature, oxygen, etc.

(continued)

Table 6-1 Key to Abbreviations *(continued)*

ED-50—effective dose to produce certain response in half the test animals
EC-50—median effective concentration
$LC_{50}s$—lethal concentration applied to surface, usually to eggs
MFO—mixed function oxidases—usually in liver tissues
TLV—threshold limit value to produce certain effect
LOEC—lowest observed effect concentration
NOEC—no observed effect concentration level
TL-50—tolerance level of certain effect for half the animals tested
T—toxic
NT—non-toxic
PT—partially toxic
B—bioassay
S—static test
CF—continuous flow aquatic test
A—acute
CH—chronic
L—laboratory test
F—field test
SB—sub–lethal test
NTE—no toxic effect (define effect)
CR—critical range in ppm, usually 24-hr test, half must remain alive
MATC—maximum acceptable toxicant concentration
IV—intravenous injection
IP—intraperitoneal injection
ELS—early life stage
LD-50 is reached when ACK_x = constant
A = factor of probability of compound reaching target
C = external concentration
K_x = rate constant related to affinity for target
EEC—estimated environment concentration
MEEC—Maximum expected environmental concentration

company, or the direct purpose of the test such as for registration. Normally, wildlife species suggested by USEPA are mallard, bobwhite, pheasant, and any mammal species expected to be affected. Avian test species are obtained from commercial breeders; mammals are usually obtained by live-trapping in the field. There may be a question of the genetic history of the test animals, but in an LD-50 test of diazinon on eight different game farm stocks of bobwhites, no differences were found to be attributable to the different stocks (Hill, Camardese, Heinz, et al. 1984). Animals taken from the wild for testing may have had prior exposure or perhaps in rare instances may have been selected for reistance.

The age of the animal can influence the effects of the toxicant; for avian testing the species recommended should be at least 16 weeks of age. Sexual differences are sometimes apparent in lethal testing and the influence of the reproductive status should be considered. The physical condition of the animals is also important, particularly as it relates to liposoluble compounds. The route of administration of the test chemical also influences the result. Doses may be administered by gavage, by capsule, or injected for LD-50 tests; or in foods and/or water for LC-50 or for chronic exposure studies (Bascietto 1985). Absorption across the gut may vary related to the compound being tested as well as the carrier. Toxic substances incorporated into natural foods will provide different results than if given in a solvent or corn oil carrier. Woodcock dosed with heptachlor as a wettable powder in a capsule or in corn oil or butter oil survived doses of 708 mg/kg. Half of those fed 2.86 ppm in earthworms died in 35 days (Stickel, Hayne, and Stickel 1965). Some wild species are capable of passing toxic substances dissolved in oil through the gut without appreciable absorption and other species are capable of regurgitating doses given orally. The physical holding conditions may also affect toxic testing: whether animals are held singly or in groups; and the ambient temperature, humidity, and light.

Hill and Hoffman (1984) have provided a review of avian models for toxicity testing. They conclude that birds are excellent models for toxicity testing because they are abundant, highly visible, and they occur in a great variety of habitats. One potential effect of holding birds in captivity, at least for some species, is the alteration in the length of the caecum as a result of changes in diet. Red grouse held in captivity for four generations showed a 52 percent decrease in the length of the caeca and 72 percent decrease in the length of the small intestine (Moss 1972). Such changes in morphology could influence the uptake and retention of toxic substances in captive birds that would vary from wild birds. Birds may also show an aversion to treated food, resulting in anorexia (Grue 1982).

Another important factor in toxicity testing is the actual mixture, isomer, or formulation used for the test. In most instances this is the formulated product that is applied to the field, but in other instances the manufactured product is used, the compound that is purchased by formulators for the final mixture sold in the retail market. On occasion it seems most appropriate to test the nearly pure compound if it is available.

AQUATIC SYSTEMS

Testing for lethal effects in aquatic systems has been well developed and voluminous literature is available on techniques, various species, and results. Toxicity, methodology, residues, and kinetics of pesticides in fish have been reviewed (Murty 1986). Another thorough review was provided by Cairns, Dickson, and Maki in 1978.

For aquatic vertebrate testing, both warm- and cold-water fish are used, usually the rainbow trout and the bluegill, but many other species have also been utilized. Goldfish or carp are not recommended because of their relative tolerance to some toxic substances. Fathead minnows have been used widely and much information is available on early life stage testing and life cycle testing.

Cairns (1986) has discussed the fallacy in attempting to select a most sensitive species for toxicity testing. Intake though the water or in food produces different results and the retention of toxins in the body varies with the route of intake (Jarvinen, Hoffman, and Thorslund 1976).

Water quality is important as is the oxygen content, pH, and temperature. Suggested temperatures for warm-water fish and DO are 25 to 2°C and 4 mg/l and 15 to 2°C and 5 mg/l.

Static tank tests or continuous flow tests can be used; both have advantages and disadvantages. In static tank tests, there is concern about the adsorption of the test chemical to the tank, volatilization, accumulation of wastes, and the maintenance of water quality during the test. In continuous flow systems, monitoring the toxin into the water is sometimes a problem, and the cost and disposal of waste water must be considered. Volatility from the surface is of concern, especially in static tank tests. Growth of microbiological organisms in the tanks and disease are factors to be considered that could alter the test results. The number of fish to be held in each tank and the contents of the tank in terms of refuge areas are important. Dominance within the tank can alter uptake by individual fish in the tank. The protocol must indicate whether waste material is to be removed, kind and amount of aeration, and any replenishment of water in the tank.

In flow-through systems, the rate of flow must be determined, particularly if it alters the swimming rate of the test fish or alters the ventilation rate. The time of exposure for most lethal tests is 24, 48, 72, or 96 hours. The solubility of the test compound in water is important and if a solvent is used, the effect of this chemical on the test results must be determined. Treatment of the fish prior to the test must also be considered in terms of disease and parasite removal, temperature acclimation, and state of nutrition. Cost is usually a factor in any testing program. Static tank tests are less costly, but may not produce adequate test data.

The major advantage of constant-flow systems is that the level of exposure remains constant and in some instances, the flow-through system is more representative of the habitat of the species being tested. The shape and size of the system determine rates of water use and ultimate costs of cleanup of toxic chemicals from the waste water. Flow rates are related to mixing and influence the test fish in terms of energy consumption and ventillation rates, that in turn may alter uptake and metabolism of the test chemical. Various mechanisms have been devised to meter the chemical into the system at a constant rate and include various pumps (usually backed up with secondary sources of power in the event of a power outage), siphons, drip systems, desorbtion from rock surfaces, and gravity feeds. A wide selection of systems is available and cost and reliability are the most important considerations. Water quality, both chemical and physical, must be monitored throughout the test program. Fish species selected for testing are related to potential commercial or sport value, forage fish value, potential exposure to the compound, availability, ease of holding and rearing in the laboratory, geographical distribution, and prior knowledge concerning sensitivity to various substances. Some species used for toxic substance testing include threadfin shad, brook and rainbow trout, northern pike, emerald shiner, fathead minnow, white sucker, channel catfish, white bass, bluegill, largemouth bass, and perch.

Many of the considerations necessary for adequate vertebrate aquatic testing also apply to testing aquatic invertebrates. One added dimension is the selection of the life stage to be tested; some invertebrates are highly sensitive to toxins in some life stages and resistant in others. Temperature may be a more critical factor for invertebrates and tanks should be maintained at normal environmental temperatures to which the species are adapted.

Some aquatic invertebrates commonly tested include copepods, shrimp, crab, oyster, polychaetes, daphnids, amphipods, crayfish, stonefly, caddisfly, mayfly, midges, snails, and planaria.

AVIAN SYSTEMS

A wide variety of species have been utilized in avian testing programs but the most common, and those recommended by USEPA are the mallard, bobwhite, and the pheasant. Coturnix quail have also been used with some frequency and most of these species were selected because of their ease in rearing, their wide distribution, and value for sport hunting. All three species used with regular frequency are available from commercial breeders with known genetic histories.

Considerations for testing include whether the tests or holding pens are in- or outdoors; acclimation to the pens; size, shape, and numbers of birds per pen; pretreatment for diseases or parasites; condition; weight; age and reproductive status; and the fasting program prior to administration of the test compound. The route of administration is important; the carrier and diet at the time of treatment could influence results.

Birds are usually fasted for 15 hours prior to treatment. LC-50 tests are influenced by the carrier and the mixture of food used. Birds may also reject food as a result of taste aversion or illness (Bennett and Schafer 1988, Grue 1982).

FAC-50 (food avoidance concentration), WAC-50 (water avoidance concentration), and EAI (effective avoidance index) have been suggested by Kononen, Hochstein, and Ringer (1987). The higher the EAI (LC-50/FAC-50 or WLC-50/WAC-50), the greater the margin of safety for the toxin.

LC-50 tests are usually done over a 5-day period and total food consumption should be measured to determine nutritional status and intake of the test chemical. Cross contamination of feed and water is of concern, especially in mallards held indoors. Precontamination of feed should also be checked. Some feeds are already contaminated with low levels of some chlorinated compounds. Birds are usually 16 weeks or older when tested. Carriers preferred are water if the chemical is soluble, or corn oil, glycol, and methyl cellulose. The total dose administered should not be more than 0.1 to 1.0 percent of the total body weight and may be given by gavage or by gelatin capsule, or if for LC-50, in treated food. Food should be treated to insure the chemical is uniformly mixed through the pellet, mash, or grain used. Usually a minimum of a 14-day observation period is used for both LD-50 and LC-50 tests. Birds are randomly assigned to treatment. Lighting may be in 16:8 LD cycles or may be continuous. Some test results show that lighting has little effect on test results for some species. Disturbances should be held to a minimum and standard cage and space requirements should minimize cage stress. USEPA has provided complete guides to avian LD-50 testing (Bascietto 1985). In addition to the three common species recommended by USEPA and *Coturnix,* others that have been tested include ring doves, king pigeons, other species of waterfowl, grouse, kestrels, eagles, screech owls, starlings, grackles, cowbirds, redwings, finches, gulls, and some seabirds.

MAMMALS

Mammals used in test programs for wildlife models have been few and most information is on the laboratory mouse, rat, and dog. USEPA simply suggests testing mammals that are to be exposed (Farringer 1985). Many of the considerations for testing avian species also apply to mammals. Laboratory practices and holding facilities are all recommended and described in the *Federal Register* and in USEPA documents (Farringer 1985).

There is greater concern for testing wild species that are live-trapped for use. Test groups are more variable, their past history is unknown, and there is greater potential for disease and parasite problems. Most wild-trapped mammals to be used for testing are held in isolation for 14 days and maintained in facilities separate from laboratory animal holding facilities. Animals are fasted before treatment and weighed to determine condition before and after testing.

Food aversion is also a problem with mammals as a result of both taste and smell. For mammals, the total dose given by gavage or orally is never more than 3 percent of the body weight. House and deer mice were tested in the laboratory for the repellency and acute oral toxicity of 933 chemicals. Approximate lethal dose, amount of food reduction, and the number of mice refusing to eat should be considered in estimating hazard indexes for wild mammals (Schafer and Bowles 1985).

LABORATORY VERSUS FIELD TESTING

Both field and laboratory testing may be appropriate for LD-50 and LC-50 tests. The advantages of trials in the laboratory include the control of physical factors, disturbances, and possible introduction of diseases, parasites, or predation. There is little interaction among the test animals, there are no extraneous foods, and dosages can be completely controlled. Field tests have the advantage of being closer to actual conditions in the environment, and wild or pen-reared animals may be more adapted to field testing and show less pen or cage stress. In field testing, usually tops must be provided to prevent avian predation, extraneous foods are available, dosages cannot be closely controlled, and diseases and parasites can become a problem. Extraneous disturbances are also possible that might result in direct losses or they might influence the test results.

There has been some work with the use of wild trapped birds and subsequent effects monitored by radiotelemetry. This is an interesting and potentially very useful technique but costs and sample sizes can be a problem. The prior history or possible pre-exposure of the test animals is not known. In terms of ultimately determining what some of the observed subtle chronic effects have on populations and recruitment, perhaps the use of telemetry might be an appropriate way to obtain useful information.

Delayed Effects

In field or laboratory testing, delayed effects must be considered, particularly in LC-50 tests of long duration. Delayed effects that might be of concern are related to nutritional stress, migration, dispersal, and reproduction. It would be difficult to assess the potential for delayed effects using LD-50 or LC-50 tests, but some combinations of toxic substances and physical parameters such as temperature, wetting, or nutritional stress might be useful.

EXAMPLES OF LETHAL EFFECTS

In aquatic systems, rotenone has been widely used to control undesirable fish species. Sensitivity varies widely. The ostracod *Cypridopsis,* the most sensitive of the invertebrate species tested, has a 96-hr LC-50 of 0.34 ng/l. More resistant invertebrates are the snail (*Heliosoma*) and the Asiatic clam (*Corbicula*) at 7.95 ng/l and 7.50 ng/l, respectively (Chandler and Marking 1982). The LC-50 for leopard frog larva was 0.5 ng/l. Fish species are highly sensitive to rotenone and there is some variation in sensitivity by species: carp 0.05 ng/l, 96-hr LC-50; bullhead, 0.39; catfish 0.164; bluegill 0.141; and largemouth bass, 0.142 ng/l 96-hr LC-50. Some aquatic invertebrates are sensitive to mirex at 2 to 3 ppb and some of the newer synthetic pyrethroids are lethal to aquatic invertebrates in the parts per trillion level (Eisler 1985a, Leahey 1985). Fathead minnows fed diets containing varied quantities of fat were tested with endrin for LC-50 levels. Those fed low-fat diets were 2.4 times more susceptible to endrin intoxication than those on high-fat diets. Fish that were starved for various periods of time were also more susceptible, about 2 times (Dave 1981). Because fish species show wide diversity in lethal responses, DDT was not recommended as a standard toxicant for bioassays (Marking 1966). The mean LC-50 for largemouth bass was 0.8 ppb; for northern redbelly bass, 68.0 ppb.

Avian testing programs have shown differences between LD-50 and LC-50 tests for a variety of compounds. Ten test compounds were administered to mallards in LD-50 and LC-50 trials. The results (Table 6.2) show some interesting changes in sensitivity.

For some toxins such as endrin there is little difference; the compound is highly toxic whether the bird might obtain it in a single dose or over a period of time. The most obvious compound for concern in the list of those

Table 6-2 Mallard LD-50 and LC-50 Test Results

Compound	Subacute Rank	Subacute LC-50 (ppm)	Acute Rank	Acute LD-50 (mg/kg)
Endrin	1	22	1	5.6
Aldrin	2	155	5	520
Dieldrin	3	169	4	381
Heptachlor	4	480	?	≥ 2000
Toxaphene	5	538	3	71
Chlordane	6	858	6	1200
Endosulfan	7	1053	2	33
DDT	8	1869	?	> 2240
Aroclor 1254	9	2699	?	>> 2000
Mirex	10	< 5000	?	> 2400

Adapted from Heinz, Hill, Stickel, et al. 1979. Environmental contaminant studies by the Patuxent Wildlife Research Center. Am. Soc. for Test. Mat. Spec. Tech. Pub. 693, pp. 9–35. Copyright ASTM. Reprinted with permission.

tested is endosulfan, where availability on or in foodstuffs over a short period of time would result in lower mortality than a high dose available at a single point in time. The same is true for toxaphene. Because of different rates of metabolism, or lack of absorption across the gut, some compounds are less toxic when added to food or given in lower doses over periods of time. In chronic studies, rates of metabolism can change as a result of MFO induction. Among four organophosphates tested with mallard ducklings, fensulfothion produced the greatest reduction in cholinesterase (ChE) activity and malathion the least change (Fleming and Bradbury 1981). The four most common avian laboratory test species were given LC-50 doses of four common toxic substances. In general, the bobwhite was the most sensitive of the four species tested (Heath, Spann, Hill, et al. 1972). See Table 6.3 for complete test results. Despite the close systematic relationship among three of the bird species, their sensitivity to the toxins is quite different.

Acute toxicities of 13 pesticides were determined for six species of birds including mallard, pheasant, coturnix, common pigeon partridge, and house sparrow. The average range of LD-50 values was almost 10-fold, suggesting that extrapolation of toxicity data across species should be avoided (Tucker and Haegele 1971).

Twenty avian species, always including the redwing and starling, were tested for toxic responses to 369 chemicals. The redwing seemed more sensitive to toxins than the starling, and both species were more sensitive

Table 6-3 Relative Toxicities of Some Chemicals to Birds

Species	PCB (1254)	Ceresan M	Chlordane	DDE	Endrin	Parathion	Dasanit
Bobwhite	604	57	331	825	14	194	35
Coturnix	2898	100	350	1355	18	44	—
Pheasant	1091	146	430	841	14	365	148
Mallard	2699	50	858	3572	22	275	43

Values are test compound LC-50s in ppm. Heath, Spann, Hill, et al. 1972, Comparative dietary toxicities to birds. U.S. Fish and Wild. Serv. Spec. Sci. Rpr. No. 152, 57 pp. Five-day diets, ten-week old birds.

than the rat (Schafer 1972). In later tests of 998 chemicals, the redwing was found to be the most sensitive of the avian species tested and may be used to test various chemicals' potentials for poisoning episodes (Schafer, Bowles, and Hurlbut 1983).

LD-50 studies of a selected group of 41 pesticides (insecticides, acaracides, fungicides, nematocides, and herbicides) were tested with the red and grey partridge in France. As a general observation, the red partridge was more resistant to most of the toxicants. For some pesticides, the LD-50 dose was quite similar, but for others the dose to produce lethal effects was two or more times greater or sometimes less (see Table 6.4). For example, phosphamidon produced an LD-50 for grey partridge of 7.8 mg/kg; for the red partridge, it was 21.7, nearly three times greater. In some instances the opposite was true; the red partridge was more susceptible. Even though these two species are in different genera it would seem that the LD-50 dosages should be more consistent. Why the red partridge should generally be more resistant to these pesticides is unknown (Grolleau and Caritez 1986).

Lethal residues in the brain were determined for four species of passerines treated with the aroclor, PCB 1254. Dosages of 1500 ppm were given daily until 50 percent of the animals on treatment died. For all species, residues of 310 ppm in the brain (w/w) was indicative of death. Residues in the brains of starlings were lower (367–469 ppm) than the average for the other three species (579 ppm): the grackle, red-winged blackbird, and cowbird (Stickel, Stickel, Dyrland, et al. 1984a). This was true for oxychlordane and nonachlor as well (Stickel, Stickel, Dyrland et al. 1983). Long-term LC-50 studies for some compounds also show accumulation in the brain sufficient to cause death. Kestrels treated with 2.8 ppm DDE in the diet died after 14 to 16 months with brain residues of 213 and 301 ppm (Porter and Weimeyer 1972). In short- and long-term

Table 6-4 LD-50 Values for Pesticides Tested on Red and
Gray Partridges

Pesticide	Grey Partridge (mg/kg)	Red Partridge (mg/kg)
More Lethal for Grey		
Aldicarb	4.5	6.7
Dimethoate	27.4	83.2
Formothion	165.7	312
Monocrotophos	1.8	4.6
Phosphamidon	7.8	21.7
Trichlorfon	110	249
More Lethal for Red		
Carbaryl	1870.5	1261.3
Fonofos	43.1	29.2
Ethyl parathion	157	48.1

Adapted from Grolleau and Caritez 1986. Toxicity, by oral
administration, of various pesticides to grey partridge and the red
partridge. Gibier. Faune Sauv. 3(2):185–196.

dosage of cowbirds, about 66 ppm (wet weight) DDT plus DDD in the brain
was indicative of death (Stickel, Stickel, and Christensen 1966).

The LC-50 for mirex in female starlings, red-winged blackbirds, and
cowbirds was reached in 9 to 12 days at 750 ppm in the diet. The brain
residue at death was 292 ppm geometric mean (w/w), and birds that died 1
to 15 days post-treatment ranged from 235 to 422 ppm in the brain (Stickel,
Gaylen, Dyland, et al. 1973). Bald eagles treated with about 80 ppm DDT
in the diet would probably die in 3 to 4 months and brain residues (DDT,
DDD) were 58 to 86 ppm in five birds that died on high dosages (Stickel,
Chura, Stewart, et al. 1966). Mallard ducklings and kestrels treated in the
laboratory in toxicity tests were more susceptible when held at low temperatures to some toxins and some dosages (Fleming, Heinz, Franson, et
al. 1985; Rattner and Franson 1984).

There is ample field evidence of lethal effects of organochlorine and
organophosphate insecticides. Brain residues are usually used to determine cause of death for organochlorines and for organophosphates. Decreases of 50 percent or more in ChE activities in the brain are indicative of
poisoning. Despite the cancellation of a number of the organochlorines,
lethal effects are still evident in a number of locations across the country.
Heptachlor has decreased productivity and caused mortality of Canada

geese (Blus, Henny, Lenhart, et al. 1984) and kestrels (Henny, Blus, and Stafford 1983) in the northwestern United States and the use of endrin to control grasshoppers and cutworms threatened the closure of the waterfowl season in 17 states (*Fish and Wildlife News* 1981).

Considerable effort has been made to understand the relationships between organochlorine body burdens and mortality in fish-eating birds, particularly herons. The most frequently found residues in carcasses of dead herons, mostly great blues, was DDE. Dieldrin was considered the most common direct cause of death. Other organochlorines found included PCBs, endrin, mirex, toxaphene, TDE, and HCB. Residues in dead birds from both coasts, the south, and the Great Lakes were analyzed (Ohlendorf, Swineford, and Locke 1981). Great blue herons from the Great Lakes states of Minnesota, Illinois, and Wisconsin had brain residues of dieldrin (wet weight) of 6.0 to 14.0 ppm. Samples were collected from 1972–1979 (Ohlendorf, Swineford, and Locke 1979). Organochlorines not only caused direct mortality in herons but also reduced reproductive success through eggshell thinning. Eggs from 243 clutches of black-crowned night-heron nests were analyzed for organochlorine contamination. Residues from eggs taken in 1972–1973 were highest from Long Island rookeries, DDE residues of 7.0 ppm wet weight in eggs. Lowest residues were from Florida, 0.30 ppm. PCBs were highest from Massachusetts, 21.0 ppm, and lowest from Florida rookeries, 0.14 ppm. Eggshells were 9.3 percent thinner in Massachusetts and 7.1 percent thinner in the New York region (Ohlendorf, Klaas, and Kaiser 1978). The contaminant most closely correlated with eggshell thinning was DDE ($r = 0.431$). Point sources of pollution in Alabama, New Mexico, and Arizona have caused high residues of DDE/DDT in birds. High PCB levels have been found in waterfowl in New York and New Jersey (Fleming, Clark, and Hennry 1983). Direct mortality as a result of organochlorine treatment was evident in an area treated with dieldrin. A survey for dead animals resulted in postmortem analyses of brain residues in a variety of wildlife species (Table 6.5). Deaths were presumed to be associated with dieldrin exposure from field treatments or industrial exposure.

Birds of prey and fish-eating birds in the Netherlands had high levels of chlorinated hydrocarbons in their bodies as early as 1964 (Koeman and Van Genderen 1969). Populations of spoonbills and terns along the Dutch coast probably declined as a result of environmental contamination by insecticides. Liver residues of dieldrin in spoonbills was as high as 6.1 ppm, and 9.1 ppm in livers of common tern.

In 1970–1971, cormorants were found dead in the Biesbosch Estuary of the Rhine and anlyzed for PCB residues. In dead birds PCBs in brain tissue were 190.0 ppm mean, wet weight, and in liver 319.0 ppm. Five birds held

Table 6-5 Brain Residues (ppm w/w) of Dieldrin in
Dead Wildlife[a]

Species	N	Geometric Mean (ppm)
Meadowlark	5	9.26
Starling	2	12.5
Robin	7	9.6
Woodcock	2	7.5
Cottonrat (hispid)	5	7.92
Cottontail	5	13.78
Shoveler	—	10.20
Greenwing	—	9.0
Lesser scaup	—	7.7, 10.6, 13.3, 16.0
Kestrel	—	9.8, 12.0
Barn owl	—	8.1
Buteo	—	4.4

[a] *Geometric means if more than one sample.*
Adapted from several tables in Stickel, Stickel, and Spann 1969.

in captivity were fed total doses of 2.3 to 9.1g of chlophen A60. Survival time was 55 days at minimum, and 124 days maximum (dosage 200 to 500 ppm per day). Brain residues ranged from 76 to 180 ppm and in liver 210 to 290 ppm wet weight. High body burdens and cold spring weather were suggested as causes of mortality (Koeman, VanVelzen-Blad, De-Vries et al. 1973).

The induction of toxicity by natural light is important related to the low-level exposure to polycyclic aromatic hydrocarbons (PAH) residues found in many aquatic environments. Enhanced photo-induced toxicity occurs in invertebrates, such as *Daphnia,* other plankton species, and fish, but not to phytoplankton such as green algae (Oris, Giesy, Alred, et al. 1984).

Most organophospates do not generally produce primary or secondary toxic effects in vertebrates if applied at recommended doses. The compound famphur is used as a topical treatment on cattle to prevent infestations of warble flies. Lethal effects were observed in the black-billed magpie that picks hair from the backs of treated cattle and also in red-tailed hawks in a form of secondary poisoning as a result of feeding on magpies. Cow hair taken from gizzards of affected magpies had residues of 4,600 ppm famphur. It has been suggested that magpie populations in some western states were reduced between 1968 and 1979, when famphur was used extensively as a topical treatment on cattle (Henny, Blus, Kolbe, et al. 1985). A bald eagle has also been found dead as a result of secondary famphur poisoning.

Indirect lethal effects of feeding on pelletized rodenticides have been demonstrated in California quail. Crops were found to be impacted with parrafin-treated pellets and birds starved to death. There was little impact of the rodenticide (Rozol) directly (Blus, Henny, and Grove 1985).

Furadan, a carbamate used on a variety of crops, has been implicated in mass deaths of a variety of birds, largely as a result of misuse and overuse. Thousands of waterfowl have been killed as a result of exposure to furadan granules used in alfalfa, vegetable, and grain fields. In one treated Texas rice field, 106 individuals of 11 species of birds were found dead. Analyses showed that ChE levels were about 30 percent reduced in dead birds compared to controls. Rice seed contained 22 to 91 ppm wet weight of furadan (Flickinger, Mitchell, White, et al. 1986). Long-billed curlews have been found to be contaminated by organochlorines and some mortality as well as possible reproductive effects have been suggested in Oregon. Curlews obtain pesticide residues on their wintering grounds as well as in breeding areas (Blus, Henny, and Krynitsky 1985a).

LETHAL EFFECTS IN THE FIELD

Birds

Endrin was still being used to treat orchards for rodent control in 1983. As a result of treatment with this highly toxic substance, a variety of wildlife species were found dead. Brain residues of over 0.8 ppm (w/w) were found in postmortem analyses of California quail, chukar partridge, barn owl, saw whet owl, flicker, goshawk, Cooper's hawk, sharp-shinned hawk, great horned owl, and house finch (Blus, Henny, Kaiser, et al. 1983).

Chlordane has also been implicated in the mortality of wildlife; two red-shouldered hawks and one barn owl were reportedly killed by chlordane in Maryland, Alabama, and Oregon. Brain residues (w/w) were 3.4 ppm for the hawks and 5.8 ppm for the owl (Blus, Pattee, Henny, et al. 1983).

Organophosphates have also caused avian mortality as a result of recommended and illegal uses in a variety of crops. Parathion applied to winter wheat fields in Texas caused mortality of Canada, snow, and white-fronted geese and other waterfowl At least 1600 dead birds were counted at one Playa lake. Acetycholinesterase decreases in the brains of birds found dead were 75 to 85 percent (White, Mitchell, Kolbe, et al. 1982).

Fenthion applied at the rate of 47 gAI/ha (grams active ingredient per hectare) for mosquito control resulted in high mortality to a variety of wildlife species including mallard, pintail, killdeer, horned lark, western meadowlark, several blackbird species, and savanna sparrow (DeWeese, McEwen, Settimi, et al. 1983). Depressed ChE levels were found in some species as long as 15 days post-treatment. Rice fields in Louisiana treated with azodrin resulted in mortality of blue- and green-winged teal, snow geese, grackles, and red-wings (White and Mitchell 1983). Percentage reduction of AChE activity averaged 82 to 89 percent in birds found dead.

Widespread illegal treatment of rice with mono- and dicrotophos distributed especially to kill birds in Texas resulted in the mortality of nearly 1100 birds of 12 different species. Average ChE activity was reduced by 87 percent and residues of the organophosphate in intestinal tracts ranged from 5.6 to 14 ppm. Treated seed was found to contain 950 ppm monochrotophos and 210 ppm dicrotophos (Flickinger, White, Mitchell, et al. 1984).

Dursban, applied four times to small ponds in California at rates of 0 to 1.0 lb per acre, resulted in 42 percent mortality of mallard ducklings on treated ponds and zero mortality on control ponds. Mortality of ducklings was independent of treatment rate (Hurlbert, Mulla, Keith, et al. 1970).

Mammals

Less work has been done in assessing field mortality of mammals. Some special groups such as bats have been studied in some depth as a result of population reduction and in some instances, endangered species status. Differential storage of organochlorines in brown fat of bats could enhance the potential for lethal effects because brown fat is metabolized rapidly at the time of arousal from hibernation when bats are in poor physiological condition and food may not be readily available as a result of bad weather conditions (Clark and Krynitsky 1983a). Gray bats (gray myotis) in Missouri were found to have died from dieldrin toxicity. Brain residues ranged up to 21 ppm (w/w) and whole-body up to 27 ppm. Lipid weight residues whole-body were as high as 970 ppm. The lowest brain dieldrin residue level in dead bats was 5.6 ppm. Juvenile bats seemed more sensitive than adults. Transport of residues from guano and dead bats to nearby streams resulted in death of aquatic invertebrates (Clark, Clawson, and Stafford 1983).

The correlation between brain and body lipid residues in bats is indicative of death caused by organochlorines. Lipid residues in brain and body of Mexican (Brazilian) free-tailed, little brown and gray (myotis) bats was measured for DDE, DDT, and dieldrin. Brain lipid residues for DDE, DDT, and dieldrin averaged 460 to 540 ppm, 12.0 ppm, and 4.6 ppm. Body lipid residues for the same compounds were 66 to 79,000 ppm, 470 ppm, and 390 ppm. The correlations between body and brain lipid residues for several bat species were all significant and ranged from $r = 0.83$ to $r = 0.98$ (Clark 1981b).

In an area treated with fenthion for mosquito control, the mortality of mammals included yellow-bellied marmot, white-tailed jackrabbit, mountain (Nuttall's) cottontail, Richardson's ground squirrel, white-footed mouse, and the porcupine (DeWeese, McEwen, Settimi, et al. 1983). A variety of birds were also found dead.

Difficulties in Estimating Mortality

Because surveys of mortality in the field are difficult and not very efficient, direct mortality as a result of the release of toxic substances into the environment has undoubtedly been underestimated. In some cases reports of mortality are several days post-treatment or release and the carcasses of small animals quickly disappear. In some instances investigators are not allowed to search for carcasses on private lands and estimates from the periphery are conservative (Flickinger, Mitchell, White, et al. 1986). Birds and mammals that are lethally exposed and do not die immediately could move from the area or seek hiding places as a result of illness. Reinvasion into areas following high mortality could increase the total death rate of the species or populations involved. For those long-lived species that accumulate lipophyllic compounds over long periods of time, the incidence of mortality could rarely be detected. The coincidence of treatment and presence of large numbers of migratory species could also enhance mortality and not be predictable so that surveys might be designed and carried out to appropriately assess lethal effects. The rapid population turnover times for some species would also tend to mask the impact of mortality from toxic substance releases. We need better techniques for the full assessment of approved treatments of crops with pesticides, for illegal uses as well as for industrial contaminants.

TESTING PROGRAMS

In the system of a hierarchial or tiered testing program, the approaches to some assessment of toxicity begin with simple laboratory tests on individual organisms to determine LD-50 or LC-50. Testing then moves to chronic studies on physiological function or reproduction, then to field tests, and in some cases to the use of microcosms. An excellent review of testing programs is provided by Cairns, Dickson, and Maki (eds.) 1978.

Microcosms

Microcosms might be developed for screening tests or in an effort to predict ultimate environmental effects once a substance is released into the open environment. In most cases microcosms have been used to determine transport and fate of a toxin introduced into the closed system and measured through time. In most instances the results from microcosms testing has not proven suitable for predicting effects in natural systems. Some estimates of the fate of the compound, particularly in multispecies systems, have been useful in examining the effects of toxins on inter- and intraspecific competition and on prey/predator systems. Many aquatic and terrestrial microcosms have been developed to test the effects of toxic substances. These range from simple soil cores or mixed flask cultures to large aquarium tanks and simulations of stream channels both in the laboratory and in the field. A review of multispecies tests has been completed, together with an extensive bibliography of methods for testing (Hammons [ed.] 1981). Testing systems are frequently selected based on the ability to replicate them, their realism, generality, and their potential application for screening new compounds, for research, or for advanced testing. Sizes, shapes, and volumes of microcosms vary greatly, but in most cases the physical factors of light, temperature, and humidity are controlled. Substrates may be sterile, either from the field or synthesized, or they may contain microorganisms and in situ toxic substances. Plants vary from phytoplankton to terrestrial annuals, agricultural crops, and even small trees. Organisms to be included are obviously related to microcosm volume and they may be selected for specific sex, age, and reproductive state. Combinations of organisms might include: vertebrates/invertebrates; protozoa/protozoa; zooplankton/zooplankton; fish/zooplankton; fish/macroinvertebrates; fish/fish; soil invertebrates/soil invertebrates; herbivores/plants; predator/prey; and other relationships such as symbionts and parasitoids.

Both the usefulness and limitations of the use of microcosms have been described (Neuhold and Ruggerio 1976). Microcosms might be useful in identifying and quantifying some ecosystem processes and components, determining the fate of materials in the environment, determining the short-term effects such as predator/prey interactions, for altering the experimental design through feed-back loops to change objectives and hypotheses, for identifying hazardous compounds in the screening process, and for determining the ultimate fate through testing and thereby eliminating the release of toxic substances into the environment even for testing purposes. Limitations to the use of microcosms are related to the comparability of microcosms to natural systems and the ability to predict dynamics of toxic substances from one to the other; the study of long-term low-level chronic effects because some microcosms are only useful for shorter periods of testing; the impact of scale related to reduction of habitat and home-range sizes for test species; microcosm replicability and reproducibility; the presence of vital and vulnerable processes of natural systems in microcosms and the length of time for the test system to reach stability; and the time it remains stable and suitable for testing purposes.

Microcosm testing should be rapid, reproducible, relatively inexpensive, unequivocal, sensitive, socially and economically relevant, and predictive. When developing the design and conduct of a microcosm test, it is important to consider whether the system is to be used for screening a test compound, or whether it is to be used for predictive purposes. One of the most obvious benefits is to test the interactions between species or among the same species, tests and results that cannot be obtained in single-species testing.

Because of their adaptability to tank testing, more types of aquatic systems have been used in toxic substance testing than terrestrial systems. Lake, pond, or stream cultures have been used, and in some instances innoculations from horse troughs or cemetery urns have been useful. Some of these aquatic systems have been in existence for 10 or more years. Aquatic systems might be used to test competition among various species of phyto- or zooplankton, or the vulnerability of various species to predation. Efficiency of capture and handling times can also be examined.

Microcosm testing in terrestrial systems has been less common, but could involve simple soil cores to determine effects of toxic compounds on CO_2 production from soil organisms. Such important ecological relationships as legume/rhizobia interactions can be tested in simple soil cores or in plant/pot systems. Plant/plant allelopathy might be analyzed in simple terrestrial microcosms, together with plant/herbivore tests. Arachnid/insect predation such as between spiders and beetles, and insect intraspecific competition among various life stages might be assessed with terrestrial microcosms.

There have been problems with the realistic simulation of complete ecosystems on a small scale and more validation and comparative data are needed to improve design and testing protocols. There have also been problems with the replicability between laboratories of well-defined microcosm tests. The simplification and scale and the short time for most tests have also presented problems in the interpretation of results. Ages and age structures of organisms within the test chambers can vary with time and some learned responses and behavioral patterns could alter the microcosm responses compared to natural systems. Some microcosms have been useful in assessing impacts on primary production, community metabolism, and nutrient cycling. There is some benefit to the use of entirely synthetic systems because they can be controlled more completely and should be more reproducible than mixed species natural systems.

Some of the earliest work with simple terrestrial microcosms involved the use of soil cores and single plant pots to determine leaching, soil loss to air, and uptake by plants (Lichtenstein 1958). Soils were treated in different ways and surfaces were tilled, planted, and fate of compounds was determined primarily into the various physical compartments of the various soil horizons (Lichtenstein and Schulz 1965). Various complexities were added to microcosms and perhaps those by Odum and Lugo (1970); Witkamp and Frank (1970); Metcalf, Cole, Wood, et al. (1979); Gile and Gillett (1979); and Gillett, Gile, and Russell (1983) are most representative. Odum and Lugo (1970) utilized soil/plant natural systems to test the effects of radiation on primary productivity by measurement of CO_2 production and exchange in small dessicators. Witkamp and Frank (1970) increased the complexity by testing lechate, and adding millepedes and snails. Metcalf, Cole, Wood, et al. (1979) combined a terrestrial and aquatic system in large jars and used salt marsh caterpillars, earthworms, slugs, isopods, and later in the trial introduced a prairie vole. Leachate and air sampling were also possible during the trials. The most complex and costly systems were developed by Gile and Gillett (1979). Gillett, Gile, and Russell (1983) tested a complete system including crickets, plants, nematodes, earthworms, isopods, mealworms, snails, and a pregnant gray-tailed vole. Tolle, Arthur, Chesson, et al. (1985) compared the results obtained from pots, microcosms, and field tests and found that microcosm data was better able to predict field uptake of fly ash elements to alfalfa, timothy, and oats. Larsen, DeNoyelles, Stay, et al. (1986) found that single-species tests coupled with some microcosm testing satisfactorily predicted the uptake and effects of atrazine on natural communities. Four-liter microcosms used to test the effects of some agricultural pesticides on wetland ecosystems showed that impacts of atrazine, fonofos, and triallate on invertebrates and plants was sufficient to advise against the contamination of wetlands with these common agricultural pesticides (Johnson 1986).

The judicious selection and use of microcosms can assist not only in the prediction of fate and transport of toxic substances in natural systems, but also to elucidate some of the inter- and intraspecific interactions that cannot be examined with single-species tests. More and more documentation is becoming available to validate microcosm models; some are supportive of further testing and others are not. So long as the microcosms are designed, developed, and analyzed to respond to specific questions they can be useful. Perhaps the most difficult area is to use simplified microcosms as predictors of fate, transport, and effects of relatively unknown toxins in natural systems. More work on validation of various microcosms as they apply to natural systems is necessary.

Models

Many numerical simulations of toxic substance fate, transport, and accumulation have been produced. Perhaps one of the most ambitious was the global model for DDT distribution and accumulation (Randers and Meadows 1971). The model included input from application rates and subsets of models for air, soil, oceans, rivers, and in the biota of these compartments. Three different estimates of degradation rates and transport were used to model various inputs of DDT to the environment. Degradation half-life in oceans was estimated as 8, 15, or 80 years. Three major conclusions were drawn as a result of manipulating the model with different constraints: DDT can move long distances from the point of application; DDT appears in higher concentrations in ocean food chains only several years after its application on land; and the level of DDT in food chains will continue to increase for several years after rates of application are decreased. In another effort to model the global distribution of DDT, it was estimated that the entire world's biota in the late 1960s contained 5.4×10^9 g of DDT. Peak accumulation in the troposphere and the oceanic mixed layer was to occur about 1970 (Woodwell, Craig, and Johnson 1971). Many other models are available and as Barnthouse (1981) has suggested, there could in principle be an infinite number of possible models for any ecosystem.

Simple models based on the chemical and physical characteristics of the compound result in estimates of distribution in various compartments of the environment. This approach has been called the calculation of fugacity (Mackay and Paterson 1981). Fugacity is related to the partial pressure of the substance and the tendency for the compound to move from one compartment to another. Using the physical characteristics of the compound, estimates can be made concerning the concentration in the various compartments following release.

There are terrestrial and aquatic ecosystem models that might be adapted to study the transport, fate, and effects of toxic substances. Some have already been adapted to examine the movement of radioactive substances in the environment (Hoffman, Miller, Schaeffer, et al. 1977), for the prediction of changes in atmospheric pollutants (Emanuel, Olson, and Killough 1980), and for terrestrial systems such as biomes (Innis 1972) and forest succession (Shugart and West 1980). Field data have also been used in attempts to model the fate of various toxic substances. Hamelink, Waybrant, and Ball (1971) described the partitioning of DDT in a pond. Giles (1970) traced the distribution of ^{35}S malathion in a forest ecosystem. The partitioning of ^{36}Cl DDT in a marsh (Meeks 1969; Eberhardt, Meeks, and Peterle 1971, Fig. 6.1) and in a meadow (Forsyth, Peterle, and Bandy 1983; Grau and Peterle 1979, Fig. 6.2) have also been studied over periods of 1 to 7 years.

Other models specific for estimation of transport of pesticides from agricultural lands have also been developed and entitled exposure analysis modeling systems (EXAMS) and field agricultural runoff monitoring

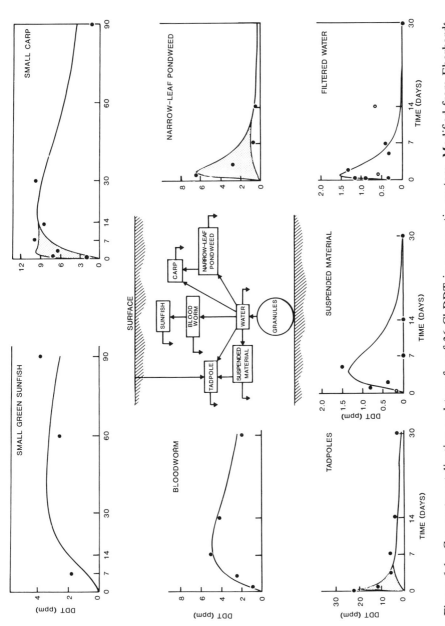

Figure 6.1 Compartmentalization and transfer of 36 Cl-DDT in an aquatic system. Modified from Eberhardt, L. L., R. L. Meeks, and T. J. Peterle. 1971. Food chain model for DDT kinetics in a freshwater marsh. *Nature* 230(5288):60–62. Reprinted by permission. Copyright © 1971 Macmillan Magazines Ltd.

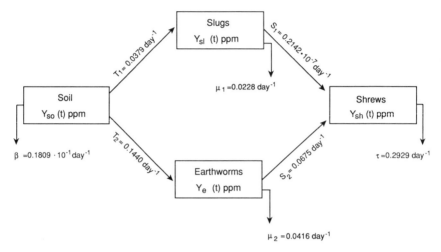

Figure 6.2   Modeling and transfer coefficients for DDT-R flow through a meadow ecosystem following treatment with 1 lb per acre of granular DDT in 1969. Modified from "A preliminary model of DDT kinetics in an old-field ecosystem." D. J. Forsyth, T. J. Peterle, and G. C. White. 1975. *Environ. Qual. Safety* Supp. Vol. III, pp. 754–759. Stuttgart: Georg Thieme Pub.

(FARM) (Pollard and Hern 1985). Others include simplified lake and stream analysis (SLSA) (Rodgers, Dickson, Saleh, et al. 1983); quantitative structure-activity relationships (QSAR) (Lien 1985); and pesticide root zone model (PRZM) (Carsel, Nixon, and Ballantine 1986).

No model has yet been found to be completely satisfactory for predicting the effects of toxic substances in the natural environment. The criteria for the selection of appropriate models has been described. The models should require a minimum degree of modification to be adapted for toxic substance predictions and biological, chemical, and physical processes should be included. The data requirements necessary should be considered in the light of time/money constraints. The model should have general applicability and should be easily validated. It should have temporal/spatial scales, be relevant to monitoring of toxic substances, be easy to use, and have social relevance related to regulatory needs. The model should also be acceptable to the scientific community (Barnthouse 1981). Models can provide useful insight into gaps and needs in data collection, but much effort is needed before they can be used to predict the impact of a specific toxic substance on the various components of the ecosystem.

7

Chronic Effects on Organisms

The effects of toxic substances on organisms may be considered in broad categories such as lethal, chronic, or no effect. Perhaps no observable effect might be more appropriate because the determination of effects must be described at all levels from effects on the whole organism, its social, behavioral, and physiological functions, and potential effects at the biochemical or cellular level. In most instances, we do not know the no-effect level, but in the design of experimental exposure or in the assessment of effects in the field we can determine what the no observable effect exposure might be. We know, for example, that organophosphates alter ChE levels in blood and brain of exposed animals. We also know in some instances what normal levels are for a particular wildlife species, and we know approximate levels that relate to mortality (Rattner 1982). In most instances we cannot define the no-effect level in terms of the physiological function of the animal. Dinman (1972) has argued that there is in fact a no-effect level and that the linking of *effect* with *deleterious* is not appropriate. To imply that a single molecule in a cell implies potential deleterious effects disregards stochastic considerations. Dinman suggests that the level of potential for activity could be set at the level of biological activity of 10^4 atoms. Measurement of effects at this level of activity would be very difficult.

REPRODUCTION

Birds

The impacts of toxins on reproduction in wildlife species have received much attention and a considerable body of literature is available. Perhaps the most often cited paper that had an impact on field and laboratory research, especially in birds, was that by Ratcliffe (1967). He was the first author to report on the effects of toxic substances on eggshell weights

157

(thickness) and as a result many of the subsequent investigations on the effects of toxic substances were related to reproduction (Fig. 7.1).

We might consider reproductive effects of toxins on several aspects or periods of the reproductive cycle. Effects may involve rates of growth and attainment of sexual maturity either physically or physiologically. Other parameters of reproductive success that may be influenced could be behavioral, physiological (including hormonal), direct lethal effects on adults, embryos, or young, and finally the reproductive patterns and success of the F_1 generation could be altered by chronic exposure of the breeding female, the embryo, or the young.

Many behavioral responses necessary to successful reproduction can be very complex and are logically related to the physiological and nutritional state of the mated pair. Toxins either directly or as an indirect influence on the endocrine system could affect competition and territoriality, mate selection, sequences of mating behavior, nest building, egg laying, incubation behavior, and feeding and care of the young (Rattner, Eroschenko, Fox, et al. 1984).

In mammals many of these factors also apply: estrus cycles might be altered and care and feeding of the young might also be changed. Imprint-

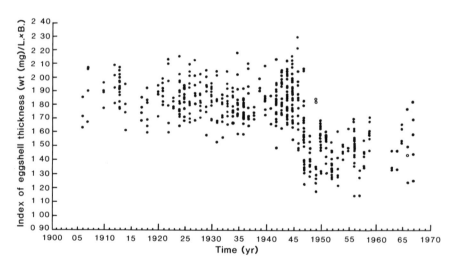

Figure 7.1 Change in ratio of eggshell weight to size in peregrine falcon eggs from Great Britain. The pattern of eggshell weights clearly shows a decline following the widespread use and dissemination of DDT during World War II. Modified from "Decrease in eggshell weight in certain birds of prey." D. A. Ratcliffe. 1967. *Nature* 215(5097):208–210. Reprinted by permission from *Nature* 215:208–210. Copyright 1967 Macmillan Magazines Ltd.

ing and learning are important early in the life history of many wildlife species, and we do not know whether toxic substance exposure might influence these behavior patterns that are important to survival and subsequent reproduction.

Egg breakage and eggshell eating have been reported in birds carrying body burdens of toxic substances, but whether this is a result of eggshell thinning or caused by some behavioral or physiological modification is not known for most species (Ratcliffe 1970). Some behavioral changes have been demonstrated experimentally that alter incubation and feeding of nestlings. Treatment of ring doves with 10 ppm PCB in the diet resulted in lowered hatchability because of erratic incubation behavior of the mated pair (Peakall and Peakall 1973). Of 36 control eggs incubated, 33 hatched. If both of the adults in the mated pair were treated with PCB, the number of eggs hatched was only 12; if only one adult was treated, hatch improved but not equal to the control success. Laughing gulls dosed with 6 mg/kg parathion spent less time in incubation on days 2 and 3 than control gulls (White, Mitchell, and Hill 1983).

There are also behavioral changes evident in young when they are exposed to toxic substances during incubation. Mallard ducklings sprayed with FLIT-MLO and fuel oil had excessive responses to fright stimuli compared to ducklings from untreated eggs (Albers and Heinz 1983). There are many aspects of reproductive behavior that could be altered by direct or indirect impacts of toxic substances. How these might influence recruitment and population change in most species is unknown.

Physiological changes resulting from the intake of toxic substances can have direct effects on reproductive success. Some toxins mimic reproductive hormones and could directly influence the normal reproductive patterns of behavior, estrus, development of the gametes, mating, fertility, incubation, gestation, and care of the young. Despite the widespread evidence of eggshell thinning as a physiological effect, the exact mechanism in unknown. Absorption, transport, and utilization of calcium during the formation of the eggshell are all potential sites of impact of DDT/DDE on the reproductive process (Cooke 1973). There was some suggestion that blockage of carbonic anhydrase activity in the shell gland might be a problem (Bitman, Cecil, Harris, et al. 1969a), but later studies showed that the levels of action were too low to cause eggshell thinning (Dvorchik, Istin, and Maren 1971). Dieldrin, DDE, and DDT were shown not to be inhibitors of carbonic anhydrase (Pocker, Beug, and Ainardi 1971). Kolaja and Hinten (1979) showed that mallard hens fed 50 ppm DDT produced eggshells weighing 12 percent less and thickness was reduced by 18 percent. They stated that DDT inhibited Ca-ATPase and this induced alteration in calcium transport resulting in thin eggshells. Peakall (1970a) has outlined the calcium transport process in birds (Fig. 7.2).

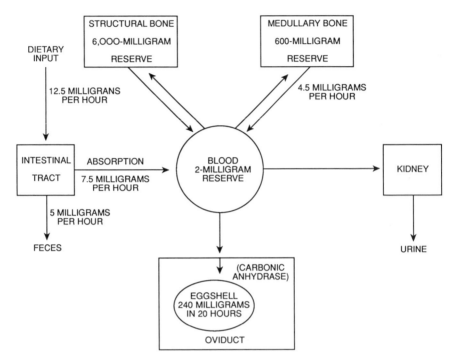

Figure 7.2 The compartmentalization and flow of calcium during the reproductive processes in birds. Toxic substances, primarily the chlorinated hydrocarbon compounds, strongly inhibit the deposition of calcium in the eggshell. Modified from "Pesticides and the reproduction of birds." D. A. Peakall. 222(4):72–78. Copyright © 1970 by *SCIENTIFIC AMERICAN,* Inc. All rights reserved.

The physiology of eggshell thinning related, primarily, to DDE contamination was discussed thoroughly and many possible pathways were considered: calcium deposition in medullary bone, mobilization and transport to the eggshell gland, actual calcium absorption across the wall of the gut, vitamin D and calcium binding, and carbonic anhydrase inhibition. Premature expulsion of the egg was also a possibility. The theory was that at least two different sites of calcium transport and deposition were being affected (Risebrough, Davis, and Anderson 1970). Although a variety of toxic substances fed to cotrnix quail and mallards produced thinner eggshells, some of the effects were related to reduced food intake, not the influence of the toxic substance. Only DDE produced long-term effects beginning only 24 hours after treatment, indicating that microsomal enzyme induction could not be important because the effect began so soon after treatment (Haegele and Tucker 1974).

Alteration in metabolism of steroids has been shown in birds exposed to DDE (Peakall 1967; 1970a, b; Lustick, Voss, and Peterle 1973; Peterle, Lustick, Nauman, et al. 1974; Fig. 7.3). Haseltine, Peterle, Nagode, et al. (1981) showed that the hormone PTH may be involved and Parsons and Peterle (1977) reported histological changes in the parathyroid glands of DDE-exposed mallards and king pigeons.

Transportation of calcium across the wall of the gut was not altered by DDE exposure in mallards, but transport in pheasants, a species that does not respond by showing eggshell thinning, was altered (Haseltine, Peterle, Nagode, et al. 1981).

How enhanced microsomal action could influence levels of hormones in a variety of species and thereby alter reproductive patterns and success is not known. Altered progesterone levels in the plasma of mourning doves reduced reproductive success as a result of 10 ppm dietary PCB treatment (Koval, Peterle, and Harder 1987, Fig. 7.4).

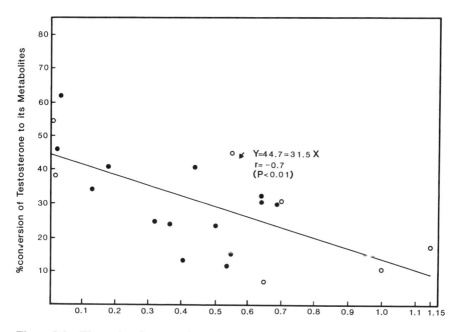

Figure 7.3   The ratio of conversion of testosterone to more polar metabolites by liver homogenates from male bobwhite quail treated with DDT to the testes/body weight ratio. This shows the potential for reproductive dysfunction caused by enhanced MFO induction. Modified from "Effects of DDT on steroid metabolism and energetics in bobwhite quail *Colinus virginianus*." S. Lustick, T. Voss, and T. J. Peterle. 1973. First Bobwhite Quail Symp., pp. 213–233. Stillwater: University of Oklahoma Press.

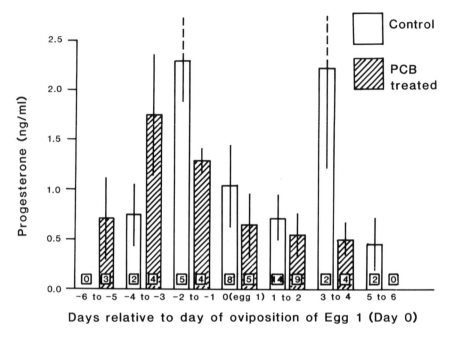

Figure 7.4   Levels of circulating progesterone in female mourning doves treated with dietary PCB at 10 ppm in relation to egg laying. PCBs may alter reproductive function and success by reduction of hormones necessary for ovulation. Modified from "Effects of polychlorinated biphenyls on mourning dove reproduction and circulating progesterone levels." *Bull. Environ. Contam. Toxicol.* 39(4):663–670. By permission of Springer-Verlag, Heidelberg.

DDE, PCB, and crude oil exposure to mallards and to mourning doves does delay egg laying and in the case of mourning doves, exposure to 40 ppm PCB in the diet inhibited nest building and reproduction for at least 30 days (Tori and Peterle 1983). Mallards treated with South Louisiana crude oil and/or DDE showed delayed egg laying, reduced hatchability, and alteration of egg size, weight, and content (Vangilder and Peterle 1980, 1981, 1983). Mallard reproduction was delayed and survival of young to 21 days was also reduced by treatment with 10 ppm Abate (Franson, Spann, Heinz, et al. 1983). Reduced prolactin levels were found in the plasma of mallard hens treated with crude oil in the diet (3 ml crude oil/100 g food) and this significantly reduced reproductive success (Cavanaugh, Goldsmith, Holmes, et al. 1983). Oil in the diet of mallard hens also reduced the levels of plasma ovarian steriod hormones, estradiol, and estrone. This resulted in delayed ovulation and irregular egg laying (Cavanaugh and Holmes 1982).

Physiologically, the pheasant, guinea fowl, and the domestic chicken do not respond to chronic exposure to chlorinated hydrocarbons by alteration in reproductive patterns or eggshell thinning (Genelly and Rudd 1956; Hunt, Azevedo, Woods, et al. 1969; Robinson 1969; Wiese, Basson, Van Der Wyver, et al. 1969; Haseltine, Peterle, Nagode, et al. 1981).

Single oral doses of 1000 μg/kg of DDT to mallard hens resulted in a 25 to 28 percent thinning in eggshells laid two days following treatment (Tucker and Haegele 1970). A single treatment of DDE at 40 ppm in the diet for 96 days resulted in reduced eggshell thickness in mallards through two reproductive seasons. The first season the shells were reduced by 15 to 20 percent, the second season by 7.4 percent (Haegele and Hudson 1974).

Exposure of Pekin ducks to 40 ppm DDE in the diet for 4 days resulted in 20 percent eggshell thinning. In addition, the breaking strength of the shell was less, water permeability was reduced, and pore area of the shell was also decreased by 30 percent (Pritchard, Peakall, Risebrough, et al. 1972).

Treatment of mallard hens and drakes with 40 ppm DDE or PCB and combined treatment showed no increased shell thinning with the addition of PCB to DDE diets. There was, however, a decrease in the number of intact eggs laid with PCB treatment (Risebrough and Anderson 1975).

Declines in raptorial species populations related to eggshell thinning was reported in 1968 (Hickey and Anderson 1968). Residues of DDE in herring gull eggs were strongly correlated (R = 0.98) with shell thickness. Shell thickness in other species also declined compared to the pre-DDT era; bald eagles by 19.8 percent, osprey by 25.1 percent, and peregrines by 26.0 percent.

Peregrines in Alaska were still reproducing in 1966, but residues of organochlorines in both birds and eggs were close to levels thought to be injurious (Cade, White, and Haugh 1968). Mean residues of DDE in eggs was 48.0 ppm (dry weight) and in adult bird fat 622.0 ppm DDE. Downy chicks contained 38.4 ppm. Among peregrine prey, spotted sandpipers and lesser yellow legs had highest DDE body burdens of 6.02 ppm. Reproductive dysfunction was predicted unless residues declined.

In the wild, reproductive success among ospreys on Long Island and in Connecticut improved when the residues of DDE and PCB declined between 1970 and 1976 (Spitzer, Risebrough, Walker, et al. 1978). Among common and red-breasted merganser eggs sampled in northern Wisconsin and Michigan, DDE residues were related to eggshell thickness (White and Cromartie 1977). Approximately 20 percent eggshell thinning seems necessary to result in significant reductions in reproductive success (Keith and Gruchy 1972).

Among ospreys and marsh harriers in Sweden, DDT and mercury were related to hatchability, but PCB was not. Hatched eggshell fragments were 15 percent thinner, and broken eggs 20 percent thinner; at 16 percent shell thinning, breakage begins and at 30 percent thinning, complete clutches are lost (Odsjo 1982).

Kestrels seem sensitive to residues of about 1.5 ppm in the egg, but for Canada geese, residues must be about 10 ppm before any effect is demonsrated on eggshell thickness (Henny, Blus, and Stafford 1983).

DDE and/or dieldrin fed to barn owls over a period of 2 years caused eggshell thinning, egg breakage, embryo mortality, and reduced production. Dieldrin alone caused eggshell thinning, but not reproductive impairment (Mendenhall, Klaas, and McLane 1983).

Shell thickness of black crowned night heron eggs taken in Colorado and Wyoming was correlated with residues of DDE; shells with DDE residues were 8.8 percent thinner than normal (McEwen, Stafford, and Hensler 1984).

Eight contaminants found in bald eagle eggs were correlated to eggshell thickness. Residues of DDE below 3 ppm w/w produced normal hatch, but residues of over 15 ppm resulted in complete clutch failure. About 10 percent shell thinning was associated with 5 ppm DDE residues in eggs (Wiemeyer, Lamont, Bunck, et al. 1984).

Aside from the bald eagle, the brown pelican has also been a dramatic example of the impacts of chlorinated hydrocarbon pesticides on reproduction or populations. Total numbers of breeding pelicans off the California coast (Anacapa, Coronados) varied from 1,125 in 1969 down to 511 in 1972, and back up to 1,286 in 1974. In those years, the number of young produced was 4 in 1969, 207 in 1972, and 1,185 in 1974 (Anderson and Anderson 1976). Over this same period, the thickness of eggshells from pelicans off the California coast as well as from the western Baja, followed the same pattern of impacts and recovery. In 1969 eggshells averaged 0.402 mm, went down to 0.393 in 1970, up to 0.438 mm in 1972, and in 1974 eggshells averaged 0.482 mm (Anderson, Jehl, Risebrough, et al. 1975). DDE residues in eggs were 1,155.3 ppm lipid weight in 1969, and 96.6 ppm in 1974. Recovery of avian reproduction and populations is difficult to predict, but when environmental contaminant levels are reduced, birds do respond and recover their numbers.

Blus (1984) reviewed the data from brown pelicans and black-crowned herons related to the prediction of reproductive failure based on eggshell thinning or egg residues. He found that egg residues produced lower effect levels than the shell thinning estimates. For pelicans, this was 3 $\mu g/g$ versus 8 $\mu g/g$, and for herons it was 12 $\mu g/g$ versus 54 $\mu g/g$.

Drastic declines in brown pelican populations on the Pacific coast were related to accumulation of chlorinated hydrocarbons and subsequent effects on reproductive success (Keith, Woods, and Hunt 1970). In wood storks, residues of 2.9 ppm in the egg resulted in less than 100 percent hatching success (Fleming, Rodgers, and Stafford 1984). Shell thickness of great blue, green-backed, and black-crowned night-herons in the Tennessee Valley were 7.5, 7.6, and 3.0 percent thinner than pre-1947 eggshells, but this did not impair reproductive success (Fleming, Pullin, and Swineford 1984).

Estuarian areas have been heavily contaminated by pesticides. Residues of various environmental contaminants, and declines in avian populations, have been evident in such large areas as Chesapeake Bay, where many species have shown residues, and simultaneous declines in reproduction and populations (Ohlendorf 1981). By 1979, there was already evidence of declines in body burdens, subsequent increased eggshell thickness, and improved reproduction.

A strong relationship was shown among DDE, PCB residues, and eggshell thickness in both white pelicans and double-crested cormorants (Anderson, Hickey, Risebrough, et al. 1969). Eggshell thickness in white pelican eggs was 4.5 percent thinner than pre-1940 eggshells, and for the cormorant there was a decrease of 8.5 percent from pre-1940 to 1965 eggshells. DDE/eggshell correlations were r = 0.98 for the double-crested cormorant and r = 0.43 for the pelican.

Eggshell thickness reduction in predatory birds in Alaska varied from none in the gyrfalcon to 21.7 percent in the tundra peregrine. Tundra peregrines had shells reduced by 16.8 percent; 7.5 percent in the Aleutian peregrines, and 3.3 percent in the rough-legged hawks (Cade, Lincer, White, et al. 1971). DDE residues followed these decreases in thickness of eggshells. In the tundra peregrine residues of DDE (lipid basis) were 889 ppm, in the taiga peregrine 673 ppm, 167 ppm in the Aleutian peregrine eggs, and 22.5 ppm in rough-legged hawk eggs. DDE residues were only 3.88 ppm in gyrfalcon eggs.

The use of heptachlor for seed treatment of wheat in Oregon and Washington has resulted in avian mortality of adults as well as contamination of eggs to levels sufficient to cause reproductive failure. Eggs from 60 nests of six different species were picked up and analyzed. Heptachlor epoxide residues were found in 35 of the eggs, and residues were high in eggs of magpie, mallard, and ring-necked pheasant. Lindane has been recommended as an alternate to heptachlor and in areas where the conversion had already taken place, no lindane residues were found in eggs (Blus, Henny, and Krynitsky 1985b).

The determination of eggshell thickness in relation to toxic substance exposure must be done in relation to the stage of incubation for some species. Mallard and kestrel eggshell thickness does change during incubation, but eggshells of black-crowned night-heron did not change throughout the incubation period. In some species eggshell changes occur in the last few days of incubation, so eggshell thickness should be used cautiously if measured during the terminal part of the incubation period. Eggshell thinning during incubation is generally considerably below that caused as a result of exposure to some toxic substances (Bunck, Spann, Pattee, et al. 1985).

Residues of DDE and PCB found in Caspian tern eggs in San Diego Bay were thought to have influenced reproductive success. There was more DDE (9.3 ppm) found in Caspian tern eggs than in elegant tern eggs (3.79). About 4.6 percent of the Caspian tern chicks died during hatching, and DDE was associated with shell thickness. Fish brought to the nests for chicks contained up to 3.9 ppm DDE (Ohlendorf, Schaffner, Custer, et al. 1985).

White-faced ibis populations in Texas declined 42 percent between 1969 and 1976. Population declines were attributed to DDE-induced eggshell thinning and direct adult mortality caused by dieldrin. DDE averaged 2.5 ppm in thin-shelled eggs and brain residues of dieldrin ranged from 5 to 25 ppm in dead and dying ibises (King, Meeker, and Swineford 1980).

Three subpopulations of bald eagles in the greater Yellowstone ecosystem responded differently to DDT contamination. The Snake Unit population existed in areas not heavily treated with organochlorines, while the Yellowstone and Continental populations were in heavily treated areas. Comparing the years 1976 through 1982 with earlier years, the number of young produced increased by 35 percent in the Yellowstone subpopulation, 67 percent in the Continental subpopulation, but only 5 percent in the Snake population, where less pesticide had been used. It takes about 5 years after use of organochlorines have been banned to demonstrate an increase in recruitment because of the time to sexual maturity for long-lived birds such as eagles (Swenson, Alt, and Eng 1986).

A succinct review of pesticides and bird populations was provided by Risebough (1986). The review deals mainly with the impacts of chlorinated hydrocarbons on avian populations, physiology, behavior, and reproduction. Some of the review also deals with PCBs. There is need for added information at three different levels: environmental levels of chlorinated hydrocarbons and their impacts on mortality; the amounts and destinations of pesticides being exported; and global estimates for production of chlorinated hydrocarbons so that mass balances might be calculated.

Sodium fluoride fed to screech owls did impair reproduction in terms of producing smaller fledglings for the first week. Birds fed 40 and 200 ppm produced smaller eggs and smaller young, but by 7 days of age, body weights and lengths were similar, except the tibiotarsus in the 200 ppm group remained shorter (Hoffman, Pattee, and Wiemeyer 1985).

Altricial nestlings of the kestrel seemed more responsive to treatments of paraquat than were young of precocial species. Depending on dose, there was some mortality and reduced growth of kestrel nestlings. Birds were dosed at 10.25 and 60 mg/kg. About 44 percent of the nestlings given the high dose died in 4 days; others on lower doses had reduced skeletal growth (Hoffman, Franson, Pattee, et al. 1985a). Doses of diazinon given in food to bobwhite quail reduced egg production at levels above 35 ppm under constant dosage (Stromborg 1982).

Heavy metals apparently have a lesser effect on avian reproductive success. Kestrels fed 10 and 50 ppm metallic lead showed no signs of eggshell thinning (Pattee 1984). Up to 10 ppm selenium in the diet did not affect mallard reproduction (Heinz, Hoffman, Krynitsky, et al. 1987). Lead and mercury fed to mallard hens at 100 ppm and 200 ppm (Ceresan at 3.1% metallic mercury) did not influence eggshell thinning nor did the metals act synergistically with DDE (Haegele, Tucker, and Hudson 1974). DDE did increase the level of uptake of lead in bone from 9.6 to 35.0 ppm w/w. Treatment of pheasant hens with 30 ppm ceresan (12.5 ppm mercury) was lethal. At 10 ppm ceresan (4.2 ppm mercury), reproductive success was reduced in terms of egg production (50–80 percent reduced) and survival of chicks to 14 days (Spann, Heath, Kreitzer, et al. 1972).

Earthworms

Regeneration of segments in earthworms exposed to mercury was reduced at 5 ppm. Worms exposed to 1 ppm Hg were not different from control worms. Control worms regenerated about 38 segments in 12 weeks and worms exposed to 5 ppm mercury in the soil regenerated about 12 segments in 12 weeks. Mercury accumulated about 21 to 22 times the level in the soil and at the higher treatment levels, there was sufficient mercury in the worms (85 ppm wet weight) to potentially present a hazard to predators feeding on worms (Beyer, Cromartie, and Moment 1985).

Mammals

There is less evidence of reproductive effects of toxic substances on mammals in the laboratory and in the field. Laboratory studies of the mouse showed higher reproductive success in terms of young produced per pair with 7 ppm DDT in the diet. Mirex at 5 ppm slightly reduced young per day and telodrin at 1 ppm produced no effect (Ware and Good 1967).

Some mammals are highly susceptible to organochlorine contamination in terms of reproductive effects. Both DDT and aldrin produced subnormal reproduction in beagle dogs (Deichmann, Macdonald, Beasley, et al. 1971). Organochlorine and PCB residues of 2 to 8 times higher than average were associated with premature births and pup mortality in California sea lions (DeLong, Gilmartin, and Simpson 1973). Ranch mink fed rations containing up to 0.58 ppm DDE from ground contaminated fish had higher embryonic losses than did control females (Gilbert 1969). PCBs also produce these reproductive effects in mink (Platonow and Karstad 1973). Mink are also apparently sensitive to DNOC. In Czechoslovakia at a mink ranch, 1707 females were impregnated and they produced an average of 3.4 young during a control year. Following spraying of a nearby orchard with Nitrosan, only 13.8 percent of the females had young or aborted, and only 60 females (3.5%) reared an average of 1.2 young (Konrad, Mouka, and Horak 1983). In the Love Canal area, 10 to 14.6 percent of human live births between 1940 and 1953 were below normal weight compared to adjacent areas, where 0.0 to 9.4 percent had below-normal weights (Viana and Polan 1984).

Treatment of laboratory rats with low chronic doses of cadmium (0.1–5.0 ppm) and lead (5.0 to 50.0 ppm) resulted in altered weight gains for females during gestation, and reduced litter sizes, survival of young, and sizes of surviving young (Herman, Kmieciak-Kolada, Szkilnik, et al. 1982).

Reproductive effects of PCB on Rhesus monkeys was demonstrated at oral doses of 2.5 and 5.0 ppm for 6 months. At 5.0 ppm, 6 of 8 monkeys conceived, but only one infant was carried to term. All monkeys conceived on the 2.5 ppm diet and 5 of 8 were born. Three of six surviving infants died in the first year (Allen and Barsotti 1976). Aroclor 1254 fed at 0.25, and 100 ppm to female white-footed mice for 3 weeks showed increased liver weights, reduced plasma corticoids, but no change in reproductive organs nor in estrous cycles (Sanders and Kirkpatrick 1977).

Effects on the Embryo

In addition to the behavioral and physiological effects related to reproduction, direct mortality of embryos does occur during gestation and incubation. Perhaps this is most evident in avian reproduction, when the surface of the egg is contaminated, usually by oil, either by direct application or by transfer from the breast feathers of the incubating adult. As little as 1 ml of Kuwait No. 2 fuel oil applied to the breast feathers of incubating herring and black-backed gulls reduced hatchability. A lesser amount, 20 μl, when applied directly to the egg, also reduced reproductive success (Lewis and Malecki 1983). Oil and a dispersant were added to water troughs in pens with incubating mallard hens. Hatchability was reduced up to 50 percent with oil alone, up to 80.2 percent with the dispersant, and 59.6 percent with the oil and dispersant mixed (Albers and Gay 1982).

Of 42 environmental contaminants tested in relation to producing embryotoxicity in mallards, used road oil was found to be most toxic to the developing embryo, followed by South Louisiana crude oil and Prudhoe Bay crude oil. Paraquat was the most toxic herbicide tested (Hoffman and Albers 1984).

Developing embryos are apparently most susceptible during the early stages of incubation from 1 to 10 days. In seabirds, as little as 1 to 2 μl of oil transferred to the egg can be embryotoxic (Albers 1982). Weathered No. 2 fuel oil placed on mallard eggs on the 8th day of incubation resulted in reduced hatchability of 78 percent for 1 μl, 46 percent for 5 μl, 42 for 10 μl, 24 for 20 μl, and none of the eggs hatched when treated with 50 μl of oil (Szaro, Coon, and Stout 1980). In eider ducks, treatment of eggs with 5 μl of oil reduced hatchability to 92 percent and with 20 μl of oil, 69 percent of the eggs hatched (Szaro and Albers 1977).

Applications of field levels of organophosphates to mallard eggs showed that parathion was most embryotoxic, followed by diazinon and malathion. Oil carrier increased the toxic effects (Hoffman and Eastin 1981b). Embryotoxicity was also evident with field treatments of lindane, toxaphene, and 2, 4-5T. Paraquat was teratogenic at half the field dose level (Hoffman and Eastin 1982). Petroleum products applied to egg surfaces are embryotoxic at 0.3 to 5.0 μl per egg. Pesticides, when applied to the egg in a non-toxic oil carrier, are 18 times more toxic than if applied in an aqueous solution because of better penetration with oil (Hoffman and Albers 1984).

Abnormal development during gestation or incubation can result in non-lethal abnormal development in young that leads to reproductive dysfunction. DDT, DDE, and methoxychlor injected into developing gull eggs resulted in abnormal development of ovarian tissue in male hatchlings (Fry and Toone 1981). If rats are exposed to phenobarbital during critical periods of gestation, testosterone levels in the brains of pups 21 days old are reduced (Gupta, Yaffe, and Shaprio 1982).

Reproductive effects may occur at many stages of the system and extend even into the next generation. Many species of wildlife have not been tested even for LD-50 calculations and we know even less about the long-term chronic effects of toxic substances on the behavior, physiology, and mortality related to the many phases of the reproductive process and ultimately on the levels of recruitment to the population.

BEHAVIOR

In addition to those behavioral effects related to reproduction, the impacts of toxic substances on other types of wildlife behavior have been studied in many unique ways. One of the most common is the response of exposed animals to physical factors in the environment, to fright stimuli, and to learning and retention of learning. The study of these subtle chronic behavioral effects can reveal potential impacts of toxic substances on individuals, recruitment, and on populations that otherwise might not be determined.

In many cases, the discovery of some alteration in behavior cannot yet be evaluated in terms of impacts on the population, but the observation of subtle behavioral changes can be indicative of more important neural or physiological changes with increased exposure.

Fish

Dark, light, temperature, and electric shock were used in a multiple behavioral test of the effects of low (1.8 μg/1) doses of toxaphene on goldfish in experimental tanks. Severe behavioral pathology was developed at this dose level and some evidence of behavioral abberations was evident at a dose of 0.44 μg/1. Some tests with TEPP produced behavioral changes at 1/20th the dose level necessary to produce a TL_m. This led the researchers to recognize (p. 245) "the folly of assuming that lack of evidence is the same as negative evidence" (Warner, Peterson, and Borgman 1966). Despite this early warning, much of the evidence for toxic substance effects on wildlife has been interpreted as negative evidence because we do not understand the full impacts of low chronic exposure on species and ecosystems.

Responses to thermal stress in fish can be altered by toxic substance exposure. Johnny darters exposed to 2.3 ppb dietary dieldrin for 30 days suffered 76.5 percent mortality when exposed to 1 degree increases in ambient temperature each day for 7 days and maintained for 4 days. Controls suffered 13 percent mortality (Silbergeld 1973). Dominance in fish apparently can influence the uptake rates of toxic substances. Survival of subdominant bluegills in a tank containing 32 mg/1 zinc was improved when flowerpot shelters were added to the tanks (Sparks, Waller, and Cairns 1972). Fish ventilatory behavior is a good indicator of not only chronic but also acute toxicity. Types of responses such as amplitude, coughs, gill purges, as well as ventilatory rates may indicate the type of toxicant to which fish are exposed in the environment (Diamond, Parson, and Gruber 1990). Fish foraging behavior and predator/prey interactions have been summarized as being mostly empirical. Models using feeding behavior related to optimal foraging and bioenergetics as well as predation sequences could show how reduced food intake could alter growth (Sandheinrich and Atchison 1990).

Birds

Locomotor activity and fright responses to various stimuli have been tested in a variety of species and young produced from treated females. Adult male bobwhites treated with a field dose (131 ppm) of carbofuran had reduced locomotor activity, food intake, and body weights when compared to control birds (Robel, Felthousen, and Dayton 1982). In *Coturnix* there was a significant reduction in avoidance response to an avian predator silhouette following treatment with ceresan M, aroclor 1254, chlordane, dieldrin, and endrin, but not with DDE. Birds recovered their normal responses except for those exposed to ceresan M and aroclor (Kreitzer and Heinz 1974). Ducklings hatched from eggs of mallard hens treated with DDE (3.0 ppm) or morsodren (0.5–3.0 ppm Hg) were hyper-responsive to maternal calls and to fright stimulus (Heinz 1975, 1976a,b). During the second year of treatment, only those ducklings from hens treated with 3.0 ppm mercury remained hyper-responsive (Heinz 1976b). Ducklings of black duck hens fed 0, 4, or 40 ppm cadmium showed different responses to fright stimuli. The 4 ppm treatment showed the highest effect when compared to 0 or 40 ppm (Heinz, Haseltine, and Sileo 1983). Chromium fed at 20 or 200 ppm to black duck hens and their ducklings showed no behavioral affects in ducklings (Heinz and Haseltine 1981). Starling males treated with 2.5 mg of dicrotophos perched 46 percent more of the total time and spent less time flying (96%), less time foraging (28%), and less time singing and displaying (59%) (Grue and Shipley 1981). Non-spatial discrimination tasks were used to determine the chronic behavioral effects of toxaphene (10 and 50 ppm) and endrin (0.1 and 1.0 ppm) on bobwhite quail. After 30 to 40 days of treatment, the birds treated with toxaphene made 50 percent more errors but they later adjusted to the intake of the toxin and performed normally. The endrin-treated birds made 36 to 139 percent more errors than control birds (Kreitzer 1980). Key pecking-food reinforcement tests with bobwhites fed dieldrin at five dosage levels from 50 to 300 μg showed that above 100 μg, the birds were slower and had fewer accurate responses than at lower dosages or in control birds (Gesell, Robel, Dayton, et al. 1979).

Chlordimeform is an important formamidine insecticide used on cotton. Potential effects on bobwhite were studied in both lethal and behavioral tests. Bobwhites were exposed to various levels of the insecticide up to 100 ppm. Those fed the higher dose moved further from fright stimulus, ate less, weighed less, and test groups had greater movements than control birds. Visual cliff performance tests also showed differences between treated and control groups (Fleming, Heinz, and Schuler 1985). In a unique study of sharp-tailed grouse, birds were fitted with neck tags and radio collars prior to administration of single oral doses of malathion and dieldrin, and subsequent release to the wild. Aside from the determination of lethal dosages, some interesting behavioral modifications resulted from sub-lethal exposures, including a greater vulnerability to predation and changes in behavior on the breeding grounds. Some dominant treated males were challenged and defeated and others ceased to participate in display on the leks following exposure. Following treatment of some males with malathion, the intensity of display and defense on the breeding grounds became more intense (McEwen and Brown 1966). Such alteration in behavior could reduce breeding success.

Mammals

Very little behavioral work has been done with wild mammals. Laboratory mice treated with both lead and the roundworm parasite (*Toxocara*) were influenced by treatment by either the heavy metal or the parasite. When given jointly, there was less effect than either treatment singly (Dolinsky, Burright, Donovick, et al. 1981). Thirty-day-old mice born from females treated during pregnancy with mercury showed fewer aggressive movements in open field tests and poorer swimming ability and coordination in water (Spyker, Sparber, and Goldberg 1972). Young children shown to have had higher lead exposure by assay of deciduous teeth have lower scores in IQ tests, suggesting that lead exposure can influence learning and intelligence as measured by standard tests; later re-analysis seemed to support the relationship (Needleman 1981; Needleman, Geiger, and Frank 1985). (This finding is still somewhat controversial.) Wild kangaroo rats were acclimated to the laboratory and exposed to seed/bead discrimination tests before and after one-time oral gavage of 5 mg/kg of methyl parathion given in corn oil. Twelve and 24 hours following treatment, they were again exposed to discrimination trials and the treated rats picked up fewer beads. The LD-50 for kangaroo rats is 97.1 mg/kg of methyl parathion (Peterle and Bentley 1989). Feed tainted with paraquat and carbofuran resulted in some aversion by wild-trapped *Microtus*. There is some suggestion that population effects may result if field exposures affect food intake of females (Linder and Richmond 1990). *Microtus* exposed to sludge amended field plots showed uptake of cadmium and subsequent alteration in locomotor and exploratory behavior. Exposed females, not males, showed inability to habituate to novel environments or they were hyperactive (Hall, Taylor, and Woods 1990).

Subtle tests of behavioral responses in the laboratory to low-level chronic exposure to toxins are exciting and interesting, but the importance of these impacts on animals living in the wild and ultimately on recruitment and populations must be demonstrated. Relevant laboratory tests must be designed or careful field observations must be made to place behavioral alterations in proper perspective in relation to the effects imposed on wildlife by increasing levels of complex mixtures of xenobiotics released into natural systems.

PHYSIOLOGICAL RESPONSES

Many of the more sophisticated physiological measurements developed for human and laboratory animal studies have been adapted to study the effects of toxic substances on wildlife. In some instances, the relationship between dose and response has been well correlated so if it is more efficient to measure the physiological response, this may be more appropriate than measuring the level of toxic substance in the organism.

This is the case for the effects of lead on several blood parameters. Dehydratase levels in blood plasma are inversely related to lead levels. Approximately 200 ppb lead in the blood of canvasback ducks reduced dehydratase levels (ALAD enzyme) by 75 percent (Dieter, Perry, and Mulhern 1976). Seventeen percent of the wild canvasbacks sampled on Chesapeake Bay had less than one-half the normal dehydratase levels in their blood.

Because one of the most ubiquitous effects of many toxic substances found in the environment is the enhancement of microsomal action in the liver, the measurement of cytochrome P-450 levels in the livers of 21-day-old nestling herring gulls might be used as a monitor of their exposure to organochlorines or polynuclear aromatic hydrocarbons.

The induction of the mixed function oxidase system and the reduction in residues during the nestling stage requires critical assessment of age in order to compare results between areas. In the Canadian study reported, residues of DDE and PCB decreased 50 fold in muscle from day 2 following hatch to day 21 (Peakall, Norstrom, Rahimtula, et al. 1986). The effect of many organic compounds on the induction of the microsomal mixed-function oxidase system (MFO) has been well studied and used to assess other physiological effects such as sleep-time induced by narcotic drugs.

Most of the physiological studies with wildlife have emphasized two major effects related to exposure to the organochlorine groups: MFO induction and changes in steroids in plasma; and the effect of organophosphates on the levels of acetylcholinesterase (AChE) in blood plasma and brain tissue.

MFO Induction and Changes in Plasma Steroids

Induction of the MFO system in the liver is measured in vivo by reduced sleep times as a result of narcotic treatment. Wild cottontail rabbits were treated with dietary PCB at 10 ppm for 10 weeks and then injected with sodium pentobarbital. Sleep times for those treated with PCB were significantly shorter, mean sleep time following the drug injection was 162.8 minutes for control animals and 116.3 minutes for PCB-treated rabbits (Zepp, Sanders, and Kirkpatrick 1974). Similar effects have also been observed in cottontails following treatment with mirex. Oral treatment of 200 ppm mirex reduced sleep time from 178.6 minutes in control to 95.5 minutes in treated rabbits (Warren, Kirkpatrick, and Young 1978). In vivo studies have also been done with domestic rabbits and laboratory rats. In vitro measurement of MFO induction has been reported for many species in response to a variety of chemicals. Male and female bobwhite quail treated with 5.0 ppm dietary DDT showed increased breakdown of testosterone and progesterone when these hormones were incubated with liver homogenates from treated birds. The conversion of progesterone in females was 54 percent and in control females it was 24.1 percent (Lustick, Voss, and Peterle 1973). The effect was more pronounced in females than in males. Earlier it had been shown that treatment of king pigeons with combinations of DDT and/or dieldrin produced similar results. The combination of DDT and dieldrin showed some synergistic effects in terms of increasing the breakdown of both testosterone and progesterone to more polar metabolites (Peakall 1967). Mallards exposed to 4,000 ppm dietary petroleum hydrocarbons showed a 25 percent increase in liver weight, a 30 percent increase in hepatic blood flow, and a 33 percent increase in the rate of clearance time of indocyanien dye from the blood (Patton and Dieter 1980). White mice and laboratory rats show similar responses to PCB treatment in terms of enlarged livers and reduced sleep times (Sanders and Kirkpatrick 1975; Sanders, Kiripatrick, and Scanlon 1977). Total plasma corticoids increased dramatically from 2.78 μg/100 ml to 157.22 μg/100 ml in mice treated with 400 ppm PCB and 50 percent food restricted (Sanders, Kirkpatrick, and Scanlon 1977). Basic differences in responses to MFO-inducing chemicals among carnivores and herbivores may be a result of evolutionary response to plant toxins ingested by herbivores but not carnivores (Vangilder and Drawer 1983). Natural selection may have allowed polyphagous herbivores to adjust their responses to intake of plant toxins and thereby they are better able to respond to xenobiotics than are strict carnivores.

The many varied effects of enzyme induction, suppression, and activation can alter the rate of uptake, transport, storage, and breakdown of toxic substances as well as the natural hormones circulating in the body of exposed organisms (Conney 1967). Feedback responses inherent in the endocrine system can be altered and result in changes in behavior, reproduction, feeding habits, nutrition, and responses to diseases. Alteration in the function and structure of endocrine organs have been reported as a result of toxic substance exposure. These effects are evident not only with exposure to organochlorines that induce MFO in the liver, but result from organophosphate treatment as well.

Bobwhites treated with 100 ppm parathion showed reduced plasma LH and reduced reproductive success (Rattner, Sileo, and Scanes 1982b). Mallards treated with dietary crude oil showed reduced levels of plasma corticosterone. The responses varied depending on the oil fraction tested (Gorsline and Holmes 1982). Plasma corticosteriod levels were reduced 72 percent in resting mallards but adrenal size remained the same following exposure to petroleum. Adrenal tissue excised from treated mallards and perfused with ACTH released about one-fifth the level of corticosteroids compared to adrenals from control mallards (Gorsline and Holmes 1982). Oil may alter the structure and function of endocrine and reproductive organs such as the adrenal gland and the ovary, and the subsequent secretion of LH and progesterone (Rattner, Eroschenko, Fox, et al. 1984).

Bobwhite quail adrenals from DDT-treated birds had different cortico/medulary ratios than control birds. Quail were orally treated with 0, 10, 50, and 150 ppm DDT and as the amount of DDT in the diet increased, the cortical/medullary ratio also increased from 1.13 to 1.39 in control birds to 2.27 to 2.72 in birds treated with 150 ppm. Adrenal body weight ratios did not change, indicating an alteration in type of tissue within the adrenal, not in adrenal size (Lehman, Peterle, and Mills 1974).

Mallards fed crude oil had delayed reproductive periods. The treated birds completed their cycle in 71 days and the control birds in 56 days. Prolactin levels in treated hens were lower and peaks occurred later than in control hens (Cavanaugh, Goldsmith, Holmes, et al. 1983).

Plasma corticosterone was increased 2 to 5 times in bobwhites treated with 100 ppm parathion and then placed in a cold room. LH levels, egg production, and body weight were also reduced (Rattner, Sileo, and Scanes 1982a).

The direct estrogenic effect of kepone was demonstrated. DeWitt (1955, 1956), early in the efforts to determine toxic substance effects on wildlife, showed a reversal of external secondary sex characteristics in pheasants treated with mirex; males became more female-like in external appearance.

The direct estrogenic effect of DDT and methoxychlor in rats was demonstrated by increased uterine weights following injection in ovarianectomized females (Welch, Levin, and Conney 1969). Reduced aggressiveness was demonstrated in male laboratory mice treated with 7 ppm dietary DDT for 20 days (Peterle and Peterle 1971).

In chicken oviducts tested in vitro, kepone acts as an estrogen by binding to estrogen receptors and by increasing albumen synthesis and indirectly plasma progesterone (Palmiter and Mulvihill 1978). Luteinizing hormone levels were somewhat reduced and the peak LH in plasma was delayed in ring doves treated with 40 ppm dietary DDE (Richie and Peterle 1979).

Histological sections of parathyroid glands from King pigeons exposed to 10 ppm dietary DDE showed a 15.6 percent increase in the number of inactive cells compared to control parathyroid glands (Parsons and Peterle 1977).

Enzyme activities have been used to determine the chronic physiological effects of a number of toxic substances. Five enzymes from five different tissues from five avian species were assayed and there was little difference found between the sexes, but some significant differences among species. Liver, kidney, and muscle enzymes were similar, but plasma enzymes were different. It is important to establish baseline levels of plasma enzymes in each species prior to utilizing this technique to assess the impact of toxic substance exposure (Franson, Murray, and Bunck 1985). Black-crowned night-herons exposed to fenthion-treated water showed no change in brain AChE activities as a result of the dermal exposure, but the plasma butyrycholinesterase activites showed that the herons had been exposed to an organophosphate (Smith, Spann, and Hill 1986). Brain ChE levels in horned larks and McCown's longspurs feeding on western cutworms in wheat fields treated with chlorpyrifos were reduced on days 3 and 9 post-spray, but by day 16 the levels were again normal. The effects of chlorpyrifos treatment for cutworm was much less than the previous use of endrin (McEwen, DeWeese, and Schladweiler 1986).

Hepatic mixed-function oxidase systems in herring gull embryos are being used to examine contaminant exposure history in wild populations and potential effects (Boersma, Ellenton, and Yagminas 1986). Embryos from herring gull colonies in the Great Lakes area were compared to a colony in the Bay of Fundy that had low body burdens of contaminants. In vitro studies of liver homogenates showed that aniline hydroxylation was significantly depressed in the embryos from the Great Lakes compared to the Bay of Fundy colonies. Organochlorine residues in eggs were negatively correlated with rates of demethylation and hydroxylation. More studies of normal oxidase functions in adults and embryos are needed before field results can be fully interpreted. Toxic substances can affect oxidase function according to species and combinations of exposures, as well as age. Differential responses were observed in mallards treated for 6, 12, and 18 weeks with either South Louisiana or Prudhoe Bay crude oil (SLCO, PBCO). A 0.15 and 1.5 percent dietary treatment with PBCO significantly reduced plasma corticosterone levels, but SLCO did not. Neither of the treatments influenced plasma thyroxine concentrations. These changes could alter the ability of the birds to respond to cold stress or to food deprivation (Rattner and Eastin 1981). Mallard ducklings hatched from hens treated with 10 ppm DDE or 2 percent SLCO survived a shorter time when exposed to cold (Vangilder and Peterle 1980). Both hyper- or hypothyroidism can be induced by DDT treatment of pigeons. Low doses of 3 mg/kg/day produced hyperthyroidal activity and doses of 54 mg/kg resulted in hypothyroidal function (Jefferies and French 1971).

Following an in-depth review of the effects of toxic substances on avian endocrine responses, Rattner, Eroschenko, Fox, et al. (1984) suggested that (p. 688) "Further research on the effects and mechanism of action of environmental contaminants on avian endocrine function is warranted." The areas in need of study include effects of organochlorines, AChE-insecticides, and petroleum products as well as heavy metals. Only with added information can we begin to assess the potential impacts of chronic exposure on the physiological function of the individual organism and ultimately on the well-being of the population and survival of the species. There is a continued challenge to study the physiological responses of organisms to environmental contaminants because the information contributes to general knowledge and potentially leads to the prediction of effects of toxins as additive stressors to biological systems (Anderson, Peterle, and Dickson 1986).

Effect of Organophosphates on Acetylcholinesterase Activity

Acetylcholinesterase activity is stongly influenced by the exposure of wildlife to the organophosphate pesticides. Measurement of ChE levels in blood and brain have shown that reductions of about 50 percent are indicative of lethal doses. The brain is considered the best tissue to analyze because it is less variable and changes more slowly than these parameters do in blood samples (Fleming 1981). AChE (acetylcholinesterase) levels in blood and brain can change as a result of ambient temperature changes and the state of nutrition in the animal, so baseline studies are necessary. Food and environmental changes may alter plasma levels by 10 to 17 percent (Rattner 1982).

The development of brain ChE differs between precocial and altricial birds, so the age of altricial nestlings is important to baseline measurements of ChE activity. Chicks of precocial birds at hatching have ChE levels more or less the same as those in adults (Grue and Hunter 1984). In nestling starlings 18 days old, about 14.1 um/g of tissue are hydrolyzed and in adult birds this is about 20 um/g of tissue (Grue and Hunter 1984). This is also true of nestling snowy and great egrets and black-crowned night-herons. Brain ChE level increased to at least 16 days of age (Custer and Ohlendorf 1989). Brain ChE levels in female bobwhites fed graded doses (0–400 ppm) of parathion were directly correlated to dose level. In micromols of ChE iodide hydrolyzed per minute per gram of tissue, the control group on day 10 was 5.6 and the 400 ppm group 1.82 μmol/min/g of tissue (Rattner, Sileo, and Scanes 1982b).

Mallard ducklings tested in the laboratory with a variety of organophosphates showed ChE depressions of 25 to 58 percent. Some mortality occurred and was most severe in fensulfothion treatment and lowest with malathion. About 8 days were required for the survivors to recover to normal ChE levels (Fleming and Bradbury 1981). Mallard adults treated with 17 ppm fenthion for 6 days showed decreased levels of ChE activity. Control birds showed 2.7 μmol/min/g of tissue wet weight and the treated birds 1.8 μmol/min/g (Eastin, Fleming, and Murray 1982).

Fenthion fed to black ducks at 21 ppm resulted in 44 to 61 percent inhibition of ChE activity in the adults.

Dicrotophos was fed to five avian species at several dosages from 3.0 to 4.0 mg/kg. Varied responses were obtained in terms of reduction of ChE activity in the brain after 18 hours. The reduction in percent of ChE activity as a result of treatment at 3.5 mg/kg was highest in the bobwhite, 54 percent; and lowest for the barn owl, 14 percent. Percentage reductions for other species were 18 percent for mallard, 25 percent for grackle, and 29 percent for starling. Treated birds recovered to at least 80 percent of normal in about 10 to 20 days (Fleming and Grue 1981).

Five different organophosphates were tested on mallard ducklings in doses from 350 mg/kg to 900 mg/kg for the various compounds. Fensulfothion was the most potent inhibitor at 48.9 percent; parathion ChE levels were 74 percent as high as controls (Fleming and Bradbury 1981). Methyl parathion fed to nuthatches in injected mealworms at 3.5 mg/kg once daily for 15 days showed 36 percent ChE inhibition in brain tissue. Regression coefficients of rectrix growth showed some effects of treatment (Herbert, Peterle, and Grubb 1989).

Some post-mortem changes in ChE do occur. They are significant at 24 to 72 hours. Japanese quail treated with 9 mg of carbofuran had brain ChE activities of 2.9 umol/min/g of brain tissue as fresh specimens, 5.5 at 24 hours, 7.3 at 48 hours, and 5.9 at 72 hours (Hill 1989). Intact birds were held at 25°C. Control bird brain ChE activities were 15.4 umol/min/g as fresh specimens and did not change up to 72 hours post-mortem. Oral dosing of white-footed mice with acephate at 50 and 100 mg/kg resulted in reduced ChE levels in the brain of 45 and 56 percent. Luteinizing hormone plasma levels were also reduced (Rattner and Michael 1985).

There is also ample field evidence that ChE levels are reduced in exposed birds following field treatment with organophosphates. In fields treated with parathion and toxaphene, there was a significant difference in the reduction in ChE levels in brain tissue of dickcissels (74%) and red-winged blackbirds (40%). This could not be explained on the basis of dietary differences in field feeding (Niethammer and Baskett 1983). Aerial application of fenthion for mosquito control resulted in mortality of birds and mammals. ChE depression was highest 2 days post-spray, but significant depression of ChE was evident in some species for 15 days post-spray (DeWeese, McEwen, Settimi, et al. 1983). Brain ChE activity was depressed in a variety of shorebirds wintering in Texas as a result of organophosphate exposure. Western sandpipers, American avocets, and long-billed dowitchers were tested and up to 43 percent inhibition was found. Approximately 20 percent is considered to be active toxicosis (Mitchell and White 1982). Blue grouse recovered in forest areas aerially sprayed with phosphamidon for spruce budworm control had blood ChE levels reduced to 54 and 58 percent. One bird recovered in 33 days; the other died (Finley 1965).

Effects of Heavy Metals

The effects of heavy metals and other toxic substances on the physiological parameters that can be measured in blood have been given a lot of attention, partially because of the ease of sampling and in some cases the direct relationship between cause and effect. This is probably most closely related in the case of lead contamination of birds, where the levels of lead in the body are positively correlated with dehydratase levels in plasma. In wild canvasback ducks collected on Chesapeake Bay, residues of 200 ppb lead in the blood reduced dehydratase levels by 75 percent (Dieter, Perry, and Mulhern 1976). This causes malfunction of the hemoglobin, and because ducks have a short erythrocyte half-life of about 40 days, physiological changes in oxygen exchanges could result from lead exposure. The relationship between lead levels and blood parameters has been used by examining urban pigeons in relationship to air quality in cities. Oral treatment of herring gulls and puffins with Prudhoe Bay crude oil at 10 to 20 mg/kg produced anemia in 4 or 5 days. In herring gulls PCV decreased by 50 percent and Heinz body counts increased from 0 percent to as high as 92 percent. Heinz bodies are granular masses in the red blood cells thought to be precipitates of oxidized hemogloblin (Leighton, Peakall, and Butler 1983). Lead contamination (4200 ppm) in waste oil fed to mallards at 0.5 percent and 4.5 percent of the diet decreased ALAD activity in red blood cells by 50 and 85 to 90 percent (Eastin, Hoffman, and O'Leary 1983). Lead fed to day-old kestrels inhibited their growth rates by the third day. Residues of 2.0 ppm (w/w) in the liver and 6.0 ppm in the kidney were indicative of impacts on growth rates (Hoffman, Franson, Pattee, et al. 1985b). Cockerels fed 1850 ppm lead in the diet for 4 weeks weighed 47 percent as much as control birds and both Hb (hemoglobin) and PCV (packed cell volume) were significantly reduced. Lead residues in the kidney were about three times higher than those found in the liver (Franson and Custer 1982). Kestrels treated with 50 ppm powdered lead had blood ALAD levels about 20 percent as high as control birds, but 10 ppm in the diet did not result in any accumulation nor in physiological effects (Franson, Sileo, Pattee, et al. 1983). Lead fed to kestrels that was biologically incorporated in cockerels at 448 ppm did not produce any physiological blood parameter changes nor any accumulation in the body after 60 days of treatment. Mallard ducklings fed 20 ppm cadmium in the diet for 12 weeks showed increased glutamic pyruvic transaminase (GPT) and reduced Hb and PCV. Liver cadmium residues were about twice that found in the diet (Cain, Sileo, Franson, et al. 1983). Mercury can also result in altered plasma chemistries when fed to *Coturnix* at subchronic levels (Hill and Soares 1984).

Salt Gland and Osmoregulation Responses

Another physiological change in wildlife species that has been of interest to toxicologists is the response of the salt gland and osmoregulation to chronic exposure to pollutants. Black surfperch injected with 200 ppm DDT had plasmotic concentrations of 368 to 375 milliosmols compared to 306 to 308 milliosmols in control fish (Waggoner and Zeeman 1975).

The primary toxic effect of the treatment of eels with either PCB or DDT was a disruption of osmoregulation. Sodium transport was affected and there was inhibition of sodium/potassium ATPase (Kinter, Merkens, Janicki, et al. 1972). There has been some conflicting evidence of the effect of toxic substances on salt gland and osmoregulation in birds. Sodium/potassium ATPases were reported to have been inhibited by DDE in vitro tests, but treatment of Pekin ducks, black guillemots, and common puffins with 10 to 250 ppm DDE showed no effects on salt gland function. Earlier tests also showed ATPases to be affected in vitro in five species of turtles (Phillips and Wells 1974). DDE, but not fenthion was shown to influence salt gland activity in in-vitro studies of ATPase activity in chicks (Rattner,

Fleming, and Murray 1983). Fenthion fed to black ducks held on saltwater resulted in increased salt gland size and increased sodium/potassium ATPase activity (Eastin, Fleming, and Murray 1982). Later, 21 ppm fenthion fed to black ducks showed no effects on osmoregulatory function (Rattner, Fleming, and Murray 1982). Mature male mallards fed various levels of DDE in the diet were later challenged with injections of concentrated salt solution. Subsequent salt excretion was not influenced by DDE treatment if birds had been held on saltwater, but mallards being held on fresh water prior to treatment were significantly less able to excrete salt following DDE exposure (Friend, Haegele, and Wilson 1973). Apparently there is still some question concerning the impact of various toxic substances on osmoregulation in birds. Perhaps dose, species, age, and the specific toxic substance may have altered results and impacts may not be general across species and toxicants.

PREDISPOSITION TO DISEASE AND OTHER FORMS OF STRESS

One of the most interesting areas of research is related to the interaction between toxic substance exposure and predisposition to diseases, parasites, and other forms of stress. This potential synergistic interaction could have major impact on population change, yet it has received little attention either in the field or in the laboratory.

Some early work on laboratory rats showed the relationship of organochlorines to the immune system. Rats fed 200 ppm DDT in drinking water for 35 days and challenged with injections of ovalalbumin showed a 30 percent decrease in antibodies to ovalalbumin and decreased spleen weights. Adrenal hypertrophy induced by surgical procedures was completely inhibited by DDT treatment (Wassermann, Wasserman, Gershon, et al. 1969).

Both laboratory and wild deer mice were shown to be responsive to the interaction of a virus, a plant growth regulator, and PCB treatment. Malnourishment also made them more susceptible to the PCB treatment effects, and some synergistic action between the plant growth regulator and PCB was evident (Porter, Hinsdill, Fairbrother, et al. 1984).

Some of these relationships could be quite complex and difficult to identify. Some toxic substances might have the same predilection for accumulation to specific tissues as disease organisms, or diseased tissue might accumulate more toxic compounds. We know that immune systems are affected and alteration of the MFO system could alter metabolism of enzymes as well as toxic compounds. We also know that chronic exposure can increase metabolic rates and require more energy intake and utilization for maintenance and perhaps less energy would be available to supress or fight diseases and parasites. The toxic substance might also change the virulence of a disease organism or alter the susceptibility of the host for infestation by a parasite.

Bobwhite quail fed the insecticide sevin at rates of single doses from 2.5 to 50 μg were found to be more susceptible to challenges of *Heterakis* (blackhead) eggs given in equal doses of 0 to 5000 eggs over a 5-day period. Quail given only parasite eggs did not develop the symptoms of the disease. Those given only the insecticide sevin showed discoloration of the liver, but those treated with both the toxin and the parasite eggs suffered 36 to 63 percent mortality (Zeakes, Hansen, and Robel 1981).

Despite immunization of channel catfish against the bacterium *Aeromonas,* 100 percent of the exposed fish died if they were also exposed to 70 mg/kg arochlor 1232 (Jones, Lewis, Eurell, et al. 1979).

Mallards exposed to either DDT or dieldrin and then challenged with doses of duck hepatitis virus (DHV) had higher mortality than control birds. Twenty-day-old ducklings fed 900 ppm DDT or 40 ppm dieldrin and the virus suffered 47 and 57 percent mortality, respectively, compared to 6 percent mortality in birds not fed any insecticide. Insecticide residues in brain tissue of birds that died of DHV were 255 percent greater in the case of DDT treatment and 1410 percent more in those fed dieldrin. These disease/pesticide relationships have also been demonstrated for PCB exposure and DHV (Friend and Trainer 1970, 1974a, b).

The relationship between air pollution and disease has been demonstrated in humans as shown by increased mortality following incidences of high air pollution events. Laboratory studies have demonstrated relationships between ozone exposure and the increased culture of bacteria from lung tissue of exposed animals. Suggestions have also been made relating air pollution to the incidence of macrophages in lung tissue of urban birds such as English sparrows and starlings. Little has been done to examine potential effects of air pollution on wildlife outside the cities (Newman 1979, Newman and Schreiber 1988).

The entire area of how toxic substances influence the ability of an animal to respond to diseases and parasites is in need of additional study and evaluation both in the laboratory and in the field.

TUMOR DEVELOPMENT AND MUTAGENIC EFFECTS

There is some evidence from monitoring programs to show higher incidences of tumors in aquatic species in polluted waters. Brown, Wolke, Brown, et al. (1979) have shown higher incidences of neoplasia in soft-shell clams in New England in the vicinity of point sources of pollution. The percentage incidence of neoplasia in clams from clean water varied from 4 to 20 percent. In an area of a No. 2 fuel oil spill, clams showed 31 percent incidence and at a dumpsite, 39 percent of the clams examined had some evidence of neoplasia. Enlarged livers, but not enhanced MFO induction were found in tumor-bearing brown bullheads from polluted waters (Fabacher and Baumann 1985). How toxic substances affect the incidence of tumor development and potential lethal effects in wildlife is not well understood.

Embryotoxic effects have been noted in fish species that result in scoliosis or spinal deformities in young as a result of low chronic exposures to such compounds as toxaphene, dylox, guthion, malathion, and parathion (McCann and Jasper 1972). Some of the PAH compounds such as pyrene, chrysene, and anthracene are embryotoxic, carcinogenic, and teratogenic when applied to mallard eggs during development, (Hoffman and Gay 1981). Western and California gull eggs were injected with 2 to 100 ppm DDT, DDE, or methoxychlor and feminization of male embryos was evident because of abnormal development of ovarian tissues and the oviduct (Fry and Toone 1981). Mirex injected into pregnant female rats at the rate of 6 mg/kg on days 8 and 15 of gestation resulted in higher incidence of cardiovascular problems in young, 27 percent stillbirths, and 17 percent mortality within 6 hours of birth (Grabowski 1981). Exposure of rats prenatally to phenobarbital resulted in reduced testosterone production later in life and possible reproductive dysfunction (Gupta, Yaffe, and Shapiro 1982). Exposure of mice prenatally to 2,4-D resulted in destruction of the Harderian gland 2 weeks after birth. Effects on the Harderian gland also are apparent from thyroidectomy (Gray, Kavlock, Chernoff, et al. 1982).

Optic abnormalities were shown in embryos of marine fish (Atlantic silverside, mummichog or killifish) at exposures of 1 to 10 mg/l, or carbaryl and malathion (Weis and Weis 1979). Multi-tiered tests beginning with bacteria and progressing through fruit flies and then to mice have been suggested for testing mutagenic effects (Lewin 1983). There is little information concerning potential mutagenic effects of toxic substances on wildlife.

CARCINOGENICITY

The relationship between toxic substance exposure and the enhanced induction of cancer in wildlife is largely unkown. Some of the polycyclic hydrocarbons have been shown to be carcinogenic and many human cancers are induced in epithelial tissues. Cultures of human keratinocytes subsequently treated with both adenovirus and chemical carcinogens do induce cancer when transplanted into nude mice. Treatment with the adenovirus alone is not sufficient to produce cancer. This type of human cell culture might be an appropriate way to test chemicals for possible carcinogenicity (Rhim, Fujita, Arnstein, et al. 1986).

An NCI study has shown that formaldehyde poses a very low threat of cancer among humans exposed to occupational levels that are below the OSHA recommended residues. There was an increase in lung cancer of about 30 percent after 20 years, but because the incidence of cancer was not correlated to the levels of exposure, the scientists reporting the study did not feel the relationship was important. Samples of work exposure to formaldehyde were rarely made until after the mid-1970s (Sun 1986c).

PHENOLOGICAL ASPECTS

An important aspect of toxic substance/wildlife study that has not been fully evaluated is the impact of phenological development or season on the effects toxic substances exert directly on exposed organisms. The timing of the actual exposure can be extremely important in determining the impact on the organism. If animals are already in some state of debilitation because of disease, parasites, or malnutrition, a toxic substance impact could be lethal. The stress of migration, molt, hibernation, aestivation, sexual maturity, and reproduction are all important to how a toxin might influence the exposed animal.

Most pesticides are applied during the growing season so exposure coincides with the breeding season for many birds and mammals. One might imagine the importance to timing of exposure to a highly susceptible predator such as the mink or otter with breeding in autumn and delayed implantation; the lack of exposure because of the timing of most applications of pesticides could be very important.

The impact of pesticide applications on birds during the season when adults are feeding nestlings can be more severe as a result of the impact on availability of insects and the transfer of toxins to young in food brought to the nest. An application of fenthion during the nestling season did not influence reproductive success in the red-winged blackbird, but nestling growth rates were reduced in treated areas (Powell 1984). Nestling starlings were more sensitive to dicrotophos doses and LD-50 levels were age-related. Nestlings showed greater ChE inhibition than adults, but they also recovered faster from chronic doses (Grue and Shipley 1984). Wild female starlings made fewer sorties for food and their young lost more weight following exposure to dicrotophos (Grue, Powell, and McChesney 1982).

The impact of how the timing of exposure on a variety of life history phases has been discussed by Grue, Fleming, Busby, et al. (1983). Factors that might influence vulnerability include the timing, rate, frequency, and formulation of the chemical application. Many organophosphates are applied in early morning and could influence birds at their peak of activity. Other factors mentioned include species sensitivity, physiological condition, and behavioral traits, all of which might change seasonally.

If exposure is high during incubation periods, the impact of external contamination of eggs has been well studied and micro-liter quantities of some toxins applied to eggs can be lethal or teratogenic to the embryo (Hoffman and Eastin 1981a,b; 1982 Hoffman, Eastin, and Gay 1982).

The sequential exposure of an animal to organochlorines, for example, can alter the uptake, metabolism, and storage. Induction of the MFO system alters the rate of breakdown of both toxins and hormones and the influence of seasonal events in such a sequence of exposures can be very important. Exposure to DDT and/or dieldrin can influence the total body burden depending on the sequence of exposure. Periods of climatic or food stress related to exposure to toxins is also important. Mobilization of fat stores at times of need can mobilize stored residues of toxic substances and produce chronic or lethal effects. Stress-induced delayed lethal effects of mirex to grackles has been described (Stickel, Gaylen, Dyrland, et al. 1973).

The transmissions of disease through insect vectors is undoubtedly influenced by pesticide treatment. This might result in reduced potential for transfer if the vector organism is reduced by pesticide treatment. However, if the vector is released by removal of predators or by lack of competition, the potential for disease transfer might be increased. Behavioral changes induced by chronic exposure might also alter the susceptibility of the host to transfer by the vector. We know that some prey species are more vulnerable to predation following exposure to toxic substances, so it seems logical to assume that hosts might also be more susceptible to their parasites following chronic exposure. Because there is high selectivity of target populations for resistance, it also seems plausible that toxic substances with differential toxicity could alter the virulence of a disease organism or alter the ability of the parasite to attack the host.

ADDITIVE MODEL FOR TOXINS

Perhaps the impacts of chronic exposure of toxic substances to wildlife should be viewed, generally, as an additive model where the effect impacts the organism as one additional environmental stress that may or may not influence the life or health of the exposed individual. All of the physical, social, behavioral, nutritional and human-induced disturbances impact the individual and in addition the kinds, amounts, timing, and sequence of xenobiotic intake can have an added influence. Whether this influence is additive, synergistic, or whether beneficial or harmful effects result cannot be predicted for wild-living species existing in complex systems.

Body burdens of organochlorines may be higher in a population of birds that is reproducing at a satisfactory recruitment rate than in another where reproduction is failing. In one instance, other added environmental stress may not be sufficiently high to demonstrate effect with the toxic substance, but in the other instance a low nutritional plane and human disturbances, or lack of habitat may result in reproductive losses with lower body burdens.

Because we are not able to measure the total environmental stress on the organism in addition to the effects of toxic substance exposure, it is difficult to provide evidence that toxins are additive stressors on animals. Body burdens of DDE in ospreys have been directly related to recruitment. Egg residues of DDE, PCB, and dieldrin have been lower in osprey nests producing two young than in nests producing no young in Long Island and Connecticut (Spitzer, Risebrough, Walker, et al. 1978). As egg residues declined from 1969 to 1977, recruitment, in terms of young per active nest, increased.

Perhaps the notion of additive stress might be shown by the productivity and DDE residues in ospreys from the Potomac River and those from the Lake Nipigon area of Ontario. Recruitment was quite similar, 0.61 to 0.80 fledglings per occupied nest along the Potomac and 0.74 to 0.79 fledglings in the Lake Nipigon area. DDE residues in eggs were quite different, 2.4 ppm (w/w) for the Potomac eggs and 4.7 ppm for the eggs analyzed from Lake Nipigon (Henny 1975). One might assume that other total stress, particularly human disturbances, would be less in the Lake Nipigon area than on the Potomac. Laboratory evidence seems to support the notion that physical and human stress on test animals can alter the effect of toxic substance. The actual validation of such a model in the field would be difficult because all influences on the organism cannot be measured and perhaps not even identified. (See Fig. 5-4 for GAS systems in birds.)

CONCLUSION

The study and identification of chronic effects of toxins on wildlife is a very interesting and productive challenge, but the ultimate demonstration of productivity or population impacts in natural systems is difficult. The relationship between exposure to toxic substances and eggshell thinning clearly demonstrated population impacts in terms of reduced recruitment and in some cases local extinction of some species (i.e., peregrines, Hickey 1969).

Table 7-1 Hypothetical Responses of Vertebrates to Chronic Pollution Stress

A. Direct pathological effects
  1. Mortality
  2. Morbidity
B. Physiological and reproductive effects
  1. Fertility
  2. Fecundity
  3. Growth, metabolism, and energetics
  4. Immunosuppression
  5. Differential effects on life functions
  6. Other factors affecting competitive ability
C. Biochemical effects
  1. Enzyme suppression or activation
  2. Enzyme kinetics
D. Genetic change
E. Behavioral or physiological effects
  1. Dormancy
    a. Hibernation
    b. Estivation
  2. Physical movement
    a. Dispersal
    b. Migration
    c. Refuging
    d. Dispersion
  3. Selective behavior (e.g., feeding, habitat selection, etc.)
F. Adaptation and resistance
  1. Induced detoxication mechanisms
  2. Altered rates of uptake and/or excretion
  3. Sequestering
  4. Behavioral adaptation
G. Indirect effects manifested through reduced home range carrying capacity, e.g., via:
  1. Direct vegetation destruction
  2. Factors affecting soil nutrients
  3. Factors affecting nutrient quality of vegetation
  4. Factors affecting climate
  5. Other factors that interrupt energy flow or otherwise alter resource relationships
H. Other effects
  1. Dysfunctional phase-shifting (in time) of life functions
  2. Preadaptation
  3. Non-adaptative change (e.g., ancillary or related to one of the above; pleiotropy)

Adapted from Lewis, R. A., and C. W. Lewis. 1979. Terrestrial vertebrate animals as biological monitors of pollution. In Monitoring environmental materials and specimen banking, *ed. N-P. Luepke, pp. 369–391. Reprinted by permission of Kluwer Academic Publishers.*

Whether we will ever be able to demonstrate the population impacts of more subtle behavioral, physiological, or anatomical effects remains to be seen. A broad and extensive list of hypothetical responses of vertebrates to chronic pollution stress has been presented (Lewis and Lewis 1979, Table 7-1) and offers some insight into areas where evidence is present and verified and other areas where we have done very little to describe, identify, and verify the effects of chronic exposure of wildlife to xenobiotics.

8

Effects on Ecosystems

The impacts of toxic substances on ecosystems, especially low level chronic effects, are difficult to describe and assess. Major catastrophes such as clear-cutting or fire can not only be easily observed, but assessment of effects can be measured. Consider the low-level application of an insecticide on part or all of the community under study and, unless there is high direct mortality of many species, impacts are difficult to observe, and even more difficult to measure. When we discuss toxic substance effects, we are immediately drawn to such hard data as LC/LD50 levels on individual organisms, yet these kinds of information cannot easily be transposed to ecosystem effects. Single species tests in the laboratory do not provide data concerning intra/inter species responses, total system productivity, metabolism, and nutrient turnover. We are essentially totally ignorant of potential impacts of chemical substances on the future genetic structure of chronically exposed populations. We know that genetic changes do result from selection for resistance, but how chronic body burdens might influence genetic structure is unknown.

Our inability to assess chronic ecosystem effect is partially due to the state of the science in terms of what characteristics to measure, and how to assess them in ever-changing environments. If chronic toxic substances effects are subtle, measurements of ecosystem characteristics with 30 to 50 percent statistical validity are not useful. Perhaps, if toxic substance effects are not obvious nor great enough to measure, we should be complacent and not be concerned about their potential negative impacts. Based on what we know about subtle, chronic effects of toxic substances on individuals, it would seem likely that these cumulative negative effects could ultimately result in chronic ecosystem impacts as well. The more we are willing to consider such effects and improve our ability to measure them, the more likely we are to successfully avoid potential catastrophic collapse of functioning ecosystems as a result of cumulative build-up of long-term chronic toxic substance inupt into the global environment.

POPULATIONS

The acute impacts of toxic substances on populations is obviously related to the dose/time continuum and the sensitivity of the species found at the site. Acute effects may be short-term as a direct result of the application or release, or they may be long-term if the compound is one that accumulates over longer periods to a lethal dose effect. Because species sensitivity varies so widely and is influenced by inherent structural, physiological, and perhaps phylogenetic relationships, the direct acute impact of a toxic substance on populations of a wide spectrum of species is difficult to predict. Population effects are related to the ecosystem structure, function, and dynamics; and to the relative abundance of the species at the time of exposure. Timing of the exposure might be at either peak or low periods of abundance for a particular species and the uptake and effects could be influenced by inter- and intraspecific competition, nutrition, body condition, territoriality, daily movements, and reproductive status. The potential invasion of an opportunistic species as a result of mortality of residents could also influence the rate of uptake in the remaining segment of the population. If complete laboratory toxicity tests are available for a given species, acute effects on populations might be predicted, but not with great precision.

Chronic, long-term effects on populations are more difficult to assess or predict. These might be in direct survivorship, in terms of the individual's ability to metabolize or sequester low-level intake, and ultimately lethal effects are manifest. Other more subtle non-lethal effects on populations might relate to disruption of breeding systems; delayed growth and sexual maturity; changes in behavior, migration, emigration, or dispersal; and alteration in the F_1 generation that could impact recruitment as a result of reproductive dysfunction or genetic selection.

One of the areas about which we know least is the potential for influence on the genetic structure of the remaining populations following direct mortality. There is potential for selection for greater or lesser hetero- or homogeneity as well as demonstrated selection for resistance (Ferguson 1967). Short-term evaluation of such changes may over- or underestimate long-term effects. Tolerance to stress or the ability of the species to respond to reduced diversity and an alteration in intra- interspecies interactions could influence population dynamics over long periods of time. The mode of adaptation of a species or population to a toxic substance might vary in terms of changes in resistance, growth, fecundity, altered food habits, or in their competitive relationships. Possible selection for or against tolerance to toxic substances may be linked to selection for or against other desirable or undesirable genetic attributes. This might result in lower or higher survival in either stable or changing ecosystems or environments. Selection response is influenced by both the intensity of selection and by the possible genetic variance, either decreased or increased, as a result of the toxic substances lethal effects.

The removal of certain cohorts of a population at one time could have a long-lasting impact on the population of long-lived species. Reductions in total recruitment as a result of a missing cohort could push the population over the threshold level to extinction as a result of normal system perturbations. Other selection factors might disrupt growth and timing of sexual maturity that is related to peaks in food resources or to optimum seasonal climatic factors suited to reproduction. This could be highly critical, for example, in some invertebrate populations that require specific foods such as pollen for attainment of sexual maturity. Population changes over long periods might also relate to the differences in response to diseases and parasites as a result of selection or altered physiological functions such as enzyme production and metabolism.

Behavioral responses have also been shown as a result of low-level chronic exposure. Fish exposed to chronic doses of toxic substances select different temperature preferenda and this might completely eliminate successful reproduction if eggs are deposited in areas of higher or lower temperature preferenda for development. We know little of F_1 generation effects other than the isolated evidence to show possible disruption of hormone production and feminization of some male birds as a result of toxic substance exposure. Alteration in genetic structure, changes in behavior, and possible lack of fertility are all possible impacts directly on the F_1 generation as a result of toxic substance exposure to the adults. Population threshold levels are not only important as they relate to possible extinction from other causes, but to transmission of diseases and parasites and to other behavioral requirements for reproduction (social functions such as leks) or to learned patterns of behavior such as migration and dispersal.

Secondary population effects must also be considered, such as control of prey populations by predators, or the pollination of plants. Other ecosystem functions such as the breakdown and transfer of nutrients could also be a secondary relationship that might change as a result of population change. There are also some unique relationships among species such as obligate parasitism, commensalism, and mutualism that could be disrupted by effects on a single species population. Life table characteristics such as survival, life expectancy, and mortality rates might be expected to change and have an impact on the structure and density of the residual population.

DIVERSITY

Ecologists have tended to discard the old maxim that diversity is related to stability, but in terms of how toxic substances impact ecosystems it seems apparent that diversity is of considerable importance in the determination of the final impact. Perhaps one of the best examples of this is in aquatic systems, where communities of different complexity and biomass were treated with the same level of a toxic substance. Partitioning among the various compartments and disappearance rates for the various systems were dependent on their total biomass and complexity (Terriere, Kiigemagi, Gerlach, et al. 1966).

Diversity must not only be considered in light of the number of species present in any community that is being impacted by toxic substances, but also the importance of the various species as they relate to energy flow and nutrient retention and transfer in the system. Function may be more important than taxonomic identification and listing of the species present. Function may not only be species related, but sex/age related as well. Consideration must be given to whether highly susceptible species have buffer species that can fulfill the same function in the system in the event of high mortality of the susceptible species. The impact on species diversity may not be great if the reduction in species composition is spread throughout the various levels of the trophic system. If the losses caused by mortality are concentrated at some specific level of the system, the reduction in diversity could be catastrophic and system collapse would occur. If diversity is reduced, subsequent enrichment of species might occur if vacant niches permit the invasion of opportunistic species. This could occur as a result of mortality of resident species, or reduced vigor and aggressiveness of the resident species to niche compression. Altered species abundance could result in either increased or decreased biomass, an effect that may be desirable or undesirable.

As a result of removal of highly sensitive species, traditional roles of interspecific relationships or predator–prey interactions could be altered and predation might increase as a result of more vulnerable prey even at reduced population levels of prey. This could further alter the species composition as an indirect result of treatment or exposure. Some species or group of species might be more important to the detoxification of an introduced substance and by the removal of these species, the rate of detoxification or sequestering of the toxin within the community might be reduced. The impacts on the system might thereby be lengthened in time and other unpredictable results might occur. The relationships among species and between species and the physical components of the environment have developed over long periods of time. Any disruption of these relationships by the removal or drastic reduction of some species could result in a long time to recovery. If reduced diversity permits the invasion of opportunistic species, the re-establishment of the original system would take even longer and might never occur. In a discussion of the measurement of inertia and resilience of ecosystems, Westman (1978) has suggested that a PS-50, (percentage similarity index) similar to an LD-50 might be developed to describe the impact of toxic substances on ecosystems. Other characteristics of resilience such as inertia, elasticity, amplitude, hysteresis, and malleability might also have application to the study and description of how toxic substances affect ecosystems (Westman 1978). Disruption of species diversity and composition can have lasting impacts on community/ecosystem development, productivity, and stability.

PRODUCTIVITY AND BIOMASS

Simply stated, productivity deals with the rate of nutrient exchange in a system and biomass is a measurement of the standing stock at any given point in time. The effects of toxic substances on ecosystems could result in both increased or decreased productivity and biomass and this might be considered either beneficial or detrimental to human interests.

For example, an increase in production of algal growth in aquatic systems used for water supplies or recreation could be considered detrimental. A similar increase in basic productivity might be beneficial if it resulted in higher productivity of terminal species in the food chain that were being harvested for food or for sport fishing. Higher rates of productivity usually imply higher biomass, but not always. In some systems with very high nutrient turnover, the biomass might never reach higher proportions because of the low total nutrient pool. Following exposure to toxins, the rate of productivity might decrease as a result of lowered metabolic rates, reduced efficiency of organic breakdown and recycling, and reduced numbers of organisms could result in reduced transfer to higher trophic levels and an accumulation of energy at producer levels of the system. There might also be a reduction in primary production as a result of lethal or chronic effects on the species at this trophic level.

The rates of nutrient/energy flow in the system are related to the transfer, accumulation, and metabolism of toxic substances. Low productivity systems would tend to retain and concentrate toxic substances over longer periods, not only as a result of low species diversity and productivity, but also because of the physical aspects of the environment. Arctic systems, for example, retain organochlorines over longer periods, not only because of low diversity and productivity, but also because of the cold snow cover and lack of photodegradation and sublimation (Brown and Brown 1970). Low productivity, low biomass systems would not be able to withstand multiple releases of toxic substances over short periods of time. Productivity might also be altered as a result of the loss of nutrients through death and leaching.

Some species may be highly important in the sequestering and retention of certain nutrients in the system and loss of these species could affect the productivity of the system over long periods if lethal effects result in nutrient loss from the system. In tests of various rates of exploitation on guppy populations exposed to dieldrin and control populations, the control group was able to respond to higher rates of exploitation by increased growth and reproduction. The populations treated with 1 ppb dieldrin showed reduced growth and reproduction; this would have led to extinction had the rate of exploitation been continuously high over long periods (Liss, Woltering, Finger, et al. 1982).

CONNECTIVITY

The chemical characteristics of a compound (solubility, volatility) and the pathways of distribution in a system influence the final fate, accumulation, and impact. If a plant or prey species is eaten by many different herbivores or predators, the potential for transfer in the system is greater. The rate of input then could directly affect more or fewer species and thereby have greater or lesser probability of reaching highly sensitive species in the system. The analysis of connectivity might be utilized to establish principles related to the point of impact in an ecosystem, as a technique for validating proposed models of interrelationships among components of ecosystems and to identify the point of entry into the system (National Academy of Sciences 1981).

Connectivity might be considered as a linear or non-linear model. In a linear model, the partitioning is constant throughout the system and effects can be related to average concentration. Because distribution is constant, the behavior of the toxic substance can be considered as that induced by the average concentration. In non-linear systems, the importance of the various pathways of concentration in the system change with the rate of concentration. Active sites of adsorption or absorption might become satiated, there might be an increase or decrease in the rates of detoxification, or the rate of predation might change because predators become satiated (National Academy of Sciences 1981).

Connectivity might be studied to search for general principles and to assist with the description (i.e., structure) of the system being affected; to test individual chemicals to determine how they couple to the ecosystem;

and if a chemical is registered and being released, the area of impact should be monitored to determine and verify the predicted behavior and to identify the unexpected.

Levins (in National Academy of Sciences 1981) has provided several examples of how connectivity might be useful in studying the impact of toxic substances of ecosystems (Fig. 8.1 a–c). There seems to be some

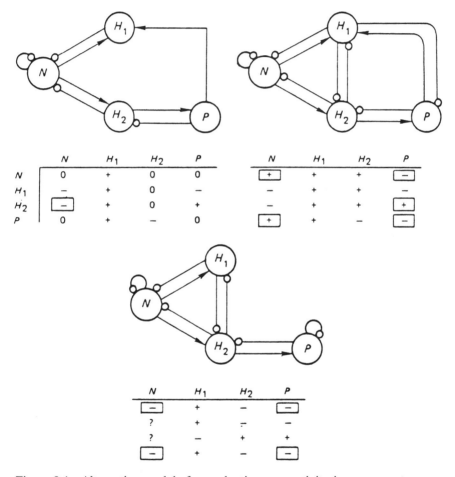

Figure 8.1 Alternative models for evaluating connectivity in an ecosystem exposed to toxic substances. Examination of different pathways in simple to complex models may be able to predict the subsequent flow and effects of toxins in ecosystems. Developed by R. Levins 1981 in *Testing for effects of chemicals on ecosystems*, pp. 97–103. Washington, DC: National Academy Press.

correlation among variables; N and P respond in the same direction when the entry of the toxic substance is through H_1 and they respond in the opposite direction for other entry modes. The positive correlation between N and P and the negative relationship between H_1 and H_2 identify the impact source as H_1.

Studies of connectivity might be used to determine and predict the pathways and impacts of toxic substances on ecosystems, but there are at least five different ecosystem properties that might prevent prediction or extrapolation. These include potential random variation in the parameters studied; an arbitrary time-dependent variation in the environment; non-linear dynamics of populations; the network structure of the community or natural selection among the species for altered predator interactions, resistance, and avoidance learning (National Academy of Sciences 1981).

RESISTANCE AND RESILIENCE

Ecosystems may respond to toxic substance input by being highly resistant or resilient. Some species within the ecosystem may be highly adapted to avoid the toxin and thereby reduce the impact of the substance on the system. There might be reduced metabolic rates or reduced feeding as adaptations to introduced toxins. Rates of detoxification might be increased to inactivate the compound, or rates of transfer, dissipation, dissolution, and diffusion within the system might be enhanced. If recolonization and reconstruction of the system is very rapid, if only a limited area is affected, the system would appear to be resistant. Bay ecosystems have been studied for long periods of time in the northern Gulf of Mexico and the various organisms at various levels of the system respond at different times with different recovery rates when impacted by toxic substances. Because of natural variability in system functions and responses, long-term studies are required to determine the impact of disturbance on equilibrium and resilience of ecosystems (Livingston 1982a,b). Resistance might be related to the sheer size of the system being impacted; if it is large it might be able to absorb a release of toxic substances without major impact. Systems might also be resistant by virtue of their ability to detoxify, sequester in sinks; or by rapid adaptation of the component species.

Resilience, or the rate and ability to return to normal stability, might be related to the type of impact, such as how the toxic substance was introduced, as a point or non-point source. It might relate to the magnitude of the impact in terms of volume, and the seasonality of the release as it relates to the productivity of the system (Fig. 8.2). If toxins were released during a period of low productivity, the toxic compound might have a more

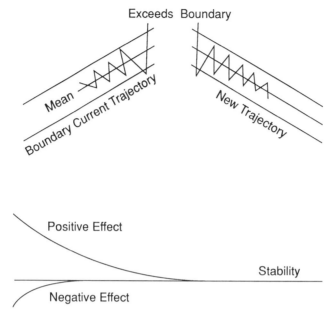

Figure 8.2   Schematic diagram of how a toxic substance may effect the trajectory of an ecosystem by impacting organisms, populations, and ecosystem processes. Increased perturbations ultimately force the system to a new trajectory by exceeding the boundary limits. Return to a stable system trajectory may be dependent on whether the perturbation is positive or negative. The pathway of return may not be mirror images.

severe impact on the system than at periods of high productivity, when many species are reproducing at maximum rates.

Resilience might vary seasonally in terms of higher or lower productivity. Positive or negative perturbations might affect the system in different ways because response to perturbations many not be mirror images, as shown above.

Seasonality as it relates to the reproductive process might also result in different trajectories of recovery following disturbance from equilibrium. Highly resistant systems could sustain more severe impacts of toxic substances if as a result of resistance the compound builds up in the system. Less resistant and more resilient systems might be less severely impacted. In stable, resistant systems that vary about some equilibria, there is some trajectory over time that will result in a different stable state. Toxic substances could alter this trajectory as a result of changes in energy flow, productivity, or species composition. Most systems have boundaries within which they normally vary; this might be considered "boundary-oriented stability." The impact of toxic substance might force the trajectory of development outside this boundary of stability and set the course of the system on another trajectory (Figure 8.2).

The return of a disturbed system to ground state is related to the amplitude of deflection from ground state, the rapidity of response to perturbation, and the rate at which any deflection is damped. The species composition of the system related to the r–k continuum is also associated with the system's resilience and resistance. Some systems' processes may be more vulnerable to disturbance than observed species effects. In an aquatic system stressed by the addition of cadmium the production/respiration ratio (P/R) decreased, there were decreases in grazing herbivores, and nighttime respiration increased as a result of the increase in fungi (Hendrix, Langner, Odum, et al. 1981).

NUTRIENT RETENTION AND TRANSFER

The retention and transfer of nutrients is related to many physical, biological, and physiological factors in the system and is site-specific. Any loss of nutrients from the system could influence subsequent productivity, function, species composition, and equilibrium. In the event of a large-scale mortality as a result of toxic substance input, the decomposer component of the system might not be capable of handling the increase in available nutrients and washout could occur. Most systems in equilibrium cannot handle a sudden increase in nutrient input and removal from the local system is the result.

Some nutrients in systems are tied up in specific organisms and if these species are more or less drastically affected by a toxic compound, then retention or removal of that particular nutrient or mineral from the system can be altered to the detriment of system stability and function. Serious imbalances of some minerals could affect the function of the entire system. Turnover times for various nutrients or elements in systems can be very long or very short and as a result, the impact of perturbation might have long- or short-term effects. The carbon cycle might take years, but the nitrogen/phosphorus cycle, especially in aquatic systems, might be completed in hours or days. Toxic substances that might influence short-term turnover times would have a more drastic impact on the system than if they influenced only long-term cycles. Recovery of species diversity might be possible if only long-term cycles were impacted. Disruptions of decomposers is most serious to mineral recycling and could alter the system in a major way. The disrupted flow of nutrients could lead to system dysfunction; and changes in trajectory, species composition, productivity, and total biomass. Should this lead to possible physical changes such as erosion of surface soils, further loss of productivity could occur and the system might not return to the same stable state for a very long period of time. The rate of forest litter breakdown is reduced by pesticide treatment (Crossley and Witkamp 1964).

Functional measurements in ecosystems might better reflect the impacts of toxic substances than structural measurements. In periphyton communities for example, measurements might be made of dry weight, ATP, chlorophyl 3, CO_2 assimilation, SO_2 assimilation, and fluxes of nutrients such as nitrogen, phosphorus, and ammonia. In aquatic systems, transparency and dissolved solids are also useful measurements related to system function.

GEOGRAPHIC SPECIFICITY

The impacts of toxic substances on wildlife must be considered in relationship to geographic specificity. This relates to physical factors of the environment in terms of the transport, fate, and accumulation of the compound in addition to the type and rate of input into the system. Ecosystems that are located in extremes of climate have low human habitation and inputs to the system are more likely to be from non-point sources, they are probably low-level, and perhaps have already been modified by metabolism or physical breakdown. Because of the extremes in physical factors, breakdown and transport might be slower in the case of arctic environments, but might be much faster in tropical areas. Concentration gradients and food-chain accumulation would be much different in non-agricultural areas, where direct application of toxins does not occur. Where human habitation is of very low density, there would be much less direct input from household use of pesticides and from other toxins in solid and liquid wastes.

The temperature gradients are very important to volatilization and disappearance rates and also influence the rate of deposition from air, rainfall, and snow. We know that organochlorines disappear more slowly from arctic situations (Brown and Brown 1970). Snow cover would reduce direct sublimation to air and would also reduce breakdown by ultraviolet light. Short growing seasons and lower metabolism of plants and animals under cold conditions would alter the kinetics of the compound within the organism. Shorter growing seasons would also reduce the rates of transfer and uptake between the compartments of the system. Many of these considerations would also apply in an opposite way to tropical systems. Aestivation as opposed to hibernation would also alter the metabolism and excretion of body burdens of toxic substances.

The geographical distribution of the species being affected must also be considered. A sensitive species might be more likely to die from low chronic doses if it existed at the fringes of its distribution where environmental factors made survival more difficult. The added impact of the toxin might result in direct mortality. Recruitment and survival might also be lower as a result of nutritional or physical stress and the added impact of toxic-substance–induced mortality might lead to greater population fluctuations and possible extinction from local habitats. Geographic specificity must also be considered in relation to migratory species that inhabit widely divergent areas and different exposures.

9

Classic Examples

A review of several classic examples of unique environmental contaminants is instructive, not only for the unusual characteristics of the compound and how it behaves in the environment and influences wildlife, but also for the sequential impact of their appearance. Although the toxicity of heavy metals had been known for decades or even centuries, the introduction of DDT, following its rediscovery as a pesticide during World War II, caused an unusual chain of events. Because of the chemical and physical characteristics of DDT, the impacts on wildlife, and the toxicity of the most common metabolite DDE, wildlife toxicology became a science. Feeding trials in the laboratory to determine physiological, behavioral, and reproductive effects, coupled with extensive field surveys and monitoring, documented how a commonly used chemical could affect the global environment. Perhaps the impact of this chemical alone and the resultant public interest is partially responsible for the environmental movement and the subsequent legislative acts to reduce the potential for general environmental contamination from industrial products.

We learned much from the laboratory and field studies of DDT and its metabolites. This information should have had a greater impact on how we understood subsequent toxic insults such as those from PCB, PBB, and the discoveries of accumulations of heavy metals such as mercury, lead, cadmium, and selenium. Many PCB studies were modeled after those done on DDT/wildlife relationships, but unfortunately the PBB incident showed a nonresponsive attitude on the part of private and public agencies. Classic cases of toxic substances in the environment should be studied and restudied in terms of possible models for the prevention of such incidents in the future and in the event of inadvertent releases, better knowledge of how to minimize the total environmental impact of these xenobiotics to both wildlife and humans.

DDT

History

One of the general findings in the case of the review of DDT by USEPA stated (*Federal Register,* 37(131), July 7, 1972, p. 13375) "The present total volume of use of DDT in this country for all purposes is an unacceptable risk to man and his environment." This decree came after about 30 years of DDT use and the release of about 1.3 billion pounds in the United States.

The disclosure of the chemical characteristics of DDT and what happened as a result its release, distribution, transport, accumulation, and incorporation into the environment was a unique process that was responsible for much of how we consider and legislate impacts of toxic substances today. Discovery of the initial impact of the effect of DDT on wildlife populations gave rise to the great impetus in research on the effects of toxic substances on wildlife, including not only pesticides but industrial contaminants and heavy metals as well. The study of DDT and its effects served as a model for all of the organochlorines that were developed later as well as for the other organics and for heavy metals.

The publication of *Silent Spring* (Carson 1962) resulted in a greater public awareness of toxic substances in the environment. The dangers to the environment were further emphasized by mass media presentations of tremoring robins, as well as by documented scientific reports of the effect of DDT on robin populations (Bernard 1963; Wallace, Etter, and Osborne 1964; Weller 1971). The impact of DDT on the reproductive process in relation to eggshell thinning was documented in the classic publication by Ratcliffe (1967).

It seems difficult to imply that population impacts on birds were evident in Great Britain by the middle 1940s, when DDT was utilized on a broad scale beginning in WW II, both in Europe and also in Great Britain. Perhaps it was a fortuitous event that the compound used most extensively initially was a chlorinated hydrocarbon that did accumulate and one that also demonstrated physiological and reproductive effects in birds. Despite the early detection of effects about 20 years after initial widespread release, it still took an additional 15 years before the compound's use was restricted in the United States.

DDT is still being used by national and international agencies abroad for control of vector-borne diseases and for certain crops. Following the ban on general use of DDT in 1972, the USEPA (1975) published a detailed review of the information leading to the decision. The review included, in addition to fish and wildlife effects, possible human effects, monitoring DDT in the environment, and the potential economic impact of withdrawing DDT from general use. Edwards (1970) and Stickel (1968) published earlier reviews of persistent pesticides in the environment.

Prior to the issuance of the ban on DDT in June 1972, a U. S. Department of Interior Hearing Examiner, following an extensive presentation of evidence for and against the continued use of DDT, issued a finding that all essential uses of DDT should be continued. The opinion and order of the EPA administrator reversed that finding. Earlier, in 1968–69, similar hearings were held in Wisconsin concerning the restricted use of DDT. Following the presentation of that evidence, the Examiner for the Wisconsin Department of Natural Resources did rule that DDT and its analogs were environmental pollutants within the definitions of Wisconsin law (Henkin, Merta, and Staples 1971, p. 206) "by contaminating and rendering unclean and impure the air, land and waters of the state and making the same injurious to public health and deleterious to fish, bird and animal life." As a result, the use of DDT was restricted in Wisconsin and in several other states prior to the general ban by USEPA in 1972.

DDT became the most used insecticide because it was, initially, effective on a broad spectrum of pest species and it was cheap. At one point, technical grade DDT was sold for as low as 17 cents per pound. Because it is still effective for some insects and it is still relatively cheap, DDT is still being used by international and national agencies for disease vector control; a mosquito abatement program using DDT was initiated in Brazil in 1990.

The actual reason for the ban on DDT may never be known, but it was perhaps a combination of medical, environmental, biological, political, and economic reasons. Carcinogenicity was an item of importance, as well as the increase in development of insect resistance. Alternatives had been developed for most DDT uses, and the little economic disruption resulted for most crops after DDT was banned. Although environmental considerations were presented in the review of the decision to ban DDT (USEPA 1975) how much the toxic impact of DDT on wildlife weighed in the decision to ban is not known.

Other important factors in the DDT story are related to its persistence in the environment, the potential for volatilization and transport to untreated areas, the lipophyllic nature of the compound and its metabolites, the toxicity of the most stable metabolite DDE, and the high variability in species responses to the chronic effects of DDT and its metabolites. All of these characteristics resulted in the potential for the study of distribution in ecosystems, accumulation in organisms, and the study of ultimate lethal and chronic effects.

Even though DDT and its metabolites have perhaps been the most researched toxic compound in relation to wildlife toxicity, there are still some unknowns and still some surprises. We do not yet understand the deposition of long-lasting toxic substances in sinks and their potential recirculation into the system and hence into the biota. There is some evidence that deep ocean particulate matter remains suspended above the ocean floor. Despite all we know about DDT/DDE, the exact mechanism of eggshell thinning is not understood. We do not yet know why pheasants fed hundreds of parts per million of DDT do not show eggshell thinning (Azevedo, Hunt, and Woods 1965), but the mallard will develop eggshell thinning with dietary treatment of 3 or 5 ppm DDE (Heath, Spann, and Kreitzer 1969). Birds of prey are also highly susceptible (Keith and Gruchy 1972). We do not yet understand why some mammalian predators such as mink show reproductive failure with low levels of DDT/DDE in the diet (Aulerich, Ringer, Iwamoto 1973), but whitetails can be fed high levels of chlorinated compounds without major impact on reproduction (Murphy and Korschgen 1970). Despite all of the basic laboratory testing, we do not have a good understanding of species-specific toxic responses. Because of widespread general environmental contamination and accumulation it doesn't seem likely that many highly sensitive species occur, but in some instances, low exposures might have not been sufficient to make them obvious.

Much of the information, both laboratory and field, concerning the effects of DDT on wildlife was summarized in the federal hearings from August 1971 to March 1972. One hundred twenty-five witnesses were called and the inquiry resulted in the production of 9,312 pages of testimony. It became apparent that this type of adversarial hearing was perhaps not the best way to produce a good scientific document for the decision makers, but the resulting USEPA document (1975) summarized the most important findings.

Effects on Mammals

The literature related to the effects of DDT on wildlife is voluminous and is still being developed. Direct lethal impacts of DDT on wild mammals were not widely demonstrated, but chronic effects, paticularly on reproduction, were suggested by the measurement of residues in such highly susceptible mammals as mink (Aulerich, Ringer, and Iwamoto 1973; Sherburne and Dimond 1969). Bats have also been found to be contaminated with potential lethal and reproductive effects residues (Clark 1981b, Clark and Krynitksky 1983a). DDT residues have been reported in a wide variety of mammals, but aside from possible subtle physiological effects, no population impacts have resulted. Accumulations in some small mammals, particularly the shrews, may have been sufficient to cause mortality or reproductive failure. Residues in wild mammalian herbivores have been low and no direct evident lethal or reproductive effects have been reported. Residues in marine mammals have been reported and in some instances they may have been related to abortion, stillbirth, or susceptibility to disease. Evidence for population effects is lacking. Premature births in California sea lions (DeLong, Gilmartin, and Simpson 1973) have been associated with organochlorine residues and alteration in metabolic rates have been demonstrated in the laboratory in short-tailed shrews (Braham and Neal 1974). The widespread impact of DDT on mammalian populations in natural systems has not been documented.

Effects on Birds

The evidence of both lethal and chronic effects of DDT on avian populations, sufficient to reduce numbers, has been well-documented from demonstration of cause and effect relationships in the laboratory, from residues in wild birds, and from the observation of lethal and chronic reproductive effects in the field. Most of these impacts have been on birds of prey, those feeding on invertebrates, fish, birds, and mammals.

Direct lethal effects were observed very early as a result of the unique relationship among Dutch elm disease, DDT spraying for beetle control, accumulation of residues by earthworms, and the predation on earthworms by robins. Widespread reduction in robin populations in urban areas being treated for Dutch elm disease control became evident (Bernard 1963). The classic publication by Ratcliffe (1967) documented the eggshell thinning phenomenon in peregrine and sparrow hawks. Eggshell thinning has now been deomonstrated in a least 54 species of 10 orders of birds (Stickel 1975). Some of this can be related to DDT or its metabolites, but other organochlorine pesticides and the industrial contaminant PCB are also contributing factors. Peakall (1970a) reviewed the impact of pesticides on avian reproduction. In review of life table data for 16 different species of birds for periods prior to and after the major use of pesticides, changes in recruitment were found in those species feeding on fish, reptiles, amphibians, and birds, but not in those avian species feeding primarily on mammals (Henny 1972). Whether this is a matter of food-chain accumulation rates or some peculiar characteristic of the reproductive physiology of the species involved is not clear. It is probably the former because experimental treatment of some avian predators that feed principally on small mammals (screech owl) has shown reproductive impairment (McLane and Hall 1972).

In addition to demonstrated lethal and reproductive effects, DDT influences avian species in many ways. The enhancement of microsomal action in the liver results in greater breakdown of hormones as demonstrated by in vitro studies (Peakall 1967; Lustick, Voss, and Peterle 1973; Richie and Peterle 1979). Alteration in enzyme production, transport, and function is also possible as a result of low chronic exposure (Dieter 1974). Bobwhites treated with 100 ppm DDT for 10 weeks showed higher liver lipid levels but no differences in body lipids nor in liver glycogen levels (Haynes 1972). Thyroid size and function are apparently influenced by DDE, as is the histology of the parathyroid (Jefferies and French 1969, 1972; Parsons and Peterle 1977).

DDT has shown a direct estrogenic activity in the avian reproductive system (Bitman, Cecil, Harris, et al. 1969a). Calcium transport and/or deposition is apparently responsible for eggshell thinning; reduced calcium levels were found in Japanese quail treated with DDT. The authors postulated that the mechanism might be related to stimulation of the liver MFO system that would degrade steriods necessary for calcification, inhibition of medullary bone deposition, the primary source of calcium shell formation, inhibition of the parathyroid and thyroid glands, inhibition of absorption of calcium across the gut, inhibition of carbonic anhydrase activity in the shell gland, and lastly a stimulation of the nervous system causing the egg to be extruded prematurely before the shell is completely formed (Bitman, Cecil, Harris, et al. 1969a,b). Reduced estradiol levels in blood plasma and possible inhibition of carbonic anhydrase activity have been reported in Japanese quail and ring doves treated with DDT (Bitman, Cecil, and Fries 1970; Peakall 1970b). Subsequently it has been suggested that the influence of DDT in eggshell thinning is not related to reductions in carbonic anhydrase function (Dvorchik, Istin, and Maren 1971; Pocker, Beug, and Ainardi 1971). Later, calcium ATPase was thought to be involved (Miller, Peakall, and Kinter 1975; Miller, Kinter, and Peakall 1979; Kolaja and Hinton 1979). A review of the eggshell thinning phenomenon was prepared in 1973 by Cooke (1973). No definitive description of how DDE influences eggshell thinning is available, but alteration in estrogens, parathyroid hormone, vitamin D, or carbonic anhydrase could be involved (Haseltine, Peterle, Nagode, et al. 1981). Alteration in the histology of the parathyroid gland has been demonstrated in species susceptible to eggshell thinning, but influence on circulating parathyroid hormone has not been demonstrated (Parsons and Peterle 1977). The question of why pheasants are not susceptible to shell thinning and mallards are highly susceptible remains despite nearly 30 years of research on the physiological effects of DDT and its metabolites.

Perhaps one of the most well-designed studies conducted to demonstrate the effect of field applications of DDT on avian reproduction was done in the northwestern United States following a special permit application of DDT for tussock moth control in several states. As a result of an emergency order by the USEPA, the U.S. Forest Service applied DDT at the rate of 0.75 lb. per acre to 426,159 acres of forested land in Oregon, Washington, and Idaho. Three hundred nest boxes were established to attract kestrels and their reproductive success was monitored both within and outside the treated areas (Henny 1977). DDE in blood plasma and in eggs were related to reduced levels of reproductive success. For various periods of the 1976 reproductive season, the number of kestrel fledglings in nests in sprayed areas was 2.33, 3.0, 2.25, and 0. In non-sprayed areas for the same periods, fledged young numbered 2.0, 3.6, 4.0, and 2.33 (Henny 1977). Residues in eggs and reproductive success was also related to eggshell thinning. In 1975 eggshells were 11.5 percent thinner and in 1976, 6.7 percent thinner than normal.

Concluding Comments on DDT

Other requests for the use of DDT have been made such as for pea weevil control in Washington, but in 1975 the USEPA denied a request from the state of Louisana to use 2.25 million pounds of DDT for control of tobbaco worm on cotton. More recent evidence of DDT contamination has been the result of residues at an industrial site in Alabama (Fleming and O'Shea 1980) and either illegal use or high local residual levels in Arizona (Fleming and Cain 1985). The approved continued use of dicofol, which contains DDT as an industrial contaminant of up to 15 percent is still presenting problems in some parts of the nation with high residues of DDT in wildlife. Until DDT contaminant levels in dicofol are reduced, or dicofol itself is controlled, the DDT problem will continue in wildlife species exposed directly and in food chains. Hall (1984) has suggested that another DDT incident such as occurred from the 1940s to 1972 and beyond would be unlikely because of the current monitoring programs, new registration procedures that require additional testing, and the closer attention to fluctuations in wildlife populations.

PCB

Background

Polychlorinated biphenyls (PCB) are industrial contaminants synthesized in 1881 and made commercially available in about 1930. The industrial fluid is usually a mixture of several isomers with different amounts of chlorine. Sometimes numerical values are given to the isomers in addition to common names. The first two digits indicate the structure of carbon atoms in the compound, 12; the second two digits indicate the percentage of chlorine atoms and can range from 1221, which is 21 percent chlorine, up to 1268 which contains 68 percent chlorine. Many common names have been used for PCB depending on the country of manufacture. These include the most common for the United States, aroclor; and for other nations, kanneclor, santhaterm, delor, fenclor, phenclor, sovol, and clophen. The only U. S. manufacturer was Monsanto Chemical Company of St. Louis, Missouri.

In terms of distribution in the environment, accumulation in food chains, and effects on wildlife, PCBs, because they are also chlorinated hydrocarbons, behave similarly to DDT and its metabolites as well as other chlorinated insecticides such as endrin, dieldrin, and others. PCBs have been found to be ubiquitous in the environment and concentrations have been found in predatory species and in aquatic systems where industrial contamination and aerial fallout occurred.

Because they are stable, heat-resistant, and have a high dielectric constant, PCBs have been used largely as coolants for large transformers called askarels. They have also been used for a great variety of other reasons where stability is necessary such as in paints, printing inks, coolants for motors, hydraulic fluids, plasticizers and plastics, as extenders for pesticide applications, caulking compounds, adhesives, and in carbonless papers (Task Force on PCB 1976). Although there was only one major U. S. producer of PCB, it was and probably still is being manufactured in other countries such as France, USSR, Japan, Italy, Czechoslovakia, and Germany.

Because of the concern over potential effects and long persistence in addition to increasing residues in the environment, U. S. production was voluntarially restricted in 1970 and all non-closed uses were banned by USEPA in 1978. From 1971 to 1977 all production was for capacitors and transformers. Production ceased in 1977 in the USA. Many transformers still in use contain PCB, but these levels were to be reduced to less than 500 ppm. No capacitors were maufactured with PCB after 1979. Approximately 1.25 billion pounds of PCB was produced in the United States before the ban; very little was imported, only about 1.5 percent (Buckley 1982, Peakall 1972). Of the total manufactured, 55 million pounds is assumed to have been degraded to harmless compounds. About 445 million pounds is assumed to be in the environment, 295 million in landfills, and 150 million pounds in water and sediments (Buckley 1982). The peak production in the United States was in 1970, when about 85 million pounds was maufactured. The federal rule to ban PCB was published in the *Federal Register* on May 31, 1979. PCBs may remain in service in transformers so long as they do not need repair or replacement. PCB may be destroyed by incineration or burial in approved EPA landfills. Replacements for transformers include high flash point silicone oils, hydrocarbon filter packs, and carbon. By 1984, all heat transfer fluids were to be less than 50 ppm PCB.

Effects on Wildlife

Although there are considerable data in the literature related to PCB residues in various wildlife species, particularly those in aquatic systems, there is not much information concerning lethal or chronic effects in terrestrial systems. The laboratory toxicity data suggest that PCBs are generally less toxic, in terms of LD-50, than is DDT, and much less toxic than, for example, endrin. Toxicity is related to the amount of chlorine present in the isomer: the higher the chlorine content, the more toxic and less easily metabolized the compound. When DDE and aroclor were fed to *Coturnix* quail simultaneously, the effect was additive, not synergistic (Heath, Spann, Kreitzer, et al. 1972). Breakdown of PCB is by oxidation, hydrolisis, photodecomposition, and biological metabolism. Generally the higher the chlorine content, the more resistant the isomer is the decomposition. This may not be true for photodecomposition. Transport of PCB in natural systems is by leaching, volatilization, and movement in air, and as a result of incomplete combustion. Aerial transport is perhaps most important. PCB has been found in air samples in Bermuda (0.65 ng/m^3); in Kingston, Rhode Island (5.8); Providence, Rhode Island (9.4); and in Chicago ($140-170$ ng/m^3) (Bidleman and Olney 1974, Paulson and Brown 1978). PCBs with lower chlorine content are also more readily leached and transported in water.

It has been estimated that approximately 80 percent of the PCB deposited in Lake Michigan is the result of aerial transport, not from tributary systems. Because of the long turnover time of Lake Michigan (90 years) the concentration factor to biota of the lake is 4×10^4. The estimated input of PCB into Lake Michigan between 1930 and 1975 was 1.5×10^5 lbs. The amount in the biota is estimated at 3.6×10^3 lbs. Dry flux PCB in Lake Michigan has been estimated at 3354 kg/year (Swain 1980). Input from rainfall is 193 to 215 ng/l. PCB residues in lake trout taken from Lake Michigan ranged from 18 to 20 mg/kg compared to 20 to 4.0 mg/kg for Lake Superior, 3.0 to 5.0 mg/kg for Lake Huron, and 6.0 to 8.0 mg/kg for Lake Ontario. In Lake Erie, coho salmon residues of PCBs were 0.5 to 1.05 mg/kg. Lake Superior is not yet in PCB equilibrium; the surplus input over loss is about 6400 to 8700 kg/year. The net increase in PCB in Lake Superior is 0.2 ng/l/year. Most of this input is from the atmosphere, between 6600 and 8300 kg/year (Swain 1980).

Sensitivity of wildlife species to PCB is quite variable. Some fish species are killed by exposures as low as 0.1 ppb (μg/l), while other species can survive concentrations of over 1,000 ppb (Eisler 1986b). Among terrestrial wildlife, some monkeys are highly sensitive; dietary treatment of 3.0 ppm can be fatal in 245 days for Rhesus monkeys and reproductive effects have been demonstrated in monkeys with dietary treatment of 2.5 ppm. Effects were manifest as resorbtion, stillbirths, and death during the first year following birth (Allen and Barsotti 1976; Carstens, Barsotti, and Allen 1979). PCBs are also highly disruptive of reproductive processes in mink and ferret (Aulerich and Ringer 1977; Bleavins, Auerlich, and Ringer 1980). Common seal populations in the Wadden Sea have decreased from about 3000 in 1950 to fewer than 500 in 1975. Tests of dietary PCBs in fish fed to captive seals showed significant decreases in reproductive success (Reijnders 1986). PCBs apparently do not influence reproductive success in cottontails (Zepp and Kirkpatrick 1976). PCB fed to wild cottontail rabbits did induce higher MFO function in the liver as measured by in vivo reduction in sleep time induced by phenobarbital (Zepp, Sanders, and Kirkpatrick 1974).

The effect of PCB on avian reproduction has been well established in the laboratory. Ring doves treated with 10 ppm showed reproductive failure into the third generation (Peakall 1972; Peakall, Lincer, and Bloom 1972). Erratic incubation behavior was also demonstrated with treatments of 10 ppm PCB in ring doves (Peakall and Peakall 1973). The impact of PCB on reproduction among wild birds is not well understood. Residues are regularly found in eggs in combination with chlorinated insecticides but the role they play in eggshell thinning is not clear. Combined treatment of aroclor 1254 and DDE showed no effect in bobwhite quail reproductive tests (Heath, Spann, Kreitzer, et al. 1972). There was no additive effect of aroclor 1254 in mallards being treated with DDE (Risebrough and Anderson 1971).

PCB residues in various wildlife species taken from the Rhine River and the coastal areas of the Netherlands in 1966 to 1968 showed a variety of PCBs such as phenchlor, aroclor, and clophen (Koeman, Ten Noever de Brauw, and deVos 1969). Based on comparisons of chemical analyses, most of the contamination in the Wadden Sea was apparently originating from the Rhine River. Lower chlorinated PCBs occurred most frequently in fish (roach) than in sea birds (eider ducks).

Little direct mortality has been associated with residues of PCB. High residues of PCB in the fat of seals in the Baltic and the coast of Holland may be related to direct mortality and/or reproductive effects. Residues of 2530 ppm w/w in blubber and 89 ppm in brain tissue of harbor seals may have caused mortality and reproductive failure (Koeman, Peeters, Smit, et al. 1972). PCB does transfer across the placenta and in milk of mammals. Considerable work has been done with laboratory and field studies of the effects of PCBs on bats. Some of these studies both from the field and laboratory were summarized by Clark (1981a). He listed 14 major die-offs of bats, but none of them was directly related to PCB residues. In one study of residues in neonate big brown bats from Maryland, PCB residues in five of the dead newly born young were thought to be sufficiently high to cause death (Clark and Lamont 1976a,b). Apparently, PCB crosses the placenta in big brown bats two or three times more readily than DDE (Clark and Lamont 1976b). A later study in the laboratory showed that feeding pregnant big brown bats mealworms containing 6.36 ppm aroclor 1260 prior to the birth of their litters did not result in higher mortality of neonates. Age of the female was thought to be a compounding factor, not PCB residues alone (Clark 1978). Brain residues thought to be indicative of death as a result of aroclor toxicity in little brown bats (*Myotis*) was 1300 to 1500 ppm (Clark and Stafford 1981). PCBs may reduce metabolic rates in bats at environmental levels (Clark and Prouty 1977). Metabolic rates are reduced in mourning doves treated with PCB and doves fed 40 ppm PCB in the diet did not reproduce in laboratory tests lasting 30 days (Tori and Mayer 1981, Tori and Peterle 1983). Mourning doves fed 10 ppm PCB showed lower circulating progesterone levels and delayed ovulation (Koval, Peterle, and Harder 1987).

The assessent of the impact of PCB on wildlife is difficult because most organisms assayed for residues contain not only PCB, but other chlorinated hydrocarbons as well. PCBs have also been shown to be contaminated with dibenzofurans, and this further complicates the assessment of toxicity related to carcinogenicity and teratogenicity. Residues in wildlife, both aquatic and terrestrial, are widespread (Task Force on PCB 1976). PCB residues in herring gull eggs were reported to be as high as 855.1 ppm dry weight in samples from Black Ant Island in Lake Ontario in 1972 (Task Force on PCB 1976). Alaska bald eagle eggs contained a median of 1.65 ppm, and those from Mainland United States, 9.7 ppm (Dustman, Stickel, Blus, et al. 1971). Arctic mammals such as seals and polar bears have also been found to be contaminated with PCB. James and Hudson Bays' polar bears contained 7.8 ppm wet weight of PCB in fat (Bowes and Jonkel 1975). PCB residues in the eggs of prairie falcons and merlins collected in Alberta between 1969 and 1975 varied from an average low of 2.97 ppm dry weight to an average high of 8.59 ppm in 28 merlin eggs analyzed in 1971. PCB residues in human fat tissue from Canada ranged from an average low of 0.499 ppm wet weight from the central region to 1.07 ppm in human samples from Ontario (Task Force on PCB 1976).

Because PCBs are highly persistent and because of their ubiquitious distribution and large quantities in the environment, they will continue to present toxic problems to wildlife for many years. Based on some estimates of PCB residues in the sediments of four of the Great Lakes (Ontario, Erie, Huron, and Superior) the total quantity of PCB residing in the sediments was about 2.15×10^6 kg. Most of this was estimated to be biologically available, between 1 and 46 cm (Task Force on PCB 1976). This will continue to present low chronic hazard to wildlife, but perhaps not lethal effects. We know that PCB does cause predisposition to disease, at least under laboratory conditions. Mallards exposed to PCBs were more susceptible to duck hepatitis virus and suffered higher mortality (Friend and Trainer 1970). We also know that PCB does affect metabolic rates and could result in higher energy demand in wildlife species with chronic body burdens. How these effects would influence recruitment and mortality is not known. Because PCBs also induce MFO activity in the liver, normal levels of steroids could be reduced and indirect effects of PCB exposure could influence reproduction. We do not know whether the potential carcinogenic, teratogenic, or mutagenic effects of PCB, including the dibenzofuran contaminants, have any effect on wildlife species and populations. We know that PCB does act as a synergist for some insecticides in invertebrate systems, but in the few tests with birds and some organochlorines, this was not evident. Whether PCB might be synergistic with other xenobiotics is not known. Despite the reduction in production as early as 1970 and the ultimate ban on PCB production in 1977, PCBs are still entering the environment from approved former uses, from incineration, from illegal dumping, and from landfills. The hazard of PCB to wildlife is still evident and the total impact cannot be assessed based on current knowledge.

PBB

Some have considered the inadvertent release of polybrominated biphenyl as the worst single environmental contamination in history (Chen 1979). This accidental release of PBB resulted from an error in shipment of a requested dairy cattle feed supplement, magnesium oxide, labeled "Nutrimaster" from the Michigan Chemical Company in St. Louis, Michigan. Apparently an error in labeling and use of similar paper bags caused the shipment of a polybrominated (PBB) fire retardant called "Firemaster" instead of Nutrimaster to the Farm Bureau Company of Battle Creek, Michigan in May 1973.

The Michigan Chemical Company, a subsidiary of Velsicol Chemical Company, began manufacturing polybrominated biphenyls to be used in the manufacture of plastics and other products in 1970. Between 1970 and

1974, approximately 11,220,000 lbs were produced. Annual production was estimated at 2.27 million kg (Sleight 1979). Dairy cattle fed additives containing magnesium apparently increase milk production and in May 1973, Fred Halbert, a dairy farmer near Delton, Michigan, ordered an increase in the additive, Nutrimaster, to the feed for his large herd. The Farm Bureau ordered the additive from Michigan Chemical Co. and received by mistake, on or about May 2, 1973, 10 to 20 50-lb bags of Firemaster that was subsequently mixed with cattle feed and distributed throughout the state. PBB is a mixture of isomers of tetra, petna, hexa, and heptabromobiphenyls with very high stability and low vapor pressure. They are somewhat less stable than PCB in the environment.

Beginning in September 1973, Halbert noted symptoms of illness in his herd and a decrease in milk production. Contact with a local veterinarian, university veterinarians, the state Department of Agriculture, and the feed company produced no satisfactory answer to his problem (Halbert and Halbert 1978). Because Halbert had been a college-trained chemical engineer, he suspected the possibility of a feed contaminant and questioned the Farm Bureau but they assured him the feed was not contaminated. Halbert conducted his own feeding trials with calves and found those fed the pelleted feed from the Farm Bureau refused to eat and some of them died. Autopsy reports suggested malnutrition. Subsequent feeding trials with laboratory mice by the Department of Agriculture resulted in death in 10 days to 2 weeks (Halbert and Halbert 1978). Despite considerable effort to determine the cause of the reduced milk production and illness in his herd, it was not until April 20, 1974, that the contamination was identified. The National Animal Disease Laboratory in Iowa had identified some latent gas chromatograph peaks in feed samples sent by Halbert and these were subsequently confirmed by the Wisconsin Alumni Research Foundation Laboratories. WARF determined the latent peaks to be bromine and the USDA Laboratory in Beltsville identified the compound as PBB and the fire retardant Firemaster. Subsequently a bag of Firemaster was found at one of the Farm Bureau plants.

Following the identification of the toxic substance, tolerance levels were established in milk and dairy products and in meat, initially at 1.0 ppm and then reduced to 0.3 ppm in meat and milk and 0.05 ppm in animal feed and eggs (Dunckel 1975; Sleight 1979). Many herds were quarantined and milk was withdrawn from the market. Appearance and effects of PBB toxicity in cattle were described (Jackson and Halbert 1974).

There were many legal suits and the Farm Bureau and the insurance companies ultimately paid about $40 million in settlement for contaminated livestock and products. A burial site was established in the Kalkaska County area of the state and then another near Mio for disposal of contaminated livestock, products, and feeds. There was much adverse publicity about contamination of dairy products and meats and importation of products from Michigan to other states and Canada was temporarily halted (Carter 1976). There were some extremely long and detailed court hearings and decisions did not always favor the plaintiff (State of Michigan Circuit Court, County of Wexford, Taloma and Taroma vs. Michigan Chemical Company et al. File 2933 1978). Some livestock was destroyed by owners without prior residue analyses and compensation was not paid.

Studies of human effects began in 1976 by New York's Mt. Sinai Hospital. General reports in 1977 of human studies revealed no widely common health problems. Early preliminary tests done on laboratory animals as well as on a variety of livestock, including calves on the Halbert farm, had shown both lethal and chronic effects. Rats, mice, rabbits, calves, and feral rats and domestic cats had apparently been killed by doses of PBB either as a primary or secondary toxin. Some of the dairy cattle feed was effectively used as a rodenticide. Effects on liver and kidney function were suggested and some evidence of carcinogenicity was reported. PBB are apparently more potent MFO inducers than are PCBs (Dent, Natter, and Gibson 1976; Sleight 1979; Garthoff, Friedman, Farber, et al. 1977). Some teratogenicity was found in embryos of laboratory mice treated with 100 ppm on days 7 through 18 of pregnancy (Chen 1979).

Despite the identification of the contaminant in April 1974 and the source of the toxic substance, contaminated livestock feed continued to be distributed throughout Michigan as a result of the contamination of the feed mixing equipment at the Farm Bureau Plant. Despite cleanups of the equipment, feed mixed in September 1974 was still contaminated at 1.1 ppm (Chen 1979). Some contaminated feed was returned to the mixing plant and in order to bag the material, it was run through the system, further contaminating the equipment. Contaminated feed was sold through the cooperative throughout most of 1974 after the PBB incident was discovered in April. The result was further widespread low-level distribution of PBB in the livestock industry, and in one case 300,000 chickens had to be destroyed because of high PBB residues from feed. Total cost of the accident was estimated at $26 to 45 million (Dunckel 1975). Monitoring of human foodstuffs did not begin until January of 1975, nearly one year after the problem was discovered. Most of the farm surveys were done on milk and usually from pooled samples. As a result, some contaminated dairy herds were never discovered or quarantined and cows with low milk production were culled and sold for meat despite PBB contamination.

Reported effects on human health were presented in numerous hearings by a legislative committee held in different locations in Michigan. Farm families told of fatigue, arthritic problems, ulcers, loss of hair and weight, vision problems, deformities, and other illnesses, but the Michigan Department of Health continued to state that there were no proven human health effects from PBB contamination. Human adipose tissue samples showed 99 percent of Lower Peninsula inhabitants and 85 percent of Upper Peninsula people had significant residues of PBB (Maugh 1982). Some liver and immune reaction deficiencies were reported by the New York Environmental Health studies done in 1976. In 1977, the Mt. Sinai study did corroborate reports of human health effects based on a survey of over 1,000 PBB-exposed Michigan residents (Selikoff 1977, Sleight 1979).

There is little information on the impact of PBB on wildlife. One person reported at one of the legislative hearings that they submitted a sample of a black bear killed that tested positive for PBB; no concentration level was given. Because of reports of mortality of dogs, cats, rats, and mice on farms, it would seem likely that there were some direct wildlife lossess due to PBB poisoning. Mink reproduction is reduced and kit survival affected at 1 ppm in the diet (Michigan State University 1976). Reproductive effects were also observed in chickens (Ringer and Polin 1977), in coturnix (Babish, Gutenmann, and Stoewsand 1975), and dietary levels of 0.3 ppm produced menstrual irregularities in monkeys (Lambrecht, Barsotti, and Allen 1978). PBBs are apparently not teratogenic in animals tested (Sleight 1979). Chen (1979) reported that residues were found in rabbits, ravens, coyotes, gulls, starlings, rats, pheasants, raccoons, deer, and bear. High residues of PBB were found in raccoon and muskrat samples taken near the Pine River, downstream from the Michigan Chemical Company in St. Louis, the manufacturers of PBB. Because of PBB contamination in fish, sections of the Pine River were closed to public fishing. The extent of contamination of wildlife thoughout Michigan as a result of the distribution of PBBs in animal feeds may never be known. Effects on humans are still being assessed and studied.

Perhaps if TSCA had been in effect at the time of development of PBB, it may have been restricted to closed uses only. But the accidental distribution could have happened regardless of the limited use regulations if they had been imposed.

A more concerned and considered response by agencies and professionals could have been offered to livestock owners following the release of the PBB in feedstuffs. There was inadequate response from private, state, and federal agencies. Based on what was already known of the distribution and effects of the chlorinated hydrocarbons and PCB, a more reasoned and enlightened response should have been possible. Requirements for testing by both TSCA and FIFRA and a formal review by EPA prior to registration might prevent such an event from occurring again.

MERCURY

Mercury is an important toxic heavy metal that is persistent in the environment, can concentrate in food chains, and is neurotoxic to all organisms. The element enters the environment from natural as well as anthropogenic origins. It volatilizes and is transported in air and returns as fallout in particulate matter, in snow and rain. It occurs as the element called quicksilver, in inorganic salts, as mercuric chloride, and as organic mercury. Methyl, phenyl, alkyl, and ethyl mercury are the most important forms. Microorganisms in soil and sediment can convert various forms of mercury to methyl mercury, which is then available for uptake by various organisms and transport in the food chain. Direct toxic effects of mercury on humans have been known for a long time. For example, it was assumed that the Mad Hatter in *Alice in Wonderland* was influenced by the mercuric salts used in the production of hats. Mercury enters aquatic systems from natural runoff from soils containing high levels of mercuric sulfides and from areas where cinnabar mines have been developed (Jenne 1970). It is estimated that the mercury content of runoff from the Kuskokwim River in Alaska is 16,700 kg of mercury per year. Mercury partitions from colder, nutrient-rich Pacific Ocean waters into air. Evidence from these supersaturated waters indicates that ocean/air mercury transport could equal total input from human-made sources (Kim and Fitzgerald 1986). Coal may contain an average of 130 ppm of mercury and when burned for heat or for fuel in power plants, this is released into the air (Hartung and Dinman 1972). Some petroleum has up to 21.0 ppm and refineries may release 64,000 lbs of mercury to the air each year. Coal burning may add 2,000 tons of mercury to the environment each year. Some is also added as a result of cement production. Other industrial sources that have or are currently adding mercury to the environment include paper mills where mercury was used as a slimicide, plating industries, milling and metal alloy production, chlorine and caustic soda production, fungicidal paints, preservatives, batteries, switches, thermometers, barometers, medicinal uses such as for blood pressure pills, in dental treatments, and in agricultural uses such as insecticides, fungicides, and in seed dressings.

Because of the widespread uses of mercury, the ratio of technological input into the environment compared to natural emissions is the highest for toxic heavy metals. The ratio is 80.0 for mercury, 70.0 for lead, 14.0 for selenium, 4.6 for zinc, and 0.9 for nickel (Harris and Hohenemser 1978). Total world production of mercury from 1963-1967 was estimated at 18 to 20 million pounds (Peakall and Lovett 1972; see Figure 9.1). Emissions from industrial, agricultural, and medicinal uses have increased levels in sinks such as ice sheets. Mercury residues in the Greenland ice sheet from the period 800 B.C. to 1952 were 60 ± 17 ng/kg and from 1952 to 1965 the level increased to 125 ± 52 ng/kg (Weiss, Koide, and Goldberg 1971). Goshawk feathers analyzed from specimens taken in Sweden between 1863 and 1946 averaged 2200 ng/gm; those taken from 1947 to 1965 averaged 29,000 ng/kg (Johnels and Westermark 1969).

A relative hazard index for some heavy metals has been calculated based on the ratio of human-made to natural occurrences of the toxic metal and the relatively toxicity. The relative hazard index of mercury is 40 to 1600, for cadmium it is 13, for lead it is 7, and for arsenic 0.7 (Harris and Hohenemer 1978). Mercury accumulates in the body and the half-life is about 70 days for a human, 1,000 days in an eel, 700 days in a pike, and 90 days in an osprey (Berry, Osgood, and St. John 1974). In humans, about 1 percent of the body burden is lost per day. In mice, this half-life is 3.7 days, in rats 15 to 70 days, and 20 days in the dog (Nelson, Byerly, Kolbye Jr., et al. 1971).

Mercury is neurotoxic; it will cross the placenta in mammals and is present in milk. It is also mutagenic. There have been several episodes of human poisoning: two in Japan, where contaminated seafood was eaten in Minimata Bay and in Niigata Bay; and an incident in Iraq, where approximately 459 deaths resulted from the use of mercury-treated seed for making bread. In the United States one family was seriously poisoned (New Mexico) when hogs were fed contaminated seed and subsequently eaten (Miller and Berg 1969, Hartung and Dinman 1972).

Wildlife losses as a result of mercury poisoning were first identified in Sweden and many publications resulted (Borg, Wanntorp, Erne, et al. 1969; Johnels and Westermark 1969; Westoo 1969). Since 1958, Swedish biologists have studied the distribution and impact of Hg in the environment. Dead birds of various species in Sweden contained 2 to 140 to 200 mg/kg of mercury in livers and kidneys (Borg, Wanntorp, Erne, et al. 1969). These included seed eaters, and predators as well as scavengers. An adult magpie fed treated seed had 200 mg/kg Hg in its liver and kidneys. Contamination of lower level invertebrates was also high in areas of industrial pollution. In an area downstream from a paper mill in Sweden, caddisflies contained 17000 ng/g mercury, isopods 1900 ng/g, and the alderfly 5500 ng/g (Johnels and Westermark 1969). Uptake of mercury by animals in aquatic systems is the result of the conversion of various forms of Hg to dimethyl or methyl forms by microbes and as a result of more acid conditions found in anaerobic stream sediments. Methyl mercury is soluble in water and becomes part of the water column, where it is taken up by living organisms and passed on in the food chain. The effects of mercury toxicity occur at all levels of the food chain from reduced photosynthesis of phytoplankton to neurotoxic effects on vertebrates. Some food-chain accumulation of mercury does result in some fish species being unacceptable for human consumption. Age, but not sex is a factor in accumulation in lake trout. One-year-old lake trout from Cayuga Lake contained 0.28 ppm mercury; those 12 years old, 0.66 ppm (Bache, Gutenmann, and Lisk 1971). A burbot from Clay Lake in the Kenora District of Ontario contained 16.65 ppm mercury (Bligh 1970). Predatory fish from the Great Lakes usually had higher levels of mercury. The walleye in Lake Erie had up to 1.43 ppm mercury; in Lake Huron, 0.28 ppm; Lake Ontario, 0.25 ppm; and for Lake St. Clair, mercury in walleye was 1.08 ppm (Bligh 1970). Mercury concentrations in an aquatic system have been examined for Lake Powell, New Mexico, and residues in water of 0.01 ppb increase to levels of 427 ppb in the walleye (See Table 9.1; Kidd, Johnson, and Garcia 1974).

Mercury is accumulated in birds, and various species that died of mercury poisoning in Sweden contained liver residues of 2 to 140 ppm (Borg, Wanntorp, Erne, et al. 1969). Seed-eating birds had residues of 140 ppm mercury (pheasant) in livers and predatory birds up to 270 ppm (tawny

Table 9-1 Concentrations of Mercury in an Aquatic Ecosystem, Lake Powell, New Mexico

Ecosystem Element	Hg Concentration $\mu g/l$
Water	0.01
Sediment	30.0
Periphyton	32.0
Plant debris	148.00
Invertebrates	10.0
Flannel-mouth sucker	99.0
Shad	42.0
Bluegill	91.0
Carp	252.0
Catfish	126.0
Walleye	427.0
Bass	314.0
Trout	84.0
Crappie	204.0

Adapted from Kidd, Johnson, and Garcia 1974.
An analysis of materials in the Elephant Butte
ecosystem. Tech. Comp. Rpt. Project
AOUONMEX. Credit New Mexico Water
Resources Research Institute.

owl) (Borg, Wanntorp, Erne, et al. 1969). Mercury seed dressing was banned in Sweden in 1966 and body burdens of mercury declined rapidly in seed eaters, but more slowly in predatory birds. Feather analyses of predatory birds showed a concentration factor over their prey of about 20 times and fish-eating birds concentrated mercury in their tissues about 3 times that of their prey. In Sweden, the content of mercury in goshawk feathers analyzed from 1863 to 1946 was 2200 ng/g; those taken from specimens collected between 1947 and 1965 was 29,000 ng/g (Johnels and Westermark 1969). Similar increases in Hg in feathers occurred in osprey and great crested grebe. Fimreite (1970) initially pointed out the potential contamination of aquatic systems in North America, particularly those related to industrial pollution. Fish residues in Lake St. Clair and the St. Clair River ranged as high as 7.09 ppm in muscle from a pumpkinseed (Fimreite, Holsworth, Keith, et al. 1971). Studies in the Prairie Provinces of Canada also showed above-normal residues in seed-eating birds and in their avian predators (Fimreite, Fyfe, and Keith 1970). Residues in the eggs of some owls, falcons, and hawks was sufficiently high to suggest possible impact on reproduction based on laboratory feeding trials with other species. The average residue in livers of predatory birds was 0.236 ppm, and the mean in seed-eating birds was 1.160 ppm (Fimreite, Fyfe, and Keith 1970). A short-eared owl had residues of 11.3 ppm Hg in its liver. Treatment of pheasants with mercury resulted in reduced egg production, hatchability, and egg weight and, in some cases, shell-less eggs were laid. Egg color was also affected (Fimreite 1971). Redtailed hawks fed contaminated domestic chicks (liver levels 3.9, 7.2, and 10.0 ppm) for 12 weeks showed mercury poisoning and those that died had liver residues of about 20 ppm (Fimreite and Karstad 1971). When mercury residues in eggs from a variety of aquatic birds from the Great Lakes and from Louisiana were compared, eggs from the Great Lakes showed generally higher residues. Mean mercury residues were 0.49 from eggs sampled in the Great Lakes region and 0.12 in eggs taken in Louisiana (Faber and Hickey 1973). Industrial contamination from both point and non-point sources seems important to the contamination of aquatic systems. Studies in northwestern Ontario showed much higher mercury residues in birds sampled from areas below a point source of mercury pollution (Table 9.2).

Differences in food habits of common waterfowl species result in variation in liver mercury residues from common environments. Waterfowl sampled on Lake St. Clair showed a mean of 1.63 in mallard livers ($N = 8$), 1.53 ppm mercury in livers of blue-winged teal ($N = 4$), and 3.18 ppm Hg in livers of lesser scaup ($N = 4$) that feed more on animal sources than do the other two species (calculated from Dustman, Stickel, and Elder 1972). Great blue herons from the same area contained up to 175 ppm mercury in

Table 9-2 Mercury (mean ppm) in Livers of Aquatic and Fish-Eating
Birds Northern Ontario

Species	Above Point Source (Wabigoon Lake)	Below Point Source (Ball Lake)
Common tern	9.08	20.7
Common merganser	6.10	50.8
Common goldeneye	2.21	13.3
Herring gull	2.10	19.3

Adapted from Fimreite, N. 1974. Mercury contamination of aquatic birds in northwestern Ontario. J. Wildl. Manage. 38(1):120–131. Copyright The Wildlife Society.

liver; common tern, 39 ppm; killdeer, 3.7 ppm; and the dunlin, 1.3 ppm (Dustman, Stickel, and Elder 1972). Direct mortality as a result of mercury poisoning has not been widespread except during the period of high usage as seed dressing, or in areas of high industrial contamination. In laboratory trials, brain residues of Hg that were indicative of lethal effects varied from 21.0 ppm in the grackle to 45.0 in the redwing. The starling and cowbird were intermediate at 44.9 and 30.9 ppm mercury in brain. Whole body residues followed the same pattern (Finley, Stickel, and Christensen 1979). In a review of the occurrence and effects of mercury in ecosystems, Peakall and Lovett (1972) suggested that seed-eating birds (because of Hg seed dressing) and birds at the top of freshwater food chains were those at highest risk. Because mercurial seed dressings have been banned, the greatest hazard remains in aquatic food chains.

Despite reduced research interest in mercury, it will continue to be an important environmental contaminant both as a result of natural leaching from the earth's crust, and from anthropogenic input in industrial, agricultural, and medical pollution. The element can accumulate in organisms, it does concentrate in the food chain, and low levels can be highly neurotoxic. We need to maintain an effort and interest in seeking greater information on the effects of mercury on wildlife in environmental systems.

Appendix A

Chemical Compounds

Common Name	Alternate Name	Class of Compound/Use
abate	temephos	organophosphorus insecticide
acephate	orthene	systemic insecticide
acetonitrile	cyanomethane	pesticide
aflatoxin	dihydroaflatoxin	natural toxin
alachlor	lasso	pre-emergence herbicide
aldicarb	temik	systemic insecticide
aldrin	HHDN	insecticide
amiton	tetram	acaricide, insecticide
amitrole	cytrol	herbicide
antu	antu	rodenticide (Norway rats)
aroclor	arochlor	(PCB) industrial
atrazine	aatrex	selective pre-post-emergence herbicide
azinphos	guthion	acaricide, insecticide
azodrin	monocrotophos	systemic-contact insecticide
sodium arsenite	atlas "A"	fungicide, herbicide, insecticide

Common Name	Alternate Name	Class of Compound/Use
arsenicals	various compounds, Paris green	insecticide/ herbicide
barbital	barbituric acid	drug, sleep-inducing
baygon	propoxur	non-systemic insecticide
BEE	butoxyethanol ester	herbicide
BHC	hexachlorocyclohexane, techncal HCH	insecticide
benzylchloride	toluene	monochloro derivative
bidrin	dicrotophos	systemic insecticide, acaricide
bifenox	mowdown	broadleaf, grass herbicide
blackleaf	nicotine	(alkaloid, sulphate) insecticide
brodifacoum	talon, havoc, klerat	anticoagulant rodenticide
bromacil	krovar	perennials herbicide
bromochlormethane	—	industrial chemical, mildly corrosive
bromophos	nexion	non-systemic insecticide
bulan	dilan, prolan	insecticide
Butoxyethanol	—	derivative of ethyl alcohol, industrial chemical
Butyl	—	organic radical, attached to many compounds
captafol	difolatan	protective non-systemic fungicide

Common Name	Alternate Name	Class of Compound/Use
captan	—	protective fungicide
carbamate	—	carbamic acid derivative insecticides
carbaryl	sevin	contact insecticide
carbofuran	furadan	contact insecticide
carbophenothion	trithion	insecticide, acaricide
ceresan, L or M	granosan	seed disinfectant, fungicide
chloralkenes	—	halogenated unsaturated organic
chlordane	belt, octachlor, chlordan	insecticide
chlordimeform	galecron	systemic acaricide
chlorfenvinphos	supona	soil, foliar insecticide
chloroflurohydrocarbon	—	propellant, solvent, alkane, atmospheric contaminant
chloroform	trichloromethane	solvent
chlorofluroethane	—	solvent, propellant, atmospheric contaminant
chloro IPC	propham	herbicide
chlorophenol		industrial, combustible liquid, neoplastigenic
chlorothion	chlorthion	insecticide
chlorpyrifos	dursban	broad spectrum insecticide
copper sulphate	blue copperas, bluestone algicide	fungicide

Common Name	Alternate Name	Class of Compound/Use
cotinine	—	metabolite of nicotine in mammals
coumaphos	co-ral	livestock insecticide, antihelmintic
cryolite	Kryocide	stomach, contact insecticide
cyanide	hydrocyanic acid	general toxin
cypermethrin	ammo, cymbush	stomach, contact insecticide
dasanit	fensulfothion	insecticide, nematicide
dalapon	Dowpon	selective herbicide (sodium salt)
DDA	—	DDT oxidation metabolite
DDD	TDE	DDT dechlorination derivative
DDE	—	DDT degradation product, common metabolite
DDMS	—	degradation product of DDD found in rats
DDMU	—	degradation product of DDT found in rats
DDNU	—	degradation product of DDD found in rats
DDOH	—	degradation product of DDT found in chicks
DDT	technical DDT	non-systemic, contact insecticide

Common Name	Alternate Name	Class of Compound/Use
DDVP	dichlorvos	contact, stomach insecticide, fumigant
deltamethrin	decis, decamethrin	stomach, contact insecticide
demeton	systox	systemic insecticide, acaricide
diallate	avadex	pre- or post-planting herbicide
diazinon	spectracide	non-systemic insecticide
dicamba	banvel	foliar, soil applied herbicide
dichlorvos	DDVP	contact, stomach insecticide, fumigant
dicofol	kelthane	non-systemic acaricide
dicrotophos	bidrin	systemic insecticide, acaricide
dieldrin	HEOD	persistent, non-systemic insecticide
diflubenzuron	dimilan	non-systemic stomach, contact insecticide
dilan	prolan, bulan	insecticide
dimefox	—	systemic acaricide, insecticide
dimethoate	cygon	contact, systemic insecticide, acaricide
dinoseb	DNBP	contact herbicide
dioxin	—	industrial contaminant, sometimes in

Common Name	Alternate Name	Class of Compound/Use
		herbicides. suspected as strongly carcinogenic, many isomers
diphacinone	ramik	anticoagulant rodenticide
diphenyl mercury	—	environmental conversion product of mercury
diquat (dibromide)	reglone	contact herbicide, desiccant
2,4,5-T	weedone	selective, post-emergence herbicide
2,4-D	weeder	systemic herbicide
Diuron	drexel	photosynthesis inhibition herbicide
DNOC	sinox	non-systemic, contact, stomach insecticide
dursban	chlorpyrifos	broad spectrum insecticide
dylox	trichlorfon	contact, stomach insecticide
endosulfan	thiodan	broad spectrum, non-systemic insecticide
endrin	—	persistent non-systemic insecticide
ester	—	organic compound, reaction of acid, alcohol, phenol
ether	—	organic, hydrocarbon radicals, dialkyl oxide

Common Name	Alternate Name	Class of Compound/Use
ethylene oxide	epoxyethane	fumigant, sterilant
famphur	warbex	systemic insecticide, used on cattle
fenitrothion	sumithion	contact insecticide
fensulfothion	dasanit	insecticide, nematocide
fenthion	baytex	contact, stomach insecticide
fenuron	fenulon, dybar	perennial, woody herbicide
fenvalerate	pydrin	broad range contact insecticide
FLIT-MLO	petroleum fraction	mosquito larvacide
fonofos	dyfonate	soil insecticide
formaldehyde	methanal	fungicide, germicide
formothion	anthio	contact, systemic insecticide
furadan	carbofuran	contact insecticide
glucuronic acid	—	aldehydro acid, part of synthetic process in body to form glucuronides
glycol	—	ethylene glycol, alcohols
gophacide	phosaretim, phorazetim	rodenticide
guthion	azinphos methyl	insecticide
haloethanes	—	halogenated aliphatic hydrocarbon with two carbons
halopropane	—	halogenated aliphatic hydrocarbon with three carbons

Common Name	Alternate Name	Class of Compound/Use
halowax	—	PCB-like compound, 1014
heptachlor	—	non-systemic, contact, stomach insecticide
IOE	—	isocytl ester, compound included in herbicides
isodrin	aldrin isomer	insecticide
isolan	primin	insecticide
kelthane	dicofol	non-systemic acaricide
kepone	chlordecone	insecticide
lindane	BHC gamma isomer	insecticide
malathion	sumitox	non-systemic insecticide, acaricide
matacil	aminocarb	insecticide, molluscicide
methane ether	methyl ether	solvent
methoxychlor	metox	contact, stomach insecticide
methyl parathion	—	non-systemic, contact, stomach insecticide
methyl phenol	—	a cresol
mevinphos	phosdrin	contact, systemic insecticide
mirex	dechlorane	stomach insecticide
monocrotophos	azodrin	systemic, contact insecticide
monuron	telvar	photosynthesis inhibition herbicide
morsodren	panogen	cyano guanidine fungicide
napthalene	—	insecticidal fumigant

Common Name	Alternate Name	Class of Compound/Use
napthylthiourca	antu	rodenticide
nicotine	(sulphate) (alkaloid)	insecticide
nitrate	—	common fertilizer component, aquatic contaminant
nitrite	—	nitrate derivative, potential carcinogen
OCDD	octachlorodioxin	isomer of dioxin, potential carcinogen
octanol	—	solvent, used to determine partition coefficient
PAH	polycyclic aromatic hydrocarbons	petroleum products, fused benzene rings, many compounds; napthalene
paraquat	gramoxone	herbicide
parathion	paraoxon	non-systemic, contact, stomach insecticide
PBB	firemaster	polybrominated biphenyl-fire retardant
PCB	many isomers, aroclor	industrial coolant, other uses
PCDD	polychlorinated dibenzo-para-dioxin	industrial contaminant, potential carcinogen
PCP	pentachlorophenol	wood preservative, defoliant, herbicide
permethrin	ambush, pounce	contact insecticide

Common Name	Alternate Name	Class of Compound/Use
PGBE	Propylene glycol butyl ester	compound used in herbicides
phenobarbital	—	sleep-inducing drug
phenol	—	aromatic hydroxl derivative from coal tar
phosdrin	mevinphos	contact, systemic insecticide
prolan	dilan, bulan	insecticide
phosphamidon	dimecron	systemic insecticide
pyrethrin	many isomers, synthetic organics, allethrin-tetramethrin	non-systemic insecticide
pyrethrum	—	botanical insecticide
pyrolan	G-22008	insecticide
rhothane	TDE	hydroxy analog of DDT-metabolite, isomer
ronnel	fenchlorphos	systemic insecticide
rotenone	mexide	selective non-systemic insecticide, picicide
rozol	chlorophacinone	rodenticide
ryania	botanical	insecticide
schradan	pestox	systemic insecticide, acaricide
sesamex	sesoxane	synergist for pyrethrins
sevin	carbaryl	contact insecticide
silica gel	dri-die, drione	insecticide
simazine	princep	pre-emergence herbicide

Common Name	Alternate Name	Class of Compound/Use
Sodium arsenite	atlas-a. kill-all	fungicide, herbicide, insecticide
sodium carbonate	soda ash	disinfectant
sodium fluoride	florocid	insecticide, phytotoxic
sodium pentobarbital	—	sleep-inducing drug
sumithion	fenitrothion	contact insecticide
TCE	trichloroethylene	solvent, sub-surface water contaminant
1080 (fluoroacetates)	fratol	rodenticide, potential vertebrate control chemical
TDE	—	rhothane isomer, metabolite of DDT insecticide
telodrin	isobenzan	insecticide
temik	aldicarb	systemic insecticide
TEPP	tetron, killmite 40	insecticide
tetrachlorophenol	Dowicide	wood preservative
thiodan	endosulfan	broad spectrum, non-systemic insecticide
thiram	arasan	protective fungicide
toxaphene	camphechlor	non-systemic, contact, stomach insecticide
triallate	avadex BW	soil herbicide
trichlorfon	dylox	contact, stomach insecticide
trihalomethane	—	any trihalogenated compound, industrial toxicants
tritox	acetonitrile	wood preservative

Common Name	Alternate Name	Class of Compound/Use
trichlorfon	dylox	contact, stomach insecticide
warfarin	ratox	anticoagulant rodenticide
xylene	—	common aromatic solvent, used for partition coefficients
zectran	mexacarbate	insecticide, acaricide
zineb	dithane Z	protectant fungicide
ziram	zerlate	protective fungicide

Appendix B

Scientific Names

Fungi
Daedalea confragosa
Polyporus spraguei
Mycena sp.
Russula sp.
Phylloporus rhodoxanthus
Armillariella mellea

Scleroderma aurantium
Rush
Juncus
Green Algae
Chlorella pyrenoidosa

Cultivated plants
Alfalfa   *Medicago sativa*
Barley   *Hordeum vulgare*
Bluegrass   *Poa*
Carrot   *Daucus carota sativa*
Clover   *Trifolium sp.*
Corn   *Zea mays*
Cotton   *Gossypium herbaceum*
Johnsongrass   *Sorghum halepense*

Lettuce   *Lactuca sativa*
Oats   *Avena sativa*
Peanut   *Arachis hypogaea*
Ryegrass   *Lolium*
Sorghum   *Sorghum vulgare*
Soybean   *Glycine max*
Timothy   *Phleum pratense*
Wheat   *Triticum aestivum*

Herbaceous plants
Goldenrod   *Solidago graminifolia*

Mosses
Holocomium
Funaria
Tortula
Byrum

Lichens
Hypogumnia
Peltigara
Cladonia rangifera
Usnea

Woody plants

Aspen   *Populus*
Elm   *Ulmus*
Fir   *Abies*
Heather   *Calluna*
Larch   *Larix*

Oak   *Quercus*
Peach   *Prunus persica*
Raspberry   *Rubus*
Spruce   *Picea*
Staghorn sumac   *Rhus typhina*

Invertebrates

Bacteria Fish bacterium   *Aromonas hydrophila*
Bacteria   *Escherichia coli*
Bacteria   *Proteus vulgaris*

Protozoa

Blackhead   *Heterakis gallinae*

Rotifera   Polychaetes   *Polychaetus*

Amphipod   *Hyalella*

Ostracod   *Eucypris*
Cypridopsis

Nematode   Dog roundworm   *Toxocara canis*

Free-living nematode   *Cephalobus perseghis*
Heteroderma radicicola

Planaria

Euplanaria
Dugesia
Protocotyla

Earthworm

Lumbricus terrestris
Eisenoides carolinensis
Dendrodrilus rubidus

Grass shrimp   *Palaemonetes vulgaris*

Slug   *Philomycus carolinianus*

Millipede   *Polydesmida; Spiro bilida; Dixidesmus erasus*

Freshwater snails   *Helix pomata; Helix aspersa; Paravitrea; Lymnaea; Helisoma; Physa*

Scud   *Gammarus pseudolimnaeus*

Asiatic clam   *Corbicula*   Mussels   *Mytilus*

Crab   *Cancer*   Soft-shell clam   *Mya arenaria*

Lobster   *Homarus*   American oyster   *Crassostrea virginica*

Isopods
Tracheoniscus rathkei
Armadillidium vulgare

Euphausiacea
Euphausia   krill

Crayfish
Crayfish   *Cambarus; Orconectes lancifer; Orconectes nais*
Red River crayfish   *Procambarus acutus acutus*
White River crayfish   *Procambarus clarkii*

Copepods
Copepods   *Diaptomus; Cyclops*
Water flea   *Daphnia magna*
Fairy shrimp   *Branchinecta*
Marine shrimp   *Penaeus duorarum*
Glass shrimp   *Palaemonetes kodiakensis*

Mud crab   *Rithropaneopeus harrisii*

Blue crab   *Callinectes sapidus*

Insects
Alderflies   *Sialis*
Mayflies   *Hexagenia; Baetis*
Grasshoppers   *Brachystola; Melanoplus*
Crickets   Field cricket   *Nemobius allardi;*
          Common cricket   *Acheta domestica*
Cockroaches   American cockroach   *Periplaneta americana;*
          Oriental cockroach   *Blatta orientalis*
          German cockroach   *Blatella germanica*
Stoneflies   *Neoperla; Aroperla; Perlesta; Acronueria*
Beetles   Carabid ground beetle   *Abacidus permundus; Abax ater; Carabus coriaceus; Carabus auratus; Pterostichus vulgaris*
          Mealworms   *Tenebrio molitor; Tribolium*
          Dutch elm beetle   *Scolytus multistriatus*
          Potato beetle   *Leptinotarsa decimlineata*
          Pea weevil   *Mylabris pisorum*
Caddis flies   *Hydroptila; Trentonius; Brachycentrus; Micrasema; Hydropsyche; Limnephilus*
Tiger moth   Salt marsh caterpillar   *Estigmene acraea*
Tobacco budworm   *Heliothis virescens*
Cutworm, western pale   *Agrotis orthogonia*

Gypsy moth   *Porthetria dispar*
Silkworm moth   silkworm   *Bombyx mori*
Spruce budworm   *Archips fumiferana; Archips argyrospila*
Tussock moth (Douglas fir)   *Orygia pseudotsugata*
Moths

Malacosma americanum	*Catocala palaeogma*
Paonias exaecatus	*Halysidota tessellaris*
Noctua c-nigrans	*Halisdota*
Keucania unipuncta	*Spilosoma*
Amphipyra pyramiddoides	

Midges
   Phantom midge   *Chaoborus punctipennis*
   Chironomus
   Pentaneura
Rust flies   Carrot rust fly   *Psila rosae*
House fly   *Musca domestica*
Fruit fly   *Drosophila melanogaster*
Horse fly   *Tabanus*
Mosquitoes   *Culex tarsalis; Anopheles; Aedes*
Fire ant   *Solenopsis invicta*
Honeybee   *Apis millifera*

Arachnida   spiders

Amphibians
   Toads   *Bufo americana; Bufo woodhousei*
   Bullfrog   *Rana catesbeiana*
   Frog   *Rana sylvatica*
   Common frog   *Rana temporaria*
   Cricket frog   *Acris crepitans*
   Leopard frog   *Rana pipiens*
   Warty newt   *Triturus cristatus*

Reptiles
   Green sea turtle   *Chelonia*
   Snapping turtle   *Cheldyra serpentina*
   Map turtle   *Graptemys geographica*
   Midland soft-shelled turtle   *Trionyx spiniferus*
   Painted turtle   *Chrysemys picta*
   Diving turtle   *Chrysemys scripta*
   Water snake   *Natrix(Nerodia)cyclopion;*
                       Natrix(Nerodia) rhombifera
   Cottonmouth   *Agkistrodon piscivorus*

Fishes
  Paddle fishes—Polyodontidae
  Gars—Lepisosteidae
    Spotted gar *Leipsosteus oculatus*
  Bowfins—Miiidae
  Herrings—Clupeidae
    Threadfin shad *Dorosoma pretenense*
    Gizzard shad *Dorosoma cepedianum*
  Anchovies—Engraulidae
  Trout, whitefish, grayling—Salmonidae
    Coho salmon *Oncorhynchus kisutch*
    Brown trout *Slamo (fario) trutta*
    Rainbow trout *Salmo gairdneri*
    Atlantic salmon (siskowet) *Salmo salar*
    Brook trout *Salvelinus fontinalis*
    Lake trout *Salvelinus namaycush*
    Lake whitefish *Coregonus clupeaformis*
  Pikes—Esocidae
    Northern pike *Esox lucius*
  Minnows and carps—Cyprinidae
    Fathead minnow *Pimephales promelas*
    Goldfish *Carassius auratus*
    Roach *Leuciscus rutilus*
    Golden shiner *Notemigonus crysoleucas*
    Carp *Cyprinus carpio*
    Emerald shiner *Notropis antherinoides*
  Suckers—Catostomidae
    White sucker *Catostomus commersoni*
    Flannelmouth sucker *Catostomus latipinnis*
  Catfishes—Ictaluridae
    Black bullhead *Ictalurus melas*
    Yellow bullhead *Ictalurus natalis*
    Channel catfish *Ictalurus punctatus*
    Brown bullhead *Ictalurus nebulosus*
  Eels—Anguillidae
    American eel *Anguilla rostrata*
  Killifishes—Cyprinodontidae
    Munnihog (killifish) *Fundulus heteroclitus*
  Livebearers—Poeciliidae
    Mosquitofish *Gambusia affinis*
    Guppy *Poecilia reticulata*
  Codfishes, hakes—Gadidae
  Sticklebacks—Gasterosteidae

Trout fishes—Percopsidae
Seabasses—Serranidae
  White bass   *Roccus chrysops*
Sunfishes—Centrarchidae
  Bluegill   *Lepomis macrochirus*
  Largemouth bass   *Micropterus salmoides*
  Smallmouth bass   *Micropterus dolomieui*
  Green sunfish   *Lepomis cyanellus*
  White crappie   *Pomoxis annularis*
  Black crappie   *Pomoxis nigromaculatus*
Perches—Percidae
  Yellow perch   *Perca flavenscens*
  Johnny darter   *Etheostoma nigrum*
  Walleye   *Stizostedion vitreum*
Drums—Sciaenidae
  Spot   *Leiostomus xanthurus*
Porgies—Sparidae
  Pinfish   *Lagodon rhomboides*
Surfperches—Embiotocidae
  Black (surf) perch   *Embiotoca hacksoni*
Sculpins—Cottidae
Mullets—Mugilidae
  Striped (grey or black) mullet   *Mugil cephalus*
Silversides—Atherinidae
  Atlantic silverside   *Menidia menidia*

Birds

Spheniscidae
  Adelie penguin   *Pygoscelis adeliae*
Gaviidae
  Red-throated loon   *Gavia stellata*
  Arctic loon   *Gavia arctica*
  Common loon   *Gavia immer*
Podicipedidae
  Eared grebe   *Podiceps nigricollis*
  Great crested grebe   *Podiceps cristatus*
  Western grebe   *Aechmophorus occidentalis*
Procellariidae
  Bermuda petrel   *Pterodroma cahow*
Hydrobatidae
  Fork-tailed storm petrel   *Oceanodroma furcata*
  Leach's storm petrel   *Oceanodroma leucorhoa*
  Sooty storm petrel   *Oceanodroma tristrami*

Pelecanidae
  American white pelican   *Pelecanus erythrorhynchos*
  Brown pelican   *Pelecanus occidentalis*
Phalacrocoracidae
  Double-crested cormorant   *Phalacrocorax auritus*
  Cormorant   *Phalocrocorax carbo*
Ardeidae
  Great blue heron   *Ardea herodias*
  Green-backed-heron   *Butorides striatus*
  Black-crowned night-heron   *Nycticorax nyticorax*
Threskiornithidae
  White-faced ibis   *Plegadis chihi*
  Spoonbill   *Platelea leucorodia*
Ciconidae
  Wood stork   *Mycteria americana*
Anserinae
  Greater white-fronted goose   *Anser albifrons*
  Snow goose   *Chen caerulescens*
  Canada goose   *Branta canadensis*
  Brant, Brent goose   *Branta bernicla*
  Green-winged teal   *Anas crecca*
  American black duck   *Anas rubripes*
  Mallard—Pekin duck   *Anas platyrhynchos*
  Northern pintail   *Anas acuta*
  Blue-winged teal   *Anas discors*
  Northern shoveler   *Anas clypeata*
  Canvasback   *Aythya valisineria*
  Lesser scaup   *Aythya affinis*
  Common eider   *Somateria mollissima*
  Common goldeneye   *Bucephala clangula*
  Common merganser   *Mergus merganser*
  Red-breasted merganser   *Mergus serrator*
Cathartidae
  Turkey vulture   *Cathartes aura*
  California condor   *Gymnogyps californianus*
Accipitridae
  Osprey   *Pandion haliaetus*
  Snail kite   *Rostrhamus sociabilis*
  Bald eagle   *Haliaeetus leucocephalus*
  Sharp-shinned hawk   *Accipter striatus*
  Cooper's hawk   *Accipiter cooperii*
  Northern goshawk   *Accipiter gentilis*
  Sparrowhawk   *Accipiter nisus*

Marsh harrier   *Circus hudsonicus*
Red-shouldered hawk   *Buteo lineatus*
Red-tailed hawk   *Buteo jamaicensis*
Rough-legged hawk   *Buteo lagopus*
American kestrel   *Falco sparverius*
Merlin   *Falco columbarius*
Peregrine falcon   *Falco peregrinus*
Gyrfalcon   *Falco rusticolus*
Prairie falcon   *Falco mexicanus*
Phasianidae
  Gray partridge   *Perdix perdix*
  Chukar   *Alectoris chukar*
  Red partridge   *Alectoris rufa*
  Japanese quail or coturnix   *Coturnix japonica*
  Domestic chicken   *Gallus domesticus*
  Ring-necked pheasant   *Phasianus colchicus*
  Red grouse   *Lagopus scoticus*
  Sage grouse   *Centrocercus urophasianus*
  Sharp-tailed grouse   *Tympanuchus phasianellus*
  Northern bobwhite   *Colinus virginianus*
  California quail   *Callipepla californica*
  Helmeted guineafowl   *Numida meleagris*
Rallidae
  American coot   *Fulica americana*
Charadriidae
  Killdeer   *Charadrius vociferus*
Recurvirostridae
  American avocet   *Recurvirostra americana*
Scolopacidae
  Lesser yellowlegs   *Totanus (Tringa) flavipes*
  Spotted sandpiper   *Actitis macularia*
  Long-billed curlew   *Numenius americanus*
  Western sandpiper   *Calidris mauri*
  Dunlin   *Calidris alpina*
  Long-billed dowitcher   *Limodromus scolopaceus*
  American woodcock   *Scolopax minor*
Laridae
  South polar skua   *Catharacta maccormicki*
  Laughing gull   *Larus atricilla*
  Ring-billed gull   *Larus delawarensis*
  California gull   *Larus californicus*
  Herring gull   *Larus argentatus*
  Western gull   *Larus occidentalis*

Glaucous-winged gull   *Larus glaucescens*
Great black-backed gull   *Larus marinus*
Caspian tern   *Sterna caspia*
Elegant tern   *Sterna elegans*
Common tern   *Sterna hirundo*
Forster's tern   *Sterna forsteri*
Black skimmer   *Rynchops niger*
Black guillemot   *Cepphus grylle*
Horned puffin   *Fratercula arctica*
Columbidae
King pigeon   *Columba livia domestica*
Ringed turtle dove   *Streptopelia risoria*
Mourning dove   *Zenaida macroura*
Tytonidae
Common barn-owl   *Tyto alba*
Strigidae
Eastern screech-owl   *Otus asio*
Great horned owl   *Bubo virginianus*
Northern saw-whet owl   *Aegolius acadicus*
Picidae
Northern flicker   *Colaptes auratus*
Alaudidae
Horned lark   *Eremophila alpestris*
Hirundinidae
Tree swallow   *Tachycineta bicolor*
Northern rough-winged swallow   *Stelgidopteryx serripennis*
Bank swallow   *Riparia riparia*
Corvidae
Black-billed magpie   *Pica pica*
American crow   *Corvus brachyrhynchos*
Hawaiian crow   *Corvus hawaiiensis*
Common raven   *Corvus corax*
Musiccapidae
Wood thrush   *Hylocichla mustelina*
American robin   *Turdus migratorius*
Sturnidae
European starling   *Sturnus vulgaris*
Emberizidae
Dickcissel   *Spiza americana*
Baird's sparrow   *Ammodezmus bairdii*
McCowan's longspur   *Calcarius mccownii*
Red-winged blackbird   *Agelaius phoeniceus*
Eastern meadowlark   *Sturnella magna*

Western meadowlark   *Sturnella neglecta*
Common grackle   *Quiscalus quiscula*
Brown-headed cowbird   *Molothrus ater*
Fringillidae
Bengalese finch   *Lonchura striata*
House finch   *Carpodacus mexicanus*

Mammals
Didelphidae
Virginia opossum   *Didelphis virginiana*
Phalangeridae
Possum   *Trichosurus vulpecula*
Primates
Rhesus monkey   *Macaca mulatta*
Soricidae
Masked shrew   *Sorex cinereus*
Northern short-tailed shrew   *Blarina brevicauda*
Talpidae
Townsend's mole   *Scapanus townsendii*
Eastern mole   *Scalopus aquaticus*
Vespertilionidae
Little brown myotis   *Myotis lucifugus*
Gray myotis   *Myotis grisescens*
Eastern pipistrelle   *Pipistrellus subflavus*
Big brown bat   *Eptesicus fuscus*
Brazilian free-tailed bat   *Tadarida brasiliensis*
Leporidae
Eastern cottontail   *Sylvilagus floridanus*
Nuttall's cottontail   *Sylvilagus nuttallii*
European rabbit, domestic   *Oryctolagus cuniculus*
Snowshoe hare   *Lepus americanus*
White-tailed jack rabbit   *Lepus townsendii*
Sciuridae
Yellow-bellied marmot   *Marmota flaviventris*
Richardson's ground squirrel   *Spermophilus richardsonii*
Geomyidae
Pocket gopher   *Thomomys*
Cricetidae
Deer mouse   *Peromyscus maniculatus*
White-footed mouse   *Peromyscus leucopus*
Hispid cotton rat   *Sigmodon hispidus*
Meadow vole   *Microtus pennsylvanicus*
Gray-tailed vole   *Microtus canicaudus*

Prairie vole *Microtus ocrogaster*
Woodland vole, pine vole *Microtus pinetorum*
Muskrat *Ondatra zibethicus*
Common hamster *Cricetus cricetus*
Muridae
   Norway rat, common rat, lab rat *Rattus norvegicus*
   House mouse, common mouse, lab mouse *Mus musculus*
Erethizontidae
   Porcupine *Erethizon dorsatum*
   Guinea pig *Cavia porcellus*
Myocastoridae
   Nutria, coypu *Myocastor coypus*
Canidae
   Domestic dog *Canis familiaris*
   Coyote *Canis latrans*
   Gray wolf *Canis lupus*
   Red fox *Vulpes vulpes*
Ursidae
   Black bear *Ursus americanus*
   Polar bear *Ursus maritimus*
Otariidae
   California sea lion *Zalophus californianus*
Procyonidae
   Raccoon *Procyon lotor*
Mustelidae
   Mink *Mustela vison*
   River otter *Lutra canadensis*
Phocidae
   Harbor seal *Phoca vitulina*
   Ringed seal *Phoca hispida*
   Gray seal *Halichoerus grypus*
   Crabeater seal *Lobodon carcinophagus*
Felidae
   Domestic cat *Felis domestica*
Cervidae
   Roe deer *Capreolus capreolus*
   Red deer, elk *Cervus elaphus*
   White-tailed deer *Odocoileus virginianus*
   Caribou *Rangifer tarandus*
   Domestic sheep *Ovis sp.*
   Domestic cow *Bos tarus*

Appendix C

Sources of Chemicals and Scientific Names

Chemicals

Analytical references standards and supplemental data: *The Pesticides and Industrial Chemicals Repository,* EPA-600/4-84-082, 1984.

Farm chemicals handbook. Willoughby, OH: Meister Publishing Company, 1986.

The toxic substances list, 1973 ed. Rockville, MD: USHEW.

Handbook of chemistry and physics. Cleveland, OH: Chemical Rubber Publishing Company, 1962.

Plants

Fernald, M. L. 1950. *Gray's manual of botany.* New York: American Book Co.

Scott, T. G., and C. H. Wasser. 1980. *Checklist of North American plants for wildlife biologists.* Washington, DC: The Wildlife Society.

Invertebrates

Ward, H. B., and G. C. Whipple. 1945. *Fresh-water biology.* New York: John Wiley & Sons.

Borror, D. J., and D. M. DeLong. 1957. *An introduction to the study of insects.* New York: Rinehart and Co.

Reptiles and amphibians

Conant, R. 1938. The reptiles of Ohio. *The American Midland Naturalist.* 20(1):1–200.

Goin, C. J., and O. B. Goin. 1971. *Introduction to herpetology.* San Francisco: W. H. Freeman and Co.

Porter, K. R. 1972. *Herpetology*. Philadelphia: W. B. Saunders Co.
Orr, R. T. 1969. *Vertebrate biology*. Philadelphia: W. B. Saunders Co.

Fishes
A list of common and scientific names of fishes from the United States and Canada. American Fisheries Society Report of Committee. Baltimore, MD: Waverly Press.

Birds
Checklist of North American birds. 1982. American Ornithological Union. Suppl. to *Auk* 99(3):1–16.

Mammals
Jones, J. K. Jr., D. C. Carter, H. H. Genoways, et al. 1982. *Revised checklist of North American mammals north of Mexico, 1982*. Occasional Paper No. 80. by The Museum Texas Tech University, Lubbock.

Appendix D

Sources of Toxicity Data for Fish and Wildlife

Eisler, R. Mirex (and other toxic substances that follow) hazards to fish, wildlife, and invertebrates. *Fish and Wildlife Service Contaminant Hazard Review Reports*. These are a series of reports reviewing the hazards of specific compounds to invertebrates and wildlife. The years of publication and report numbers and the toxin are listed as follows:

Mirex	March 1985	85(1.1)
Cadmium	July 1985	85(1.2)
Carbofuran	August 1985	85(1.3)
Toxaphene	August 1985	85(1.4)
Selenium	October 1985	85(1.5)
Chromium	January 1986	85(1.6)
Polychlorinated biphenyls	April 1986	85(1.7)
Dioxins	May 1986	85(1.8)
Diazinon	August 1986	85(1.9)
Mercury	April 1987	85(1.10)
Polycyclic Aromatic Hydrocarbons	May 1987	85(1.11)
Arsenic	January 1988	85(1.12)
Chlorpyrifos	March 1988	85(1.13)
Lead	April 1988	85(1.14)
Tin	January 1989	85(1.15)
Index to Species	February 1989	85(1.16)
Pentachlorophenol	April 1989	85(1.17)
Atrazine	May 1989	85(1.18)
Molybdenum	August 1989	85(1.19)
Boron	April 1990	85(1.20)

Heath, R. G., J. W. Spann, E. F. Hill, et al. 1972. *Comparative dietary toxicities of pesticides to birds*. U. S. Fish and Wildlife Service Special Science Report. Wildlife No. 152. Washington, DC.

Hill, E. F. 1971. Toxicity of selected mosquito larvicides to some common avian species. *J. Wildl. Manage*. 35(4):757–762.

Hill, E. F., and M. B. Camardese, 1986. Lethal dietary toxicities of environmental contaminants and pesticides to coturnix. U. S. Fish and Wildlife Service Technical Report 2. Washington, DC.

Hill, E. F., R. G. Heath, J. W. Spann, et al. 1975. Lethal dietary toxicities of environmental pollutants to birds. U. S. Fish and Wildlife Service Special Science Report Wildlife No. 191. Washington, DC.

Hoffman, D. J., and P. H. Albers. 1984. Evaluation of potential embryotoxicity and teratogenicity of 42 herbicides, insecticides, and petroleum contaminants to mallard eggs. *Arch. Environ. Contam. Toxicol.* 13(1):15–27.

Hudson, R. H., R. K. Tucker, and M. A. Haegele. 1984. *Handbook of toxicity of pesticides to wildlife,* 2nd ed. U. S. Fish and Wildlife Service Resour. Pub. 153. Washington, DC.

Johnson, W. W., and M. T. Finley. 1980. *Handbook of acute toxicity of chemicals to fish and aquatic invertebrates*. U. S. Fish and Wildlife Service Resour. Pub. 137. Washington, DC.

Murty, A. S. 1986. *Toxicity of pesticides to fish*. Vols. I and II. Cleveland, OH: C.R.C. Press.

Rudd, R. L., and R. E. Genelly. 1956. *Pesticides: their use and toxicity in relation to wildlife*. Cal. Dept. Fish and Game, Game Bull. No. 7. Sacramento.

Schafer, E. W. 1972. The acute oral toxicity of 369 pesticidal, pharmaceutical, and other chemicals to wild birds. *Toxicol. Appl. Pharma*. 21(3):315–330.

Schafer, E. W., Jr., and W. A. Bowles, Jr. 1985. Acute oral toxicity and repellency of 933 chemicals to house and deer mice. *Arch. Environ. Contam. Toxicol*. 14(1):111–129.

Schafer, E. W., Jr., W. A. Bowles, Jr., and J. Hurlbut. 1983. The acute oral toxicity, repellency, and hazard potential of 998 chemicals to one or more species of wild and domestic birds. *Arch. Environ. Contam. Toxicol.* 12(3):355–382.

Smith, G. J. 1987. *Pesticide use and toxicology in relation to wildlife: organophosphorus and carbamate compounds*. U. S. Fish and Wildlife Service Resour. Pub. 170. Washington, DC.

Tucker, R. K., and D. G. Crabtree. 1970. *Handbook of toxicity of pesticides to wildlife*. U. S. Fish and Wildlife Service Resour. Pub. No. 84. Washington, DC.

USDA. 1968. *The toxicity of herbicides to mammals, aquatic life, soil microorganisms, beneficial insects and cultivated plants., 1950–65, a list of selected references.* Lib. List No. 87. Natl. Agric. Lib. Washington, DC.

USEPA 1971. *Water quality criteria data book, Vol. 3. Effects of chemicals on aquatic life. Selected data from the literature through 1968.* Water Pollution Cont. Series. 18050GWV05/71. Sects. A, B, C, D.

Literature Cited

Abbott, D. C., R. B. Harrison, J. O'G. Tatton, et al. 1966. Organochlorine pesticides in the atmosphere. *Nature* 211(5046):259–261.

Acree, F., Jr., M. Beroza, and M. C. Bowman, 1963. Codistillation of DDT with water. *J. Agr. Food Chem.* 11(4):278–280.

Adams, L., M. G. Hanavan, N. W. Hosley, et al. 1949. The effects on fish, birds, and mammals of DDT used in the control of forest insects in Idaho and Wyoming. *J. Wildl. Manage.* 13(3):245–254.

Addison, R. F., and T. G. Smith. 1974. Organochlorine residue levels in Arctic ringed seals: variation with age and sex. *Oikos* 25(3):335–337.

Adkisson, P. L., G. A. Niles, J. K. Walker, et al. 1982. Controlling cotton's insect pests: a new system. *Science* 216(4541):19–22.

Albers, P. H. 1982. Effects of oil on *Anas* reproduction: a review and discussion. In *The effects of oil on birds,* pp. 78–96. Stone Harbor, NJ: Wetlands Institute.

Albers, P. H., and M. L. Gay. 1982. Effects of a chemical dispersant and crude oil on breeding ducks. *Bull. Environ. Contam. Toxicol.* 29(4):404–411.

Albers, P. H., and G. H. Heinz. 1983. FLIT-MLO and No. 2 fuel oil: effects of aerosol applications to mallard eggs on hatchability and behavior of ducklings. *Environ. Res.* 30(2):381–388.

Alexander, M. 1981. Biodegradation of chemicals of environmental concern. *Science* 211(4478):132–138.

Allen, J. R., and D. A. Barsotti. 1976. The effects of transplacental and mammary movement of PCBs on infant Rhesus monkeys. *Toxicol.* 6(3):331–340.

Ames, P. L. 1966. DDT residues in the eggs of the osprey in the north-eastern United States and their relation to nesting success. *J. Appl. Ecol.* (Suppl. 3):87–97.

Anderson, D. W., and I. T. Anderson. 1976. Distribution and status of brown pelicans in the California current. *American Birds* 30(1):3–12.

Anderson, D. W., and F. Gress 1983. Status of a northern population of California brown pelicans. *Condor* 85(1):79–88.

Anderson, D. W., and J. J. Hickey. 1972. Eggshell changes in certain North American birds. *Proc. Int. Ornith Cong.* 15:514–540.

Anderson, D. W., and J. J. Hickey. 1976. Dynamics of storage of organochlorine pollutants in herring gulls. *Environ. Pollut.* 10(3):183–200.

Anderson, D. W., J. J. Hickey, R. W. Risebrough, et al. 1969. Significance of chlorinated hydrocarbon residues to breeding pelicans and cormorants. *Canada. Field Nat.* 83(2):91–112.

Anderson, D. W., J. R. Jehl, Jr., R. W. Risebrough, et al. 1975. Brown pelicans: improved reproduction off the southern California Coast. *Science* 190(4216):806–808.

Anderson, D. W., J. E. Mendoza, and J. O. Keith. 1976. Seabirds in the Gulf of California: a vulnerable international resource. *Nat. Resour. J.* 16(3):483–505.

Anderson, D. W., T. J. Peterle, and K. L. Dickson. 1986. Contaminants: neglected and forgotten challenges. *Trans. N. A. Wildl. Nat. Resour. Conf.* 51:550–561.

Anderson, J., P. E. Lichtenstein, and W. Wittingham. 1970. Effect of *Mucor alternans* on the persistence of DDT and dieldrin in culture and in soil. *J. Econom. Ent.* 63(5):1595–1599.

Antommaria, P., M. Corn, and L. DeMaio. 1965. Airborne particulates in Pittsburgh: association with p,p'-DDT. *Science* 150(3702):1476–1477.

Atlas, E., and C. S. Giam. 1981. Global transport of organic pollutants: ambient concentrations in the remote marine atmosphere. *Science* 211(4478):163–165.

Aulerich, R. J., and R. K. Ringer. 1977. Current status of PCB toxicity to mink and effects on their reproduction. *Arch. Environ. Contam. Toxicol.* 6(2/3):279–292.

Aulerich, R. J., R. K. Ringer, and S. Iwamoto. 1973. Reproductive failure and mortality in mink fed Great Lakes fish. *J. Repro. Fertil.* (Suppl. 19):365–376.

Azevedo, J. A., Jr., E. G. Hunt, and L. A. Woods, Jr. 1965. Physiological effects of DDT on pheasants. *Calif. Fish and Game* 51(4):276–293.

Babish, J. G., W. H. Gutenmann, and G. S. Stoewsand. 1975. Polybrominated biphenyls: tissue distribution and effect on hepatic microsomal enzymes in Japanese quail. *J. Agr. Food Chem.* 23(5):879–882.

Bache, C. A., W. H. Gutenmann, and D. J. Lisk. 1971. Residues of total mercury and methylmercuric salts in lake trout as a function of age. *Science* 172(3986):951–952.

Back, R. C. 1985. The Temik story. *Science* 230(4728):885–886.

Bailey, S., and P. J. Bunyan. 1972. Interpretation of persistence and effects of polychlorinated biphenyls in birds. *Nature* 236(5340):34–36.

Baker, M. F. 1967. Studies of possible effects of Mirex baits on bobwhite quail and other birds. *Proc. Ann. Conf. S. E. Assn. Game and Fish Comm.* 18:153–160.

Balcomb, R. 1983. Secondary poisoning of red-shouldered hawks with carbofuran. *J. Wildl. Manage.* 47(4):1129–1132.

Ballatori, N., and T. W. Clarkson. 1982. Developmental changes in the bilary excretion of methylmercury and glutathione. *Science* 216(4541):61–63.

Barnett, D. C. 1950. The effect of some insecticide sprays on wildlife. *Proc. Ann. Conf. West. Assoc. State Game and Fish Comm.* 30:125–134.

Barnthouse, L. W. 1981. Mathematical models useful in chemical hazard assessment. In *Method for ecological toxicology: a critical review of laboratory multispecies tests,* ed. A. S. Hammons, pp. 156–168. EPA-560/11-80-026.

Bart, J. 1975. The effects of Dimilin on birds. In *The environmental impact of Dimilin (TH-6040) on a forest environment.* Lake Ontario Environ. Lab. Report 210. Oswego, NY.

Bascietto, J. 1985. *Avian dietary LC-50 test.* USEPA-540/9-85-008.

Batcheler, C. L. 1982. Quantifying "bait quality" from number of random encounters required to kill a pest. *N. Z. J. Ecol.* 5:129–139.

Baumgartner, F. M. 1948. A preliminary study of the effects of certain insecticides upon wildlife in north central Oklahoma. *Proc. Oklahoma Acad. Sci.* 28:6–10.

Benedict, W. V., and W. L. Baker. 1963. Pesticides in forestry—a review of current practices. *J. Forest.* 61(5):340–344.

Bengston, S. A., and A. Sodergren. 1974. DDT and PCB residues in airborne fallout and animals in Iceland. *Ambio* 3(2):84–86.

Bennett, R. S., and D. W. Shafer. 1988. Procedure for evaluating the potential ability of birds to avoid chemically contaminated food. *Environ. Contam. Toxicol.* 7(5):359–362.

Benton, A. H. 1951. Effects on wildlife of DDT used for control of Dutch elm disease. *J. Wildl. Mange.* 15(1):20–27.

Berg, W., A. Johnels, B. Sjostrand, et al. 1966. Mercury content in feathers of Swedish birds from the past 100 years. *Oikos* 17(1):71–83.

Bernard, R. F. 1963. *Studies of the effects of DDT on birds.* Michigan State University Mus. Pub. Biol. Ser. 2(3):155–192.

Berry, J. W., D. W. Osgood, and P. A. St. John. 1974. *Chemical villains: a biology of pollution.* St. Louis: C. V. Mosby Co.

Berteau, P. E., and R. E. Chiles. 1978. Studies on the inhalation toxicity of two phosphoramidothioate insecticides to rodents and quail. *Toxicol. Appl. Pharmacol.* 45(1):232(abstract).

Bevenue, A., J. N. Ogata, and J. W. Hylin. 1972. Organochlorine pesticides in rainwater, Oahu, Hawaii, 1971–1972. *Bull. Environ. Contam. Toxicol.* 8(4):238–241.

Beyer, N. 1983. The smoke that settled over Palmerton, N.J. *Audubon* 9:14–16.

Beyer, W. N., R. L. Chaney, and B. M. Mulhern. 1982. Heavy metal concentrations in earthworms from soil amended with soil sewage. *J. Environ. Qual.* 11(3):381–385.

Beyer, W. N., E. Cromartie, and G. B. Moment. 1985. Accumulation of methylmercury in the earthworm, *Eisenia foetida,* and its effect on regeneration. *Bull. Environ. Contam. Toxicol.* 35(2):157–162.

Beyer, W. N., and A. J. Krynitsky, 1989. Long-term persistence of dieldrin, DDT, and heptachlor expoxide in earthworms. *Ambio* 18(5):271–273.

Beyer, N. W., O. H. Pattee, L. Sileo, et al. 1985. Metal contamination in wildlife living near two zinc smelters. *Environ. Pollut.* Series A. 38:63–86.

Bidleman, T. F., and C. E. Olney. 1974. Chlorinated hydrocarbons in the Sargasso Sea atmosphere and sea water. *Science* 183(4142):516–518.

Bitman, J. H. C. Cecil, and G. F. Fries. 1970. DDT-induced inhibition of avian shell gland carbonic anhydrase: a mechanism for thin eggshells. *Science* 168(3931):594–596.

Bitman, J., H. C. Cecil, S. J. Harris, et al. 1969a. Estrogenic activity of o,p'-DDT in the mammalian uterus and avian oviduct. *Science* 162(3851)371–372.

Bitman, J. , H. C. Cecil, S. J. Harris, et al. 1969b. DDT induces a decrease in eggshell calcium. *Nature* 224(5241):44–46.

Bleavins, M. R., R. J. Aulerich, and R. K. Ringer. 1980. Polychlorinated biphenyls (Aroclors 1016 and 1242): effects on survival and reproduction in mink and ferrets. *Arch. Environ. Contam. Toxicol.* 9(5):627–635.

Bligh, E. G. 1970. *Mercury and the contamination of freshwater fish.* Freshwater Inst. Mss. Rpt. Series N. 1088. Winnipeg, Manitoba.

Blus, L. J. 1984. DDE in birds' eggs: comparison of two methods for estimating critical levels. *Wilson. Bull.* 96(2):268–276.

Blus, L. J., C. J. Henny, and R. A. Grove. 1985. Effects of pelletized anticoagulant rodenticides on California quail. *J. Wildl. Dis.* 21(4):391–395.

Blus, L. J., C. J. Henny, and R. A. Grove. 1989. Rise and fall of endrin usage in Washington State fruit orchards: effects on wildlife. *Environ. Pollut.* 60(3/4):331–349.

Blus, L. J., C. J. Henny, T. E. Kaiser, et al. 1983. Effects on wildlife from the use of endrin in Washington State orchards. *Trans. N. A. Wildl. Nat. Resour. Conf.* 48:159–174.

Blus, L. J., C. J. Henny, and A. J. Krynitsky. 1985a. Organochlorine-induced mortality and residues in long-billed curlews from Oregon. *Condor* 87(4):563–565.

Blus, L. J., C. J. Henny, and A. J. Krynitsky. 1985b. The effects of heptachlor and lindane on birds, Columbia Basin, Oregon and Washington, 1976–1981. *Sci. Tot. Environ.* 46(Nov.):73–81.

Blus, L. J., C. J. Henny, C. J. Lenhart, et al. 1979. Effects of heptachlor-treated cereal grains on Canada geese in the Columbia Basin. In *Manage. Biol. of Pacific Flyway Geese: a Symposium,* ed. R. L. Jarvis and J. C. Bartonek, pp., 105–116. Oregon State University Bookstores, Corvallis.

Blus, L. J., C. J. Henny, D. J. Lenhart, et al. 1984. Effects of heptachlor- and lindane-treated seed on Canada geese. *J. Wildl. Manage.* 48(4):1097–1111.

Blus, L. J., O. H. Pattee, C. J. Henny, et al. 1983. First records of chlordane-related mortality in wild birds. *J. Wildl. Manage.* 47(1):196–198.

Blus, L. J., C. S. Staley, C. J. Henny, et al. 1989. Effects of organophosphorus insecticides on sage grouse in southeastern Idaho. *J. Wildl. Manage.* 53(4):1139–1146.

Boellstorff. D. E., H. M. Ohlendorf, D. W. Anderson, et al. 1985. Organochlorine chemical residues in white pelicans and western grebes from the Klamath Basin, California. *Arch. Environ. Contam. Toxicol.* 14(4):485–493.

Boersma, D. C., J. A. Ellenton, and A. Yagminas. 1986. Investigation of the hepatic mixed-function oxidase system in herring gull embryos in relation to environmental contaminants. *Environ. Toxicol. Chem.* 5(3):309–318.

Boersma, P. D. 1986. Ingestion of petroleum by seabirds can serve as a monitor of water quality. *Science* 231(4736):373–376.

Borg, K., H. Wanntorp, K. Erne, et al. 1969. Alkyl mercury poisoning in terrestrial Swedish wildlife. *Viltrevy* 6(4):301–379.

Bowes, G. W., and C. J. Jonkel. 1975. Presence and distribution of polychlorinated biphenyls (PCB) in arctic and subarctic marine food chains. *J. Fish. Res. Bd. Canada* 32(11):2111–2123.

Boyd, C. E., S. B. Vinson, and D. E. Ferguson. 1963. Possible DDT resistance in two species of frogs. *Copeia* 1963(2):426–429.

Braestrup, L. J. Clausen, and O. Berg. 1974. DDE. PCB, and aldrin levels in Arctic birds of Greenland. *Bull. Environ. Contam. Toxicol.* 11(4):326–332.

Braham, H. W., and C. M. Neal. 1974. The effects of DDT on energetics of the short-tailed shrew. *Bull. Environ. Contam. Toxicol.* 12(1):32–37.

Bramble, W. C., and W. R. Byrns. 1958. Use of powerline right-of-way by game after chemical brush control. *Pa. Game News.* 29:19–25.

Brattsten. L. B., C. W. Holyoke, Jr., J. R. Leeper, et al. 1986. Insecticide resistance: challenge to pest management and basic research. *Science* 231(4743):1255–1260.

Brewerton, H. V. 1969. DDT in fats of antarctic animals. *N. Z. J. Sci.* 12(2):194–199.

Brown, J. F., Jr., D. L. Bedard, M. J. Brennan, et al. 1987. Polychlorinated biphenyl dechlorination in aquatic sediments. *Science* 236(4802):709–712.

Brown, N. J., and A. W. A. Brown. 1970. Biological fate of DDE in a sub-arctic environment *J. Wildl. Manage.* 34(4):929–940.

Brown, R. A., and H. L. Huffman, Jr. 1976. Hydrocarbons in open ocean water. *Science* 191(4229):847–849.

Brown, R. S., R. E. Wolke, C. W. Brown, et al. 1979. Hydrocarbon pollution and the prevalence of neoplasia in New England soft-shell clams (*Mya arenaria*). In *Animals as monitors of environmental Pollutants,* pp. 41–51. Washington, DC: National Academy of Sciences.

Bruce, W. N., G. C. Decker, and J. G. Wilson. 1966. The relationship of the levels of insecticide contamination of crop seeds to their fat content and soil concentration of aldrin, heptachlor and their epoxides. *J. Econom. Ent.* 59(1):179–181.

Bruggers, R. L., M. M. Jaeger, J. O. Keith, et al. 1989. Impact of fenthion on nontarget birds during quelea control in Kenya. *Wildl. Soc. Bull.* 17(2):149–160.

Buckley, E. H. 1982. Accumulation of airborne polychlorinated biphenyls in foliage. *Science* 216(4545):520–522.

Buckner, C. H., and B. A. McLeod. 1975. The impact of insecticides on small forest mammals. In *Aerial control of forest insects in Canada,* M. L. Prebble ed., pp. 314–318. Ottawa, Canada: Department of the Environment.

Buckner, C. H., B. B. McLeod, and R. G. Lidstone. 1975. *The effects of experimental application of Dimilin upon selected forest fauna*. Chemical Control Research Institute Report CC-X-97. Ottawa, Ontario, Canada.

Bullister, J. L., and R. F. Weiss. 1983. Anthropogenic chlorofluoromethanes in Greenland and Norwegian seas. *Science* 221(4607):265–268.

Bunck, C. M., J. W. Spann, O. H. Pattee, et al. 1985. Changes in eggshell thickness during incubation: implications for evaluating the impact of organochlorine contaminants on productivity. *Bull. Environ. Contam. Toxicol.* 35(2):173–182.

Bunyan, P. J., and P. I. Stanley. 1983. The environmental cost of pesticide usage in the United Kingdom. *Agr. Ecosys. Environ.* 9(2):187–209.

Burge, W. D. 1971. Anaerobic decomposition of DDT in soil: acceleration by volatile compounds of alfalfa. *J. Agr. Food. Chem.* 19(2):375–378.

Cade, T. J., J. L. Lincer, C. M. White, et al. 1971. DDE residues and eggshell changes in Alaskan falcons and hawks. *Science* 172(3986):955–957.

Cade, T. J., C. M. White, and J. R. Haugh. 1968. Peregrines and pesticides in Alaska. *Condor* 70(2):170–178.

Cain, B. W. 1981. Nationwide residues of organochlorine compounds in wings of adult mallards and black ducks, 1979–1980. *Pest. Monit. J.* 15(3): 128–134.

Cain, B. W., L. Sileo, J. C. Franson, et al. 1983. Effects of dietary cadmium on mallard ducklings. *Environ. Res.* 32(2):286–297.

Cairns, J., Jr. 1986. The myth of the most sensitive species. *Biosci.* 36(10):670–672.

Cairns, J., Jr., K. L. Dickson, and A. W. Maki, eds. 1978. Estimating the hazard of chemical substances to aquatic life. Philadelphia, PA: ASTM Spec. Tech. Pub. 657. 278 pp.

Capen, D. E. 1977. Evaluating the impact of pesticides on the white-faced ibis in Utah. *Proc. Conf. Colonial Waterbird Group.* 1977:196–201.

Carsel, R. F., W. B. Nixon, and L. G. Ballantine. 1986. Comparison of pesticide root zone model predictions with observed concentrations for the tobacco pesticide metalaxyl in unsaturated zone soils. *Environ. Toxicol. Chem.* 5(4):345–353.

Carson, R. 1962. *Silent spring*. Boston: Houghton Mifflin.

Carstens, L. A., D. A. Barsotti, and J. R. Allen. 1979. Exposure of infant Rhesus macaques (*Macaca mulatta*) to polychlorinated biphenyl (PCB). In *Animals as monitors of environmental pollutants*, pp. 339–355. Washington, DC: National Academy of Sciences.

Carter, L. J. 1976. Michigan's PBB incident:chemical mix-up leads to disaster. *Science* 192(4236):240–243.

Cavanaugh, K. P., A. R. Goldsmith, W. N. Holmes, et al. 1983. Effects of ingested petroleum on the plasma prolactin levels during incubation and on the breeding success of paired mallard ducks. *Arch. Environ. Contam. Toxicol.* 12(3):335–341.

Cavanaugh, K. P., and W. N. Holmes. 1982. Effects of ingested petroleum on plasma levels of ovarian steroid hormones in photostimulated mallard ducks. *Arch. Environ. Contam. Toxicol.* 11(4):503–508.

Chacko, C. I., J. L. Lockwood, and M. Zabik. 1966. Chlorinated hydrocarbon pesticides: degradation by microbes. *Science* 154(3751):893–895.

Chandler, J. H., Jr., and L. L. Marking. 1982. Toxicity of rotenone to selected aquatic invertebrates and frog larvae. *Prog. Fish Cult.* 44(2):78–80.

Chen, E. 1979. *PBB: an American Tragedy.* Englewood Cliffs, NJ: Prentice-Hall, Inc.

Chisholm, R. D, and L. Koblitsky. 1959. Accumulation and dissipation of pesticide residues in soil. *Trans. N. A. Wildl. Conf.* 24:118–123.

Christensen, H. E. (ed.). 1973. *The toxic substances list, 1973 edition.* Rockville, Md: U.S. Dept. H. E. W., NIOSH.

Clark, D. R., Jr. 1978. Uptake of dietary PCB by pregnant big brown bats (*Eptesicus fuscus*) and their fetuses. *Bull. Environ. Contam. Toxicol.* 19(6):707–714.

Clark, D. R., Jr. 1981a. *Bats and environmental contaminants: a review.* Washington, DC: USFWS Special Scientific Report No. 235.

Clark, D. R., Jr. 1981b. Death in bats from DDE, DDT, or dieldrin: diagnosis via residues in carcass fat. *Bull. Environ. Contam. Toxicol.* 26(3):367–374.

Clark, D. R., Jr., R. L. Clawson, and C. J. Stafford. 1983. Gray bats killed by dieldrin at two additional Missouri caves: aquatic macroinvertebrates found dead. *Bull. Environ. Contam. Toxicol.* 30(2):214–218.

Clark. D. R., Jr., and A. J. Krynitsky. 1983a. DDE in brown and white fat of hibernating bats. *Environ. Pollut. Series A* 31(4):287–299.

Clark, D. R., Jr., and A. J. Krynitsky. 1983b. DDT: recent contamination in New Mexico and Arizona? *Environ.* 25(5):27–31.

Clark, D. R., Jr., and T. G. Lamont. 1976a. Organochlorine residues and reproduction in the big brown bat. *J. Wildl. Manage.* 40(2):249–254.

Clark, D. R., Jr. and T. G. Lamont. 1976b. Organochlorine residues in females and nursing young of the big brown bat (*Eptesicus fuscus*). *Bull Environ. Contam. Toxicol.* 15(1):1–8.

Clark. D. R., Jr., and R. M. Prouty. 1977. Experimental feeding of DDE and PCB to female big brown bats (*Eptesicus fuscus*). *J. Toxicol. Environ. Health* 2(4):917–928.

Clark, D. R., Jr., and C. J. Stafford. 1981. Effects of DDE and PCB (Aroclor 1260) on experimentally poisoned female little brown bats (*Myotis lucifugus*): lethal brain concentrations. *J. Toxicol. Environ. Health* 7(6):925–934.

Clarkson, T. W. 1969. Isotope exchange methods in the study of the biotransformation of organomercurial compounds in experimental animals. In *Chemical fallout*, eds. M. W. Miller and C. G. Berg, pp. 274–296. Springfield, IL: C. C. Thomas.

Clawson, S. G., and M. F. Baker. 1959. Immediate effects of dieldrin and heptachlor on bobwhites. *J. Wildl. Manage.* 23(2):215–219.

Cliath, M. M., and W. F. Spencer. 1972. Dissipation of pesticides from soil by volatilization of degradation products. I. Lindane and DDT. *Environ. Sci. Tech.* 6(10):910–914.

Coats, J. R., M. Symonik, S. P. Bradbury, et al. 1989. Toxicology of synthetic pyrethroids in aquatic organisms: an overview. *Environ. Toxicol. Chem.* 8(8):671–679.

Coburn, D. R., and R. Treichler. 1946. Experiments on toxicity of DDT to wildlife. *J. Wildl. Manage.* 10(3):208–216.

Colvin, B. A., P. L. Hegdal, and W. B. Jackson. 1988. Review of non-target hazards associated with rodenticide use in the U.S.A. *Bull. OEPP/EPPO* 18:301–308.

Conney, A. H. 1967. Pharmacological implications of microsomal enzyme induction. *Pharma. Rev.* 19(3):317–366.

Cooke, A. S. 1971. Selective predation by newts on frog tadpoles treated with DDT. *Nature* 229(5282):275–276.

Cooke, A. S. 1973. Shell thinning in avian eggs by environmental pollutants. *Environ. Pollut.* 4(2):85–152.

Cope, O. B., and P. F. Springer. 1958. Mass control of insects: the effects on fish and wildlife. *Bull. Ent. Soc. Amer.* 4(1):52–56.

Cope, W. G., J. G. Wiener, and R. G. Rada. 1990. Mercury accumulation in yellow perch in Wisconsin seepage lakes: relation to lake characteristics. *Environ. Toxicol. Chem.* 9(7):931–940.

Cottam, C., and E. Higgins. 1946. *DDT: its effects on fish and wildlife*. U.S. Fish and Wildlife Service Circular 11. Washington, DC.

Couch, L. K. 1946. Effects of DDT on wildlife in a Mississippi bottom woodland. *Trans. N. A. Wildl. Conf.* 11:323–329.

Cox, J. L. 1970. Low ambient level uptake of 14C-DDT by three species of marine phytoplankton. *Bull. Environ. Contam. Toxicol.* 5(3):218–221.

Creaven, P. J., D. V. Parke, and R. T. Williams. 1965. A fluorimetric study of the hydroxylation of biphenyl *in-vitro* by liver preparations of various species. *Biochem J.* 96(3):879–885.

Crossley, D. A., and M. Witcamp. 1964. Effects of pesticide on biota and breakdown of forest litter. *Trans. Int. Congress of Soil Sci.* 8:887–892.

Custer, T. W., and H. M. Ohlendorf. 1989. Brain cholinesterase activity of nestling great egrets, snowy egrets, and black-crowned night-herons. *J. Wildl. Disease.* 25(3):359–363.

Czuczwa, J. M., B. D. McVeety, and R. A. Hites. 1984. Polychlorinated dibenzo-p-dioxins and dibenzofurans in sediments from Siskowit Lake, Isle Royale. *Science* 226(4674):568–569.

Dahlen, J. H., and A. O. Haugen. 1954. Acute toxicity of certain insecticides to the bobwhite quail and mourning dove. *J. Wildl. Manage.* 18(4):477–481.

Dahlgren, R. B., and R. L. Linder. 1971. Effects of polychlorinated biphenyls on pheasant reproduction, behavior and survival. *J. Wildl. Manage.* 35(2):315–319.

Dave, G. 1981. *Influence of diet and starvation on toxicity of endrin to fathead minnows (Pimephales promelas).* EPA-600/S3-81-048.

Davies, C. S., and R. J. Richardson. 1980. Organophosphorus compounds. In *Experimental and clinical neurotoxicity,* ed. P. S. Spencer and H. H. Schamberg, pp. 527–544. Baltimore, MD: Williams and Wilkins.

Day, K. E. 1989. Acute, chronic and sublethal effects of synthetic pyrethroids on freshwater zooplankton. *Environ. Toxicol. Chem.* 8(5):411–416.

Deichmann, W. B., W. E. MacDonald, A. G. Beasley, et al. 1971. Subnormal reproduction in beagle dogs induced by DDT and aldrin. *Ind. Med. Surg.* 40(2):10–20.

Deichmann, W. B., W. E. MacDonald, and D. A. Cubit. 1971. DDT tissue retention: sudden rise induced by the addition of aldrin to a fixed DDT intake. *Science* 172(3980):275–276.

DeLong, R. L., W. G. Gilmartin, and J. G. Simpson. 1973. Premature births in California sea lions: association with high organochlorine pollutant residue levels. *Science* 181(4105):1168–1170.

Delp, C. J. 1986. Pesticide resistance management is a key to effective pest control. *Biosci.* 36(2):101–102.

Demoute, J-P. 1989. A brief review of the environmental fate and metabolism of pyrethroids. *Pestic. Sci.* 27(4):375–385.

Dent, J. G., K. J. Netter, and J. E. Gibson. 1976. Effects of chronic administration of polybrominated biphenyls on parameters associated with hepatic drug metabolism. *Res. Commun. Chem. Pathol. Pharmacol.* 13(1):75–82.

Dewees, D. C. 1986. *Asbestos in buildings: an economic investigation.* Washington, DC: Resources for the Future.

DeWeese. L. R., R. R. Cohen, and C. J. Stafford. 1985. Organochlorine residues and eggshell measurements for tree swallows (*Tachycineta bicolor*) in Colorado. *Bull. Environ. Contam. Toxicol.* 35(6):767–775.

DeWeese, L. R., C. J. Henny, R. L. Floyd, et al. 1979. *Response of breeding birds to aerial sprays of trichlorfon (Dylox) and carbaryl (Sevin-4-oil) in Montana forests.* U. S. Fish and Wildlife Service Special Scientific Report on Wildlife No. 222.

DeWeese. L. R., L. C. McEwen, G. L. Hensler, et al. 1986. Organochlorine contaminants in Passeriformes and other avian prey of the peregrine falcon in the western United States. *Environ. Toxicol. Chem.* 5(7):675–693.

DeWeese, L. R., L. C. McEwen, L. A. Settimi, et al. 1983. Effects on birds of fenthion aerial application for mosquito control. *J. Econom. Ent.* 76(4):906–911.

DeWitt, J. B. 1955. Effects of chlorinated hydrocarbon insecticides upon quail and pheasants. *J. Agr. Food. Chem.* 3(8):672–676.

DeWitt, J. B. 1956. Chronic toxicity to quail and pheasants of some chlorinated insecticides. *J. Agr. Food Chem.* 4(10):863–866.

Diamond, J. M., M. J. Parson, and D. Gruber. 1990. Rapid detection of sublethal toxicity using fish ventilatory behavior. *Environ. Toxicol. Chem.* 9(1):3–11.

Dieter, M. P. 1974. Plasma enzyme activities in coturnix quail fed graded doses of DDE, polychlorinated biphenyl, malathion, and mercuric chloride. *Toxicol. Appl. Pharmacol.* 27(1):86–98.

Dieter, M. P., and L. J. Ludke. 1975. Studies on combined effects of organophosphates and heavy metals in birds. I. Plasma and brain cholinesterase in Coturnix quail fed methyl mercury and orally dosed with parathion. *Bull. Environ. Contam. Toxicol.* 13(3):257–262.

Dieter, M. P., and L. J. Ludke. 1978. Studies on combined effects of organophosphates and heavy metals in birds. II. Plasma cholinesterase in quail fed morsodren and orally dosed with parathion or carbofuran. *Bull. Environ. Contam. Toxicol.* 19(4):389–395.

Dieter, M. P., M. C. Perry, and B. M. Mulhern. 1976. Lead and PCB's in canvasback ducks: relationship between enzyme levels and residues in birds. *Arch. Environ. Contam. Toxicol.* 5(1):1–13.

Dimond, J. B., G. Y. Belyea, R. E. Kadunce, et al. 1970. DDT. residues in robins and earthworms associated with contaminated forest soil. *Canad. Entomol.* 102(9):1122–1130.

Dindal, D. L. 1970. Accumulation and excretion of Cl-36 DDT in mallard and lesser scaup ducks. *J. Wildl. Manage.* 34(1):74–92.

Dindal, D. L., and T. J. Peterle. 1968. Wing and body tissue relationships of DDT and metabolite residues in mallard and lesser scaup ducks. *Bull. Environ. Contam. Toxicol.* 3(1):37–48.

Dinman, B. D. 1972. "Non-concept" of "no-threshold": chemicals in the environment. *Science* 175(4021):495–497.

Dolinsky, Z. S., R. G. Burright, P. J. Donovick, et al. 1981. Behavioral effects of lead and *Toxocara canis* in mice. *Science* 213(4512):1142–1144.

Dover, M. J., and B. A. Croft. 1986. Pesticide resistance and public policy. *Biosci.* 36(2):78–85.

Dunckel, A. E. 1975. An updating of the polybrominated biphenyl disaster in Michigan. *J. Amer. Vet. Med. Assoc.* 167(1):838–841.

Dustman, E. H., L. F. Stickel, L. J. Blus, et al. 1971. The occurrence and significance of polychlorinated biphenyls in the environment. *Trans. N. A. Wildl. Nat. Resour. Conf.* 36:118–133.

Dustman, E. H., L. F. Stickel, and J. B. Elder. 1972. Mercury in wild animals, Lake St. Clair, 1970. In *Environmental mercury contamination,* ed. R. Hartung and B. D. Dinman, pp.46–52. Ann Arbor, MI: Ann Arbor Science Publications.

Dvorchik, B., H. M. Istin, and T. H. Maren. 1971. Does DDT inhibit carbonic anhydrase? *Science* 172(3984):728–729.

Eastin, W. C., Jr., W. J. Fleming, and H. C. Murray. 1982. Oganophosphate inhibition of avian salt gland Na,K-ASTPase activity. *Comp. Biochem. Physiol.* 73C(1):101–107.

Eastin, W. C., Jr., D. J. Hoffman, and C. T. O'Leary. 1983. Lead accumulation and depression of a aminolevulinic acid dehydratase (ALAD) in young birds fed automotive waste oil. *Arch. Environ. Contam. Toxicol.* 12(1):31–35.

Eberhardt, L. L., R. L. Meeks, and T. J. Peterle. 1971. Food chain model for DDT kinetics in a freshwater marsh. *Nature* 230(5288):60–62.

Ecobichon, D. J., and P. W. Saschenbrecker. 1968. Pharmacodynamic study of DDT in cockerels. *Canad. J. Physiol. Pharmaco.* 46(5):785–794.

Edwards, C. A. 1970. Persistent pesticides in the environment. *Crit. Rev. Environ. Contam.* 1(1):7–78.

Eisler, R. 1985a. *Mirex hazards to fish, wildlife, and invertebrates: a synoptic review*. U. S. Fish and Wildlife Service Contam. Hazard Rev. Rpt. No. 1.

Eisler, R. 1985b. *Carbofuran hazards to fish, wildlife and invertebrates: a synoptic review*. U. S. Fish and Wildlife Service Contam. Hazard Rev. Rpt. No. 3.

Eisler, R. 1986a. *Dioxin hazards to fish, wildlife, and invertebrates: a synoptic review*. U. S. Fish and Wildlife Service Contam. Hazard Rev. Rpt. No. 8.

Eisler, R. 1986b. *Polychlorinated biphenyl hazards to fish, wildlife and invertebrates: a synoptic review*. U. S. Fish and Wildlife Service Contam. Hazard Rev. Rpt. No. 7.

Eisler, R., and J. Jacknow. 1985. *Toxaphene hazards to fish, wildlife, and invertebrates: a synoptic review*. U. S. Fish and Wildlife Service Contam. Hazard Rev. 4.

Elder, D. L., and S. W. Fowler. 1977. Polychlorinated biphenyls: penetration into the deep ocean by zooplankton fecal pellet transport. *Science* 197(4302):459–461.

Elliott, M. 1989. The pyrethroids: early discovery, recent advances and the future. *Pestici. Sci.* 27(4):337–351.

Ellis, D. H., L. R. DeWeese, T. G. Grubb, et al. 1989. Pesticide residues in Arizona peregrine falcon eggs and prey. *Bull. Environ. Contam. Toxicol,* 42(1):57–64.

Emanuel, W. R., J. S. Olson, and G. G. Killough. 1980. The expanded use of fossil fuels by the U. S. and the global carbon dioxide problem. *J. Environ. Manage.* 10(1):37–49.

Eng. R. L. 1952. A two-summer study of the effects on bird populations of chlordane bait and aldrin spray as used for grasshopper control. *J. Wildl. Manage.* 16(3):326–337.

Eyer, J. R., L. R. Faulkner, and R. T. McCarty. 1953. *The effect of toxaphene and DDT on geese in cotton fields*. New Mexico Agricultural and Mechanical College Press. Bulletin 1078.

Fabacher, D. L., and P. C. Bauman. 1985. Enlarged livers and hepatic microsomal mixed-function oxidase components in tumor-bearing brown bullheads from a chemically contaminated river. *Environ. Toxicol. Chem.* 4(5):703–710.

Faber, R. H., and J. J. Hickey. 1973. Eggshell thinning, chlorinated hydrocarbons, and mercury in inland aquatic bird eggs, 1969 and 1970. *Pest. Monit. J.* 7(1):27–36.

Fahey, J. E., D. W. Hamilton, and R. W. Rings. 1952. Longevity of parathion and related insecticides in spray residues. *J. Econom. Ent.* 45(4):700–703.

Farage-Elawar, M., and B. M. Francis. 1987. Acute and delayed effects of fenthion in young chicks. *J. Toxicol. Environ. Health* 21(4):455–469.

Farage-Elawar, M., and B. M. Francis. 1988. Effects of multiple dosing of fenthion, fenithrothion, and desbromoleptophos in young chicks. *J. Toxicol. Environ. Health* 23(2):217–228.

Farmer, W. J., K. Igue, W. F. Spencer, et al. 1972. Volatility of organochlorine insecticides from soil: 1. Effect of concentration, temperature, air flow rate, and vapor pressure. *Soil Sc. Soc. Amer. Proceed.* 36(3):443–447.

Farringer, R. 1985. *Wild mammal toxicity test.* USEPA 540/9-85-004. 16 pp.

Ferguson, D. E. 1963. In less than 20 years/Mississippi Delta wildlife developing resistance to pesticides. *Agric. Chem.* 18(9):32–34.

Ferguson, D. E. 1967. The ecological consequences of pesticide resistance in fishes. *Trans. N. A. Wildl. Nat. Resour. Conf.* 32:103–107.

Ferguson, D. E., and C. C. Gilbert. 1967. Tolerances of three species of anuran amphibians to five chlorinated hydrocarbon insecticides. *Miss. Acad. Sci.* 13:135–138.

Ferguson, D. E., J. L. Ludke, and G. G. Murphy. 1966. Dynamics of endrin uptake and release by resistant and susceptible strains of mosquitofish. *Trans. Amer. Fish. Soc.* 95(4):335–344.

Fimreite, N. 1970. Mercury uses in Canada and their possible hazards as sources of mercury contamination. *Environ. Pollut.* 1(2):119–131.

Fimreite, N. 1971. *Effects of dietary methylmercury on ringnecked pheasants.* Canadian Wildlife Service Occasional Paper No. 9. 39 pp.

Fimreite, N. 1974. Mercury contamination of aquatic birds in Northwestern Ontario. *J. Wildl. Manage.* 38(1):120–131.

Fimreite, N., R. W. Fyfe, and J. A. Keith. 1970. Mercury contamination of Canadian Prairie seed eaters and their avian predators. *Canad. Field Nat.* 84(3):269–276.

Fimreite, N., W. N. Holsworth, J. A. Keith, et al. 1971. Mercury in fish and fish-eating birds near sites of industrial contamination in Canada. *Canad. Field Nat.* 85(3):211–220.

Fimreite, N., and L. Karstad. 1971. Effects of dietary methyl mercury on red-tailed hawks. *J. Wildl. Manage.* 35(2):293–300.

Finley, M. T., M. P. Dieter, and L. N. Locke. 1976. Lead in tissues of mallard ducks dosed with two types of lead shot. *Bull. Environ. Contam. Toxicol.* 16(3):261–269.

Finley, M. T., W. H. Stickel, and R. E. Christensen. 1979. Mercury residues in tissues of dead and surviving birds fed methylmercury. *Bull. Environ. Contam. Toxicol.* 21(1/2):105–110.

Finley, R. B., Jr. 1965. Adverse effects on birds of phosphamidon applied to a Montana forest. *J. Wildl. Manage.* 29(3):580–591.

Finnegan, J. K., H. B. Haag, and P. S. Larson. 1949. Tissue distribution and elimination of DDD and DDT following oral administration to dogs and rats. *Proc. Soc. Explor. Biol. Med.* 72(1):357–360.

Fish and Wildlife News, 1981. Army cutworms-endrin. (U.S.D.I.) Oct./Nov.:3.

Fisher, A. L., H. H. Keasling, and F. W. Schueler. 1952. Estrogenic action of DDT and some analogues. *Fed. Proc.* 11(1):345.

Fleming, W. E., and I. M. Hawley. 1950. A large-scale test with DDT to control the Japanese beetle. *J. Econom. Ent.* 43(5):586–590.

Fleming, W. J. 1981. Recovery of brain and plasma cholinesterase activities in ducklings exposed to organophosphorus pesticides. *Arch. Environ. Contam. Toxicol.* 10(2):215–229.

Fleming, W. J., and S. P. Bradbury. 1981. Recovery of cholinesterase activity in mallard ducklings administered organophosphorus pesticides. *J. Toxicol. Environ. Health.* 8(5/6):885–897.

Fleming, W. J., and B. W. Cain. 1985. Areas of localized organochlorine contamination in Arizona and New Mexico. *Southwest Nat.* 30(2):269–277.

Fleming, W. J., D. R. Clark, Jr., and C. J. Henny. 1983. Organochlorine pesticides and PCB's: a continuing problem in the 1980s. *Trans. N. A. Wildl. Nat. Resour. Conf.* 48:186–199.

Fleming, W. J., H. de Chacin, O. H. Pattee, et al. 1982. Parathion accumualtion in cricket frogs and its effect on American kestrels. *J. Toxicol. Environ. Health.* 10(6):921–927.

Fleming, W. J., and C. E. Grue. 1981. Recovery of cholinesterase activity in five avian species exposed to dicrotophos, an organophosphorus pesticide. *Pest. Biochem. Physiol.* 16(2):129–135.

Fleming, W. J., G. H. Heinz, J. C. Franson, et al. 1985. Toxicity of Abate 4E (Temephos) in mallard ducklings and the influence of cold. *Environ. Toxicol. Chem.* 4(2):193–199.

Fleming, W. J., G. H. Heinz, and C. A. Schuler. 1985. Lethal and behavioral effects of chlordimeform in bobwhite. *Toxicol.* 36(1):37–47.

Fleming, W. J., and T. J. O'Shea. 1980. Influence of a local source of DDT pollution on statewide DDT residues in waterfowl wings, Northern Alabama, 1978–79. *Pest. Monitor. J.* 14(3):86–89.

Fleming, W. J., B. P. Pullin, and D. M. Swineford. 1984. Population trends and environmental contaminants in herons in the Tennessee Valley, 1980–81. *Colonial Waterbirds* 7:63–73.

Fleming, W. J., J. A. Rodgers, Jr., and C. J. Stafford. 1984. Contaminants in wood stork eggs and their effects on reproduction, Florida 1982. *Colonial Waterbirds* 7:88–93.

Flickinger, E. L. 1979. Effects of aldrin exposure on snow geese in Texas rice fields. *J. Wildl. Manage.* 43(1):94–101.

Flickinger, E. L., and K. A. King. 1972. Some effects of aldrin-treated rice on Gulf Coast wildlife. *J. Wildl. Manage.* 36(3):706–727.

Flickinger, E. L., C. A. Mitchell, D. H. White, et al. 1986. Bird poisoning from misuse of the carbamate Furadan in a Texas rice field. *Wildl. Soc. Bull.* 14(1):59–62.

Flickinger, E. L., D. H. White, C. A. Mitchell, et al. 1984. Monocrotophos and dicrotophos residues in birds as a result of misuse of organophosphates in Matagorda County. *Texas. J. Assoc. Off. Anal. Chem.* 67(4):827–828.

Forsyth, D. J., and T. J. Peterle. 1973. Accumulation of chlorine-36 ring-labeled DDT residues in various tissues of two species of shrew. *Arch. Environ. Contam. Toxicol.* 1(1):1–17.

Forsyth, D. J., T. J. Peterle, and L. W. Bandy. 1983. Persistence and transfer of ^{36}Cl DDT in the soil and biota of an old-field ecosystem: a six-year balance study. *Ecology* 64(6):1620–1636.

Forsyth, D. J., T. J. Peterle, and G. C. White. 1975. A preliminary model of DDT kinetics in an old-field ecosystem. In *Environ. Qual. Safety* Supp. Vol. 3, pp. 754–759. eds. F. Coulston and F. Korte, Stuttgart: Georg Thieme Pub.

Fowle, C. D. 1966. The effects of phosphamidon on birds in New Brunswick forests. *J. Appl Ecol.* (Suppl 3):169–170.

Fowle, C. D. 1972. *Effects of phosphamidon on forest birds in New Brunswick.* Canadian Wildlife Service Report Ser. 6. 25 pp.

Franks, E. C. 1973. Life expectancies of five passerine species in the DDT era. *Amer. Birds.* 27(3):571–572.

Franson, J. C., and T. W. Custer. 1982. Toxicity of dietary lead in young cockerels. *Vet. Human Toxicol.* 24(6):421–423.

Franson, J. C., H. L. Murray, and C. Bunck. 1985. Enzyme activities in plasma, kidney, liver, and muscle of five avian species. *J. Wildl. Disease.* 21(1):33–39.

Franson, J. C., L. Sileo, O. H. Pattee, et al. 1983. Effects of chronic dietary lead on American kestrels (*Falco sparverius*). *J. Wildl. Disease* 19(1):110–113.

Franson, J. C., J. W. Spann, G. H. Heinz, et al. 1983. Effects of dietary ABATE on reproductive success, duckling survival, behavior, and clinical pathology in game-farm mallards. *Arch. Environ. Contam. Toxicol.* 12(5): 529–534.

Friend, M., M. A. Haegele, and R. Wilson. 1973. DDE: interference with extra-renal salt excretion in the mallard. *Bull. Environ. Contam. Toxicol.* 9(1):49–53.

Friend, M., and D. O. Trainer. 1970. Polychlorinated biphenyl: interaction with duck hepatitis virus. *Science* 170(3964):1314–1316.

Friend, M., and D. O. Trainer. 1974a. Experimental DDT–duck hepatitis virus interaction studies. *J. Wildl. Manage.* 38(4):887–895.

Friend, M., and D. O. Trainer. 1974b. Experimental dieldrin-duck hepatitis virus interaction studies. *J. Wildl. Manage.* 38(4):896–902.

Frost, A. 1938. Effect upon wildlife of spraying for control of gipsy moths. *J. Wildl. Manage.* 2(1):13–16.

Fry, D. M., and C. K. Toone. 1981. DDT-induced feminization of gull embryos. *Science* 213(4510):922–924.

Gakstatter, J. H., and C. M. Weiss. 1967. The elimination of DDT-C14, dieldrin C14 and Lindane C14 from fish following a single sublethal exposure in aquaria. *Trans. Amer. Fish. Soc.* 96(3):301–307.

Galbreath, E. H. 1965. The toxic effects of Mirex to certain selected species of wildlife. Master's thesis, University of Georgia, Athens.

Garthhoff, L. H., L. Friedman, T. M. Farber, et al. 1977. Biochemical changes caused by ingestion of Aroclor 1254 (a commercial polychlorinated biphenyl mixture) or Firemaster BP-6 (a commercial polybrominated biphenyl mixture). Suppl. Toxic Substances Pt. 2 Serial No 95-28. pp. 1298–1331. Washington, DC: U. S. Government Printing Office.

Genelly, R. E., and R. L. Rudd. 1956. Effects of DDT, toxaphene and dieldrin on pheasant reproduction. *Auk* 73(4):529–539.

George, J. L., and D. E. H. Frear. 1966. Pesticides in the Antarctic. *J. Appl. Ecology* (Suppl.) 3:155–167.

Gesell, G. G., R. J. Robel, A. D. Dayton, et al. 1979. Effects of dieldrin on operant behavior of bobwhites. *J. Environ. Sci. Health.* B14(2):153–170.

Gianessi, L. P. 1986. A national pesticide usage data base (mimeo). Washington. DC: Resources for the Future.

Gilbert, F. F. 1969. Physiological effects of natural DDT residues and metabolites on ranch mink. *J. Wildl. Manage.* 33(4):933–943.

Gilbertson, M., and L. Reynolds. 1974. DDE and PCB in Canadian birds, 1969 to 1972. Canadian Wildlife Service Occasional Paper 19.

Gile, J. D., and J. W. Gillett. 1979. Fate of ^{14}C-dieldrin in a simulated terrestrial ecosystem. *Arch. Environ. Contam. Toxicol.* 8(1):107–124.

Giles, R. H., Jr. 1970. The ecology of a small forested watershed treated with the insecticide malathion-S35. *Wildl. Monog.* 24.

Gillett, J. W., T. H. Chan, and L. C. Terriere. 1966. Interactions between DDT analogs and microsomal epoxidase systems. *J. Agr. Food. Chem.* 14(6):540–545.

Gillett, J. W., J. D. Gile, and L. K. Russell. 1983. Predator-prey (vole–cricket) interactions: the effects of wood preservatives. *Environ. Toxicol. Chem.* 2(1):83–93.

Gish, C. D., and N. J. Chura. 1970. Toxicity of DDT to Japanese quail as influenced by body weight, breeding condition, and sex. *Toxicol. Appl. Pharmacol.* 17(4):740–751.

Goodrum, P. D., and V. H. Reid. 1956. Wildlife implications of hardwood and brush controls. *Trans. N. A. Wildl. Conf.* 21:127–141.

Gorsline, J., and W. N. Holmes. 1982. Suppression of adrenocortical activity in mallard ducks exposed to petroleum-contaminated food. *Arch. Environ. Contam. Toxicol.* 11(4):497–502.

Grabowski, C. T. 1981. *Pesticide effects on prenatal cardiovascular physiology.* EPA-600/S1-80-032.

Grau, B. L., and T. J. Peterle. 1979. Compartmentalization of ^{14}C-DDT in an experimental old-field plot. *Bull. Environ. Contam. Toxicol.* 22(6):846–853.

Gray, L. E., Jr., R. J. Kavlock, N. Chernoff, et al. 1982. Prenatal exposure to the herbicide 2,4-dichlorophenyl-p-nitrophenyl ether destroys the rodent Harderian gland. *Science* 215(4530):293–294.

Grolleau, G., and J. L. Caritez. 1986. Toxicity, by oral administration, of various pesticides to grey partridge (*Perdix perdix L.*) and the red partridge (*Alectoris rufa L.*). *Gib. Faune Sauv.* 3(2):185–196.

Grue, C. E. 1982. Response of common grackles to dietary concentrations of four organophosphate pesticides. *Arch. Environ. Contam. Toxicol.* 11(5):617–626.

Grue, C. E. 1985. Pesticides and the decline of Guam's native birds. *Nature* 316(6026):301.

Grue, C. E., W. J. Fleming, D. G. Busby, et al. 1983. Assessing hazards of organophosphate pesticides to wildlife. *Trans. N. A. Wildl. Nat. Resour. Conf.* 48:200–220.

Grue, C. E., and C. C. Hunter. 1984. Brain cholinesterase activity in fledgling starlings: implications for monitoring exposure of songbirds to ChE inhibitors. *Bull. Environ. Contam. Toxicol.* 32(3):282–289.

Grue, C. E., G. V. N. Powell, and M. J. McChesney. 1982. Care of nestlings by wild female starlings exposed to an organophosphate pesticide. *J. Appl. Ecology* 19(2):327–335.

Grue, C. E., and B. K. Shipley. 1981. Interpreting population estimates of birds following pesticide applications—behavior of male starlings exposed to an organophosphate pesticide. *Stud. Avian Biol.* 6:292–296.

Grue, C. E., and B. K. Shipley. 1984. Sensitivity of nestling and adult starlings to dicrotophos, an organophosphate pesticide. *Environ. Res.* 35(2):454–465.

Gundlach, E. R., P. D. Bohem, M. Marchand, et al. 1983. The fate of Amoco Cadiz oil. *Science* 216(4606):122–129.

Gunther, L. A., and L. R. Jepson. 1960. *Modern insecticides and world food production*. New York: John Wiley and Sons.

Gupta, C., S. J. Yaffe, and B. H. Shapiro. 1982. Prenatal exposure to phenobarbital permanently decreases testosterone and causes reproductive dysfunction. *Science* 216(4546):640–642.

Guzman, J. A., and T. Guardia. 1978. Effects of an organophosphorus insecticide on the cholinesteratic activities of *Bufo arenarum* (H). *Bull. Environ. Contam. Toxicol.* 20(1):52–58

Haegele, M. A., and R. H. Hudson. 1973. DDE effects on reproduction of ring doves. *Environ. Pollut.* 4(1):53–57.

Haegele, M. A., and R. H. Hudson. 1974. Eggshell thinning and residues in mallards one year after DDE exposure. *Arch. Environ. Contam. Toxicol.* 2(4):356–363.

Haegele, M. A., and R. H. Hudson. 1977. Reduction of courtship behavior induced by DDE in male ringed turtle doves. *Wilson Bull.* 89(4):593–601.

Haegele, M. A., and R. K. Tucker. 1974. Effects of 15 common environmental pollutants on eggshell thickness in mallards and coturnix. *Bull. Environ. Contam. Toxicol.* 11(1):98–102.

Haegele, M. A., R. K. Tucker, and R. H. Hudson. 1974. Effects of dietary mercury and lead on eggshell thickness in mallards. *Bull. Environ. Contam. Toxicol.* 11(1):5–11.

Halbert, F , and S. Halbert. 1978. *Bitter harvest*. Grand Rapids, MI. W. B. Erdmans.

Hall, A. T., D. H. Taylor, and P. E. Woods. 1990. Effects of municipal sludge on locomotor activity and exploratory behavior of meadow voles (*Mircotus pennsylvanicus*). *Environ. Toxicol. Chem.* 9(1):31–36.

Hall, R. J. 1984. Pesticides and wildlife: will there be any more DDTs? *Bull. Ent. Soc. Amer.* 30(4):3–6.

Hall, R. J., S. D. Haseltine, and P. H. Geissler. 1989. Monitoring contaminant exposure: relative concentrations of organochlorines in three tissues of American black ducks. *Environ. Monit. Res.* 13(1):11–19.

Hall, R. J., and E. Kolbe. 1980. Bioconcentration of organophosphorus pesticides to hazardous levels by amphibians. *J. Toxicol. Environ. Health* 6(4):853–860.

Hamelink, J. L., and R. C. Waybrant. 1973. Factors controlling the dynamics of non-ionic synthetic organic chemicals in aquatic environments. Technical Report No 44, Purdue University, West Lafayette, IN.

Hamelink, J. L., R. C. Waybrant, and R. C. Ball. 1971. A proposal: exchange equalibria control the degree chlorinated hydrocarbons are biologically magnified in lentic environments. *Trans. Amer. Fish. Soc.* 100(2):207–214.

Hamilton, G. A., and P. I. Stanley. 1975. Further cases of poisoning of wild geese by an organophosphorus winter wheat seed treatment. *Wildfowl* 26:49–54.

Hammond, A. L. 1971. Mercury in the environment: natural and human factors. *Science* 171(3973):788–789.

Hammons, A. S., ed. 1981. Methods for ecological toxicology: a critical review of laboratory multispecies tests. 307 pp. Available from: NTIS, Springfield, VA; ORNL 5708; EPA 560/11-80-026.

Hansch, C. 1969. Quantitative approach to biochemical structure-activity relations. *Accounts Chem Res.* 2(8):232–239.

Hansch, C., and T. Fujita. 1964. p-o-pi analysis. A method for the correlation of biological activity and chemical structure. *J. Amer. Chem Soc.* 86(8):1616–1626.

Hansen, R. J., P. R. Parrish, J. I. Lowe, et al. 1971. Chronic toxicity, uptake, and retention of Aroclor 1254 in two estuarine fishes. *Bull. Environ. Contam. Toxicol.* 6(2):113–119.

Hanson, W. R. 1952. Effects of some herbicides and insecticides on biota of North Dakota marshes. *J. Wildl. Manage.* 16(3):299–308.

Haque, R., D. W. Schmedding, and V. H. Freed. 1974. Aqueous solubility, adsorption, and vapor behavior of polychlorinated biphenyl Aroclor 1254. *Environ. Sci. Tech.* 8(2):139–142.

Harris, B. K. 1951. The effects of toxaphene poisoned grasshoppers upon pheasant chicks. *N. D. Outdoors* 13(8):12.

Harris, R. C., and C. Hohenemser. 1978. Mercury: measuring and managing the risk. *Environ.* 20(9):25–36.

Hart, A. D. M. 1990. The assessment of pesticide hazards to birds: the problem of variable effects. *Ibis* 132:(2):192–204.

Hartung, R., and B. D. Dinman. 1972. *Environmental mercury contamination.* Ann Arbor, MI: Ann Arbor Science Publications.

Harvey, G. R., H. P. Miklas, V. T. Bowen, et al. 1974. Observations on the distribution of chlorinated hydrocarbons in Atlantic Ocean organisms. *J. Marine Res.* 32(2):103–118.

Harvey, G. R., W. G. Steinhauer, and J. M. Teal. 1973. Polychlorobiphenyls in North Atlantic Ocean water. *Science* 180(4086):643–644.

Haseltine, S. D., T. J. Peterle, L. Nagode, et al. 1981. Physiology of the eggshell thinning response to DDE. *Trans. Int. Cong. Game Biol.* 12:237–243.

Haya, K. 1989. Toxicity of pyrethroid insecticides to fish. *Environ. Toxicol. Chem.* 8(5):381–391.

Haynes, R. J. 1972. Effects of DDT on glycogen and lipid levels in bobwhites. *J. Wildl. Manage.* 36(2):518–523.

Health Effects Research Laboratory. 1987. The ORD health research program on drinking water disinfectants and their byproducts: an issue paper prepared for a SAB program review. Health Effects Research Lab mimeo, 50 pp. USEPA, Cincinnati, OH.

Heath, R. G., J. W. Spann, E. F. Hill, et al. 1972. *Comparative dietary toxicities of pesticides to birds.* U. S. Fish and Wildlife Service Special Scientific Report No. 152, 57 p.

Heath, R. G., J. W. Spann, and J. F. Kreitzer. 1969. Marked DDE impairment of mallard reproduction in controlled studies. *Nature* 224(5214):47–48.

Heath, R. G., J. W. Spann, J. F. Kreitzer, et al. 1972. Effects of polychlorinated biphenyls on birds. *Proc. Int. Ornith. Cong.* 15:475–485.

Hegdal, P. L., and B. A. Colvin. 1988. Potential hazard to eastern screech owls and other raptors of brodifacoum bait used for vole control in orchards. *Environ. Toxicol. Chem.* 7(2):245–260.

Heinz, G. H. 1974. Effects of low dietary levels of methyl mercury on mallard reproduction. *Bull. Environ. Contam. Toxicol.* 11(4):386–392.

Heinz, G. 1975. Effects of methylmercury on approach and avoidance behavior of mallard ducklings. *Bull. Environ. Contam. Toxicol.* 13(5):554–564.

Heinz, G. H. 1976a. Behavior of mallard ducklings from parents fed 3ppm DDE. *Bull. Environ. Contam. Toxicol.* 16(6):640–645.

Heinz, G. H. 1976b. Methylmercury: second year feeding effects on mallard reproduction and duckling behavior. *J. Wildl. Manage.* 40(1):82–90.

Heinz, G. H., and S. D. Haseltine. 1981. Avoidance behaviour of young black ducks treated with chromium. *Toxicol. Letters* 8:307–310.

Heinz, G. H., S. D. Haseline, and L. Sileo. 1983. Altered avoidance behavior of young black ducks fed cadmium. *Environ. Toxicol. Chem.* 2(4):419–421.

Heinz, G. H., E. F. Hill, W. H. Stickel, et al. 1979. Environmental contaminant studies by the Patuxent Wildlife Research Center. A.S.T.M. Spec. Tech. Pub. 693, pp. 9–35.

Heinz, G. H., D. J. Hoffman, A. J. Krynitsky, et al. 1987. Reproduction in mallards fed selenium. *Environ. Toxicol. Chem.* 6(6):423–433.

Henderson, C., Q. H. Pickering, and C. M. Tarzwell. 1959. Relative toxicity of ten chlorinated hydrocarbon insecticides to four species of fish. *Trans. Amer. Fish Soc.* 88(1):23–32.

Hendrix, P. F., C. L. Langner, E. P. Odum, et al. 1981. Microcosms as test systems for the ecological effects of toxic substances: an appraisal with cadmium. Program Summary U.S. EPA 600/S3-81-036, Washington DC.

Henkin, H., M. Merta, and J. Staples. 1971. *The environment, the establishment and the law.* Boston: Houghton Mifflin Co.

Henny, C. J. 1972. An analysis of the population dynamics of selected avian species with special reference to changes during the modern pesticide era. U.S. Fish and Wildlife Service Wildlife Research Report 1, 99 pp.

Henny, C. J. 1975. Research, management, and status of the osprey in North America (pp. 199–222). *World Conf. Birds of Prey* (Vienna).

Henny, C. J. 1977. Birds of prey, DDT, and tussock moths in Pacific Northwest. *Trans. N. A. Wildl. Nat. Resour. Conf.* 42:397–411.

Henny, C. J., J. R. Bean, and R. W. Fyfe. 1976. Elevated heptachlor epoxide and DDE residues in a merlin that died after migrating. *Canad. Field Nat.* 90(3):361–363.

Henny, C. J., and L. J. Blus. 1986. Radiotelemetry locates wintering grounds of DDE-contaminated black-crowned night-herons. *Wildl. Soc. Bull.* 14(3):236–241.

Henny, C. J., L. J. Blus, E. H. Kolbe, et al. 1985. Organophosphate insecticide (famphur) topically applied to cattle kills magpies and hawks. *J. Wildl. Manage.* 49(3):648–658.

Henny, C. J., L. J. Blus, A. J. Krynitsky, et al. 1984. Current impact of DDE on black-crowned night-herons in the intermountain west. *J. Wildl. Manage.* 48(1):1–13.

Henny, C. J., L. J. Blus, and C. J. Stafford. 1983. Effects of heptachlor on American kestrels in the Columbia Basin, Oregon. *J. Wildl. Manage.* 47(4):1080–1087.

Henny, C. J., and G. B. Herron. 1989. DDE, selenium, mercury, and white-faced ibis reproduction at Carson Lake, Nevada. *J. Wildl. Manage.* 53(4):1032–1035.

Henny, C. J., C. Maser, J. O. Whitaker, Jr., et al. 1982. Organochlorine residues in bats after a forest spraying with DDT. *Northwest Sci.* 56(4):329–337.

Henny, C. J., and D. L. Meeker. 1981. An evaulation of blood plasma for monitoring DDE in birds of prey. *Environ. Pollut.* (Series A)25(4):291–304.

Henny, C. J., F. P. Ward, K. E. Riddle, et al. 1982. Migratory peregrine falcons, *Falco peregrinus,* accumulate pesticides in Latin America during winter. *Canad. Field Nat.* 96(3):333–338.

Heppleston, P. B. 1973. Organochlorines in British grey seals. *Marine Pollut. Bull.* 4(3):44–45.

Herbert, G. B., and T. J. Peterle. 1990. Heavy metal and organochlorine compound concentrations in tissues of raccoons from east-central Michigan. *Bull. Environ. Contam. Toxicol.* 44(2):331–338.

Herbert, G. B., T. J. Peterle, and T. C. Grubb. 1989. Chronic dose effects of methyl parathion on nuthatches: cholinesterase and ptilochronology. *Bull. Environ. Contam. Toxicol.* 42(4):471–475.

Herman, S. G., and J. B. Burger. 1979. Effects of a forest application of DDT on non-target organisms. *Wildl. Monog.* 69, 62 pp.

Herman, S. G., R. L. Garrett, and R. L. Rudd. 1969. Pesticides and the western grebe. In *Chemical fallout,* eds. M. W. Miller and G. G. Berg, pp. 24–53. Springfield, IL: C. C. Thomas.

Herman, Z. S., K. Kmieciak-Kolada, R. Szkilnik, et al. 1982. Chronic toxicity of lead and cadmium: III. Effects of chronic intoxication on the reproductive function of the F-1 generation and on the central nervous system of the F-2 generation of rats. U.S. EPA Washington DC, 600/S-1-82-006,

Hickey, J. J., ed. 1969. *Peregrine falcon populations: their biology and decline.*Madison: University of Wisconsin Press.

Hickey, J. J., and L. B. Hunt. 1960. Initial songbird mortality following a Dutch elm disease control program. *J. Wildl. Manage.* 24(3):259–265.

Hickey, J. J., J. A. Keith, and F. B. Coon. 1966. An exploration of pesticides in a Lake Michigan ecosystem. *J. Appl. Ecol.*(Suppl) 3:141–154.

Hill, E. F. 1971. Toxicity of selected mosquito larvicides to some common avian species. *J. Wildl. Manage.* 35(4):757–762.

Hill, E. F. 1989. Divergent effects of postmortem ambient temperature on organophosphorus- and carbamate-inhibited brain cholinesterase activity in birds. *Pest. Biochem. Physiol.* 33(3):264–275.

Hill, E. F., M. B. Camardese, G. H. Heinz, et al. 1984. Acute toxicity of diazinon is similar for eight stocks of bobwhite. *Environ. Toxicol. Chem.* 3(1):61–66.

Hill, E. F., and W. J. Fleming. 1982. Anticholinesterase poisoning of birds: field monitoring and diagnosis of acute poisoning. *Environ. Toxicol. Chem.* 1(1):27–38.

Hill, E. F., R. G. Heath, J. W. Spann, et al. 1975. Lethal dietary toxicities of environmental pollutants to birds. U.S. Fish and Wildlife Service Special Scientific Report 191, 61 pp.

Hill, E. F., and D. J. Hoffman. 1984. Avian models for toxicity testing. *J. Amer. Coll. Toxicol.* 3(6):357–376.

Hill, E. F., and J. H. Soares, Jr. 1984. Subchronic mercury exposure in coturnix and a method of hazard evaluation. *Environ. Toxicol. Chem.* 3(3):489–502.

Hill, E. F., J. W. Spann, and J. D. Williams. 1977. Responsiveness of 6 to 14 generations of birds to dietary dieldrin toxicity. *Toxicol. Appl. Pharmacol.* 42(2):425–431.

Hill, I. R. 1985. Effects on nontarget organisms in terrestrial and aquatic environments. In *The pyrethroid insecticides,* ed. P. J. Leahey, pp. 151–162. London, U. K.: Taylor and Francis.

Hirano, M. 1989. Characteristics of pyrethroids for insect pest control in agriculture. *Pesticid. Sci.* 27(4):353–360.

Hitchcock, M., and S. D. Murphy. 1967. Enzyme reduction of 0,0-(4-nitrophenyl) phosphorothioate, 0,0-diethyl 0-(4-nitrophenyl) phosphate, and 0-ethyl 0-(4-nitrophenyl) benzene thiophosphate by tissues from mammals, birds and fishes. *Biochem. Pharmacol.* 16(9):1801–1811.

Hoffman, D. J., and P. H. Albers. 1984. Evaluation of potential embryo toxicity and teratogenicity of 42 herbicides, insecticides and petroleum contaminants to mallard eggs. *Arch. Environ. Contam. Toxicol.* 13(1):15–27.

Hoffman, D. J., and W. C. Eastin, Jr. 1981a. Effects of industrial effluents, heavy metals, and organic solvents on mallard embryo development. *Toxicol. Letters* 9(1):35–40.

Hoffman, D. J., and W. C. Eastin, Jr. 1981b. Effects of malathion, diazinon, and parathion on mallard embryo development and cholinesterase activity. *Environ. Res.* 26(2):472–485.

Hoffman, D. J., and W. C. Eastin, Jr. 1982. Effects of lindane, paraquat, toxaphene, and 2,4,5-trichlorophenoxyacetic acid on mallard embryo development. *Arch. Environ. Contam. Toxicol.* 11(1):79–86.

Hoffman. D. J., W. C. Eastin, Jr., and M. L. Gay. 1982. Embryotoxic and biochemical effects of waste crankcase oil on birds' eggs. *Toxicol. Appl. Pharm.* 63(2):230–241.

Hoffman, D. J., J. C. Franson, O. H. Pattee, et al. 1985a. Biochemical and hematological effects of lead ingestion in nestling American kestrels (*Falco sparverius*). *Comp. Biochem. Physiol.* 80C(2):431–439.

Hoffman, D. J., J. C. Franson, O. H. Pattee, et al. 1985b. Survival, growth, and accumulation of ingested lead in nestling American kestrels (*Falco sparverius*). *Arch. Environ. Contam. Toxicol.* 14(1):89–94.

Hoffman, D. J., J. C. Franson, O. H. Pattee, et al. 1985c. Survival, growth, and histopathological effects of paraquat ingestion in nestling American kestrels (*Falco sparverius*). *Arch. Environ. Contam. Toxicol.* 14:495–500.

Hoffman. D. J., and M. L. Gay. 1981. Embryotoxic effects of benzo[a]pyrene, chrysene, and 7,12-dimethyl benz[a]anthracene in petroleum hydrocarbon mixtures in mallard ducks. *J. Toxicol. Environ. Health.* 7(5):775–787.

Hoffman. D. J., O. H. Pattee, and S. N. Wiemeyer. 1985. Effects of fluroide on screech owl production: teratological evaluation, growth, and blood chemistry in hatchlings. *Toxicol. Letters.* 26(1):19–24.

Hoffman, F. O., C. W. Miller, D. L. Shaeffer, et al. 1977. Computer codes for the assessment of radionuclides released to the environment. *Nuclear Safety* 18(3):343–354.

Hoffman, R. S., R. G. Janson, and F. Hartkorn, 1958. Effect on grouse populations of DDT spraying for spruce budworm. *J. Wildl. Manage.* 22(1):92–93.

Hoffman, R., and R. D. Curnow. 1973. Toxic heavy metals in Lake Erie herons. *Proc. Conf. Grt. Lakes Res.* 16:50–53.

Hom, W., R. Risebrough, A. Sintar, et al. 1974. Deposition of DDE and polychlorinated biphenyls in dated sediments of the Santa Barbara Basin. *Science* 184(4142):1197–1199.

Hooper, A. D., and J. M. Hester. 1955. A study of thirty-six streams that were polluted by agricultural insecticides in 1950. Alabama Dept. Conser. Fish, Rpt. 2, 13 pp.

Hope, C. E. 1949. The effect of DDT on birds and the relation of birds to the spruce budworm *Archips fumiferans* Clem. In *Forest spraying and some effects of DDT*. Canad. Dept. Lands For. Biol Bull. 2, pp. 57–62.

Horne, R. A. 1972. Biological effects of chemical agents. *Science* 177(4055):1152–1153.

Hotchkiss, N., and R. H. Pough. 1946. Effects on forest birds of DDT used for gypsy moth control in Pennsylvania. *J. Wildl. Manage.* 10(6):202–207.

Hudson, R. H., R. K. Tucker, and M. A. Haegele. 1984. *Handbook of toxicity of pesticides to wildlife*. U. S. Fish and Wildlife Service Resource Pub. 153, 90 pp.

Hunt, E. G., J. A. Azevedo, Jr., L. A. Woods, Jr., et al. 1969. The significance of residues in pheasant tissues resulting from chronic exposures to DDT. In *Chemical fallout,* eds. M. W. Miller and G. G. Berg, pp. 335–360. Springfield IL: C. C. Thomas.

Hunt, E. G., and A. I. Bischoff. 1960. Inimical effects on wildlife of periodic DDD applications to Clear Lake. *Calif. Fish and Game* 46(1):91–106.

Hurlbert, S. H., M. S. Mulla, J. O. Keith, et al. 1970. Biological effects and persistence of Dursban in freshwater ponds. *J. Econom. Ent.* 63(1):43–52.

Innis, G. S. 1972. *Simulation models of grassland and grazing lands.* Prep. 35. Grassland Biome, Natural Resources Ecology Lab. Fort Collins, CO: Colorado State University.

Jacknow, L., J. L. Ludke, and N. C. Coon. 1986. *Monitoring fish and wildlife for environmental contaminants: the national contaminant biomonitoring program.* U.S.F.W.S. Fish and Wildlife Leaflet 4, 15 pp.

Jackson, T. F., and F. L. Halbert. 1974. A toxic syndrome associated with the feeding of polybrominated biphenyl-contaminated protein concentrate to dairy cattle. *J. Amer. Vet. Med. Assoc.* 165(5):437–439.

Jarvinen, A. W., M. J. Hoffman, and T. W. Thorslund. 1976. Toxicity of DDT food and water exposure to fathead minnows. USEPA, Duluth Water Qual. Lab. EPA-600/3-76-114, 68 pp.

Jefferies, D. J. 1967. The delay in ovulation produced by p,p′-DDT and its possible significance in the field. *Ibis* 109(2):266–272.

Jefferies, D. J., and M. C. French. 1969. Avian thyroid: effect of p,p′-DDT on size and activity. *Science* 166(3910):1278–1280.

Jefferies, D. J., and M. C. French. 1971. Hyper- and hypothyroidism in pigeons fed DDT: an explanation for the 'thin eggshell' phenomenon. *Environ. Pollut.* 1(3):235–242.

Jefferies, D. J., and M. C. French. 1972. Changes induced in the pigeon thyroid by p,p′-DDE and dieldrin. *J. Wildl. Manage.* 36(1):24–30.

Jenne, E. A. 1970. Atmospheric and fluvial transport of mercury. In *Mercury in the environment,* pp. 40–45. U.S. Geol. Survey Prof. Paper 713. Washington, DC.

Jensen, S., A. G. Johnels, M. Olsson, et al. 1969. DDT and PCB in marine animals from Swedish waters. *Nature* 224(5216):247–250.

Johnels, A. G., and T. Westermark. 1969. Mercury contamination of the environment in Sweden. In *Chemical fallout,* eds. M. W. Miller and G. G. Berg, pp. 221–241. Springfield, IL. C. C. Thomas.

Johnson, B. T. 1986. Potential impact of selected agricultural chemical contaminants on a northern prairie wetland: a microcosm evaluation. *Environ. Toxicol. Chem.* 5(5):473–485.

Johnson, W. W., and M. T. Finley. 1980. Handbook of acute toxicity of chemicals to fish and aquatic invertebrates. U. S. F. W. S. Resource Pub. 137, 98 pp.

Johnston, D. W. 1974. Decline of DDT residues in migratory songbirds. *Science* 186(4166):841–842.

Jones, D. H., D. H. Lewis, T. E. Eurell, et al. 1979. Alteration of the immune response of channel catfish *Ictalurus punctatus* by polychlorinated biphenyls. In *Animals as monitors of environmental pollutants,* pp.385–386. Washington, DC: National Academy of Sciences.

Jones. L. W. 1952. Stability of DDT and its effects on microbial activities in soil. *Soil Sci.* 73:237–241.

Kania, H. J., and J. O'Hara. 1974. Behavioral alterations in a simple predator-prey system due to sublethal exposure to mercury. *Trans. Amer. Fish. Soc.* 103(1):134–136.

Kanitz, S., C. Costello, and P. Orlando. 1971. Effects of radiation on the decomposition of organochlorine pesticide residues in foods. *Gig. Med. Prev.* 12(1):51–57 (Italian).

Keith, J. A. 1966. Reproduction in a population of herring gulls (*Larus argentatus*) contaminated by DDT. *J. Appl. Ecol.* (Suppl.) 3:57–70.

Keith, J.A., and I. M. Gruchy, 1972. Residue levels of chemical pollutants in North American birdlife. *Proceed. Int. Ornith. Cong.* 15:437–454.

Keith, J. O. 1966. Insecticide contaminations in wetland habitats and their effects on fish-eating birds. *J. Appl. Ecol.* (Suppl.) 3:71–85.

Keith, J. O. 1968. Considerations sur les residus d'insecticides chez les oiseaux piscivores et dans leurs biotopes. *Aves* 5(1):28–41.

Keith, J. O. 1969. Variations in the biological vulnerability of birds to insecticides. In The *biological impact of pesticides in the environment,* ed. J. W. Gillett, pp. 36–39. Environ. Health Sci. Ser. No. 1. Corvallis: Oregon State University.

Keith, J. O. 1978. Synergistic effects of DDE and food stress on reproduction in brown pelicans and ring doves. Ph.D. diss., The Ohio State University, Columbus.

Keith, J. O., R. M. Hansen, and A. L. Ward. 1959. Effect of 2,4-D on abundance and foods of pocket gophers. *J. Wildl. Manage.* 23(2):137–145.

Keith, J. O., and M. S. Mulla. 1966. Relative toxicity of five organophosphorus mosquito larvacides to mallard ducks. *J. Wildl. Manage.* 30(3):553–563.

Keith, J. O., L. A. Woods, Jr., and E. G. Hunt. 1970. Reproductive failure in brown pelicans on the Pacific Coast. *Trans. N. A. Wildl. Nat. Resour. Conf.* 35:56–63.

Kelsall, J. P. 1950. A study of bird populations in the apple orchards of the Annapolis Valley, Nova Scotia with special reference to the effects of orchard sprays upon them. *Canad. Wildl. Serv. Wildl. Manage. Bull.* ser. 2., No 1. 69 pp.

Kidd, D. E., G. V. Johnson, and J. D. Garcia. 1974. An analysis of mercurials in the Elephant Butte ecosystem. Tech. Comp. Rpt. Proj. A-040 NMEX., New Mexico Water Res. Int. New Mexico State University, Las Cruces.

Kierdorf, U., and H. I. Kierdorf. 1990. Chronic fluoride toxicosis in game animals. *Trans. Int. Cong. Game Biol.* 20: in press.

Kim, J. P., and W. F. Fitzgerald. 1986. Sea-air partitioning of mercury in the equatorial Pacific Ocean. *Science* 231(4742):1131–1133.

King, K. A., D. R. Blankinship, E. Payne, et al. 1985. Brown pelican populations and pollutants in Texas 1975–1981. *Wilson Bull.* 97(2):201–214.

King, K. A., and E. L. Flickinger. 1977. The decline of brown pelicans on the Louisana and Texas Gulf Coast. *Southwestern Nat.* 21(4):417–431.

King, K. A., D. L. Meeker, and D. M. Swineford. 1980. Whitefaced ibis populations and pollutants in Texas, 1969–1976. *Southwestern Nat.* 25(2):225–240.

Kinter, W. B., L. S. Merkens, R. H. Janicki, et al. 1972. Studies on the mechanism of toxicity of DDT and polychlorinted biphenyls (PCBs): disruption of osmoregulation in marine fish. *Environ. Health Perspec.* 1(April):169–173.

Klein, W. 1979. Organohalogenated compounds in plants. In *Monitoring environmental materials and specimen banking,* ed. N-P. Luepke, pp. 354–368. Boston: Martinus Nijhoff.

Knedel, C. F. 1951. Spraying and wildlife. *N.D. Outdoors* 14:12–15.

Knopf, F. L., and J. C. Street. 1974. Insecticide residues in white pelican eggs from Utah. *Wilson Bull.* 86(4):428–434.

Koeman, J. H., W. H. M. Peeters, C. J. Smit, et al. 1972. Persistent chemicals in marine mammals. *TNO-Nieuws* 27:570–578.

Koeman, J. H., M. C. Ten Noever de Brauw, and R. H. deVos. 1969. Chlorinated by Phenyls in Fish, Mussels, and Birds from the River Rhine and the Netherlands Coastal Area. *Nature* 221(5186):1126–1128.

Kolaja, G. J., and D. E. Hinton. 1979. DDT-induced reduction in eggshell thickness, weight, and calcium is accompanied by calcium ATPase inhibition. In *Animals as monitors of pollutants,* pp. 309–318. Washington, DC: National Academy of Sciences.

Kononen, D. W., J. R. Hochstein, and R. K. Ringer. 1987. Avoidance behavior of mallards and northern bobwhite exposed to carbofuran-contaminated food and water. *Environ. Toxicol. Chem.* 6(1):41–50.

Konrad, J., J. Mouka, and I. Horak. 1983. Some negative aspects of the use of chemicals in agriculture connected with the health problems of minks. In *Czech/Amer. Symp. Toxic Effects of Chem. Environ. Contam. upon Prod. amd Reprod. Ability in Free-living Animals,* ed. P. Kacmar, pp. 130–133. Kosice: Czechoslovakia University of Veterinary Medicine.

Korschgen, L. J. 1970. Soil–food-chain–pesticide wildlife relationships in aldrin-treated fields. *J. Wild. Manage.* 34(1):186–199.

Kosian, P., A. Lemke, K. Studders, et al. 1981. The precision of the ASTM bioconcentration test. USEPA-600/S3-81-022, Washington, DC.

Koval, P. J., T. J. Peterle, and J. D. Harder. 1987. Effects of polychlorinated biphenyls on mourning dove reproduction and circulating progesterone levels. *Bull. Environ. Contam. Toxicol.* 39(4):663–670.

Kozlick, F. M. 1946. The effects of DDT on birds. *Passenger Pigeon.* 8(4):99–103.

Kreitzer, J. F. 1980. Effects of toxaphene and endrin at very low dietary concentrations on discrimination, acquisition and reversal in bobwhite quail, *Colinus virginianus. Environ. Pollut.* Series A 23(3):217–230.

Kreitzer, J. F., and G. H. Heinz. 1974. The effect of sublethal dosages of five pesticides and a polychlorinated biphenyl on the avoidance response of coturnix quail chicks. *Environ. Pollut.* 6(1):21–29.

Kreitzer, J. F., and J. W. Spann. 1973. Tests of pesticidal synergism with young pheasants and Japanese quail. *Bull. Environ. Contam. Toxicol.* 9(4):250–256.

Kuhr, R., A. Davis, and E. F. Taschenberg. 1972. DDT residues in a vineyard soil after 24 years of exposure. *Bull. Environ. Contam. Toxicol.* 8(6):329–333.

Kunze, F., A. A. Nelson, O. G. Fitzhugh, et al. 1949. Storage of DDT in the fat of the rat. *Fed. Proc.* 8(1):311.

Lambrecht, L. K., D. A. Barsotti, and J. R. Allen. 1978. Responses of nonhuman primates to a polybrominated biphenyl mixture. *Environ. Health Perspect.* 23 (April):139–145

Langford, R. R. 1949. The effect of DDT on the natural fauna of the forest exclusive of insect pests. In *Forest spraying and some effects of DDT. Canadian Department of Lands and Forestry Biol. Bull.* No. 2, pp. 13–18.

Larsen, D. P., F. DeNoyelles, Jr., F. Stay, et al. 1986. Comparisons of single species, microcosm, and experimental pond responses to atrazine exposure. *Environ. Toxicol. Chem.* 5(2):179–190.

Leahey, J. P., ed. 1985. *The pyrethroid insecticides.* London: Taylor and Francis.

Lehman, J. W., T. J. Peterle, and C. M. Mills. 1974. Effects of DDT on bobwhite quail (*Colinus virginlatus*) adrenal gland. *Bull. Environ. Contam. Toxicol.* 11(5):407–414.

Leighton, F. A., D. B. Peakall, and R. G. Butler. 1983. Heinz-body hemolytic anemia from the ingestion of crude oil: a primary toxic effect in marine birds. *Science* 220(4599):871–873.

Leonard, C. S. 1942. The effects of pyrethrins on certain mammals. *J. Econom. Entomol.* 35(2):261–264.

Lewin, R. 1983. NAS study highlights chemical mutagens. *Science* 219(4590):1304–1305.

Lewis, R. A., and C. W. Lewis. 1979. Terrestrial vertebrate animals as biological monitors of pollution. In *Monitoring environmental materials and specimen banking,* ed. N-P. Luepke, pp. 369–391. Boston: Martinus Nijoff.

Lewis, S. J., and R. A. Malecki. 1983. Effects of egg oiling on Larid productivity and population dynamics. *Auk* 101(3):584–592.

Lichtenstein, E. P. 1958. Movement of insecticides in soils under leaching and non-leaching conditions. *J. Econom. Ent.* 51(3):380–383.

Lichtenstein, E. P. 1959. Absorption of some chlorinated hydrocarbon insecticides from soils into various crops. *J. Agr. Chem. Food Chem.* 7(6):430–433.

Lichtenstein, E.P., and K. R. Schulz. 1959. Persistence of some chlorinated hydrocarbon insecticides as influenced by soil types, rate of application and temperature. *J. Econom. Ent.* 52(1):124–131.

Lichtenstein, E. P., and K. R. Schulz. 1965. Residues of aldrin and heptachlor in soils and their translocation into various crops. *J. Agr. Food Chem.* 13(1):57–63.

Lien, E. J. 1985. Molecular structure and different modes of exposure affecting transport and toxicities of chemicals: QSAR analysis. *Environ. Toxicol. Chem.* 4(3):259–271.

Lindberg, S. E., G. M. Lovett, D. D. Richter, et al. 1986. Atmospheric deposition and canopy interactions of major ions in a forest. *Science* 231(4734):141–145.

Linder, G., and M. E. Richmond. 1990. Feed aversion in small mammals as a potential source of hazard reduction for environmental chemicals: agrichemical case studies. *Environ. Toxicol. Chem.* 9(1):95–105.

Lindsdale, J. M. 1931. Facts concerning the use of thallium in California to poison rodents—its destructiveness to game birds, song birds, and other valuable wildlife. *Condor* 33(3):92–106.

Liss, W. J., D. M. Woltering, S. E. Finger, et al. 1982. Organization and adaption of aquatic laboratory ecosystems exposed to the pesticide dieldrin. USEPA-600/S3-82-050.

Livingston, M. L. 1952. Parathion poisoning in geese. *J. Amer. Vet. Med. Assoc.* 120(898):27.

Livingston, R. J. 1982a. Long-term biological variability and stress in coastal ecosystems, pp. 52–56. USEPA-600/3-82-034.

Livingston, R. J. 1982b. Long-term variability in coastal ecosystems: background noise and environmental stress. In *Ecological stress and the New York Bight: Science and management,* pp. 605–620. Columbia: SC: Est. Res. Fed.

Lloyd-Jones, C. P. 1971. Evaporation of DDT. *Nature* 229(5279):65–66.

Longcore, J. R., J. D. Heyland, A. Reed, et al. 1983. Contaminants in greater snow geese and their eggs. *J. Wildl. Manage.* 47(4):1105–1109.

Ludke, J. L. 1977. DDE increases the toxicity of parathion to coturnix quail. *Pest. Biochem. Physiol.* 7(1):28–33.

Luepke, N-P. ed. 1979. *Monitoring environmental materials and specimen banking.* Boston: Martinus Nijhoff.

Lustick, S., T. Voss, and T. Peterle. 1973. Effects of DDT on steroid metabolism and energetics in bobwhite quail (*Colinus virginianus*). In *First National Bobwhite Quail Symposium,* eds. J. A. Morrison and J. C. Lewis, pp. 213-233. Stillwater, OK: Oklahoma University Press.

McArn, G. E., M. L. Boardman, R. Munn, et al. 1974. Relationship of pulmonary particles in English sparrows to gross air pollution. *J. Wildl. Disease* 10(4):335–340.

McArthur, M. L. B., G. A. Fox, D. B. Peakall, et al. 1983. Ecological significance of behavioral and hormonal abnormalities in breeding ring doves fed an organochlorine chemical mixture. *Arch. Environ. Contam. Toxicol.* 12(3):343–353.

McCann, J. A., and R. L. Jasper. 1972. Vertebral damage to bluegills exposed to acutely toxic levels of pesticides. *Trans. Amer. Fish. Soc.* 101(2):317–322.

McDermid, A. M. 1946. DDT poisoning in mink. *Amer. Fur Breeder* 19:40 41.

McEwen, L. C. 1982. Review of grasshopper pesticides vs. rangeland wildlife habitat. In *Proceedings of the 1981 Wildlife–Livestock Relationships Symposium* 10, eds. J. M. Peek and P. D. Dalke, pp. 362–382. Moscow: University of Idaho.

McEwen, L. C., and R. L. Brown. 1966. Acute toxicity of dieldrin and malathion to wild sharp-tailed grouse. *J. Wildl. Manage.* 30(3):604–611.

McEwen, L. C., L. R. DeWeese, and P. Schladweiler. 1986. Bird predation on cutworms (Lepidoptera:Noctuidae) in wheat fields and chlorpyrifos effects on brain cholinesterase activity. *Environ. Toxicol.* 15(1):147–151.

McEwen, L. C., C. J. Stafford, and G. L. Hensler. 1984. Organochlorine residues in eggs of black-crowned night-herons from Colorado and Wyoming. *Environ. Toxicol. Chem.* 3(3):367–376.

McLane, M. A. R., and L. C. Hall. 1972. DDE thins screech owl eggshells. *Bull. Environ. Contam. Toxicol.* 8(2):65–68.

Mackay, D., and Y. Cohen. 1976. Prediction of volatilization rate of pollutants in aqueous systems. In *Symposium on the non-biological transfer and transformation of pollutants. on land and water: processes and critical data required for predictive description* (Abstracts). Bethesda, MD: National Bureau of Standards.

Mackay, D., and S. Paterson. 1981. Calculating fugacity. *Environ. Sci. Tech.* 15(9):1006–1014.

Maddy, K. T. 1983. Pesticide usage in California and the United States. *Agric. Ecosyst. Environ.* 9(2):159–172.

Marking, L. L. 1966. *Evaluation of p,p'DDT as a reference toxicant in bioassays.* Investigations in Fish Control Resource Public. 14, U.S. Dept. Interior, Washington, DC, 10 pp.

Marshall, E. 1985a. San Joaquin flooded with water researchers. *Science* 230(4728):920–921.

Marshall, E. 1985b. The rise and decline of Temik. *Science* 229(4720):1369–1371.

Marshall, E. 1986a. High selenium levels confirmed in six states. *Science* 231(4734):111.

Marshall, E. 1986b. OMB and Congress at odds over cancer risk policy. *Science* 233(4764):618.

Marx, J. L. 1977. Chitin synthesis inhibitors: new class of insecticides. *Science* 197(4304)1170–1172.

Matsumura, F. 1975. *Toxicology of insecticides.* New York: Plenum Press.

Maugh, T. H., II. 1982. Just how hazardous are dumps? *Science* 215(4532):490–493.

Maugh, T. H., II. 1984. Acid rain's effects on people assessed. *Science* 226(4681):1408–1410.

Meeks, R. L. 1968. The accumulation of ^{36}Cl ring-labeled DDT in a freshwater marsh. *J. Wildl. Manage.* 32(2):376–398.

Mendelssohn, H., and U. Paz. 1977. Mass mortality of birds of prey caused by azodrin, an organophosphorus insecticide. *Biol. Conserv.* 11(3):163–170.

Mendenhall, V. M., E. E. Klaas, and M. A. R. McLane. 1983. Breeding success of barn owls (*Tyto alba*) fed low levels of DDE and dieldrin. *Arch. Environ. Contam. Toxicol.* 12(2):235–240.

Mendenhall, V. M., and L. F. Pank. 1980. Secondary poisoning of owls by anticoagulant rodenticides. *Wildl. Soc. Bull.* 8(4):311–315.

Menzie, C. M. 1966. Metabolism of pesticides. U.S. Fish and Wildlife Service Special Scientific Report Wildl. No. 96, 274 pp.

Menzie, C. M. 1980. Metabolism of pesticides: update III. U. S. Fish and Wildlife Service Special Science Report Wildl. No. 232, 709 pp.

Metcalf, R. L., L. K. Cole, S. G. Wood, et al. 1979. *Design and evaluation of a terrestrial model ecosystem for evaluation of substitute pesticide chemicals.* USEPA-600/3-79-004. Corvallis, OR, 20 pp.

Michigan State University Agricultural Experiment Station. 1976. MSU research on PBBs. Michigan in Action Info. Serv., Michigan State University, East Lansing, MI, 11 pp.

Miller, D. S., W. B. Kinter, and D. B. Peakall. 1976. Enzymatic basis for DDE-induced eggshell thinning in a sensitive bird. *Nature* 259(5539):122–124.

Miller, D. S., D. B. Peakall, and W. B. Kinter. 1975. Biochemical basis for DDE-induced eggshell thinning in ducks. *Fed. Proc. Fed. Amer. Soc. Exp. Biol.* 34(3):811.

Miller, M. W., and G. G. Berg, eds. 1969. *Chemical fallout: current research on persistent pesticides.* Springfield, IL. C. C. Thomas.

Mills, J. A. 1973. Some observations on the effects of field applications of fensulfothion and parathion on bird and mammal populations. *Proc. N. Z. Ecol. Soc.* 20:65–71.

Mitchell, C. A., and D. H. White. 1982. Seasonal brain acetylcholinesterase activity in three species of shore birds overwintering in Texas. *Bull. Environ. Contam. Toxicol.* 29(3):360–365.

Mitchell, R. T. 1946. Effects of DDT spray on eggs and nestlings of birds. *J. Wildl. Manage.* 10(3):192–194.

Mlot, C. 1985. Managing pesticide resistance. *Biosci.* 35(4):216–218.

Mohr, R. W., H. S. Telford, E. H. Peterson, et al. 1951. *Toxicity of orchard insecticides to birds.* Washington Agricultural Experimental Station Circular No. 170, 22 pp.

Moore, N. W., and D. A. Ratcliffe. 1962. Chlorinated hydrocarbon residues in the egg of a peregrine falcon (*Falco peregrinus*) from Perthshire. *Bird Study* 9(4):242–244.

Moore, N. W., and C. H. Walker. 1964. Organic chlorine insecticide residues in wild birds. *Nature* 201(4924):1072–1073.

Moriarty, F. 1972. Pollutants and food-chains. *New Sci.* 53(787):594–596.

Moriarty, F. 1988. *Ecotoxicology: the study of pollutants in ecosystems,* 2nd ed. New York: Academic Press, Inc.

Moss, R. 1972. Effects of captivity on gut lengths in red grouse. *J. Wildl. Manage.* 36(1):99-104.

Mulla, M. S., J. O. Keith, and F. A. Gunther. 1966. Persistence and biological effects of parathion residues in waterfowl habitats. *J. Econom. Entmol.* 59(5):1085–1090.

Mulla, M. S., G. Majori, and A. A. Arata. 1979. Impact of biological and chemical mosquito control agents on nontarget biota in aquatic ecosystems. *Residue Rev.* 71:121–173.

Munger, J. W., C. Tiller, and M. R. Hoffman. 1986. Identification of hydroxymethanesulfonate in fog water. *Science* 231(4735):247–249.

Murphy, D. A., and L. J. Korschgen. 1970. Reproduction, growth, and tissue residues of deer fed dieldrin. *J. Wildl. Manage.* 34(4):887–903.

Murty, A. S. 1986. Toxicity of pesticides to fish. Vols. I and II. Cleveland, OH: C. R. C. Press.

Nash, R. G., W. G. Harris, and C. Lewis. 1973. Soil pH and metallic amendment effects on DDT conversion to DDE. *J. Environ. Qual.* 2(3):390–394.

National Academy of Sciences. 1977. *Nitrogen oxides.* Committe on the Medical and Biological Effects of Environmental Pollutants. Washington, DC: National Academy of Sciences.

National Academy of Sciences. 1979. *Animals as monitors of environmental pollutants.* National Academy of Sciences Natural Resource Council. Washington, DC.

National Academy of Sciences. 1980. Mineral tolerance of domestic animals. N. R. C. Committee on Animal Nutrition. Washington, DC: National Academy of Sciences.

National Academy of Sciences 1981. Testing for the effects of chemicals on ecosystems. Report by the Committee to Review Methods for Ecotoxicology. Committee on Natural Resources, National Research Council, Washington, DC: National Academy Press.

National Research Council of Canada. 1986. *Pyrethroids: their effects on aquatic and terrestrial ecosystems.* NRCC Publ. No. 24376. Ottawa, Canada.

Nauman, L. E. 1969. Endocrine response to DDT and social stress in the male mallard duck. Ph.D. diss., The Ohio State University, Columbus.

Needleman, H. L. 1981. Studies in children exposed to low levels of lead. USEPA-600/S1-81-066.

Needleman, H. L., S. K. Geiger, and R. Frank. 1985. Lead and IQ scores: a reanalysis. *Science* 227(4688):701–704.

Neill, D. D., H. D. Muller, and J. V. Shutze. 1971. Pesticide effects on the fecundity of the gray partridge. *Bull. Environ. Contam. Toxicol.* 6(6):546–551.

Nelson, A. L., and E. W. Surber. 1947. DDT investigations by the Fish and Wildlife Service in 1946. U. S. Fish and Wildlife Service Special Scientific Report No. 41, 8 pp.

Nelson, N., T. C. Byerly, A. C. Kolbye, Jr., et al. ed. 1971. Hazards of mercury. Special report to Sec. Pesticide Advisory Committee, Dept. H. E. W. Study Group on Mercury Hazards. *Environ. Res.* 4(1):1–69

Nettles, V. F. 1976. Organophosphate toxicity in wild turkeys. *J. Wildl. Dis.* 12(4):560–561.

Neuhold, J. M., and L. F. Ruggerio, ed. 1976. *Ecosystem processes and organic contaminants: research needs and an interdisciplinary perspective.* National Sciences Foundation Supt. Doc. Washington, DC: U. S. Government Printing Office, 44 pp.

Newman, J. R. 1979. The effects of air pollution on wildlife and their use as biological indicators. In *Animals as monitors of pollutants,* pp. 223–232. Washington, DC: National Academy of Sciences.

Newman, J. R., and R. K. Schreiber. 1988. Air pollution and wildlife toxicology: an overlooked problem. *Environ. Contam. Toxicol.* (5)7:381–390.

Niethammer, K. R., R. D. Atkinson, T. S. Baskett, et al. 1985. Metals in riparian wildlife of the lead mining district of southeastern Missouri. *Arch. Environ. Contam. Toxicol.* 14(2):213–223.

Neithammer, K. R., and T. S. Baskett. 1983. Cholinesterase inhibition of birds inhabiting wheat fields treated with methyl parathion and toxaphene. *Arch. Environ. Contam. Toxicol.* 12(4):471–475.

Neithamner, K. R., D. H. White, T. S. Baskett, et al. 1984. Presence and biomagnification of organochlorine chemical residues in oxbow lakes of northeastern Louisiana. *Arch. Environ. Contam. Toxicol.* 13(1):63–74.

Nuroteva, P., M. Lodenius, and S. L. Nuroteva. 1979. Decrease in the mercury levels of *Esox lucius*(L.) and *Abramis farenus* (L.) (Teleostei) in the Hameenkyro watercourse after the phenylmercury ban in Finland. *Aquilo Ser. Zoo.* 19:97–100.

Oberheu, J. C. 1972. The occurrence of mirex in starlings collected in seven southeastern states. *Pest. Monit. J.* 6(1):41–42.

O'Brien, R. D. 1967. *Insecticides: action and metabolism.* New York. Academic Press.

Odsjo, T. 1982. Eggshell thickness and levels of DDT, PCB, and mercury in eggs of osprey (*Pandion haliaetus (L.)*) and marsh harrier (*Circus aeruginousus (L.)* in relation to their breeding success and population status in Sweden. Ph.D. diss., University of Stockholm, Sweden.

Odum, E. P., and R. A. Norris. 1949. Effect of DDT on birds in Georgia pecan orchards with a note on late summer census methods. *J. Wildl. Manage.* 13(4):415–417.

Odum, H. T., and A. Lugo. 1970. Metabolism of forest floor microcosms. In *Tropical rain forest,* ed. H. T. Odum, pp. 135–154. Washington, DC: United States Atomic Energy Commission.

Ohlendorf, H. M., and W. J. Fleming. 1988. Birds and environmental contaminants in San Francisco and Chesapeake Bays. *Mar. Pollut. Bull.* 19(9):487–495.

Ohlendorf, H. M., F. C. Schaffner, T. W. Custer, et al. 1985. Reproduction and organochlorine contaminants in terns at San Diego Bay. *Colonial Waterbirds.* 8(1):42–53.

Oris, T. J., J. P. Giesy, P. M. Alred, et al. 1984. Photoinduced toxicity of anthracene in aquatic organisms: an environmental perspective. In *The biosphere: problems and solutions,* ed. T. N. Veziroglu, pp. 639–658. Amsterdam: Elsevier Science.

O'Shea, T. J., R. L. Brownell, Jr., D. R. Clark, Jr., et al. 1980. Organochlorine pollutants in small cetaceans from the Pacific and South Atlantic Oceans. *Pest. Monitor. J.* 14(2):35–46.

O'Shea, T. J., W. J. Fleming, III, and E. Cromartie. 1980. DDT contamination at Wheeler National Wildlife Refuge. *Science* 209(4455):509–510.

O'Shea, T. J., J. F. Moore, and H. I. Kochman. 1984. Contaminant concentrations in manatees in Florida. *J. Wildl. Manage.* 48(3):741–748.

O'Sullivan, D. A. 1976. Norway: victim of other nations' pollution. *Chem. Eng. News* 54(25):15–16.

Palmiter, R. D., and E. R. Mulvihill. 1978. Estrogenic activity of the insecticide kepone on the chicken oviduct. *Science* 201(4353):356–358.

Parsons, A. H., and T. J. Peterle. 1977. DDE and avian eggshell thinning: ultrastructural evidence of decreased parathyroid activity. *Poul. Sci.* 56(5):1745.

Pattee, O.H. 1984. Eggshell thickness and reproduction in American kestrels exposed to chronic dietary lead. *Arch. Environ. Contam. Toxicol.* 13(1):29–34.

Pattee, O. H., M. R. Fuller, and T. E. Kaiser. 1985. Environmental contaminants in eastern Cooper's hawk eggs. *J. Wildl. Manage.* 49(4):1040–1044.

Patton. J. F., and M. P. Dieter. 1980. Effects of petroleum hydrocarbons on hepatic function in the duck. *Comp. Biochem. Physiol.* 65C(1):33–36.

Paulson, A. J., and D. T. Brown. 1978. PCBs: their environmental significance and distribution in Rhode Island. Narragansett. University of Rhode Island Marine Technical Report No. 68, 25 pp. Available from University of Rhode Island, Narragansett.

Peakall, D. B., 1967. Pesticide-induced enzyme breakdown of steroids in birds. *Nature* 216(5114):505–506.

Peakall, D. B. 1970a. Pesticides and the reproduction of birds. *Sci. Amer.* 222(4):72–78.

Peakall, D. B. 1970b. p,p′DDT: effect on calcium metabolism and concentration of estradiol in the blood. *Science* 168(3931):592–594.

Peakall, D. B. 1972. Polychlorinated biphenyls: occurrence and biological effects. *Residue Rev.* 44:1–21.

Peakall, D. B., and J. R. Bart. 1983. Impacts of aerial application of insecticides on forest birds. *CRC Crit. Rev. in Environ. Control.* 13:117-165.

Peakall, D. B., J. L. Lincer, and S. E. Bloom. 1972. Embryonic mortality and chromosomal alterations caused by Aroclor 1254 in ring doves. *Environ. Health Perspec.* 1(April):103–104.

Peakall, D. B., and R. J. Lovett. 1972. Mercury: its occurrence and effects in the environment. *Biosci.* 22(1):20–25.

Peakall, D. B., R. J. Norstrom, A. D. Rahimtula, et al. 1986. Characterization of mixed-function oxidase systems of the nestling herring gull and its implications for bioeffects monitoring. *Environ. Toxicol. Chem.* 5(4):379–385.

Peakall, D. B., and M. L. Peakall. 1973. Effect of a polychlorinated biphenyl on the reproduction of artificially and naturally incubated dove eggs. *J. Appl. Ecol.* 10(3):863–868.

Pearce, P. A 1971 Side effects of forest spraying in New Brunswick. *Trans. N. A. Wildl. Nat. Resour. Conf.* 36:163–170.

Peterle, A. F., and T. J. Peterle. 1971. The effect of DDT on aggression in laboratory mice. *Bull. Environ. Contam. Toxicol.* 6(5):401–405.

Peterle, T. J. 1966. The use of isotopes to study pesticide translocation in natural environments. *J. Appl. Ecol.* (Suppl.). 3:181–191.

Peterle, T. J. 1969. DDT in Antarctic snow. *Nature* 224:620.

Peterle, T. J., and R. Bentley. 1989. Effects of a low OP dose on seed/bead discrimination in the kangaroo rat, *Diopodomys*. *Bull. Environ. Contam. Toxicol.* 43(1):95–100.

Peterle. T. J., S. I. Lustick, L. E. Nauman, et al. 1974. Some physiological effects of dietary DDT on mallard, bobwhite quail, and domestic rabbits. *Trans Int. Cong. Game Biol.* 11:457–478.

Phillips, J. B., and M. R. Wells. 1974. Adenosine triphosphate activity in liver, intestinal mucosa, cloacal bladder, and kidney tissue of five turtle species following *in vitro* treatment with 1,1,1-trichloro-2,2-bis(p-chlorophenyl) ethane (DDT). *J. Agr. Food Chem.* 22(3):404–407.

Pierce, C. C., and M. T. Clegg. 1915. Strychnine sulfate. Its effect on California valley quail. *Public Health Rpt.* 30(50):3601–3604. Reprint 314.

Pillmore, R. E., and R. B. Finley, Jr. 1963. Residues in game animals resulting from forest and range insecticide applications. *Trans. N. A. Wildl. Nat. Resour. Conf.* 28:409–422.

Pimentel, D., and L. Levitan. 1986. Pesticides: amounts applied and amounts reaching pests. *Biosci.* 36(2):86–91.

Platonow, N. S., and L. H. Karstad. 1973. Dietary effects of polychlorinated biphenyls on mink. *Canad. J. Comp. Med.* 37(4):391–400.

Pocker, Y., W. M. Beug, and V. R. Ainardi. 1971. Carbonic anhydrase interaction with DDT, DDE, and dieldrin. *Science* 174(4016):1336–1339.

Pollack, U. F. 1929. Arsenical poisoning in the field. *Vet. J.* 85(Sept.):372–377.

Pollard, J. E., and S. C. Hern. 1985. A field test of the EXAMS model in the Monongahela River. *Environ. Toxicol. Chem.* 4(3):361–369.

Pope, G. G., and P. Ward. 1972. The effects of small applications of an organophosphorus poison, fenthion, on the weaver-bird *Quelea quelea*. *Pestici. Sci.* 3:197–205.

Porter, R. D., and S. N. Wiemeyer. 1972. DDE at low dietary levels kills captive American kestrels. *Bull. Environ. Contam. Toxicol.* 8(4):193–199.

Porter, W. P., R. Hinsdill, A. Fairbrother, et al. 1984. Toxicant–disease–environment interactions associated with suppression of immune system, growth, and reproduction. *Science* 224(4652):1014–1017.

Post, G. 1949. Two new insecticides: the present knowledge of the effect of toxaphene and chlordane on game birds in Wyoming. *Wyom. Wildl. Mag.* (May):1–7.

Powell, G. V. N. 1984. Reproduction by an altricial songbird, the red-winged blackbird, in fields treated with the organophosphate insecticide fenthion. *J. Appl. Ecol.* 21(1):83–95.

Prestt, I. 1966. Studies of recent changes in the status of some birds of prey and fish-feeding birds in Britain. *J. Appl.* Ecol. (Suppl.) 3:107–112.

Pritchard, J. B., D. B. Peakall, R. W. Risebrough, et al. 1972. DDE-induced eggshell thinning in white Pekin ducks (*Anas platyrhynchos*): structural, physiological, and biochemical studies. *Bull. Mt. Des. Biol Lab.* 12:77–79.

Prouty, R. M., and C. M. Bunck. 1986. Organochlorine residues in adult mallard and black duck wings, 1981–1982. *Environ. Monit. Ass.* 6(1):49–57.

Randers, J., and D. L. Meadows. 1971. System simulation to test environmental policy: a sample study of DDT movement in the environment. Systems Dynamics Group. Massachusetts Institute of Technology Cambridge, MA, 56 pp.

Ratcliffe, D. A. 1967. Decrease in eggshell weight in certain birds of prey. *Nature* 215(5097):208–210.

Ratcliffe, D. A. 1970. Changes attributable to pesticides in egg breakage frequency and eggshell thickness in some British birds. *J. Appl. Ecol.* 7(1): 67–115.

Rattner, B. A. 1982. Diagnosis of anticholinesterase poisoning in birds: effects of environmental temperature and underfeeding on cholinesterase activity. *Environ. Toxicol. Chem.* 1(4):329–335.

Rattner, B. A., and W. C. Eastin, Jr. 1981. Plasma corticosterone and thyroxine concentrations during chronic ingestion of crude oil in mallard ducks. *Comp. Biochem. Physiol.* 68C(2):103–107.

Rattner, B. A., V. P. Eroschenko, G. A. Fox, et al. 1984. Avian endocrine responses to environmental pollutants. *J. Expt. Zool.* 232(3):683–689.

Rattner, B. A., W. J. Fleming, and H. C. Murray. 1982. Osmoregulation and salt gland Na, K-ATPase activity following exposure to the anticholinesterase fenthion. *Physiol.* 25(4):228(abst.).

Rattner, B. A., W. J. Fleming, and H. C. Murray. 1983. Osmoregulatory function in ducks following ingestion of the organophosphorus insecticide fenthion. *Pest. Biochem. Physiol.* 20(2):246–255.

Rattner, B. A., and J. C. Franson. 1984. Methyl parathion and fenvalerate toxicity in American kestrels: acute physiological responses and effects of cold. *Canad. J. Physiol. Pharm.* 62(7):787–792.

Rattner, B. A., and S. D. Michael. 1985. Organophosphorus insecticide induced decrease in plasma luteinizing hormone concentration in white-footed mice. *Toxicol. Letters* 24(1):65–69.

Rattner, B. A., L. Sileo, and C. G. Scanes. 1982a. Hormonal responses and tolerance to cold of female quail following parathion ingestion. *Pest. Biochem. Physiol.* 18(1):132–138.

Rattner, B. A., L. Sileo, and C. G. Scanes. 1982b. Oviposition and the plasma concentrations of LH, progesterone, and corticosterone in bobwhite quail (*Colinus virginianus*) fed parathion. *J. Reprod. Fert.* 66(1):147–155.

Reichel, W. L., S. K. Schmeling, E. Cromartie, et al. 1984. Pesticides, PCB, and lead residues and necropsy data for bald eagles from 32 states—1978–1981. *Environ. Monit. Assoc.* 4(4):395–403.

Reidinger, R. F., Jr. 1976. Organochlorine residues in adults of six southwestern bat species. *J. Wildl. Manage.* 40(4):677–680.

Reijnders, P. J. H. 1986. Reproductive failure in common seals feeding on fish from polluted coastal waters. *Nature* 324(6096):456–457.

Reinert, R. E. 1970. Pesticide concentrations in Great Lakes fish. *Pest. Monit. J.* 3(4):233–240.

Reinert, R. E., D. Stewart, and H. L. Seagran. 1972. Effects of dressing and cooking on DDT concentrations in certain fish from Lake Michigan. *J. Fish. Res. Bd. Cana.* 29(5):525–529.

ReVelle, C., and P. ReVelle. 1974. *Sourcebook on the environment—the scientific perspective.* Boston: Houghton Mifflin.

Rhim, J. S., J. Fujita, P. Arnstein, et al. 1986. Neoplastic conversion of human keratinocytes by adenovirus 12SV40 virus and chemical carcinogens. *Science* 232(4748):385–388.

Rice, C. P., and H. C. Sikka. 1973. Uptake and metabolism of DDT by six species of marine algae. *J. Agr. Food Chem.* 21(2):148–152.

Richie, P. J., and T. J. Peterle. 1979. Effect of DDE on circulating luteinizing hormone levels in ring doves during courtship and nesting. *Bull. Environ. Contam. Toxicol.* 23(1/2):220–226.

Richmond, M. L., C. J. Henny, R. L. Floyd, et al. 1979. Effects of Sevin-4-oil, Dimilin and Orthene on forest birds in northeastern Oregon. Pacific Southwest Forest and Range Experimental Station Research Paper PSW-148.

Ringer, R. K., and D. Polin. 1977. The biological effects of polybrominated biphenyls on avian species. *Fed. Proc.* 36(6):1894–1898.

Risebrough, R. W. 1969. Chlorinated hydrocarbons in marine ecosystems. In *Chemical fallout*, eds. M. W. Miller and G. G. Berg, pp. 5–23. Springfield, IL. C. C. Thomas.

Risebrough, R. W., and D. W. Anderson. 1971. Aroclor 1254 did not increase effect of DDT in thinning mallard eggshells. *PCB Newslett.* 3:17.

Risebrough, R. W., and D. W. Anderson. 1975. Some effects of DDE and PCB on mallards and their eggs. *J. Wildl. Manage.* 39(3):508–513.

Risebrough, R. W., R. J. Huggett, J. J. Griffin, et al. 1968. Pesticides: trans-Atlantic movements in the northeast trades. *Science* 159(3820):1233–1235.

Risebrough. R. W., D. B. Menzel, D. J. Martin, Jr., et al. 1967. DDT residues in Pacific sea birds: a persistent insecticide in marine food chains. *Nature* 216(5115):589–591.

Robel, R. J., R. W. Felthousen, and A. D. Dayton. 1982. Effects of carbamates on bobwhite food intake, body weight, and locomotor activity. *Arch. Environ. Contam. Toxicol.* 11(5):611–615.

Roberts, L. 1982. California's fog is far more polluted than acid rain. *Biosci.* 32(10):778–779.

Robinson, J. 1969. Organochlorine insecticides and bird populations in Britain. In *Chemical fallout,* eds. M. W. Miller and G. G. Berg, pp. 113–173. Springfield, IL: C. C. Thomas.

Rodgers, J. H., Jr., K. L. Dickson, F. Y. Saleh, et al. 1983. Use of microcosms to study transport, transformation, and fate of organics in aquatic systems. *Environ. Toxicol. Chem.* 2(2):155–167.

Rosato, P., and D. E. Ferguson. 1968. The toxicity of endrin resistant mosquito fish to eleven species of vertebrates. *Biosci.* 18(8):783–784.

Rosene, W., Jr. 1965. Effects of field applications of heptachlor on bobwhite quail and other wild animals. *J. Wildl. Manage.* 29(3):554–580.

Rubin, M., H. R. Bird, N. Green, et al. 1947. Toxicity of DDT to laying hens. *Poult. Sci.* 26(4):410–413.

Rudd, R. L., and R. E. Genelly. 1955. Avian mortality from DDT in California rice fields. *Condor* 57(1):117–118.

Rudd, R. L., and R. E. Genelly. 1956. *Pesticides: their use and toxicity in relation to wildlife.* California Department of Fish and Game Bulletin 7, 209 pp.

Samiullah, Y., and K. C. Jones. 1990. Deer antlers as pollution monitors in the United Kingdom. *Trans. Int. Cong. Game Biol.* 20:in press.

Sanders, O. T., and R. L. Kirkpatrick. 1975. Effects of polychlorinated biphenyl (PCB) on sleeping times, plasma corticosteroids, and testicular activity of white footed mice. *Environ. Physiol. Biochem.* 5:308–313.

Sanders, O. T., and R. L. Kirkpatrick. 1977. Reproductive characteristics and corticoid levels of female white-footed mice fed *ad libitum* and restricted diets containing a polychlorinated biphenyl. *Environ. Res.* 13(3):358–363.

Sanders, O. T., R. L. Kirkpatrick, and P. F. Scanlon. 1977. Polychlorinted biphenyls and nutritional restriction: their effects and interactions on endocrine and reproductive characteristics of male white mice. *Toxicol. Appl. Pharmacol.* 40(1):91–98.

Sandheinrich, M. B., and G. J. Atchison. 1990. Sublethal toxicant effects on fish foraging behavior: empirical vs. mechanistic approaches. *Environ. Toxicol. Chem.* 9(1):107–119.

Sawicka-Kapusta, K., J. Kozlowski, and T. Sokolowska. 1986. Heavy metals in tits from polluted forests in southern Poland. *Environ. Biol.* (Ser. A):42:297–310.

Scanlon, P. F. 1979. Ecological implications of heavy metal contamination of roadside habitats. *Proc. S. E. Assoc. Fish and Wildl. Agenc.* 33:136–145.

Schafer, E. W. 1972. The acute oral toxicity of 369 pesticidal, pharmaceutical, and other chemicals to wild birds. *Toxicol. Appl. Pharma.* 21(3):315–330.

Schafer, E. W., Jr., and W. A. Bowles, Jr. 1985. Acute oral toxicity and repellency of 933 chemicals to house and deer mice. *Arch. Environ. Contam. Toxicol.* 14(1):111–129.

Schafer. E. W., Jr., W. A. Bowles, Jr., and J. Hurlbut. 1983. The acute oral toxicity, repellency, and hazard potential of 998 chemicals to one or more species of wild and domestic birds. *Arch. Environ. Contam. Toxicol.* 12(3):355–382.

Schreiber, R. W., and R. L. DeLong. 1969. Brown pelican status in California. *Aud. Field Notes* 23(1):57–59.

Schriesheim, A., and I. Kirshenbaum. 1981. The chemistry and technology of synthetic fuels. *Amer. Sci.* 69(5):536–542.

Seabloom, R. W., G. L. Pearson, L. W. Oring, et al. 1973. An incident of fenthion mosquito control and subsequent avian mortality. *J. Wildl. Disease* 9(1):18–20.

Seba, D. B., and E. F. Corcoran. 1969. Surface slicks as concentrators of pesticides in the marine environment. *Pest. Monit. J.* 3(3):190–193.

Selikoff, I. J. 1977. PBB health survey of Michigan residents. November 4–10, 1976. Initial report of findings to Governor Milliken. Mt. Sinai School of Medicine, City University of New York, NY.

Serafin, J. A. 1984. Avian species differences in intestinal absorption of xenobiotics (PCB, dieldrin, Hg2+). *Comp. Biochem. Physiol.* 78C(2):491–496.

Sherburne, J. B., and J. B. Dimond. 1969. DDT persistence in wild hares and mink. *J. Wildl. Manage.* 33(4):944–948.

Shugart, H. H., Jr., and D. C. West. 1980. Forest succession models. *Biosci.* 30(5):308–313.

Siegel, H. S. 1980. Physiological stress in birds. *Biosci.* 30(8):529–534.

Silbergeld, E. K. 1973. Dieldrin. Effects of chronic sublethal exposure on adaptation to thermal stress in freshwater fish. *Environ. Sci. Tech.* 7(9):846–849.

Sileo, L., and W. N. Beyer. 1985. Heavy metals in white-tailed deer living near a zinc smelter in Pennsylvania. *J. Wildl. Disease.* 21(3):289–296.

Singh, H. B., L. J. Salas, A. Smith, et al. 1981. Atmospheric measurements of selected hazardous organic chemicals. USPEA-600/S3-81-032, 7 pp.

Sladen, W. J. L., C. M. Menzie, and W. L. Reichel. 1966. DDT residues in Adelie penguins and a crabeater seal from Antarctica: ecological implications. *Nature* 210(5037):670–673.

Sleight, S. D. 1979. Polybrominated biphenyls: a recent environmental pollutant. In *Animals as monitors of pollution,* pp. 366–374. Washington, DC: National Academy of Sciences.

Smith, G. J. 1987. *Pesticide use and toxicology in relation to wildlife: organophosphorus and carbamate compounds.* U. S. Fish and Wildlife Service Resources Publication 170, 171 pp.

Smith. G. J., J. W. Spann, and E. F. Hill. 1986. Cholinesterase activity in black-crowned night-herons exposed to fenthion-treated water. *Arch. Environ. Contam. Toxicol.* 15(1):83–86.

Smith, T. M., and G. W. Stratton. 1986. Effects of synthetic pyrethroid insecticides on nontarget organisms. *Resid. Rev.* 97:93–120.

Sodergren, A., and S. Ulfstrand. 1972. DDT and PCB relocate when caged robins use fat reserves. *Ambio* 1(1):36–40.

Spann, J. W., R. G. Heath, J. F. Kreitzer, et al. 1972. Ethyl mercury p-toluene sulfonanilide: lethal and reproductive effects in pheasants. *Science* 175(4019):329–331.

Sparks, R. E., W. T. Waller, and J. Cairns, Jr. 1972. Effect of shelters on the resistance of dominant and submissive bluegills (*Lepomis macrochirus*) to a lethal concentration of zinc. *J. Fish. Res. Bd. Canad.* 29(9):1356–1358.

Spencer, W. F., and M. M. Cliath. 1972. Volatility of DDT and related compounds. *J. Agr. Food Chem.* 20(3):645–649.

Spitzer, P. R., R. W. Risebrough, W. Walker II, et al. 1978. Productivity of ospreys in Connecticut–Long Island increases as DDE residues decline. *Science* 202(4365):333–335.

Springer, P. F., and J. R. Webster. 1951. Biological effects of DDT applications on tidal salt marshes. *Trans. N. A. Wildl. Conf.* 16:383–397.

Spyker, J. M., S. B. Sparber, and A. M. Goldberg. 1972. Subtle consequences of methylmercury exposure: behavioral deviations of offspring of treated mothers. *Science* 177(4049):621–623.

Stanley, P. I., and P. J. Bunyan. 1979. Hazards to wintering geese and other wildlife from use of dieldrin, chlorfenvinphos, and carbophenothion as wheat seed treatments. *Proc. R. Soc. Lond. B. Biol. Sci.* 205(1158):31–35.

Stearns, C. R., J. T. Griffiths, W. R. Bradley, et al. 1951. Concentration of parathion vapor in groves after spraying and effects of vapor on small animals. *Citrus Mag.* 13:22–23.

Stegeman, J. J., P. J. Kloepper-Sams, and J. W. Farrington. 1986. Monooxygenase induction and chlorobiphenyls in the deep-sea fish, (*Coryphaenoides armatus*). *Science* 231(4743):1287–1289.

Stehn, R. A., J. A. Stone, and M. E. Richmond. 1976. Feeding response of small mammal scavengers to pesticide-killed arthropod prey. *Amer. Midl. Nat.* 95(1):253–256.

Stendell, R. C., W. N. Beyer, and R. H. Stehn. 1989. Accumulation of lead and organochlorine residues in captive American kestrels fed pine voles from apple orchards. *J. Wildl. Disease* 25(3):388–391.

Stevenson, H. M. 1972. Florida region-pesticides. *Amer. Birds* 26(3):593.

Stewart, R. E., J. B. Cope, C. S. Robbins, et al. 1946. Effects of DDT on birds at the Patuxent Wildlife Refuge. *J. Wildl. Manage.* 10(3):195–201.

Stickel, L. F. 1946. Field studies of a *Peromyscus* population in an area treated with DDT. *J. Wildl. Manage.* 10(3):216–218.

Stickel, L. F. 1968. *Organochlorine pesticides in the environment.* U. S. Fish and Wildlife Service Special Scientific Report on Wildlife No 119, 32 pp.

Stickel, L. F. 1973. Pesticide residues in birds and mammals. In *Environmental pollution by pesticides,* ed. C. A. Edwards, pp. 254–312. London: Plenum Press.

Stickel, L. F., N. J. Chura, P. A. Stewart, et al. 1966. Bald eagle pesticide relations. *Trans. N. A. Wildl. Nat. Resour. Conf.* 31:190–204.

Stickel, L. F., and L. I. Rhodes. 1970. The thin eggshell problem. In *Biological impact of pesticides in the environment,* ed. F. W. Gillett, pp. 31–35. Corvallis: Oregon State University Environmental Health Science Series 1.

Stickel, L., and W. Stickel 1969. Distribution of DDT residues in tissues of birds in relation to mortality, body condition and time. *Ind. Med. Surg.* 38(5):44–53.

Stickel, L. F., W. H. Stickel, and R. Christensen. 1966. Residues of DDT in brains and bodies of birds that died on dosage and survivors. *Science* 151(3717):1549–1551.

Stickel, L. F., W. H. Stickel, R. A. Dyrland, et al. 1983. Oxychlordane, HCS 3260, and nonachlor in birds:lethal residues and loss rates. *J. Toxicol. Environ. Health* 12(4/6):611–622.

Stickel, L. F., W. H. Stickel, M. A. R. McLane, et al. 1977. Prolonged retention of methyl mercury by mallard drakes. *Bull. Environ. Contam. Toxicol.* 18(4):393–400.

Stickel, W. H. 1965. Delayed mortality of DDT-dosed cowbirds in relation to disturbance. In *The effects of pesticides on fish and wildlife.* USFWS Circ. 226, pp. 17.

Stickel, W. H. 1975. Some effects of pollutants in terrestrial ecosystems. In *Ecological toxicology research,* eds. A. D. McIntyre and C. F. Mills, pp. 25–74. New York:Plenum Press.

Stickel, W. H., W. E. Dodge, W. G. Sheldon, et al. 1965. Body condition and response to pesticides in woodcocks. *J. Wildl. Manage.* 29(1):147–155.

Stickel, W. H., J. A. Gaylen, R. A. Dyrland, et al. 1973. Toxicity and persistence of mirex in birds. In *Pesticides and the environment: a continuing controversy,* pp. 437–467. North Miami, FL: Symposia Specialists.

Stickel, W. H., D. W. Hayne, and L. F. Stickel. 1965. Effects of hepatchlor-contaminated earthworms on woodcocks. *J. Wild. Manage.* 29(1):132–146.

Stickel, W. H., L. F. Stickel, and F. B. Coon. 1970. DDE and DDD residues correlate with mortality of experimental cowbirds. In *Pesticides symposia,* ed. W. P. Deichmann, pp. 287–294. Miami, FL: Helios and Associates.

Stickel, W. H., L. F. Stickel, R. A. Dyrland, et al. 1984a. Aroclor 1254 residues in birds: lethal levels and loss rates. *Arch. Environ. Contam. Toxicol.* 13(1):7–13.

Stickel, W. H., L. F. Stickel, R. A. Dyrland, et al. 1984b. DDE in birds: lethal levels and loss rates. *Arch. Environ. Contam. Toxicol.* 13(1):1–6.

Stickel, W. H., L. F. Stickel, and J. W. Spann. 1969. Tissue residues of dieldrin in relation to mortality in birds and mammals. In *Chemical fallout,* eds. M. W. Miller and G. G. Berg, pp. 174–204. Springfield, IL. C. C. Thomas.

Stone, W. B. 1979. Poisoning of wild birds by organophosphate and carbamate pesticides. *N. Y. Fish and Game J.* 26(1):37–47.

Stone, W. B., E. Kiviat, and S. A. Butkas. 1980. Toxicants in snapping turtles. *N. Y. Fish and Game J.* 27(1):39–50.

Storer. T. I. 1946. DDT and wildlife. *J. Wildl. Manage.* 10(3):181–183.

Street, J. C., and A. D. Blau. 1966. Insecticide interactions affecting residue accumulation in animal tissues. *Toxicol. Appl. Pharma.* 8(3):497–504.

Stromborg, K. L. 1977. Seed treatment pesticide effects on pheasant reproduction at sublethal doses. *J. Wildl. Manage.* 41(4):632–642.

Stromborg, K. L. 1981. Reproductive tests of diazinon on bobwhite quail. In *Avian and mammalian wildlife toxicology,* eds. D. W. Lamb and E. E. Kenaga, pp. 19–30. ASTM Spec. Tech. Pub. 757.

Stromborg, K. L., C. E. Grue, J. D. Nichols, et al. 1988. Postfledging survival of European starlings exposed as nestlings to an organophosphorus insecticide. *Ecology* 69(3):590–601.

Stromborg, K. L., L. C. McEwen, and T. Lamont. 1984. Organophosphate residues in grasshoppers from sprayed rangeland. *Chem. Ecol.* 2(1):39–45.

Strong, L. A. 1938. Insect and pest control in relation to wildlife. *Trans. N. A. Wildl. Conf.* 3:543–547.

Sun, M. 1984. Pests prevail despite pesticides. *Science* 226(4680):1293.

Sun, M. 1986a. Acid rain plan draws mixed reviews. *Science* 231(4736):333.

Sun, M. 1986b. EPA proposes ban on asbestos. *Science* 231(4738):542–543.

Sun, M. 1986c. Formaldehyde poses little risk, study says. *Science* 231(4744):1365.

Surber, E. W., and O. L. Meehean. 1931. Lethal concentrations of arsenic for certain aquatic organisms. *Trans. Amer. Fish. Soc.* 61:225–239.

Swain, W. R. 1980. An ecosystem approach to the toxicology of residue forming xenobiotic organic substances in the Great Lakes. In *Working Papers for the Committee on Revised Methods for Ecotoxicology,* pp.193–257. Washington, DC: National Academy of Sciences.

Swenson, J. E., K. L. Alt, and R. L. Eng. 1986. Ecology of bald eagles in the greater Yellowstone ecosystem. *Wildl. Monog.* 95, 46 pp.

Sykes, P. W., Jr. 1985. Pesticide concentrations in snail kite eggs and nestlings in Florida. *Condor* 87(3):438.

Szaro, R. C., and P. H. Albers. 1977. Effects of external applications of No. 2 fuel oil on common eider eggs. In *Fate and effects of petroleum hydrocarbons in marine systems and organisms,* ed. D. A. Wolfe, pp. 164–167. New York: Pergamon Press.

Szaro. R. C., N. C. Coon, and W. Stout. 1980. Weathered petroleum: effects on mallard egg hatchability. *J. Wildl. Manage.* 44(3):709–713.

Tabor, E. C. 1966. Contamination of urban air through the use of insecticides. *New York Acad. Sci.* 28(5):569–578.

Tagatz, M. E., P. W. Borthwick, J. M. Ivey, et al. 1976. Effects of leached mirex on experimental communities of estuarine animals. *Arch. Environ. Contam. Toxicol.* 4(4):435–442.

Talmage, S. S., and B. T. Walton. 1991. Small mammals as monitors of environmental contaminants. *Rev. Environ. Contam. Toxicol.* 119:47–145.

Tangley, L. 1984. Contaminated groundwater linked with disease. *Biosci.* 34(5):292.

Tarrant, K. R., and J. O'G. Tatton. 1968. Organochlorine pesticides in rainwater in the British Isles. *Nature* 219(5155):725–727.

Tarshis, I. B. 1981. Uptake and depuration of petroleum hydrocarbons by crayfish. *Arch. Environ. Contam. Toxicol.* 10(1):79–86.

Tarzwell, C. M. 1947. Effects of DDT mosquito larvaciding on wildlife. *Public Health Rpt.* 62(15):525–554.

Taskforce on PCB. 1976. Background to the regulation of polychlorinated biphenyls (PCB) in Canada. Technical Report 76-1. Environment Canada, Ottawa. 169 pp.

Tatton, J. O'G. and J. H. A. Ruzicka. 1967. Organochlorine pesticides in Antarctica. *Nature* 215(5099):346–348.

Terriere, L. C., Y. Kiigemagi, A. R. Gerlach, et al. 1966. The persistence of toxaphene in lake water and its uptake by aquatic plants and animals. *J. Arg. Food Chem.* 14(1):66–69.

Thompson, N. P., and R. L. Emerman. 1974. Interaction of p,p'DDT with histomoniasis in bobwhites. *Bull. Environ. Contam. Toxicol.* 11(5):474–482.

Thompson, N. P., P. W. Rankin, and D. W. Johnston. 1974. Polychlorinated biphenyls and p,p'DDE in green turtle eggs from Ascension Island, South Atlantic Ocean. *Bull. Environ. Contam. Toxicol.* 11(5):399–406.

Tolle, D. A., M. F. Arthur, J. Chesson, et al. 1985. Comparison of pots versus microcosms for predicting agroecosystem effects due to waste amendment. *Environ. Toxicol. Chem.* 4(4):501–509.

Tori, G. M., and L. P. Mayer. 1981. Effects of polychlorinated biphenyls on the metabolic rates of mourning doves exposed to low ambient temperatures. *Bull. Environ. Contam. Toxicol.* 27(5):678–682.

Tori, G. M., and T. J. Peterle. 1983. Effects of PCBs on mourning dove courtship behavior. *Bull. Environ. Contam. Toxicol.* 30(1):44–49.

Tragardh, I. 1935. The economic possibilities of aeroplane dusting against forest insects. *Bull. Entomol. Res.* 26(Pt. 4):487–495.

Trefry, J. H., S. Metz, R. P. Trocine, et al. 1985. A decline in lead transport by the Mississippi River. *Science* 230(4724):439–441.

Tucker, R. K., and D. G. Crabtree. 1970. *Handbook of toxicity of pesticides to wildlife.* Bureau of Sport Fisheries and Wildlife, Resource Publication 84, 131 pp.

Tucker, R. K., and H. A. Haegele. 1970. Eggshell thinning as influenced by method of DDT exposure. *Bull. Environ. Contam. Toxicol.* 5(3):191–194.

Tucker, R. K., and M. A. Haegele. 1971. Comparative acute oral toxicity of pesticides to six species of birds. *Toxicol. Appl. Pharma.* 20(1):57–65.

USEPA. 1971. *Water quality criteria data book. Vol. 3: Effects of chemicals on aquatic life.* USEPA, Washington, DC.

USEPA. 1975. *DDT: A review of scientific and economic aspects of the decision to ban its use as a pesticide.* EPA 540/1-75-022. Washington, DC.

USEPA. 1980. *Environmental outlook, 1980.* EPA 600/8-80-003. Washington, DC.

Vangilder, L. D., and E. P. O. Drawer. 1983. Reproductive effects of toxic substances on wildlife: an evolutionary perspective. In *Czechoslovakian/American Symposium on the Effects of Chemical Environmental Contamination upon Production and Reproductive Ability in Free-living Animals,* ed. P. Kacmar, pp. 250–260. Kosice: Czechoslovakia University of Veterinary Medicine.

Vangilder, L. D., and T. J. Peterle. 1980. South Louisiana crude oil and DDE in the diet of mallard hens: effects on reproduction and duckling survival. *Bull. Environ. Contam. Toxicol.* 25(3):23–28.

Vangilder, L. D., and T. J. Peterle. 1981. South Louisana crude oil or DDE in the diet of mallard hens: effects on egg quality. *Bull. Environ. Contam. Toxicol.* 26(6):328–336.

Vangilder, L. D., and T. J. Peterle. 1983. Mallard egg quality: enhancement by low levels of petroleum and chlorinated hydrocarbons. *Bull. Environ. Contam. Toxicol.* 30(1):17–23.

Van Velzen, A. C., W. B. Stiles, and L. F. Stickel. 1972. Lethal mobilization of DDT by cowbirds. *J. Wildl. Manage.* 36(3):733–739.

Veith, G. D., D. L. DeFoe, and B. V. Bergstedt. 1979. Measuring and estimating the bioconcentration factor of chemicals in fish. *J. Fish Res. Bd. Canad.* 36(19):1040–1048.

Veith, G. D., K. J. Macek, S. R. Petrocelli, et al. 1980. An evaulation of using partition coefficients and water solubility to estimate bioconcentration factors of organic chemicals in fish. In *Aquatic toxicology,* eds. J. G. Eaton, P. R. Parrish, and A. C. Hendrick, pp. 116–129. Philadelphia: ASTM.

Vianna, N. J., and A. K. Polan. 1984. Incidence of low birth weight among Love Canal residents. *Science* 226(4679):1217–1219.

Waggoner, J. P., III, and M. G. Zeeman. 1975. DDT: short-term effects on osmoregulation in black surfperch (*Embiotoca jacksoni*). *Bull. Environ. Contam. Toxicol.* 13(3):297–300.

Walker, C. H. 1983. Pesticides and birds—mechanisms of selective toxicitity. *Agric. Ecocyst. Environ.* 9(2):211–226.

Wallace, G. J., A. G. Etter, and D. R. Osborne. 1964. Spring mortality of birds following fall spraying of elms. *Mass. Audubon* 48(3):116–120.

Ward, J. C. 1931. Thallium poisoning in migratory birds. *J. Amer. Pharm. Assoc.* 20:1272–1276.

Ware, G. W., B. J. Esteson, and W. P. Cahill. 1974. DDT moratorium in Arizona—agricultural residues after 4 years. *Pest. Monit. J.* 8(2):98–101.

Ware, G. W., and E. E. Good. 1967. Effects of insecticides on reproduction in the laboratory mouse II. Mirex, telodrin and DDT. *Toxicol. Appl. Pharmacol.* 10(1):54–61.

Warner, R. E., K. K. Peterson, and L. Borgman. 1966. Behavioural pathology in fish: a quantitative study of sublethal pesticide toxication. *J. Appl. Ecol.* (Suppl.) 3:223–247.

Warren, R. J., R. L. Kirkpatrick, and R. W. Young. 1978. Barbiturate-induced sleeping times, liver weights, and reproduction of cottontail rabbits after mirex ingestion. *Bull. Environ. Contam. Toxicol.* 19(2):223–228.

Wassermann, M., D. Wassermann, Z. Gershon, et al. 1969. Effects of organochlorine insecticides on body defense systems. *Annal. N. Y. Acad. Sci.* 160(1):393–401.

Weber, R. E., R. W. Hartgrove, W. C. Randolph, et al. 1973. Toxicity studies in endrin-susceptible and resistant strains of pine mice. *Toxicol. Appl. Pharma.* 25(1):42–47.

Weibel, S. R., R. B. Weidner, J. M. Cohen, et al. 1966. Pesticides and other contaminants in rainfall and runoff. *J. Amer. Water Works Assoc.* 58(8):1075–1084.

Weeks, M. H., M. A. Lawson, R. A. Angerhofer, et al. 1977. Preliminary assessment of the acute toxicity of malathion in animals. *Arch. Environ. Contam. Toxicol.* 6:23–31.

Weil, C. S. 1952. Tables for convenient calculation of median effective dose (LD50 or ED50) and instructions in their use. *Biometrics* 8(3):249–263.

Weis, P., and J. S. Weis. 1979. Congenital abnormalities in estuarine fishes produced by environmental contaminants. In *Animals as monitors of environmental pollutants,* pp. 94–107. Washington, DC: National Academy of Sciences.

Weiss, D., B. Whitten, and D. Leddy. 1972. Lead content of human hair (1871–1971). *Science* 178(4056):69–70.

Weiss, H. V., M. Koide, and E. D. Goldberg. 1971. Mercury in a Greenland ice sheet: evidence of recent input by man. *Science* 174(4010):692–694.

Welch, R. M., W. Levin, and A. II. Conney. 1969. Effects of chlorinated insecticides on steroid metabolism. In *Chemical fallout,* eds. M. W. Miller and G. G. Berg, pp. 390–407. Springfield, IL. C. C. Thomas.

Weller, M. W. 1971. Robin mortality in relation to Dutch elm disease control programs on the Iowa State University Campus. *Iowa St. J. Sci.* 45(3):471–475.

Weseloh, D. V., T. W. Custer, and B. M. Braune. 1989. Organochlorine contaminants in eggs of common terns from the Canadian Great Lakes, 1981. *Environ. Pollut.* 59(2):141–160.

Westman, W. E. 1978. Measuring the inertia and resilience of ecosystems. *Biosci.* 28(11):705–710.

Westoo, G. 1969. Methylmercury compounds in animal foods. In *Chemical fallout,* eds. M. W. Miller and G. G. Berg, pp. 75–93. Springfield, IL. C. C. Thomas.

White, D. H., and E. Cromartie. 1977. Residues of environmental pollutants and shell thinning in merganser eggs. *Wilson Bull.* 89(4):532–542.

White, D. H., W. J. Fleming, and K. L. Ensor. 1988. Pesticide contamination and hatching success of waterbirds in Mississippi. *J. Wildl. Manage.* 52(4):724–729.

White, D. H., K. A. King, C. A. Mitchell, et al. 1979. Parathion causes secondary poisoning in a laughing gull breeding colony. *Bull. Environ. Contam. Toxicol.* 23(1/2):281–284.

White, D. H., K. A. King, C. A. Mitchell, et al. 1986. Trace elements in sediments, water, and American coots (*Fulica americana*) at a coal-fired power plant in Texas, 1979–1982. *Bull. Environ. Contam. Toxicol.* 36(3):376–383.

White, D. H., and A. J. Krynitsky. 1986. Wildlife in some areas of New Mexico and Texas accumulate elevated DDE residues, 1983. *Arch. Environ. Contam. Toxicol.* 15(2):149–157.

White, D. H., and C. A. Mitchell. 1983. Azodrin poisoning of waterfowl in rice fields in Louisiana. *J. Wildl. Disease* 19(4):373–365.

White, D.H., C. A. Mitchell, and E. F. Hill. 1983. Parathion alters incubation behavior of laughing gulls. *Bull. Environ. Contam. Toxicol.* 31(1):93–97.

White, D. H., C. A. Mitchell, E. J. Kolbe, et al. 1982. Parathion poisoning of wild geese in Texas. *J. Wildl. Disease* 18(3):389–391.

White, D. H., C. A. Mitchell, and C. J. Stafford. 1985. Organochlorine concentrations, whole body weights, and lipid content of black skimmers wintering in Mexico and in South Texas, 1983. *Bull. Environ. Contam. Toxicol.* 34(4):513–517.

White, D. H., C. A. Mitchell, L. D. Wynn, et al. 1982. Organophosphate insecticide poisoning of Canada geese in the Texas panhandle. *J. Field Ornith.* 53(1):22–27.

White, D. H., and J. T. Seginak. 1990. Brain cholinesterase inhibition in songbirds from pecan groves sprayed with phosalone and disulfoton. *J. Wildl. Dis.* 26(1):103–106.

White, D. H., J. T. Seginak, and R. C. Simpson. 1990. Survival of northern bobwhites in Georgia: cropland use of pesticides. *Bull. Environ. Contam. Toxicol.* 44(1):73–80.

Whitehead. F. E. 1934. *The effects of arsenic, as used in poisoning grasshoppers, upon birds.* Oklahoma Agricultural Experimental Station Bulletin 218, 55 pp.

Wiemeyer, S. N., C. M. Bunck, and A. J. Krynitsky. 1988. Organochlorine pesticides, polychlorinated biphenyls, and mercury in osprey eggs—1970–79—and their relationships to shell thinning and productivity. *Arch. Environ. Contam. Toxicol.* 17(6):767–787.

Wiemeyer, S. N., R. M. Jurek, and J. F. Moore. 1986. Environmental contaminants in surrogates, foods, and feathers of California condors (*Gymnogyps californianus*). *Environ. Monit. Assess.* 6(1):91–111.

Wiemeyer, S. N., A. J. Krynitsky, and S. R. Wilbur. 1983. Environmental contaminants in tissues, foods and feces of California condors. In *Vulture biology and management,* eds. S. R. Wilbur and J. A. Jackson, pp. 427–439. Berkley: University of California Press.

Wiemeyer, S. N., and R. D. Porter. 1970. DDE thins eggshells of captive American kestrels. *Nature* 227(5259):737–738.

Wiemeyer, S. N., T. G. Lamont, C. M. Bunck, et al. 1984. Organochlorine pesticide, polychlorobiphenyl, and mercury residues in bald eagle eggs—1969–79—and their relationships to shell thinning and reproduction. *Arch. Environ. Contam. Toxicol.* 13(5):529–549.

Wiese, I. H., C. J. Basson, J. H. Van Der Wyver, et al. 1969. Toxicology and dynamics of dieldrin in the crowned guiena fowl (*Numida meleagris L.*). *Phytophyl.* 1:161–176.

Wilcox, H., and T. Coffey. 1978. Environmental impacts of difluorobenzuron (Dimilin) insecticide. ERA Lab. Report. Oswego, NY, 18 pp.

Williams, R., and A. V. Holden. 1973. Organochlorine residues from plankton. *Marine Pollut. Bull.* 4(7):109–111.

Wilson, R., and E. A. C. Crouch. 1987. Risk assessment and comparisons: an introduction. *Science* 236(4799):267–270.

Witkamp, M., and M. L. Frank. 1970. Effects of temperature, rainfall, and fauna on transfer of 137Cs, K, Mg, and mass in consumer–decomposer microcosms. *Ecology* 51(3):465–474.

Wood, J. M. 1974. Biological cycles for toxic elements in the environment. *Science* 183(4129):1049–1052.

Woodard, G., R. R. Ofner, and C. M. Montgomery. 1945. Accumulation of DDT in the body fat amd its appearance in the milk of dogs. *Science* 102(2642):177–178.

Woodwell, G. M. 1961. The persistence of DDT in forest soil. *For. Sci.* 7(3):194–196.

Woodwell, G. M., P. P. Craig, and H. A. Johnson. 1971. DDT in the biosphere: where does it go? *Science* 174(4014):1101–1107.

Woodwell, G. M. and F. T. Martin. 1964. Persistence of DDT in soils of heavily sprayed forest stands. *Science* 145(3631):481–483.

Woodwell, G. M., C. F. Wurster, and P. A. Isaacson. 1967. DDT residues in an east coast estuary: a case of biological concentration of a persistent insecticide. *Science* 156(3776):821–824.

Wright, B. S. 1965. Some effects of heptachlor and DDT on New Brunswick woodcocks. *J. Wildl. Manage.* 29(1):172–185.

Wurster, C. F., Jr. 1969. Chlorinated hydrocarbon insecticides and avian reproduction: how are they related? In *Chemical fallout,* eds. M. W. Miller and G. G. Berg, pp. 368–389. Springfield, IL. C. C. Thomas.

Wurster, C. F., and D. B. Wingate. 1968. DDT residues and declining reproduction in the Bermuda petrel. *Science* 159(3818):979–981.

Wurster, D. H., C. F. Wurster, Jr., and W. N. Strickland. 1965. Bird mortality following DDT spray for Dutch elm disease. *Ecology* 46(4):488–499.

Yablokov, A. Soviet Environment. *Toledo Blade,* January 22,1990.

Young, H. F., A. Hulsey, and R. Moe, 1952. Effects of certain cotton insecticides on the mourning dove. *Proc. Arkansas Acad. Sci.* 1952:43–50.

Zahm, G. R. 1986. Kesterson Reservoir and Kesterson National Wildlife Refuge: history, current problems and management alternatives. *Trans. N. A. Wildl. Nat. Resour. Conf.* 51:324–329.

Zeakes, S. J., M. F. Hansen, and R. J. Robel. 1981. Increased susceptibility of bobwhites (*Colinus virginianus*) to *Histomonas meleagridis* after exposure to Sevin insecticide. *Avian Disease* 25(4):981–987.

Zepp, R. L., and R. L. Kirkpatick. 1976. Reproduction in cottontails fed diets containing a PCB. *J. Wildl. Manage.* 40(3):491–495.

Zepp, R. L., Jr., O. T. Sanders, and R. L. Kirkpatrick. 1974. Reduction of pentobarbital-induced sleeping times in PCB-treated cottontail rabbits. *Bull. Environ. Contam. Toxicol.* 12(5):518–521.

Zimmerman, F. R. 1938. Poison effects on wildlife. *Wiscon. Conserv. Bull.* 3:9–15.

Zinkl, J. G., J. Rathert, and R. R. Hudson. 1978. Diazinon poisoning in wild Canada geese. *J. Wildl. Manage.* 42(2):406–408.

Index